HUMAN RIGHTS AND SOCIAL JUSTICE SERIES

EDITORS: KAREN BUSBY AND RHONDA HINTHER

1. *The Idea of a Human Rights Museum*
   Karen Busby, Adam Muller, and Andrew Woolford, editors

THE IDEA OF A
Human Rights Museum

EDITED BY KAREN BUSBY, ADAM MULLER, AND ANDREW WOOLFORD

UMP
University of Manitoba Press

University of Manitoba Press
Winnipeg, Manitoba
Canada R3T 2M5
uofmpress.ca

Printed in Canada
Text printed on chlorine-free, 100% post-consumer recycled paper

19 18 17 16 15   1 2 3 4 5

Cover image: Design sketch of the Canadian Museum for Human Rights
by Antoine Predock
Cover and interior design: Jess Koroscil

Library and Archives Canada Cataloguing in Publication

The idea of a human rights museum / Karen Busby, Adam
Muller, and Andrew Woolford, editors.

(Human rights and social justice series, 2291-6024 ; 1)
Includes bibliographical references.
Issued in print and electronic formats.
ISBN 978-0-88755-782-8 (pbk.)
ISBN 978-0-88755-471-1 (pdf).
ISBN 978-0-88755-469-8 (epub)

1. Canadian Museum for Human Rights. 2. Human rights—Museums—
Social aspects. 3. Human rights—Museums—Political aspects. 4. Museum
architecture. 5. Museum exhibits. I. Busby, Karen, 1958–, author, editor
II. Woolford, Andrew, 1971–, author, editor III. Muller, Adam, 1968–, author,
editor IV. Title: Human rights museum. V. Series: Human rights and social
justice series ; 1

AM101.W45I34 2015   323.074'712743   C2015-903490-6
                                                C2015-903491-4

The University of Manitoba Press gratefully acknowledges the financial support
for its publication program provided by the Government of Canada through the Canada
Book Fund, the Canada Council for the Arts, the Manitoba Department
of Culture, Heritage, Tourism, the Manitoba Arts Council,
and the Manitoba Book Publishing Tax Credit.

FSC
www.fsc.org
MIX
Paper from
responsible sources
FSC® C016245

CONTENTS

CURATORIAL CHALLENGES

PARALLELS AND OBLIGATIONS

LIST OF ILLUSTRATIONS

THE IDEA OF
A HUMAN RIGHTS
MUSEUM

INTRODUCTION

Karen Busby, Adam Muller, and Andrew Woolford

When the Canadian Museum for Human Rights (CMHR) opened its doors in the fall of 2014, it realized many of the ambitions of its visionary originator, Winnipeg businessman and philanthropist Israel ("Izzy") Asper. Asper launched his private initiative in April 2003, but his ambitions were shared by many Canadians who, individually as well as collectively through their professional unions, charitable organizations, and places of work, donated funds to supplement those provided by the Canadian and Manitoban governments to bring this institution to life. The CMHR, via its special emphasis on Canadian human rights history and challenges, which it aims to place in a global context, seeks to inspire new generations of human rights proponents and leaders while serving as an important hub for scholarly work on human rights triumphs and tragedies.

Over the past two decades, self-identified human rights museums have opened around the world; they even established their own organization in 2010, the Federation of International Human Rights Museums. Some institutions, such as the Kigali Memorial Centre in Rwanda and the Maison des Esclaves in Senegal, focus on specific gross human rights abuses while others, such as the Museo Memoria y Tolerancia in Mexico City, promote a human rights culture but are not responses to specific events. As various contributors to this volume observe,[1] the specific missions of these institutions range from social reconciliation, reparation, symbolic memorialization, calling to action, or providing the opportunity for what Piotr Cywinski, director of the Auschwitz-Birkenau State Museum, describes in an interview with contributor Amanda Grzyb as a "deep private individual experience." These missions can shift in response to the evolving concerns of an ever-changing present. As Ruth Phillips acknowledges in her contribution, "the mandates of museums and heritage organizations are historically specific and change over time. Imposed through the oversight of government departments and the museum boards and administrators whom they appoint, they reflect priorities that those bodies identify as necessary to the creation of an informed citizenry." We find this commitment to informed citizenship highlighted in the CMHR's statutory mandate, which states that the museum will enhance the public's understanding of human rights, promote respect for others, and encourage reflection and dialogue.

This book grew out of a successful year-long seminar series organized in 2011–12 by the three editors of this volume under the auspices of the University of Manitoba's Centre for Human Rights Research. Titled *Critical Conversations on the Idea of a Human Rights Museum*, it was open to the public and podcasted. Manitobans were rightly excited about the unusual building then under construction at the edge of Winnipeg's downtown, but they wanted to be better informed about the controversies swirling around so many aspects of the structure, including building cost overruns, exhibition content, allegations of political and board interference, and high staff turnover rates. Many shared contributor David Petrasek's view that, "where the risks of manipulation are too high, and the promise of curatorial independence and courage too low, we should be sceptical about the value of a human rights museum." In 2008, the federal government announced that, while the CMHR would become a national museum and the Canadian government would pick up its operating costs, the balance of the building costs would have to be raised privately. Although addressing several long-standing worries about the museum, and relieving some of its financial burden, nationalization of the CMHR raised a series of new concerns, notably over the effects that federal oversight would have on museum content and on the precise emplotment of the human rights narrative that it would tell. Carter captures something of these anxieties when she asks: "Is this new generation of museums deployed as a political instrument to promote the interests of the state or as a forum for dialogue to enrich civil society?" Some scepticism was certainly warranted on this score, since the same government responsible for funding the operating budget of the museum and appointing its board had also cut funding for human rights advocacy and research elsewhere and consistently denied the brutal realities of Canadian settler colonialism.[2] Against this complex and politically charged backdrop, the seminar series proved to be an ideal forum for engaged and informed discussion of the idea of a human rights museum, and it sustained nuanced conversations about the CMHR's mission, architecture, curatorial praxis, and decision-making and pedagogical approaches. These conversations are reflected in the majority of this volume's contributions, which were solicited from participants in the seminar series and, though refined and enlarged, deliberately kept compact in order to reflect the provisional and forward-looking qualities of the original oral presentations.

THE STORY OF A BUILDING
Museum buildings are not passive frames for exhibits; rather, their designers work to create environments that complement the ideas behind what ends up on display, architectural form enhancing exhibit content. Sometimes this complementarity arises from taking an old structure and renewing it, changing its relationship in the present to its past. For example, contributors Jorge Nállim and Stephan Jaeger both describe how repurposed buildings such as the Space of Memory and Human Rights, (which formerly housed a notorious site for human rights violations, the Navy School of Mechanics) in Buenos Aires, and the Museum of Military History in Dresden juxtapose an earlier use—a torture site and an arsenal, respectively—with a new broadly humanitarian and didactic one. Sometimes, though, complementarity arises from preserving aspects of a building's original form, as in the example cited by Petrasek of the neo-Renaissance Peace Palace in The Hague, built in 1913 as the first modern statement against war yet evoking memories of a gilded age of European diplomacy. Museum buildings can display and reinforce specific attitudes. So, for example, the orderly geometry of modernist-inspired designs such as the Museum of Tolerance in Los Angeles and the Newseum in Washington, DC, suggests confidence, rationality, and progress. Such buildings can also generate affect, producing feelings to complement those arising from visitors' experiences of their contents. Hence, the unpredictable eclecticism of some postmodern museum buildings such as the United States Holocaust Memorial Museum or Antoine Predock–designed Canadian Museum for Human Rights can be experienced viscerally, leaving their visitors feeling off kilter and emotionally overwhelmed. In contrast, the Smithsonian's National Museum of the American Indian in Washington, with its "distinctive curvilinear form, evoking a wind-sculpted rock formation," is much more calming.[3] Whether repurposed, modern, postmodern, or derived from some other style, a museum's mission entwines

with its building's history, rituals, location, façade, and interior design. If, as Renzo Piano has said, "architecture is not just the art of making buildings; it is also the art of telling stories,"[4] then a museum's building is also its most permanent exhibit.

The Canadian Museum for Human Rights is purposefully located near the convergence of two large rivers on a site that was a meeting place for Indigenous peoples—especially the Anishinaabe, Cree, Dene, and Dakota—for thousands of years. The Forks, as it is locally known, then became the site of an important fort during the colonial fur-trade era. Following the signing of a treaty between the Canadian government and Anishinaabe and Cree leaders in 1871, the land was used by a railway company. Most immigrants coming to Winnipeg before the 1970s arrived by train at this location. Where better than a historic site of intergroup dialogue and exchange to place a museum committed to fostering conversations about human rights?

The building site proved to be the location of a rich archaeological deposit because frequent spring flooding both discouraged sub-surface usages and embedded artifacts in the clay "gumbo" left behind by receding floodwater. Construction of the CMHR was delayed for almost a year so that an archaeological dig could be conducted in order to assess the site's historical and cultural significance. The CMHR consulted with the Province of Manitoba, Indigenous groups, and the management entity of The Forks before undertaking the dig. Almost 600,000 artifacts were recovered.[5] Nonetheless, some people believe that more archaeological oversight was required since only 2 percent of the fill actually removed from the site was sifted for artifacts. Criticisms of the CMHR's archaeological mitigation plan by Leigh Syms, the former curator of archaeology for the Manitoba Museum, for example, faulted the museum for spending too little time and money on its archaeological review, calling the mitigation process "the worst case of legal destruction of the rich heritage that I have had the misfortune to witness."[6] In her response to Syms's criticisms, Angela Cassie, the CMHR's director of communications, pointed out that the museum had indeed complied with all federal and provincial heritage requirements in its archaeological review and that Aboriginal stakeholders had been involved in the review process throughout, with Elders providing direction for the handling and care of recovered artifacts and, as a way of honouring the land, ceremonially depositing medicine bags in holes dug for the museum's pilings and caissons.[7] The 2 percent of fill sifted by archaeologists was twice the amount required by Manitoba's heritage policy for a project of this kind, and the museum building itself was designed to sit atop pilings and caissons to ensure that the sub-surface was minimally disturbed and thus is available for archaeological excavation in the future, should the need arise. Dissatisfaction with these provincial standards persists, however, and one of the more important consequences of criticisms of the CMHR's archaeological mitigation plan has been the renewal of efforts to strengthen Canadian provincial and federal heritage policies concerning site excavations.

Good architecture responds to the genius of a place. The Denver Art Gallery pays homage to its mountainous home. The Michael Lee-Chin Crystal addition to the Royal Ontario Museum in Toronto, which protrudes over a busy thoroughfare, welcomingly reflects the street and reveals the museum's interior. The highly reflective blue surface of the tallest building in Boston, the John Hancock Tower, mirrors surrounding structures, especially the historic Trinity Church, and on sunny days it blends with the sky and modestly disappears. Winnipeg is located on an extremely flat, low-lying flood plain, and, while it is one of the coldest cities in the world with a population over 600,000, paradoxically it enjoys intense sunshine on most days. There are no buildings located close to the CMHR. The building thus responds to the genius of its place—the absence of anything other than the sun and the cold—by using light-absorbing white stone on the north and east walls and mutely reflective tempered glass on the south and west walls. These materials, and the unusual geometric planes of the building, respond to the extraordinary transformations in light, temperature, and atmospheric effects that characterize its prairie home. The effect is mesmerizing.

A building's façade tells the spectator what is happening inside. A church's spire points us toward the divine, whereas a mosque's symmetrical layout and repeating themes suggest Allah's infinite power and wisdom. The "jagged brutal aesthetic"[8] of the wedge incorporated into the Dresden military history museum discussed by Stephan Jaeger embodies that museum's desire to move away from glorifying warfare and toward a more complete inquiry into its horrors with a view to preventing them in future. So what does the exuberant postmodern façade of the CMHR tell us? Four large stone roots form the base of the building, representing its connection to the earth. Three of them have top surfaces designed to be planted with indigenous prairie tall grass, intended to symbolize all human beings as children of the earth; the other is stepped, allowing it to serve as an outdoor amphitheatre. Half of the building is protectively clad in a mountain

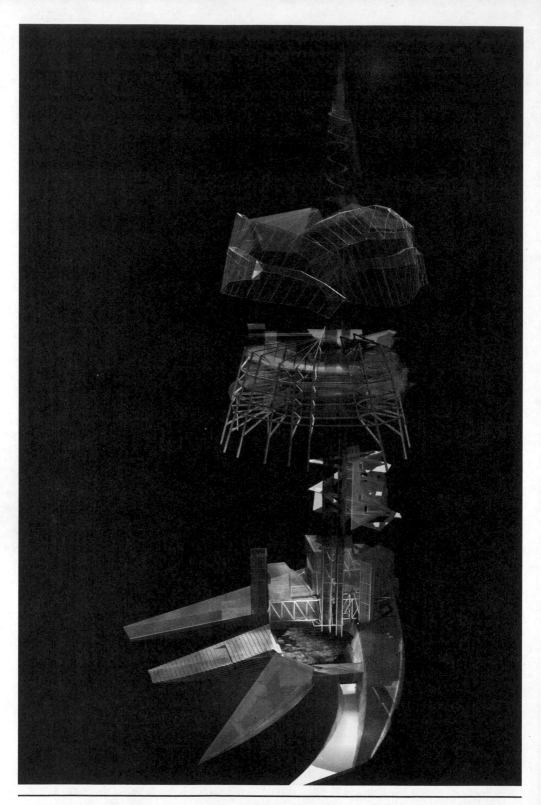

1. CMHR architectural elements.

2. Cross-section of CMHR building.

3. Alabaster walkway.

of locally quarried Tyndall limestone, its mass and great age (its surface often contains traces of fossilized sea life) serving to balance and anchor the most dramatic portion of the building's façade, the so-called Cloud. This consists of UV-reflective glass panels specially imported from Germany, some 1,200 individual glazed panels in all, which from some perspectives appears as a large dove, the symbol of peace, embracing the museum. The Tower of Hope, a glass spire jutting high above the Cloud, sits atop the building, blending into the sky and speaking for one of the museum's main ambitions, to cultivate hope for a just and more equitable future.

A typical visitor will enter the museum by walking through the canyon formed by two of the four stone roots that anchor the building. The cement walls of the canyon have been dyed brown to emphasize the sense of the museum growing organically out of the clay in which the structure is embedded. Following admission, the visitor can go to the Garden of Contemplation. Eight-sided grey basalt columns and floors suggest the violent but spent energy of a volcano, and its greenery suggests regeneration. Time spent in the garden is intended to give visitors the chance to gather strength for what lies ahead. They then start the "human rights journey" by ascending a serpentine walkway through eleven galleries, the specifics and conceptual evolution of which are documented by Karen Busby in her contribution here. This walkway is reminiscent of the Guggenheim Museum in New York, where one floor spirals into another without clear stratification between levels. Although the CMHR's exhibits are not arranged in any temporally linear succession, its design is intended to achieve a kind of thematic and affective trajectory. Its website notes that "ramps of glowing alabaster criss-cross galleries designed to challenge, motivate and uplift," and the journey is supposed to take the visitor "from darkness to light."[9] One would expect a human rights museum to be especially attentive to "universal design principles," the term given by architect Ronald L. Mace to built environments designed to be maximally usable by everyone.[10] A gently sloping walkway facilitates access for most visitors to the CMHR, and those who wish to go directly to a particular exhibit can take an elevator and thus avoid the long path.

Finally, the visitor will arrive at the Tower of Hope, again symbolizing enlightenment and brighter tomorrows. However, as contributor Chris Powell explains in his critique of the CMHR's thematizations, the museum's decision to give such prominence to an affirmation of hope remains in some ways highly problematic given the complex and uneven global history of human rights, a history that seems poorly served by any such reductively teleological and triumphalist narrative. Powell's concerns resonate along-side work by the influential French cultural historian Pierre Nora on what he calls "les lieux de mémoire," sites of memory where the past becomes crystallized through the production of narratives reflecting the prevailing ideological preoccupations of the present, concerns saturated with anxiety about the fragility and persistence of our personal and collective identities. Nora's list of memory sites includes museums, archives, monuments, festivals, and cemeteries, and they all work by "producing, manifesting, establishing, constructing, decreeing, and maintaining by artifice and by will a society deeply absorbed in its own transformation and renewal."[11] That is, according to Nora, it is by engaging with such sites that a collectivity comes to understand itself as such. It thus becomes possible to see the CMHR not as a disinterested observer of "Canada's human rights journey" but rather as one node in the complex network of institutions and practices that gives shape to and reinforces the public's idea of what it means to be Canadian. The CMHR is what Carol Duncan and Alan Wallach identify as a "transactional" space, "the site of a symbolic transaction between the visitor and the state," the latter investing its actual and symbolic capital in exchange for the production of an identity (i.e., "Canadian") and an idea of civic virtue.[12] Powell is right to be concerned that the CMHR risks making it too easy for Canadians to feel good about themselves, their history, and their government.

"CONTROVERSY WILL BE THE FIRST PERSON TO COME TO OUR DOOR EVERY DAY"[13]

Anyone following the occasionally tortured evolution of the CMHR since it was officially created by amendments to the Museums Act in 2008 can be forgiven for having thought that it might never see the light of day. As Dirk Moses makes clear in his contribution to this volume, the controversial roots of the museum extend even further back in time, to 1998 and the widely publicized failure of efforts to have a Holocaust gallery included in the Canadian War Museum. This failure encouraged Izzy Asper, who had already funded the creation of a Human Rights and Holocaust Studies program through his charitable foundation, to begin working on a plan for "an all-inclusive Canadian genocide museum," one that would refer to a broad range of atrocities and human rights abuses, including those committed by the Canadian government, such as the internment of Japanese Canadians during the Second World War.

From the first, though, the Holocaust was intended to be given pride of place in the CMHR. This was no doubt a legacy of the earlier Canadian War Museum controversy and the absence of a national Holocaust memorial, as well as a reflection of the private conviction of Asper and many others, then as today, that there is profound moral-instructional value in the example of the Holocaust for Canada and a wider world struggling to come to terms with the proliferation of gross human rights violations. As the idea of a human rights museum was beginning to come into clearer focus in the early 2000s, the world was still struggling to make sense of the complicated political and moral legacies of the spectacularly horrific genocides and episodes of "ethnic cleansing" that had recently taken place in Bosnia (1992–95) and Rwanda (1994). Working from the conviction that learning about the Holocaust could help to forestall subsequent atrocities (a conviction contested here by David Petrasek), and initially with the support of a variety of stakeholder groups, including representatives of Canada's Armenian, Ukrainian, and Indigenous communities,[14] Asper and others fundraising for the museum proceeded to refine their idea of the museum. At this time, the museum was still a private undertaking not formally dependent on public funding, though it was receiving some limited financial support from all three levels of government (municipal, provincial, and federal), with more being promised. Nevertheless, fundraising for the CMHR was slow going, and it showed no signs of getting any easier in the immediate future.

Asper died in 2003, just a few months after announcing the project. It was then taken over by his daughter Gail, who continued to struggle both to raise the required funds and to clarify the aims and scope of her father's museum. Matters were greatly helped by the 2008 decision of the federal government to make the CMHR a federal institution. This decision considerably eased (but did not eliminate) the financial pressure on the museum's planners, but in return the government required that they act on a number of recommendations set forth in the report to the Minister of Canadian Heritage issued by an exploratory committee established a year earlier to make clear what the government expected from this takeover. Prominent among these expectations was the government's desire for the museum to speak for all Canadians, not just for a few "special interests." The report thus recommended the creation of a Content Advisory Committee (CAC),[15] the ambitions and operations of which are documented in Ken Norman's chapter in this volume.

The CAC played a key role in refining the idea of the CMHR. As Norman explains, the CAC used both open forums and targeted conversations with individuals and groups held across the country, with participants being invited to share their human rights stories and thoughts about what the CMHR should include. Although well attended and successful in promoting the museum, and though deepening CAC members' awareness of the richness of human rights issues across Canada, it remains unclear exactly how museum planners have incorporated this diversity into the CMHR's actual exhibits.[16] Nor is it clear to what extent the CMHR has acted on the recommendations made in the CAC's final report, such as ensuring that "persons from Indigenous Peoples and Quebec, with knowledge and expertise, are available within the Museum to contribute to all aspects of exhibit development, communication, and programming, including at senior levels."[17] Although the museum has periodically hired Aboriginal researchers/curators, the high rate of staff turnover and failure to fill many other planned-for positions[18] have hindered continuity in Indigenous exhibition planning and design, and limited such oversight at the level of senior management. Also, no Quebec specialist has been appointed as either a manager or a researcher/curator, another key recommendation of the CAC, though the implications of this absence for the CMHR's coverage of Quebec's distinct rights and culture remain unclear since the museum has instead depended for guidance on the judgments of external recognized experts in these fields.

THE IDEA OF INDIGENOUS RIGHTS IN CANADA

The Canadian Museum for Human Rights cannot avoid grappling with issues related to the mistreatment of Indigenous peoples in Canada; indeed, its need to do so is stressed in several of the CAC report's major recommendations. This need is especially urgent given the museum's location in Winnipeg, the city with the largest Aboriginal population in Canada. As a settler-colonial nation,[19] Canada rests on the elimination of Indigenous groups from the moral-imaginative and geographical landscapes, whether through practices of forced removal, assimilation, and extermination or through the occlusion of settler colonialism's horrors from official and popular representations of the country's past. The structure of settler colonialism persists in Canada, meaning that the CMHR, in its efforts to represent historical and ongoing human rights violations against Indigenous peoples, also faces the challenge of decolonizing its own practices.[20]

Meeting this challenge is difficult, not least because, as Jennifer Carter and Ruth Phillips note in their contributions, museums have been tied historically to colonial practices of cultural appropriation and misrepresentation. Indeed, for Phillips, a paradox arises from the fact that, even as museums have been complicit in disrupting the intergenerational transmission of Indigenous knowledge via their often unsanctioned appropriation and display of artifacts, they have also proven to be useful repositories of that knowledge and have played an important role in the restoration of Indigenous culture and ongoing processes of political empowerment. The CMHR is located at the heart of this contradictory terrain and set of tensions. How should such a museum represent Indigenous peoples in an honest, collaborative, and critical manner? What resources must it dedicate to this task? How should Indigenous peoples be engaged in this task? Will the museum adequately confront and do justice to the violence and trauma associated with Canada's historical and contemporary treatment of Indigenous peoples?

This last question came to prominence in the summer of 2013 when a combination of events sparked a broad public discussion of genocide in Canada. The first was an article published by a postdoctoral researcher at Guelph University, Ian Mosby, that detailed government-sponsored biomedical and nutritional experiments on Indigenous children at six Canadian residential schools as well as in northern Manitoba Indigenous communities. Soon after CBC Radio reported on the story, debate about Canada's historical treatment of Indigenous peoples was reignited.[21]

By this time, the Truth and Reconciliation Commission of Canada had entered its fourth year of hearing survivors' testimony about the violence, degradation, and suffering of Indian residential schools. But the thought of malnourished children being used as test subjects for vitamin supplements, as well as fortified flour that caused anemia, struck a chord with the public. It was in this context that scholars and activists provoked a debate about settler-colonial genocide in Canada. This group included former grand chief of the Assembly of First Nations Phil Fontaine, who, with his co-authors Michael Dan and Bernie Farber, called on Ottawa to acknowledge Canada as its sixth officially recognized genocide, alongside the Holocaust and the Holodomor, and genocides in Srebrenica, Armenia, and Rwanda.[22]

When a reporter from the *Winnipeg Free Press* read Fontaine and his co-author's editorial in the *Toronto Star* about genocide in Canada, she decided to ask the CMHR whether or not the term "genocide" would be used to refer to the experiences of Canada's Indigenous peoples. She was told that it would not, and on the basis of this response, as well as drawing on comments from two of the editors of this volume, she published an article largely critical of the museum for this oversight.[23] The CMHR felt blindsided by this criticism and worried that either its Indigenous curator or the editors of this volume had leaked the story to the press. The primary source of this worry was the chapter written by the curator, which was supposed to have been included in this volume. The chapter, it turns out, had not been vetted through formal museum channels and featured criticism of the CMHR's practices in relation to certain planned Indigenous exhibits. (The chapter made no mention of the genocide issue.) The curator's chapter was subsequently withdrawn from this volume on the grounds that it did not comply with CMHR policy concerning publication of curators' work pertaining to the museum, and the unfortunate consequence is that our volume contains less Indigenous content than we had originally planned. Of greater concern, however, is that an opportunity was lost to foster dialogue about settler colonialism in Canada and about the role and responsibilities of the CMHR in representing the destructive and ongoing consequences of settler-colonial relations with Canada's Indigenous peoples. The curator, who left the museum shortly after these events, has now published elsewhere about her experiences.[24]

Communication between the editors and the CMHR allowed the parties to overcome misunderstandings and make this volume a place for this sort of dialogue. The CMHR has generously contributed an afterword so that its perspectives, experiences, and goals can be made clearer. In this sense, our volume serves to host a conversation both with the CMHR and about the idea of a human rights museum. Rather than simply seeking to tear the museum down immediately after it has opened its doors, we endeavour here to demonstrate the complexity and contingency inherent in the idea of a human rights museum, understood both on its own terms and in relation to a wide range of other institutions around the world all wrestling in some way with traumatic memory. Our goal in preparing and editing this volume, in short, is not to score cheap points by attempting to fuel or endorse identity-driven criticisms of the CMHR and its curatorial strategies. Such challenges too often are insufficiently grounded in the realities of the museum's actual ambitions and praxis, excessively parochial, undertheorized, and spiteful. Instead, our aim is to critically interrogate some of the many promises inherent in, as well as the key challenges facing, this extraordinary institution and its generally thoughtful and well-meaning staff.

Some appreciation of the complexity of Indigenous representation is required when one begins to think through the variety of ways in which

Indigenous issues are exhibited in the CMHR. There is Indigenous content in each of the CMHR's ten galleries, more details about which can be found in Karen Busby's contribution. As well, the museum's two temporary galleries feature Indigenous exhibits from time to time. Some of the primary content in the main galleries includes collaborative efforts to represent Indigenous peoples as resurgent, defined not solely by their suffering but also by their survivance.[25] Thus, visitors will learn not only about residential schools but also about living traditions of Indigenous human rights and spirituality, and about how these traditions remain salient.

Residential schools are also exhibited in the CMHR in at least two different places: the Breaking the Silence and Canadian Journeys galleries. As noted above, these two galleries do not refer to residential schools, or any other aspect of Canadian settler colonialism, as genocide, in part, we are told, because the phrase "settler-colonial genocide" requires a level of reading competence above the Grade 9 level at which all CMHR text panels are written. In her contribution here, curator and gallery director Mary Reid provides a more extended discussion of the difficulty associated with determining the appropriate wording for text panels, especially when they are required to convey information about traumatic events and experiences. Not only reading level but also length is an issue for those charged with writing this kind of text, since such explanatory aids are typically required to be no more than 150 words long (and many must be even shorter). Of course, for those who argue that the term "genocide" *simpliciter* is applicable to the Canadian context,[26] the qualifier "settler colonial," which one supposes increases the level of difficulty of the phrase, is not required at all. In particular, for those scholars who have sought to revive Raphael Lemkin's originary insights into the concept of genocide,[27] what matters is that Canada sought to destroy Indigenous groups as groups, not whether or not this ambition was achieved through physical, biological, or cultural means or some combination thereof. The CMHR might still be able to provoke discussion of these and other interpretations of genocide in Canada, however, through its presentation of the Phil Fontaine editorial as part of its Indian residential school exhibit or by encouraging public discussion of the Truth and Reconciliation Commission's final report, which labels the Indian residential school regime as cultural genocide. The CMHR is also a partner in the National Research Centre (NRC) on Truth and Reconciliation hosted by the University of Manitoba. The NRC will receive the massive testimonial archive accumulated by the Truth and Reconciliation Commission over the course of its mandate, and undoubtedly it will actively encourage further public and scholarly reflection on this issue. It is simply too soon to conclude that the CMHR will entirely shy away from the issue of genocide in Canada.

But questions about how Indigenous peoples can and should be represented must still be addressed. In this volume, Adam Muller, Struan Sinclair, and Andrew Woolford examine plans for the Indian residential schools exhibition in the CMHR and consider whether leading-edge digital technologies of the sort increasingly used in museums generally, but especially in evidence in non-artifactual "ideas museums" such as the CMHR, could better represent residential schools when gallery space is limited. They argue that virtual and augmented realities can allow museums to advance knowledge of and empathy for the victims of atrocities in a manner that is flexible, immersive, and collaborative. The last point is particularly important for the project that they propose, which employs a highly self-reflexive and adaptable "participatory design" methodology to build a virtual Indian residential school. But their assumption is not that this technology is de facto a panacea for ideas museums. Instead, and given the vast sums of money currently being spent by museums such as the CMHR on virtual and augmented reality installations, they acknowledge the need to gauge the effectiveness of digitally mediated representations of atrocity in order to assess the degree to which they are indeed producing their desired effects.

Ruth Phillips is also interested in the potential of the CMHR to represent Indigenous peoples in a manner that redresses imbalances and injustices too long characteristic of museum practice. She locates the CMHR in a broader "national set" of Canadian museums intended to educate the Canadian public. Considered within this set, the CMHR must therefore be interrogated about the sort of work it is expected to do. What gaps is it intended to fill in our representations of Canada's past, present, and future? Specifically, which narratives about Canada and its relations with Indigenous peoples are to be included? And how might museums redress their prior failings in attempting to represent Indigenous peoples? For Phillips, the CMHR can offer a sort of redress, but it must do so in contrast to, rather than in step with, the precedents set by the rest of Canada's federal museum network. In the end, Phillips worries that though the CMHR presents Indigenous peoples as institutional "hosts," it also risks diluting their stories in a fragmented and cursory manner, thereby failing to live up to the promise of focused and sustained redress.

FROM CONSENSUS TO DISSENSUS

Debate over the CMHR's Indigenous content and refusal to designate Canadian settler colonialism as genocidal arose in the wake of a series of other controversies that called into question differing aspects of the museum's representational, design, and public relations strategies as well as the wider implications of its political and financial underpinnings. The most influential and arguably most damaging of these disputes, which, as Helen Fallding shows in her chapter, has garnered by far the most concentrated journalistic media coverage of the museum, centred on what she terms the "relentless" charges of preferential treatment leveraged against the CMHR by elements of the Ukrainian Canadian community because of the museum's devotion of an entire gallery to the Holocaust. Charges by groups such as the Ukrainian Canadian Civil Liberties Association that the CMHR was preferentially elevating Jewish suffering over that of other groups quickly degenerated into charges and counter-charges of racism and intolerance. The debate was soon joined by members of other groups, including those representing Slovak, Lithuanian, Polish, and Armenian Canadians, who expressed concerns that their own historical traumas were being marginalized or relegated to second-class status because of the square footage that the museum was allotting to them.[28] Commentators began to see the competitive aspects of these claims as signalling another manifestation of what historian Antony Polonsky, in a related context, has called the "suffering Olympics."[29]

What many have missed in their diagnoses of these disagreements is that the CMHR has gone out of its way not to be viewed as a commemorative institution. From its perspective, the museum's job is not to memorialize suffering of any kind but to educate the public about the history of human rights and Canada's specific contributions to that history (e.g., the vital role played by Canadian jurist John Peters Humphrey in drafting the Universal Declaration of Human Rights). Unlike some museums, the CMHR is not closely linked to specific historical traumas or distinct attempts at national reconciliation and redress. Instead, as already noted, its mission statement expressly indicates that the museum has three primary tasks: (1) to preserve and promote Canadian heritage, (2) to contribute to Canadian collective memory, and (3) to inspire research and learning.[30] Likewise, Section 15 of the Museums Act, the federal legislation responsible for specifying the terms and limits of the CMHR's legal existence, states only that the museum exists "to enhance the public's understanding of human rights, to promote respect for others and to encourage reflection and dialogue."[31] In public presentations, CMHR curators have done their best to avoid the language of commemoration, and indeed that word has been assiduously avoided in the museum's press releases and other public pronouncements.

However, the ambition of its planners to have the CMHR reject any commemorative role and serve with neutrality as a kind of "honest broker" in its curatorial practice has not proven as straightforwardly realizable as first hoped. Most obviously, this is because of the museum's unavoidable dependence on memory, which serves to anchor its representational practice. That the memories present in the museum's exhibitions are often traumatic should come as no surprise given the CMHR's interest in explaining the reasons for continuing to champion the cause of human rights at home and abroad, reasons rooted in the ongoing exploitation of human vulnerabilities.[32] It is worth acknowledging, though, that the museum won't focus solely on catastrophes but will also exhibit content that details uplifting human rights success stories, thereby expressing hope for our shared future. So, for example, CMHR curator/researcher Armando Perla explains in his chapter that, while the museum's migrant worker exhibit contains accounts of the abuses suffered by this highly vulnerable (since largely invisible) group of employees, whose efforts are vital for successful Canadian food production, it also contains accounts of what he terms "mobilization," bottom-up and frequently successful attempts to secure these workers' health and dignity. As examples of mobilization, Perla discusses efforts by advocates to provide English and French language classes for foreign workers and the staging of rural health clinics and workshops by groups such as Occupational Health Clinics for Ontario Workers.

Thus the stories that the museum tells, and exactly how it tells them, speak for Canada's official memory and by extension for where the histories of the nation's various cultural groups fit (or fail to fit) within this national "metanarrative." Chris Weedon and Glenn Jordan have argued that "in recent decades, collective memory in national contexts has been challenged and augmented by a range of interest groups, often not previously included in hegemonic constructions of the nation, who are fighting to have their histories acknowledged, documented and commemorated, with the aim, in part, of reshaping national stories."[33] It is against the backdrop of these struggles for recognition—which themselves should be understood as attempts to contest the official discourse of national identity and thus as struggles for inclusion—that we should try to make sense of the various identity-based challenges to the CMHR's exhibition plans. Conceived of in this way, the museum's failure, say, to incorporate in its permanent exhibitions an account of the situation in the Middle East involving Israel and the Palestinians can be acknowledged as a significant problem. The latter's occlusion from the CMHR implicitly conveys the twin messages that, from the perspective of the nation and its government, one of the most pressing human rights challenges of our time is not really "our" problem and that its victims living among us are not really part of our "imagined community."

To remember collectively, then, is de facto to commemorate, the CMHR's rejection of the latter notwithstanding. As a public, indeed as a properly *national,* institution in a multicultural country such as Canada, the CMHR will perform its commemorative role by recalling particular histories in a shared setting to promote reflection on who we are as a nation and on how, given this putative identity, we can best promote social justice and preserve human dignity at home and abroad. The museum, in short, will work to explain what we as Canadians are and need to become. But, of course, what the factional symbolic violence surrounding the CMHR has revealed is that not just our collective memory but also our collective identity continues to be contested in light of a past not fully shared. The role of the CMHR moving forward, then, will be not to distance itself from these controversies but to embrace them fully as an active participant. In the future, the museum must do more than merely stage controversy in the guise of a disinterested host.

CHANGING THE FUTURE

As a global human rights learning resource, the CMHR bears a responsibility to ensure the accuracy, integrity, and credibility of its research and collected knowledge. The museum strives to serve as a trusted international source for human rights learning, at all times encouraging critical engagement with museum scholarship and content. It thus makes sense to follow the recommendation made by Angela Failler and Roger Simon in their contribution here and view the CMHR less as a museum *of* and more as a museum *for* human rights. That is, it must be understood as having been established not only to record and display but also to elaborate, defend, and advocate the importance of human rights and the victims of their abuse. More than this, via its presentation of potentially unsettling "difficult knowledge," incidents of unimaginable traumatic violence, the museum must seek to change those who visit it, not necessarily by telling them exactly what to make of what they see, but rather by encouraging them to see for themselves and then act accordingly. Providing roadmaps for action is thus a crucial component of the CMHR's pedagogical mission and explains the composition of its Actions Count gallery, which models successful attempts by Canadians to secure human dignity, and its Inspiring Change gallery, which explicitly seeks to motivate museumgoers to change their world for the better.

A large banner proclaiming "Change begins with you" was hung on the stone façade of the museum during the building's construction. This message and a slightly longer and different version ("Most museums explore the past. This one changes the future") will also be conveyed by other media, including billboards, posters placed in prominent locations such as Winnipeg's airport, and national newspapers. If its mission is to change the future, then obviously the museum will need to do more than just host a litany of past wrongs. It will also need to do more than explain to its visitors the meanings of the events and histories that it puts on display. As Failler and Simon, Petrasek, Powell, and Grzyb all variously argue in their contributions, such explanations might yield an illusion of understanding that could lead, in fact, either to complacency or to overconfidence in our ability to shape the future. Petrasek, for example, contends that the clear focus of hindsight can give the mistaken impression that past events were somehow foreseeable, thus ignoring the uniqueness and unpredictability of atrocities. There is no certainty, he goes on to say, that historical understanding will foster respect for human rights moving forward, especially when the story of human rights is rendered under an "illusion of progress" suggesting that human rights have triumphed, as well as an "illusion of permanence" leading us to believe that these rights are here to stay. Powell's contribution adds to the concerns raised by Petrasek. In his view, the illusions that Petrasek identifies are inevitable consequences of a "top-down" human rights narrative wherein these rights serve as emblems for enlightenment and progress, as if they have been bestowed on us by a higher power (e.g., God, the state, law). Powell cautions against relying on such a narrative, preferring instead a constructivist and pragmatic approach highlighting "bottom-up" struggles that create human rights in a manner that is relationally dynamic, contextually contingent, and unfinished. His hope for the future of the CMHR is that, despite its investments in such top-down narratives, space will be found both within and outside the museum's walls for bottom-up narratives of human rights to emerge, take shape, and counter hegemonic representations that treat human rights as abstractions fully realizable only under the terms of the Canadian status quo.

Powell's framing of the tension between top-down and bottom-up narratives raises questions about how human rights museum exhibits should go about calling those who view them to action. Grzyb addresses this issue directly in her chapter, which examines comparative genocide exhibits through three case studies: the Kigali Memorial Centre's comparative genocide exhibit *Wasted Lives* (2004); the United States Holocaust Memorial Museum's temporary exhibit on genocide and intervention *From Memory to Action: Meeting the Challenge of Genocide* (2009–present); and the Museo Memoria y Tolerancia's exhibitions *Memory and Tolerance* (2010). Her analysis shows how national and political visions of the future are incorporated into a museum's call to action, and like Powell she advocates that human rights museums instead provide opportunities for dialogue about "the nature of action itself." Like Failler and Simon, Grzyb thinks that the CMHR needs to create spaces that succeed in allowing visitors not so much to *learn about* as to *learn from* the past. However, as George Jacob reminds us in his discussion of India's Khalsa Heritage Centre, it is not always easy to generalize about what "learning" is or how best to cultivate it institutionally, particularly in locations where a significant proportion of the population is formally illiterate. Indeed, museum planners constantly need to keep in view multiple forms of literacy, not all of them reducible to reading competence, and thus a wide variety of ways to instruct and learn. Jacob also rightly cautions against viewing emerging technologies as a pedagogical panacea, particularly in environments in the developing world where digital literacy rates are low and programming and installation costs cannot easily be borne. Instead, Jacob uses the example of the Khalsa Heritage Centre to show how the incorporation by museum designers of local craft productions and traditional representational forms and media, albeit recontextualized and cross-pollinated in modern gallery settings, can produce even in non-print-literate visitors profound somatic and emotional effects, and thereby knowledge of a different but still valuable kind.[34] The Khalsa Heritage Centre exemplifies precisely the sort of multiplatform curatorial approach that Jennifer Carter sees as the hallmark of what she calls successful "progressive museographical practice."

CODA

As the CMHR undergoes critical evaluation by the scholars and members of the public who pass through its doors, both its programming and its exhibits will be scrutinized, not always kindly. It is important for our readers to understand the contents of this volume as located simultaneously within and without this critical-evaluative frame. This project, the first book-length study of the Canadian Museum for Human Rights, has its roots in (and seeks to disclose salient aspects of) discussions that preceded the museum's opening and thus focused on to the "idea" of the CMHR rather than its instantiation. It thus testifies to the museum's possibility and promise, as well as any number of potential pitfalls, while serving as an important repository for information concerning its conceptual evolution and developmental process. One thing that has become acutely apparent to us in working on the museum and with its curators over the past several years is just how much of a moving target it is, how the ground on which our understanding rests can change quickly underfoot. The picture of the CMHR that we paint here is perhaps therefore best understood as necessarily provisional and incomplete, though for all that it is still likely to reward those readers who seriously entertain the criticisms and reservations that accompany it.

In order to guide readers through the varied arguments and multiple case studies discussed by this volume's contributors, we have settled on a four-part structure bookended by this introduction, itself intended to provide readers with some idea of our orientation to the material that we present here, and an afterword written by Jodi Giesbrecht and Clint Curle from the CMHR, which responds to this project as a whole. Each section of the book is loosely arranged thematically, though we expect that readers will notice many parallels and resonances among works in different sections. The volume's first section, "The Idea of a Human Rights Museum," traces the complex history of the CMHR and provides a critical reading of the evolution of the museum's conceptualization and public self-representation. This section also raises important questions concerning the general utility of the idea of human rights, both historically and in the present, addressed later in the volume by several other contributors. The second section, "Spatialization and Design," moves from the abstract to the concrete by considering the physical structure of the CMHR, reflecting on what this unique and occasionally awkward arrangement of space means for the curation and design of exhibits on human rights. This section allows readers to witness the museum evolve and become recognizable in its present form as the architect's idea of it sharpens and solidifies. Chapters also explain what the museum contains, at the same time giving us reason to be circumspect about the arrangement of its contents as well as the technologies used to display them and engage visitors. The third section, "Curatorial Challenges," looks at the practice of curation and considers many of the risks and issues facing those who attempt to represent "difficult knowledge" in museums. Care has been taken to juxtapose broader accounts that consider curatorial practice generally or theoretically with those focused more narrowly on the museology of human rights or the CMHR's own curatorial praxis. The final section, "Parallels and Obligations," places the museum in a comparative context by examining other museums elsewhere in the world and asking what the CMHR and its visitors can learn from them. Its emphasis on obligations arises from the sense in these final contributions of the enormous importance of the work of raising human rights consciousness at home and abroad, and of the need to do this job well. Given the kind of material and experiences discussed and put on display by the CMHR, it is important to learn what has worked and what has not (and why) from the attempts made by others elsewhere to do so. This final section gives readers some reason to be circumspect concerning the CMHR's stronger claims to uniqueness, even as it provides reasons to be optimistic about the institution's prospects.

We remain profoundly grateful to CMHR staff, especially to Clint Curle and the museum's curatorial staff, past and present, for their patience and willingness to work with us, helping us to conceptualize the institution at different stages of its development and filling us in on all relevant aspects of their working lives. We recognize that both our critical scrutiny and the fluid character of the museum's exhibition plans have not made their jobs any easier. This fluidity is due to several factors, including a design process that has required successive back-and-forth negotiations/consultations with the museum's design firm, Ralph Applebaum Associates. It is also a consequence of a flexible approach to curation that has been able to respond with varying degrees of success and rapidity to scholarly input as well as public and political pressure received on a rolling basis, sometimes out of the blue. Without exception, and notwithstanding our disagreements and concerns, we have not encountered a person working for the CMHR, from former president and CEO Stuart Murray on down, who has not tried to make the museum a place that people will want to visit and that will promote social justice and the defence of human rights everywhere. While goodwill of this kind certainly is not enough to guarantee the CMHR's success, without it the museum would surely and completely fail.

As for the matter of success and failure, it is vital to remember that the museum's opening marks not the end of its development but an important beginning. To judge the CMHR as a finished product following the commencement of its public operations would be premature, unhelpful, and unfair. Like any good museum, but especially one devoted to cruel indignities that continue to proliferate domestically and abroad, the CMHR must continue to grow and evolve. In order to do its job properly, it must remain perpetually a work in progress. It is our sincere hope that the arguments presented here on the idea of a human rights museum will contribute meaningfully to this progress.

NOTES

1   Most explicitly Jennifer Carter, Amanda Grzyb, Jorge Nállim, Ruth Phillips, and Stephan Jaeger.

2   Prime Minister Stephen Harper has publicly stated that "we also have no history of colonialism." He made this statement during a press conference at the 2009 G20 meetings in Pittsburgh, and it is quoted in Jennifer Henderson and Pauline Wakeham, "Colonial Reckoning, National Reconciliation? Aboriginal Peoples and the Culture of Redress in Canada," *ESC: English Studies in Canada* 35, 1 (2009): 1.

3   "Architecture and Landscape: The Architectural Design Process," National Museum of the American Indian website, http://nmai.si.edu/visit/washington/architecture-landscape/.

4   Renzo Piano, "Renzo Piano: The World's Leading Builder of Museums," 2005, Architexturez Network, http://network.architexturez.net/pst/az-cf-121478-1081139197.

5   Angela Cassie, "Letter to Association of Manitoba Archaeologists," 2010, Association of Manitoba Archeologists website, http://www.assocmanarch.com/12.html; Mireille Lamontagne, "Museum Archaeological Dig a Goldmine of Information," 2013, Canadian Museum for Human Rights blog, http://museumforhumanrights.ca/explore/blog/museum-archaeological-dig-goldmine-information#.UpeCN41bHpU.

6   Leigh Syms, "Accelerated Destruction of First Nations Heritage Beneath the Canadian Museum of Human Rights, 2009," 2010, Association of Manitoba Archaeologists website, http://www.assocmanarch.com/12.html.

7   Cassie, "Letter."

8   Jan Otakar Fischer, as quoted in Alex Bozikovic, "Germany's First War Museum since Fall of Berlin Wall Stirs Mixed Emotions," *Globe and Mail*, 23 February 2011.

9   https://humanrights.ca/about/mandate-and-museum-experience.

10   Joan M. Mcguire, Sally S. Scott, and Stan F. Shaw, "Universal Design and Its Applications in Educational Environments," *Remedial and Special Education* 27, 3 (2006): 166–75.

11   Pierre Nora, "Between Memory and History: Les lieux de mémoire," *Representations* 26, 1 (1989): 12.

12   Carol Duncan and Alan Wallach, "The Universal Survey Museum," *Art History* 3, 4 (1980): 457.

13   Stuart Murray, CMHR CEO, at the first Critical Conversations seminar, 9 September 2011.

14   Constituencies later highly critical of elements of the plans finally settled on by the CMHR's planners.

15   *Report to the Minister of Canadian Heritage on the Canadian Museum for Human Rights* (Ottawa: Library and Archives Canada, 2008).

16   They have generated, however, a substantial repository of recorded oral testimony that will be accessible to interested parties through the CMHR's archive.

17   *Report to the Minister,* 28.

18   Owing in part to budget shortfalls because of building cost overruns and fundraising difficulties.

19   Patrick Wolfe, "Settler Colonialism and the Elimination of the Native," *Journal of Genocide Research* 8, 4 (2006): 387–409; Lorenzo Veracini, *Settler Colonialism: A Theoretical Overview* (New York: Palgrave Macmillan, 2010).

20   Amy Lonetree, *Decolonizing Museums: Representing Native America in National and Tribal Museums* (Chapel Hill: University of North Carolina Press, 2012); Linda Tuhiwai Smith, *Decolonizing Methodologies: Research and Indigenous Peoples* (New York: Zed Books, 1999).

21   Ian Mosby, "Administering Colonial Science: Nutrition Research and Human Biomedical Experimentation in Aboriginal Communities and Residential Schools, 1942–1952," *Histoire sociale/Social History* 46, 91 (May, 2013): 145–72.

22   Phil Fontaine, Michael Dan, and Bernie Farber, "A Canadian Genocide in Search of a Name," *Toronto Star,* 19 July 2013.

23   Mary Agnes Welch, "CMHR Rejects Genocide for Native Policies," *Winnipeg Free Press,* 26 July 2013, http://www.winnipegfreepress.com/local/cmhr-rejects-genocide-for-native-policies-217061321.html.

24. Tricia Logan, "National Memory and Museums: Remembering Settler Colonial Genocide of Indigenous Peoples in Canada" in *Remembering Genocide,* ed. Nigel Eltringham and Pam MacLean (New York: Routledge, 2014), 112–130.

25   Gerald Vizenor, *Survivance: Narratives of Native Presence* (Lincoln: University of Nebraska Press, 2008).

26   Damien Short, "Cultural Genocide and Indigenous Peoples: A Sociological Approach," *International Journal of Human Rights* 14, 6 (2010): 833–48; Andrew Woolford, "Ontological Destruction: Genocide and Aboriginal Peoples in Canada," *Genocide Studies and Prevention: An International Journal* 4, 1 (2009): 81–97.

27   Douglas Irvin-Ericson, "Genocide, 'Family of Mind,' and the Romantic Signature of Raphael Lemkin," *Journal of Genocide Research* 15, 3 (2013): 273–96; A. Dirk Moses, ed., *Colony, Empire, Genocide: Conquest, Occupation, and Subaltern Resistance in World History* (New York: Berghahn, 2008); Michael A. McDonnell and A. Dirk Moses, "Raphael Lemkin as Historian of Genocide in the Americas," *Journal of Genocide Research* 7, 4 (2005): 501–29; Short, "Cultural Genocide."

28   "Protest Grows over Holocaust 'Zone' in Canadian Museum for Human Rights," *Globe and Mail,* 14 February 2011, http://www.theglobeandmail.com/arts/protest-grows-over-holocaust-zone-in-canadian-museum-for-human-rights/article566190/.

29   Roger Cohen, "The Suffering Olympics," *New York Times,* 30 January 2012.

30   See http://humanrights.ca/about-museum#.Uwy9TXlX5AR.

31   http://laws-lois.justice.gc.ca/eng/acts/M-13.4/page-6.html#docCont.

32   Bryan S. Turner, *Vulnerability and Human Rights* (University Park: Pennsylvania State University Press, 2006).

33   Chris Weedon and Glenn Jordan, "Collective Memory: Theory and Politics," *Social Semiotics* 22, 2 (2012): 144.

34   For more on the "epistemic value" of our emotions, see Satya Mohanty's discussion of Naomi Scheman's "Anger and the Politics of Naming" in his *Literary Theory and the Claims of History* (Ithaca, NY: Cornell University Press, 1997).

THE IDEA OF A HUMAN RIGHTS MUSEUM

GROUNDING THE CANADIAN MUSEUM FOR HUMAN RIGHTS IN CONVERSATION

CHAPTER 1

Ken Norman

In January 2009, I accepted an invitation from the acting chief executive officer of the Canadian Museum for Human Rights (CMHR) to become a member of a new body called the Content Advisory Committee (CAC). The *Report to the Minister of Canadian Heritage on the Canadian Museum for Human Rights* had called for creation of the CAC: "It is recommended that an independent group of human rights scholars, specialists and leaders be appointed to elicit relevant information from individuals, organizations and groups. The CAC would work closely with CMHR staff for the purposes of ensuring that the Board and CMHR have the capacity and authority to acknowledge conflict, provide a balanced perspective and acknowledge and manage controversy. The members of the CAC should be chosen to play the role of advisors rather than advocates for special interest groups."[1] For the purposes of this discussion, I will focus on the mandate given to the CAC in the first sentence of this recommendation. The second sentence speaks to the *Report to the Minister*'s envisioning of a long "operating" role for the CAC.[2] However, as it turned out, the CAC was given only a preliminary finite task: "to listen to Canadians in a public engagement process and offer our expert advice on what we heard."[3] The CAC was disbanded shortly after filing its *Final Report* in May 2010.

In our planning meetings in early 2009, there was much debate on the point of our public engagement process. Were our community consultations an exercise in acquiring a "collection" for the CMHR? Were they primarily a public relations exercise in building support for the CMHR? Or were they less about listening, collecting, and pitching and more about public engagement? We landed on the final proposition: "Our role in assisting the Museum to develop content is remarkable. In a break from museum convention—where the authority tends to be firmly in the hands of museum 'experts,' to the exclusion of all others—there was a space created for knowledge contributions from the public as well as from the Content Advisory Committee."[4] We established as a key modality in our cross-Canada tour, beginning on 27 May 2009 in my home city, Saskatoon, a very public roundtable exercise. In advance of our visit to a city, an evening public forum was advertised in local media. The venue would be an accessible site such as a library or community hall. After showing a short video, we spent about an hour and a half facilitating discussions around tables of eight or so people. Facilitators asked what those at the table would like to experience in the CMHR. We hoped that participants in the roundtables would feel that they were engaged with us in that discussion.[5]

My strong support for this conversational exercise was generally informed by three different phases of my professional life. First was my fresh memory of disconcerting experiences as a member of two successive advisory committees established by Friends of the Canadian Museum for Human Rights beginning in 2005, with experts talking with designers and consultants in boardrooms with the doors closed as if one need not look elsewhere for knowledge of human rights. Second were my rewarding years as a human rights law teacher guided by Yeats's insight that education is not the filling of a pail but the lighting of a fire.[6] Third was my stint as the first chief commissioner of the Saskatchewan Human Rights Commission, where my statutory mandate to promote human rights—amounting to little more than a few speeches and boxes of pamphlets—gained little apparent ground in fostering a human rights culture in the province. Thus, I was predisposed to the idea that, if the "for human rights" in the CMHR's name was to have life, one would have to find ways to engage people respectfully, to kindle the fire of a human rights culture in them.

Specifically, I had just read three books with historical and theoretical insights that had stoked such a fire within me. First, Lynn Hunt's *Inventing Human Rights: A History*[7] illustrated how, in the eighteenth century, because of the advent of the epistolary novel in Europe, empathy for the suffering of other human beings spread beyond insular communities, resulting in the rejection of torture as a punishment and slavery as a practice. Reading Hunt's book brought to mind Richard Rorty's contention that "pragmatists argue from the fact that the emergence of the human rights culture seems to owe nothing to increased moral knowledge, and everything to hearing sad and sentimental stories."[8] The lesson for the CMHR that I took from this claim was the prospect of finding ways to spark a more expansive understanding of suffering humanity in all of its diversity—of growing a human rights culture—through the use of personal stories to achieve an empathic appreciation of what it might be like to walk in the shoes of the other.[9]

Second, Johannes Morsink's *Inherent Human Rights: Philosophical Roots of the Universal Declaration*[10] drew from debates in the Third Committee of the United Nations preceding proclamation of the Universal Declaration of Human Rights (UDHR) for the proposition that human rights are fundamental moral birthrights of our common humanity, knowable by everyone:[11] "It is through their moral sentiments that people discover the metaphysical universality of human rights."[12] For me, the epistemological point here was fundamental. Scholars and curators had no trumping claim to knowledge in answering the contested question, what are human rights? *Everyone* had the right to contribute to the content of human rights discourse. With this theoretical guidance, it seemed to me that the CAC was clearly seeking knowledge from just the right people by democratizing the CMHR's content development process in our public engagement tour.

Third, reading Amartya Sen's *The Idea of Justice*,[13] I was taken by his conception of human rights discourse as a public conversation of a particular kind, an exercise in "open impartiality," which "not only admits but requires consideration of the views of others."[14] "Human rights," Sen claims, "are ethical claims constitutively linked with the importance of human freedom, and the robustness of an argument that a particular claim can be seen as a human right has to be assessed through the scrutiny of public reasoning, involving open impartiality."[15] His Smithsonian idea of "open impartiality" is a call for reasoned public argument in dealing with conflicting claims seeking common ground and rejecting the lazy relativism of "you are right in your community and I am right in mine."[16] Sen explains that the UDHR's grand moral proclamations frame public debates around what is to be done about perceived violations of human rights.[17]

Of course, such conversations can result in dissonance. However, as Sen notes, Bernard Williams has argued that "disagreement does not necessarily have to be overcome."[18] What *is* required is open acknowledgement that there are plural and competing reasons for what is to be done in the name of human rights—"all of which have claims to impartiality and

4. Cover of the Content Advisory Committee's *Final Report*.

5. At the museum's 2010 Olympics booth.

which nevertheless differ from—and rival—each other."[19] Sen's commitment to such a possibly dissonant public conversation—seeking common human rights ground across vast differences of conviction and life experience—struck me as setting exactly the right *raison d'être* for the CAC's cross-Canada public engagement tour and for the CMHR to take to heart.[20]

Running alongside the roundtables were two other elements in the CAC's journey: "bilaterals" and oral history videos. We held bilateral meetings with individuals and groups whom members of the CAC "felt would be critical to hear from in order fully to understand human rights in Canada."[21] A room near each bilateral meeting room was set up for on-camera interviews in order to preserve for the CMHR some of the remarkable stories and insights offered to us in the bilaterals. Using videos, rather than simply transcribing testimonies, was a deliberate choice in order to demonstrate the power of the medium of film and of the arts generally to capture and stretch people's imaginations regarding the experiences of the other.

As the months of our public engagement tour came to an end, we chose to convey the key messages of our CAC conclusions in two ways. First, the cover page of our *Final Report* speaks volumes on our central epistemological stance. Second, we made the following recommendation: "The Museum should use the arts to illustrate the richness of the human soul and of reflection, its dark zones, and the multiple ways in which human beings transcend their realities and thereby seek survival.... The overall tone of art featured in the Museum should be inspirational—it should show how individuals have resisted discrimination and sought to obtain justice against all odds."[22] Support for this position is found in the recent United Nations Declaration on Human Rights Education and Training. Article 6 provides the following:

1. Human rights education and training should capitalize on and make use of new information and communication technologies, as well as the media, to promote all human rights and fundamental freedoms.

2. The arts should be encouraged as a means of training and raising awareness in the field of human rights.

As a demonstration of how video might be used to this end, CAC member and filmmaker Sylvia Hamilton undertook to edit our oral history interviews into a short video. This piece, *A Canadian Conversation*,[23] has many such engaging clips. In particular, with regard to Kofi Annan's assertion about human rights being found in the hearts and minds of human beings, captured on the cover page of our *Final Report,* the video has this scene. At a school in Iqaluit, we took this epistemological point seriously by providing students with the opportunity to step up to our camera and complete the sentence "Everyone has the right to...." Among an array of responses, surprisingly but delightfully, the video shows one child asserting that "Everyone has the right to dream."

The CMHR's booth at the 2010 Vancouver Winter Olympics took up this inclusive demonstration in democratizing the human rights knowledge question by providing visitors with an opportunity to complete the same sentence. This quickly became the booth's most popular feature. More recently, in September 2012, a fundraising golf tournament—the Dufresne Play for a Purpose tournament at the Glendale Golf and Country Club, Winnipeg, for Friends of the Canadian Museum for Human Rights—followed suit. This charity tournament dedicated itself to generating funds for Friends over the next three years. Golfers were given an opportunity to fill in a similar poster. The website of Friends posted a picture of three golfers holding up a sign saying, "Everyone has the right to a job."

As has been forcefully put recently, a community consultation, such as the CAC's public engagement tour or any such physical effort or social media openness to conversation by the CMHR, "requires honesty, trust, equality, respect and the development of long-term reciprocal relationships" if it is "to be successful."[24] The CAC was very much alive to the need for our public engagement tour not to be just a flash in the pan. Rather, we hoped that our journey, from sea to sea to sea, would lead to the development of long-term reciprocal conversations with Canadians as praxis for the CMHR. So we made this recommendation: "The contacts developed through the CAC public engagement sessions in 2009/10 form a significant base for continuing to involve Canadians in the Museum, although steps should be taken to include those who may not yet have had the opportunity to be heard."[25]

The jury is out on whether the CMHR will be brave enough to offer its researchers and curators the rewards and risks of such a stimulating continuing conversation with Canadians. The Australian National Museum offers an example of this sort of courage. I attended the second annual conference of the Federation of Independent Human Rights Museums (FIHRM), convened at the Slavery Museum in Liverpool in October 2011. Adele Chynoweth, curator of the National Museum of Australia, presented a paper showing how seriously that museum has taken the opportunity to engage in a difficult Australian conversation. She created a page on the museum's website offering a blog—a forum—for "Forgotten Australians," the half million or so non-Aboriginal children who had been kept in orphanages or other out-of-home institutions over the past century.[26] The invitation to Forgotten Australians was to share personal narratives and thoughts as well as to contribute suggestions for artifacts for the museum. This blog was a precursor to a current "living history" exhibition entitled *Inside: Life in Children's Homes and Institutions*. Chynoweth moderated the blog, which resulted in an "astounding" rate of participation by former Forgotten Australians. For example, in June 2011, the website's blog had 18,000 visits:

> Forgotten Australians used the site to share artwork, poems, song writing, personal testimonies both written and digitally recorded, re-connect with family members from whom they were separated as a result of being institutionalised. They also met, online, former inmates of their former institutions and some as a result organised legal class actions against past providers of institutional care. Forgotten Australians use the website to post notices concerning pending protest actions. Also, many children who were institutionalised do not have photographs of themselves as children and so the site has been used by Forgotten Australians to share photographs. Some of those who grew up in the same institutions have recognised themselves in these.[27]

Chynoweth's paper concludes with the observation that "the National Museum's exhibition blog created a safe site for Forgotten Australians and as a result became a popular site which fulfilled some of the social and legal needs of the Forgotten Australians. Contributions to the website may also have been used to identify other opportunities for the National Museum to further assist the achievement of social justice through human rights activism."[28]

As I have noted, the virtual CMHR has taken up the CAC's inclusive "Everyone has the right…" offering, allowing people to speak a few words of their own truths and to submit their own stories. With regard to public engagement, the CMHR's website *does* utilize social media, with Twitter, Facebook, Flickr, YouTube, and an RSS news feed and blog. However, the RSS news items are about developments with regard to the CMHR. The "news" does not carry live feeds from any human rights NGOs on current human rights situations. Furthermore, there is no hyperlink to human rights NGOs let alone information on how to contact them, not even Nobel Peace Laureate or Amnesty International. Bluntly put, this is a clear signal to those interested in engagement in current events in human rights that the CMHR is not a kindred spirit. Such a message undercuts the CMHR's inclusive statutory mandate to grow a culture of human rights.

The CMHR's Twitter and Facebook accounts *do* flag notable UN and other human rights "observance occasions" and some current human rights campaigns, such as the White Ribbon Campaign to end violence against women, which has special resonance in Canada on 6 December, the anniversary of the Montreal Massacre.[29] It is also worth noting that the CMHR's social media sites *are* open to non-automated comments from the public.

To its credit, the CMHR live-streamed its second annual public meeting, held at Sisler High School in Winnipeg on 6 December 2012. A chain of tweets tracked each notable moment in the meeting's progress up to the question period, including some testimony from three students about the lessons of the Montreal Massacre and a riveting performance by the school's dance ensemble.[30] People *were* invited to submit questions via social media. A staff member at the end of the meeting put a couple of such questions to the floor, prompting the public's response.

That said, however, as of this writing the CMHR's social media sites only occasionally record supportive notes and display very few dialogues in which the CMHR plays any sort of provocative, let alone facilitative, role. And, given the robust exchanges found all over the Internet with regard to human rights issues, as people make their voices heard on perceived injustices, almost everything found on the CMHR's social media pages seems to be guided by, with apologies to Johnny Mercer and Bing Crosby, an accentuation of the positive.[31] One Facebook friend noticed this absence of serious dialogue: "I'm kinda shocked that this website has not really made a comment or a statement of what's currently happening between Isreal [sic] and Palestine??? You would think this is something they should be taking [sic] about as soon as it started happening." And, to date, the blog remains largely used as a vehicle for CMHR professionals to post short promotional pieces about their work and solicit comments. Save for some barbed remarks on the "Holocaust versus Holodomor square footage" controversy that has managed to generate more heat than light in the aftermath of the CAC's *Final Report*,[32] there has been nothing approaching a critical exchange of views, beyond a note or two, among visitors to the

6. Billboard illuminated in the dark outside the museum.

RT @cbcmanitoba: Come down to the #CBChumanlibrary listen to Real people with Real conversations for you to take part in...

7. Twitter screen shot, January 2013.

site.[33] A brutal denunciation from the Ukrainian Canadian Civil Liberties Association in this sorry episode has recently been hyperlinked, but left unanswered, by the CMHR's Facebook site.[34]

In sum, on the question of what the future might hold, there seems to be some indication that the virtual CMHR has some readiness to initiate a continuing conversation with Canadians on difficult human rights subjects. The open question is where, on the spectrum from none to some and beyond, will the virtual and the physical CMHR come to stand?

In an interview on 12 September 2012 by columnist Dan Lett at the *Winnipeg Free Press* News Café, James Moore, the Minister of Canadian Heritage, made the sobering point that he has *repeatedly* cautioned the CMHR's CEO and Board of Trustees that the CMHR must not "be a source of division."[35] Is this an instruction to avoid controversy? If so, then there is reason to doubt whether the CMHR will take seriously its statutory mandate to grow a culture of human rights in this country. If not, and one *can* construe this cautionary admonition by focusing on the word *source,* then why would the minister have seen fit to repeat his message? A similar sobering note was sounded in a CBC investigative piece of 30 November 2012 alleging that political interference has produced dramatic staff turnover rates at the CMHR: "Staff have been told to include more 'positive stories' and to curtail criticisms of issues touching on current government policy."[36] In his opening address to the 2012 annual conference of the Federation of International Human Rights Museums, David Fleming, the president of FIHRM, urged member organizations—including the CMHR—to take seriously their "duty to represent all sections of society, to challenge standard narratives of history and exorcise the 'dark side of the national past.' This raises the question of how museums respond to contemporary issues."[37]

I have argued that grounding the CMHR in conversation is an essential foundation for its project. Such conversations can be filled with light or dark. But they are always worth having. Figure 6 and 7 are two signs that the CMHR agrees. And a third occured on 15 May 2014 when the *Winnipeg Free Press* published an item under the headline "Transgender Allies Protest: Feminist Author's CMHR Turn Deplored." A spokesperson for the local transgender community challenged the CMHR for providing the iconic feminist, Germaine Greer, with a platform from which to speak on the ground that she was no friend of their struggle for human rights. The CMHR's forthright response was to note that "'the museum's role is to inspire human-rights conversations. This is why we agreed to become the venue for the Fragile

Freedoms lecture series,' said Maureen Fitzhenry, the museum's media-relations manager."[38]

Facilitating empathic connection is a necessary element if the CMHR is to deliver on the promise made in its name by the word *for*. Simon Baron-Cohen has argued recently in *The Science of Evil: On Empathy and the Origins of Cruelty* that "empathy itself is the most valuable resource in our world."[39] And I know of no better way for empathy to emerge than through conversation. Listening to—learning from—real people in real conversations is surely the heart of the matter. This is what the CAC experienced in our roundtable public engagement sessions. This is what I know as a human rights teacher. Such "I and Thou"[40] conversations and their digital simulacra—in both the light and the dark—hold the most promise of growing a culture of human rights via the physical and virtual CMHR.

NOTES

1   *Report to the Minister of Canadian Heritage on the Canadian Museum for Human Rights* (Ottawa: Library and Archives Canada, 2008), 17.

2   Ibid., Annex A, i.

3   *Content Advisory Committee Final Report to the Canadian Museum for Human Rights* (Ottawa: Library and Archives Canada, 2010), 3.

4   Ibid.

5   Ibid., 7.

6   See http://www.teacherleaders.org/node/4176.

7   Lynn Hunt, *Inventing Human Rights: A History* (New York: W.W. Norton and Company, 2007).

8   Richard Rorty, "Human Rights, Rationality, and Sentimentality," in *On Human Rights: The 1993 Oxford Amnesty Lectures,* ed. Susan Hurley and Stephen Shute (New York: Basic Books, 1993), 112–34. Also see page 4 of http://web1.uct.usm.maine.edu/~bcj/issues/three/rorty.html.

9   Just how the CMHR might address this insight is discussed by Angela Failler and Roger Simon in their chapter in this volume. They argue that, in presenting "difficult knowledge," the CMHR eschews the model of "learning about" from experts and embraces curatorial presentations that involve "learning from" the other by taking his or her story into our own lives and then acting as though it really mattered.

10   Johannes Morsink, *Inherent Human Rights: Philosophical Roots of the Universal Declaration* (Philadelphia: University of Pennsylvania Press, 2009).

11   Ibid., 67, cited in the CAC's *Final Report*, 17n3.

12   Ibid., 59. For a critique of such an ideal metaphysical starting point, see Christopher Powell's chapter in this volume. Powell, from the perspective of an academic social scientist inspired by a vision of a radically egalitarian, inclusive, and emancipated society, argues

that human rights struggles are always socially constructed, situated in concrete historical struggles for justice.

13   Amartya Sen, *The Idea of Justice* (Cambridge, MA: Harvard University Press, 2009).

14   Ibid., 114–2, 126 for this quotation.

15   Ibid., 365–66.·

16   Ibid., x.

17   Ibid., 357, cited in the CAC's *Final Report,* 17n3.

18   Ibid., 14.

19   Ibid., 12.

20   I thank Angela Failler for drawing my attention to Jacques Rancière's related concept of dissensus as being the heart of a democratic public discourse to be celebrated, where those included and those excluded engage in a "dispute over what is given and about the frame within which we sense something is given." Jacques Rancière, *Dissensus: On Politics and Aesthetics,* ed. and trans. Steven Corcoran (London: Continuum, 2010), 9.

21   The CAC's *Final Report,* 7n3.

22   Ibid., 64.

23   Available on the CMHR's website and/or on YouTube at http://www.youtube.com/ watch?v=dYNhBYTDEVW.

24   Laurajane Smith and Kalliopi Fouseki, "The Role of Museums as 'Places of Social Justice': Community Consultation and the 1807 Bicentenary," in *Representing Enslavement and Abolition in Museums: Ambiguous Engagements,* ed. Laurajane Smith et al. (London: Routledge, 2011), 4–5. Helen Fallding's chapter in this volume makes a similar point about the virtues of openness: "A human rights museum should model the transparency that we expect from our governments and that underpins the security of many of our other rights."

25   The CAC's *Final Report,* 13n3.

26   Adele Chynoweth, "Online Activism, the National Museum of Australia Exhibition Website: Inside: Life in Children's Homes," http://www.fihrm.org/conference/conference2011. html#papers.

27   Ibid.

28   Ibid.

29   http://humanrightsmuseum.ca/explore/blog/white-ribbon-campaign.

30   https://twitter.com/cmhr_news.

31   http://www.lyrics007.com/Bing%20Crosby%20Lyrics/Ac-Cent-Tchu-ate%20The%20Positive%20Lyrics.html.

You've got to accentuate the positive
Eliminate the negative
Latch on to the affirmative
Don't mess with Mister In-Between

32   Fallding notes in this volume that eighteen of thirty-one articles about the CMHR, in national publications, "were preoccupied with the Holodomor debate."

33   "Raising Awareness of the Holodomor in Canada and Around the Globe," posted by Clint Curle, Researcher, *7 Comments,* 31 July 2012, http://humanrightsmuseum.ca/explore/blog/raising-awareness-holodomor-canada-and-around-globe.

34   https://www.facebook.com/canadianmuseumforhumanrights.

35   http://www.winnipegfreepress.com/cafe/.

36   http://www.cbc.ca/news/canada/manitoba/story/2012/11/30/mb-human-rights-museum-staff-quit-winnipeg.html.

37   As reported by Rebecca Atkinson, "The Myth of the Apolitical Museum," *Museums Journal: Blog,* 17 October 2012, http://www.museumsassociation.org/museums-journal-blog/17102012-political-museum-liverpool.

38   http://www.winnipegfreepress.com/local/Transgender-allies-protest-259342471.html.

39   Simon Baron-Cohen, *The Science of Evil: On Empathy and the Origins of Cruelty* (New York: Basic Books, 2011), 153.

40   Martin Buber, *I and Thou,* trans. Ronald Gregor Smith (New York: Scribner, 2000).

PROTECTING HUMAN RIGHTS AND PREVENTING GENOCIDE: THE CANADIAN MUSEUM FOR HUMAN RIGHTS AND THE WILL TO INTERVENE

CHAPTER 2

A. Dirk Moses

The Canadian Museum for Human Rights (CMHR) has stimulated controversy and extensive debate since it was first proposed a decade ago, but only recently has a nuanced discussion of its origins and development taken place. Hitherto, its contested foundation was ascribed to stock characters scripted into standard plots and framed by familiar literary genres: a creation myth revolving around the Asper family's epic struggle to establish a world-class institution in the teeth of fierce, even anti-Semitic, opposition;[1] a disaster story about the imposition on an unwilling public of a crypto-Holocaust museum at taxpayers' expense;[2] or a parable about the regrettable yet predictable ethno-political consequences of a fatally flawed project.[3] Whatever the reading, the drama was anchored by its actors' intentions, even though any complex social and political conjuncture cannot be ascribed solely to their conscious acts of will. Despite the fact that any drama is staged in a particular theatre, it is witnessed in multiple locations and rendered significant by diverse contexts not necessarily known to or controlled by its participants, whose own motivations are similarly informed by intersecting discourses.[4] The explicit point of contention in discussions of the CMHR is patent: the commemorative effect of privileging

Holocaust memory. Less obvious are questions about the museum's present and future. What is the point of the CMHR? What purpose should it serve now and in the future? Closer inspection of these questions sheds light on the underlying issues animating museum-related debate.

The CMHR's website gives some clues about these underlying issues. The museum "is envisioned as a … centre of learning where Canadians and people from around the world can engage in discussion and commit to taking action against hate and oppression." Its purpose, following the Museum Act, "is to explore the subject of human rights, with special but not exclusive reference to Canada, in order to enhance the public's understanding of human rights, to promote respect for others and to encourage reflection and dialogue."[5] Time and again, the museum's senior staff have responded to complaints from ethnic community leaders about perceived commemorative biases by insisting that theirs is not a backward-looking genocide museum but a future-oriented "ideas museum." As such, the CMHR proposes to take visitors on a "journey … about learning, empowerment, and action. We will shine light in dark corners; amplify the voices of those who have been silenced, and encourage people to take a stand for human rights."[6] The museum has a mandate not only to educate Canadians but also to elevate their moral lives.

In keeping with this agenda, the CMHR also participates in the broader Western discourse about genocide prevention. For example, in early 2013, it co-sponsored a conference on Prevention of Mass Atrocities at which Clint Curle, its head of stakeholder relations, delivered a paper.[7] The conference's list of distinguished participants indicated the thickness of this discourse in Canada. They included, among diplomats and NGO representatives, members of the Will to Intervene Project of the Montreal Institute for Genocide and Human Rights Studies at Concordia University. Launched in 2007 with local human rights warrior-hero General Roméo Dallaire as a senior fellow, the institute strives to realize the Responsibility to Protect (R2P) agenda by "mobilizing the will to intervene," the title of its modestly described "ground-breaking 2009 policy report."[8] Consistent with the Canadian spirit of the agenda, R2P stems from a Canadian-initiated ad hoc International Commission on Intervention and State Sovereignty that in 2001 issued a report that led to extensive debates about, and innovations in, humanitarian intervention within the UN system.[9]

In stimulating such developments, the Canadian government was building on deeply held views of the nation's human rights culture. For decades, Canadians have prided themselves on their unique historical commitment to the articulation and defence of human rights. Never forgotten is John Humphrey, the Canadian diplomat who authored the first draft of the UN Declaration on Human Rights and led the Human Rights Division of the United Nations,[10] or that the country pioneered human rights protections for its citizens, an achievement propelled by the imperative to negotiate individual and group rights between the majority anglophone and minority francophone and Indigenous populations.[11] Performing the cultural norm, some Canadians style themselves as "human rights activists," thereby acquiring an aura of dissent while working as well-heeled lawyers close to the establishment. This high-minded commitment extends to all social and institutional strata. According to Rhoda E. Howard-Hassmann, the Canada Research Chair in International Human Rights at Wilfrid Laurier University, civic leaders embody a distinctive human rights culture: they are "compassionate Canadians."[12] Consequently, because Canada is a global "human rights leader," its citizens ask whether their government will "live up to its responsibility to protect?"[13]

As always with such national self-images, reality seldom reflects the ideal. In 2012, for instance, Canada was sharply criticized by the United Nations, Amnesty International, and Human Rights Watch for multiple failings with respect to Indigenous peoples, refugees, and the environment. In response, a government spokesman impatiently dismissed their reports and appealed to the idealized collective self-image: "we are proud of the work we've done to advance freedom, democracy, human rights and the rule of law at home and around the world."[14] The evidence suggests that in Canada, as elsewhere, economic interests trump human rights norms when they clash. The Canadian government's interest in R2P stemmed in part from its 1999 investigation of the involvement of a Canadian energy company in Sudan, where forced population relocations to secure oil fields were alleged.[15] This scruple did not stop Canada from signing a trade agreement with China in 2012 that could prejudice Indigenous interests in areas where Chinese capital is invested, especially in the Alberta tar sands.[16] Worse still, the Canadian government has spent millions fighting Indigenous legal action over discriminatory federal funding of Aboriginal children on reserves.[17]

These and other derogations from human rights ideals are more than blemishes on an otherwise spotless record. They point to a tension within the R2P doctrine itself, namely that the Western states that invoke it to justify military intervention in other countries in the name of morality either gained their dominant positions in the international system through centuries of colonialism or themselves are the children of such empires, like

Canada and Australia. Either way, Western states must deny this violence and symbolically repeat it in order to maintain their dominance.[18] All of these states are predicated on settler-colonial genocides: the large-scale elimination of Indigenous peoples and seizure of their lands.[19] Consequently, admitting this violent and exploitative past and the structural imperatives that persist in any settler colony—namely, the "logic of elimination" that breaks up Indigenous collectivities so that settler societies can replace them—remains a considerable conceptual and emotional challenge.[20]

The CMHR reflects this conceptual blockage in its exhibits—as it must as a state institution. Preventing the truth that dare not speak its name is the museum's unstated, ineluctable purpose. For all the horrors perpetrated in the past, the museum incarnates the liberal subjectivity of the remediating individual who will make a better future. To undertake this future work, the individual in question cannot be a structurally flawed subject with recidivist tendencies regarding Indigenous peoples. Accordingly, the museum posits a whiggish narrative of Canadian and global human rights improvement while simultaneously displacing the genocide question onto other parts of the world, even though Canada's Truth and Reconciliation Commission on the residential school abuse of Indigenous children is considering it.[21]

The CMHR needs to cover genocides that occurred beyond Canadian borders for another reason, notwithstanding official denials that genocide remembrance falls within the museum's remit. Not only for the sake of human rights in Canada did its head of stakeholder relations visit Armenia in the company of Zoryan Institute leaders to establish links with the Armenian Genocide Museum in Yerevan and give assurances that the CMHR would not bow to Turkish denial of the genocide.[22] Given Canada's migration history and official multiculturalism, the domestic imperative for genocide commemoration is a political and financial issue because important electoral constituencies need to be placated and essential private donations secured. How this pressure affects the museum's exhibits is the contentious issue. Just as these constituencies—"stakeholders" in the museum's parlance—insist that their particular historical trauma should be chosen as the paradigmatic genocide or human rights violation, so too they posit particular prevention agendas: never again should their group's distinctive mistreatment, exile, internment, or attempted destruction be repeated.

Beyond shared banalities about toleration and anti-discrimination characteristic of multiculturalist protocols, these agendas differ in subtle but significant ways. What is the evil to be prevented by mobilizing the will to intervene? The answer depends on whom you ask. To proponents of the museum's Holocaust gallery, anti-Semitism is the burning question of our time and demands commensurate priority.[23] For Ukrainian Canadians, communist oppression and Russian aggression are the pressing issues, while Armenians think that the Turkish negation of their genocidal experience is the ongoing scandal.[24] It is the uncertain future, just as much as the troubled past, about which these groups argue. Needless to say, though, any projection into the future necessarily requires the past for lessons and orientation; even a forward-looking ideas museum cannot cut itself off from historical continuities because, as already noted, it institutionalizes a progressive narrative. What, then, comprises the archive that will shape the will to intervene at the CMHR?

The evidence suggests an ad hoc eclecticism driven by domestic pressures rather than a systematic and coherent vision for the museum—hence the public controversy. It is all too easy for community leaders and others to pick holes in museum management's justificatory statements. In what follows, I briefly reconstruct how the CMHR became the site at which the contrapuntal social pressures exerted by compassionate Canadians were negotiated to produce a flawed compromise and an incoherent message that has subsequently satisfied few of those concerned about the museum's capacity to contribute to the promotion of human rights. Setting sail with a lofty vision, the museum's legitimacy is foundering on the shoals of forces summoned into existence by its ham-fisted combination of hubris and naïveté.

FALSE STARTS

The origins of this tragic drama can be found in various places, among them the desire of organized Canadian Jewry to promote Holocaust memory after the disappointing outcome of war crimes prosecutions against Ukrainian veteran migrants in the 1980s and the feeling that other Canadians callously ignored Jewish suffering. Also a factor was the equally intense Ukrainian Canadian sense of social abjection in light of First World War internment experiences, the subsequent forgetting of Stalin's crimes against Ukrainians, and the perceived Jewish attempt to prosecute Ukrainian veteran migrants for war crimes. For Jewish and Ukrainian Canadians, the country needed to atone for these and other sins of commission and omission; memory was also to perform the redemptive task of ensuring that never again would this persecution and forgetting recur.

For Jewish groups, gaining public recognition of the Holocaust became an extension of the extant tradition of the Anti-Defamation League's combatting anti-Semitism by opposing racism and bigotry generally. Including the Holocaust in the mandate was straightforward because it was understood as "the ultimate expression of antisemitism," itself "the longest hatred": the Holocaust became coded as the ultimate hate crime.[25] Accordingly, the lesson to draw was toleration, famously embodied in the Museum of Tolerance of the Simon Wiesenthal Center in Los Angeles. For such institutions, the universal and the particular harmonized foremost in the protection of Jews as the universal victims: if Jews were endangered, then everyone else was as well, meaning that they also became steadfast Zionists, as the mission of the Simon Wiesenthal Center and statements of Canadian Jewish leaders indicate.[26]

By the 1990s, Jewish Canadian community leaders were looking to emulate Holocaust commemoration in other countries, such as the Holocaust Memorial Museum in Washington, DC, and the popular Holocaust exhibition in London's Imperial War Museum. A successful campaign of advocacy had Canadian provinces institute a Holocaust Memorial Day, making it relevant for all Canadians by drawing human rights lessons through memory. Thus, the Manitoba legislation of 2000 states that it "is an opportune day to reflect on and educate about the enduring lessons of the Holocaust and to reaffirm a commitment to uphold human rights and to value the diversity and multiculturalism of Manitoban society."[27] In many ways, this initiative reflected the agenda of the League for Human Rights of B'nai Brith and its representative, David Matas, who, along with Liberal Party politician and fellow attorney Irwin Cotler, led the effort to prosecute Ukrainian Canadian migrant veterans.[28] Matas's 1992 article "Remembering the Holocaust Can Prevent Future Genocides" extolled the league's Holocaust and Hope program, which later became part of a teachers' guide for Holocaust Memorial Day.[29]

In contrast, an unsuccessful campaign between 1996 and 1998 aimed to have a Holocaust gallery included in a reformed Canadian War Museum. Museum officials looked to Jewish and Dutch veterans as fundraising sources, and again the link was made to a wider agenda: the Holocaust gallery could address "intolerance, prejudice and the dehumanizing of other ethnic groups which lie behind not only past wars but current issues such as 'ethnic cleansing' in Yugoslavia, Rwandan atrocities, and many other problems which Canadian peacekeepers are called on to address."[30] Jewish leaders weighed in with the atonement message. Historian and past president of the Canadian Jewish Congress (CJC) Irving Abella, who had written about the Canadian government's shunning of Jewish refugees in the Second World War, wanted to include the "whole dirty story."[31] For their part, veterans bitterly opposed the notion because the projected gallery—which would be by far the largest—might detract from their own stories. In 1998, a parliamentary commission also rejected the idea but mooted the possibility of an independent Holocaust museum.[32] Subsequent efforts to have the government establish a Holocaust memorial, exhibit, or museum in the national capital, Ottawa, did not yield the desired results either; in 2000, another parliamentary committee decided against such a proposition after public hearings during which other Canadian groups, including the Canadians for a Genocide Museum (CGM) coalition led by attorney James Kafieh, pushed for a broadly conceived museum about genocide or crimes against humanity. "It's not fair for any community to be reduced to being a footnote in somebody else's museum," he said.[33]

THE DEALS ARE CUT

By all accounts, the Winnipeg-based media tycoon Israel Asper was shocked by the fierce opposition to the war museum's mooted Holocaust gallery.[34] Accordingly, in 1997 he established a Human Rights and Holocaust Studies Program in Winnipeg in the now familiar mode of promoting toleration by using the Holocaust to illuminate rights violations generally.[35] As Lyle Smordin, the past president of B'nai B'rith Canada put it, including other cases of intolerance was "a perfect complement. It shows by example that horrific events in history, even to some smaller degree, get repeated again." The advantage of this approach lay in the possibility of building a broad social constituency and donor base by involving other Canadians, such as Japanese Canadians who had been interned during the Second World War.[36] The key group to appease was the main Ukrainian Canadian organization, the Ukrainian Canadian Congress (UCC), which purported to represent the one million Canadians of Ukrainian descent.[37]

Asper's deputy, Moe Levy, brokered the deal, promising the UCC, in a letter in 2003, that the Asper Foundation proposal was for "an all-inclusive Canadian genocide museum" that would house exhibits on many human rights abuses, including those perpetrated by Canadian governments. Levy's letter continued: "As you are aware, the CMHR goes well beyond a genocide museum. The CMHR's objective is to recognize and celebrate human rights as the foundation for human equality, dignity and freedom." The sweetener was the promise that the "Ukrainian Famine/Genocide" of

1932–33 would feature "very clearly, distinctly, and permanently," as would the internment of Ukrainians in the First World War. In return, Levy requested a letter of support to include in the media package.[38]

The UCC was grateful that the Ukrainian story would finally be told in what they understood to be a separate Ukrainian gallery. "The museum will be the first place in the world where the famine will be given attention," exulted the UCC's executive director, Ostap Skrypnyk.[39] Having secured its goal, the UCC left the CGM coalition, more attracted to the projected museum's memorial function than to its human rights agenda. The Armenian Canadian leadership likewise regarded the Asper proposal in these terms and remained ambivalent about the CGM. On the whole, the Armenian leaders tried to have it both ways, cleaving to a traditional alliance with Jewish community groups while pleading for the genocide concept to include their experience.[40]

Reflecting on this moment in 2013, and particularly on Levy's letter, federal heritage minister James Moore observed that "there were a lot of pitches that were made to a lot of Canadians based on specific atrocities or based on ethnicities that you'll get your square footage if you can help us out with 20 or 50 grand from the people that you know." Indeed, Levy was encouraging ethnic communities to tell their stories and raise money as part of the pitch that Asper's foundation had accumulated sufficient community backing and funds to warrant government support. "We believe the people who pay should have a say in how it is run," he said in 2003.[41] Moore criticized the practice as "ultimately destructive of the entire enterprise because that's not how institutions should decide their mandate, based on auctioning of square footage."[42]

Another symbolically significant stakeholder was the Indigenous community: First Nations, Métis, and Inuit peoples whose suffering entered the public domain in the 1990s. By the time that Asper was lobbying for his museum after 2000, Indigenous issues had become politically significant, with lawsuits against the state forcing negotiations that culminated in the Indian Residential Schools Settlement Agreement of 2006, which provided for a compensation process, support measures, commemorative activities, and establishment of the Truth and Reconciliation Commission.[43] Asper was reportedly sympathetic to Indigenous issues, though an Indigenous dimension was not part of the original museum blueprint. Relations between Indigenous leaders and the Jewish community could have been strained after David Ahenakew, a former chief of the Assembly of First Nations, made anti-Semitic remarks at an Indigenous gathering in 2002, but prompt criticism by other leaders opened the door for high-level contacts. Sensing a mutually beneficial arrangement, Asper successfully applied for Department of Heritage money—some $25,000—to hire the national chief of the Assembly of First Nations, Phil Fontaine, to generate Indigenous support for the museum and offer advice about Indigenous content. By all accounts, Fontaine performed well in this role, convincing other Aboriginal leaders to write supportive letters to the prime minister.[44]

The new Indigenous-Jewish relationship, at least at the leadership level, soon deepened. Fontaine addressed CJC events, and the CJC national president addressed the Assembly of First Nations in 2005, agreeing on an anti-racism agenda. "By working together with allies like the Canadian Jewish Congress, we present an ever more formidable defence against those who would cause us harm due to malignant racism," said Fontaine. "Our organizations have much in common. We are both dedicated to the preservation of our languages, our cultures and to the development of a national community which celebrates diversity and seeks justice for our people." For their part, Jewish leaders pledged support for Indigenous causes that they admitted had not been high on their agenda in the past. CJC head Ed Morgan went so far as to say that First Nations and Jews shared the "full gamut of discrimination from jokes to genocide."[45] This was the only time that the genocide link was made by a Jewish communal leader. The CMHR had secured Indigenous support by promising substantial attention to Indigenous issues at the expense of the genocide question. Anti-racism was promoted over anti-colonialism. Fontaine was rewarded for his collaboration and criticism of Ahenakew as the CJC supported his campaign for a government apology for the residential school policy.[46]

Yet another stakeholder was the Jewish community, which had sought an official government Holocaust museum or gallery since the 1990s. That the CMHR should fulfill this dream was made clear by the Asper Foundation press announcement of the project in 2003:

> You may ask why there is a focus on the Holocaust in the
> Consequences Gallery. The Holocaust represents a singular,
> unprecedented event in human history. Though other
> systematic mass murders of specific groups in the multi-
> millions represented great evil, many scholars around the
> world are of the opinion that the Holocaust is unique in its
> breadth and depth. It is the first and only time in history that

an entire people across the planet (referred to by the Nazis as "world Jewry") were openly targeted for annihilation for the sole purpose of their religion by a democratically elected modern government of one of the most advanced, cultured, and intellectual countries in the world. Almost two thirds of European Jewry, one third of world Jewry, were murdered because of government-sanctioned prejudice based on ignorance, fear and misunderstanding. European Jewish civilization was effectively wiped off the face of the planet.[47]

This was the common-sense understanding of Holocaust memory for Canadian Jews: as a warning against the consequences of anti-Semitism. In other Asper Foundation formulations, remembering the Holocaust was also a means of preventing genocide generally. Similar statements were made over the years to reassure Jewish donors that the Holocaust would not be diluted in the general human rights story in the CMHR.[48]

THE DEAL

The museum remained a private initiative with some government funding until 2008, when it was formally taken over by the federal government. Its construction commenced the next year along with detailed consideration of its contents. This nationalization presented the Asper project—now led by Israel's daughter Gail after his death in 2003—with a dilemma: although less of a financial burden, how could content control be retained, especially regarding the Holocaust gallery's centrality?[49] The intrigues that transpired between 2006 and 2009 are difficult to untangle based on the public record. Parallel processes seem to have been working contrapuntally. In the first place, the nationalization process required specific, transparent procedures. Thus, in late 2007, the government appointed an advisory committee to report a year later, *inter alia,* on "the scope and content" of the museum. The *Report to the Minister of Canadian Heritage on the Canadian Museum for Human Rights,* as it was called, has long been forgotten but reveals significant concerns. Its fifth recommendation was that "members of the CAC [Content Advisory Committee] should be chosen to play the role of advisors rather than advocates for special interest groups," a stipulation forced by the realization of "widespread concern identified through consultations with Canadians that the CMHR could be unduly influenced by political activities or special interest groups, in a manner that could affect the integrity and balance of its public offerings."[50] Its seventeenth recommendation focused on the "Aboriginal people in Canada," whose experience "is a notable exception to Canada's achievements as a champion of human rights." The report recommended that "this real and perceived paradox must be addressed openly and forthrightly. It is also important to note that Aboriginal people are neither recent immigrants nor an ethno-cultural group. They are unique in Canada and healing and reconciliation are required." Its survey of Canadians indicated that only 7 percent favoured a Holocaust focus. Canadians preferred an equal treatment of historical injustice and contemporary issues.[51]

These recommendations threatened to overturn the project of linking the Holocaust and human rights. Felicitously for the Aspers, it was the adamantly pro-Israel Conservative Party leader, Stephen Harper, who had agreed to make their museum a national priority in the 2006 national election, during which their family-owned newspaper, the *National Post,* supported his campaign.[52] Former Liberal prime minister Jean Chrétien—Asper had been a Liberal Party stalwart—also lent support. The stars were aligned. The legislation that converted the Asper-led project into a national museum of the Canadian state was accompanied by the legally non-binding but declarative statement that "[t]he first national museum to be located outside of the National Capital Region, the CMHR is to be built in Winnipeg. It will house the largest museum gallery in Canada devoted to the subject of the Holocaust."[53] Harper was honoured with the CJC's Saul Hayes Human Rights Award in 2009.[54]

I have not been able to determine how the seventeen members of the CAC were chosen. Its 2010 report states that "[m]any of its members had been part of a previous Human Rights Advisory Committee established in 2005 by the Friends of the Canadian Museum for Human Rights to provide guidance during the planning process of the Museum, or part of its successor, the Friends Content Advisory Committee." The report notes further that "the initial advisors to the Friends and the exhibition designers Ralph Appelbaum and Associates for the Exhibit Master Plan (2005) were Yude Henteleff, Constance Backhouse, David Matas, Ruth Selwyn and Ken Norman."[55] Henteleff, like Matas, a lawyer and Asper confidant, was also a B'nai B'rith leader, serving on its Advisory Board on National Holocaust Task Force Leadership.[56] These figures, with the exception of Selwyn, "led the story-gathering tour across Canada" on which the report was based, the idea being to have the museum incorporate Canadians' human rights stories in its exhibition. Lord Cultural Services, involved in the

Asper project "from the early stages," ran the seventeen-city tour at which public meetings were held.[57]

As might be expected, the report bears a remarkable resemblance to Matas's views. Those who repeated the Asper Foundation and B'nai B'rith line were accorded disproportionate space in the report. Summaries of the interviews conveniently supported the B'nai B'rith vision and the Asper vision.[58] No effort was made to conceal Matas's involvement in the story-gathering process, and no reader would have been surprised to come to the report's fifteenth recommendation, which simply repeated the gist of his statements and cited two of his papers in the accompanying endnote.[59]

DOUBLE DEALING?

For all that, as Moe Levy said, "it was never ever meant *strictly* to be a Holocaust museum," indicating the inherent instability of the proposed union of the Holocaust and human rights.[60] Museum opponents sensed the incoherence from the beginning. For example, already in 2003, the Ukrainian Canadian Civil Liberties Association (UCCLA), founded in the mid-1980s to campaign against the war crimes prosecutions, declined to follow the UCC's endorsement of the project, instead sharing the position of the CGM coalition to advocate thematically organized exhibits that did not privilege any group's memory.[61] Their suspicion about Asper's intentions did not mean that the museum's human rights mission was cynical rhetoric concealing its Holocaust essence; the Jewish linking of human rights to communal experiences of persecution is sincere, indeed a venerable tradition stretching back at least a century. Even so, subsequent development of the museum did not inspire confidence that it was essentially a human rights institution either—despite its name.

As might be expected, the UCCLA and UCC complained bitterly about the CAC report, which ignored Ukrainian Canadian testimony and communist crimes entirely. They launched a relentless public campaign against its recommendations between 2010 and 2012 that mobilized politicians who could point to the state's official 2008 recognition of the Holodomor as a genocide.[62] A professional poll commissioned by the Canadians for Genocide Education (CGE, the rebadged CGM) and the UCCLA found that some 60 percent of respondents preferred a genocide gallery that did not favour any case, echoing the 2008 report overturned two years later by the CAC.[63] Buckling under the pressure, the CMHR established connections with the Holodomor museum in Ukraine and gave assurances about the Ukrainian presence in the exhibit.[64] Lindy Ledohowski, a Ukrainian

Canadian literature academic and daughter of businessman, Ukrainian honorary consul, and museum donor Leo Ledohowski, was invited to join the museum's Board of Trustees.[65]

At the same time, academic consultations undermined the original rationale for the Holocaust's presence in the museum, namely that the United Nations had passed the Universal Declaration of Human Rights in 1948 as a reaction to the Holocaust.[66] Committed to the Holocaust gallery for political and financial reasons, the museum management came up with an alternative justification: the Holocaust was the most-studied and best-known human rights violation and would therefore make the ideal subject to exemplify the lessons about abuse of state power. Consequently, its contents were amended to include non-Jewish victims of the Nazis and an exhibit on Raphael Lemkin, the Polish Jewish lawyer who coined the genocide concept, which showed how he explained the Holocaust and other genocides.[67]

The Ukrainian campaign and these changes set off alarm bells in the Jewish community. Jewish journalists were soon voicing concerns about the possible threats to the Holocaust gallery.[68] "We as a community are going to feel extremely resentful if efforts to eliminate a permanent Holocaust Gallery are successful," wrote Rhonda Spivak, editor of the *Winnipeg Jewish Review*.[69] Catherine Chatterley, a recent (non-Jewish) PhD graduate and founder of the one-person Canadian Institute for the Study of Antisemitism, complained that, "increasingly, today, people and institutions are conflating the Holocaust (or Shoah) with the general brutality of Nazi Germany, misleading the public and students into thinking that the Holocaust included any number of groups who suffered under the Third Reich."[70] For Chatterley, as for Irwin Cotler, anti-Semitism was a unique ideology that posed a "very real threat" today.[71] It was lamentable, therefore, that universities were replacing Holocaust studies with genocide studies.[72]

There was no doubting the level of anxiety. "There is a growing inclination toward insensitivity to Jewish concerns, whatever those concerns may be," wrote the editor of the *Jewish Independent* in a leader entitled "Shoah's Uniqueness." Indeed, the present atmosphere reeked of anti-Semitism: "In media and in private conversations, there is a discernible attitude that 'we've heard enough of you,' that the *Holocaust is just one of many genocides,* and your incessant need to differentiate your experience is tiresome, self-absorbed and (perhaps, ultimately, if usually implicitly) 'the very root of the troubles you bring upon yourselves.'"[73] A reading suggesting that "the Holocaust is just one of many genocides" was anti-Semitic because it refused to recognize the objective fact of the Holocaust's unique-ness as the ultimate denouement of anti-Semitism and paradigmatic hate crime. Chatterley chimed in with a similar sentiment: "Whether people like it or not, and regardless of their own personal feelings and collective grievances, the Holocaust is a catastrophic transformative event in western history and it is unique because its antecedents are 2,000 years old and yet still persist today. One cannot say that about the ideologies at work in other genocides."[74] These statements confuse interpretation and facts and lead to predictable rancour. Thus, when Winnipeg literature scholar and museum supporter Adam Muller wrote a balanced article in the *Winnipeg Jewish Review* called "Nazi Genocide Has Multiple Causes, Antisemitism Is Not Single Cause" (itself a response to an article by Chatterley), he was denounced in its pages for the heresy of supposedly doubting that anti-Semitism was the sole historical truth of the Shoah.[75] "Antisemitism remains a lethal threat to Jewish survival today," wrote one of his critics, local law professor Bryan Schwartz. The CMHR was a player in this cosmic struggle against evil: "When its exhibits address the Holocaust, will it fully and fairly convey the Jewish dimension of the Holocaust? Or will students learn little or nothing of how Nazi antisemitism draws on a long and tragic history of hatred and mistreatment of Jews, how hatred of the Jew was the fundamental and driving cause of the Holocaust, and how antisemitism remains a problem today in most parts of the world, even to a limited but still significant extent in Canada today?" Schwartz concluded by accus-ing Muller of disrespecting "the memory of the murdered, the feelings of survivors and the cause of seeking and preserving historical truth" by "downplaying of the importance of hatred of Jews as the central cause and Jewishness in the experience of the victims."[76] Muller had done no such thing; he had simply pointed to contemporary Holocaust scholarship that highlighted other contextual factors of the Holocaust, but such nuance was lost on readers concerned with preventing a second Holocaust.

Israel Asper himself led the conflation of factual and interpretive differences when he attacked reporting that suggested the Arab-Israeli conflict "is about territory and Jerusalem and Palestinian statehood and alleged refugees." Never one to mince words, he thought instead that "[h]onest reporting would tell you that it is a war to destroy Israel and kill or expel or subjugate all the Jews."[77] It is impossible to say what he would have made of the reformed Holocaust gallery had he lived to wit-ness the controversy that his project had caused. Judging by his "strident" Zionism, it is reasonable to suppose that he would have shared the general alarm about perceived anti-Semitism and dilution of the gallery's Jewish content.[78]

Even more unhappy were Ukrainian Canadians. The museum's memorandum of understanding with the Memorial in Commemoration of Famines' Victims in Kyiv did not convince the UCCLA. "This is a positive thing, but the bottom line is 'Where is it going to go?'" asked Lubomyr Luciuk. "What's that actually going to mean in terms of square metres and number of exhibits?" As noted above, the UCCLA argued that a "publicly funded museum should not raise the suffering of one community above all others," meaning that neither should the Holodomor be singled out.[79] A site inspection by UCC officials in February 2013 led to consternation when they realized that no distinct Ukrainian gallery was envisaged, thereby violating their understanding of Asper-Levy's 2003 commitment. This outcome should have been obvious from an official ninety-two-page CMHR document on the gallery profiles from September 2012 that did not foresee the anticipated Ukrainian gallery. Worse still, a small panel devoted to the Holodomor was adjacent to the public toilets. UCC officials were "shocked to discover how shamefully Ukrainian Canadian and Ukrainian themes are to be presented in this national institution."[80] Luciuk agreed: "To think that one of the worst crimes against humanity will be put on a light table that may be seldom used is frankly insulting."[81] In effect, their decade of lobbying had come to naught.

In response, the CMHR disputed the claim about the toilet proximity and noted that Ukrainian content features in many of the museum's twelve galleries: "We're not saying, here's the Ukrainian thing, here's the Rwandan thing.... It's not like a collection of grievances. Instead we're trying to raise the importance of human rights for everyone, and we're using different examples, so the Ukrainian Canadian stuff is scattered throughout three different galleries."[82]

Indeed, "Ukrainian Canadian stuff" appears in the Holocaust gallery as one of Lemkin's cases of genocide. Although no doubt the case, these points do not appreciate how dispersing Ukrainian experiences throughout the museum can be experienced as a psychic dispersion, especially when the UCC expectation was of a unified presentation that could function as a site of mourning and public commemoration. UCC president Steve Andrusiak made plain the anxiety when he acknowledged that, while the CMHR might mention the Holodomor, there was no guarantee that it would not do so in the future: "Displays can change, shrink, eventually disappear." In contrast, "a gallery would signal permanence." The gallery issue had become, effectively, an analogical genocidal anxiety.[83] Still, Lindy Ledohowski and Rhonda Hinther, the head of exhibits research at the CMHR and an academic expert on Ukrainian Canadians, had presumably signed off on the exhibits, indicating differences of opinion within migrant communities.[84] And the Holodomor remains one of the five genocides recognized by the Canadian Parliament and the museum (the Armenian genocide, Holocaust, Holodomor, Rwanda, and Srebrenica massacre in Bosnia), though the status of Guatemala is uncertain since its contested legal recognition as genocide.[85] What is more, in 2009 Ukrainians and other groups founded Tribute to Liberty to lobby and raise money for a memorial in the national capital to victims of "totalitarian communism," just as over the decades they have erected monuments to Ukrainian heroes and suffering.[86]

There were still other dissatisfied citizens. Palestinian Canadians also voiced concerns about their omission. "Our story is an excellent story to educate Canadians about human rights. How would anyone take that museum seriously if they don't hear the Palestinian story?" asked Rana Abdulla.[87] In response to media questioning, the museum said that a Palestinian children's art project might be included, deftly depoliticizing the issue.[88] A prominent museum critic who supported the Palestinian view is James Kafieh, chair of the CGE. The CGE submission to a CMHR roundtable discussion in 2009 argued that Indigenous suffering warranted a privileged position because of its intrinsic relationship to Canada: "It is our position that the genocide of Canada's First Nations and Inuit is the only case of genocide that deserves special status in the CMHR as this genocide happened in Canada and is a defining aspect of all that Canada is today. Our prosperity is premised on the resources taken from and then denied to our First Nations and Inuit. In addition, this human rights museum is to be built on their stolen land."[89] Here was an anti-colonial manifesto that recognized settler colonialism's logic of elimination and challenged the CMHR's liberal anti-racism, suggesting a link between the Palestinian experience of dispossession, occupation, and exile and Indigenous Canadians' experiences. It is no surprise that Kafieh's recommendation to weight the exhibits "towards lesser-known cases of human rights abuses and genocide that have been historically marginalized or neglected" was ignored.[90] To have taken up the spirit of the CGE submission would have been to connect the dots of material already planned for the museum in a manner inconsistent with its unstated aim. Thus, Lemkin's eight-pronged typology of genocidal policies is exemplified in relation to some cases about which Lemkin wrote, including the Aboriginal Tasmanians, but not to Canadian First Nations, their logical and natural application in the Winnipeg context. Their experience is not one of the five officially recognized genocides, an exclusion unlikely to change with the fresh evidence of independent investigations that appeared in 2012 and 2013. The notorious residential schools, the subject of the Truth and Reconciliation Commission, were lethal for thousands of First Nations children, who died of disease or disappeared entirely while in government and church care.[91]

Adding to the genocide file, research came out in mid-2013 about government experiments on malnourished First Nations children between 1942 and 1952 that Phil Fontaine, Michael Dan, and Bernie Faber called genocidal. "The time has come for Canada to formally recognize a sixth genocide," they declared, "the genocide of its own aboriginal communities; a genocide that began at the time of first contact and that was still very active in our own lifetimes; a genocide currently in search of a name but no longer in search of historical facts."[92] They were ignored.

At the same time, the CMHR's decision to prevent curators from using the term "settler-colonial genocide" for the Indigenous exhibits created a firestorm of controversy. For the first time, Indigenous leaders publicly raised the genocide question, berating the museum for its presumptuousness. Although museum management said that designating any genocide lay outside its competence and remit—pointing to the five official ones—it added that the exhibit would note that Indigenous people used the term. For their part, Indigenous leaders noticed that this was a choice to interfere with curatorial expertise, for the museum was denoting Cambodia and Guatemala as genocides despite their lack of parliamentary recognition.[93] If it was going to take the federal government to recognize past policies as genocidal for the museum to follow, then Indigenous people would be waiting a long time.[94]

CONCLUSION: LEGITIMACY IN QUESTION

The conceptual blockage preventing this recognition lies in the fact that, as a museum spokesperson said in March 2013, "[t]he inclusion of a stand-alone holocaust gallery is a defining feature of the museum" because it is the most studied genocide.[95] This reasoning falls foul of Avishai Margalit's injunction about the "dangers of biased silence": just because something is better remembered does not make it more significant. What is more, he continues, "because they are likely to be better remembered, the atrocities of Europe will come to be perceived as morally more significant than atrocities elsewhere. As such, they claim false moral superiority."[96] Now, it could be argued—as museum defenders have—that centralizing the Holocaust in this way illuminates other genocides and human rights violations. So why is it not happening in this case?

We know that the museum plans for its visitors to feel "proud of Canada's apology" to Indigenous citizens.[97] They might have been the occasional victims of government abuse but not settler-colonial genocide, and ultimately toleration will benefit all; it is an achievement about which all can feel pride. Accordingly, in July 2012, museum management decided to replace the planned Peace Forum gallery on contemporary issues with one featuring "more positive Canadian content."[98] We also know that a year later curators were forbidden from using the term "genocide" for Indigenous content, and, after calling for the public to come forward with information about the "Sixties Scoop" in which about 20,000 Indigenous children were apprehended for placement in white foster families, the museum unceremoniously downgraded the planned full exhibit on the scandal to a few photographs on a touch-screen display panel.[99] Not for nothing did many staff leave the museum in 2012 and 2013, feeling "defeated" by executive violation of their autonomy.[100] The Holocaust's analogical capacity for solidarity, vaunted by David Matas, has not activated the CMHR in the case of Indigenous genocide, even though it accords with Lemkin's definition and the UN Genocide Convention.[101] Instead, the Nazi experience is presented as the paradigmatic human rights abuse with which to understand other such abuses, functioning as a screen memory. Jewish Canadians such as Bernie Faber and Michael Dan who do draw links between the Jewish and First Nations experiences are not backed by the *Canadian Jewish News,* which is more concerned with the size of the Holocaust gallery. Accompanying a group of elders of the Assembly of Manitoba Chiefs on a preview "spirit tour" of the CMHR—in which "any mention of residential schools, forced removal of children, or genocide" was "notably absent"—Dan observed that it "was like being in a room full of Holocaust survivors."[102] Faber has worked closely with Fontaine to advance the cause of recognition.[103]

The museum's failure to follow Faber and Dan, still less to internalize what First Nations leaders are saying, has accompanied successive flawed justifications for the Holocaust's central placement. Clint Curle now argues that Germany and the Holocaust were exemplary because they "bear structural resemblance to modern nation-states today," which holds "special relevance for countries like Canada"—an argument made by Sheldon

Howard, director of government relations at B'nai B'rith, to a parliamentary committee in 2000.[104] It does not take much reflection to see how this line of reasoning could bring down the house of cards constructed in Winnipeg. To invoke the European state's development over the centuries necessarily entails acknowledging its dependence on military and imperial expansion since the early modern period, an expansion that resulted in the deaths of millions of non-Europeans along with the foundations of states like Canada. European civilization has expanded via genocide.[105]

The CMHR's blindness is also a function of human rights language itself. Such language is not well equipped to analyze founding violence, structural inequality, and collective victimization. What Australian historian Tony Barta calls "relations of genocide" lie beyond its field of vision.[106] And that is why Indigenous genocide is incommensurable with the R2P agenda: the states that invented it in the nineteenth century—above all, Britain and France—were the world's prime imperialists and founders of settler colonies that dispossessed and often exterminated Indigenous peoples. Because R2P focuses mainly on Western powers preventing or stopping genocide in other countries in the future, it screens out the violence that it took (and takes) to establish these liberal democracies in the first place.[107]

Indigenous Canadian intellectuals understand this point. Robert Falcon Ouellette, program director for the Aboriginal Focus Programs at the University of Manitoba, observes that "Canadians ... believe we go over to other countries in order to stop these genocides from happening." It was difficult for Canadians to contemplate that their country was culpable in this way. "I don't think the Canadian public is ready to hear that message, and I don't think the Canadian government could be promoting that in their own museum."[108] The evidence suggests that he is correct. Consider journalist Larry Krotz's observation that the genocide appellation "is troubling to many, not least because it equates perpetrators such as the Nazis, Stalin and Ottoman Turks with our own Canadian government and its colonial predecessors—ourselves and our ancestors."[109] Fellow journalist Doug Saunders agrees that "many Canadians would be outraged to see their country put in the same column as Nazi Germany."[110]

The liberal discourse on human rights is in fact predicated historically on the triumph of that liberal state which is the outcome of those colonizing processes. It is no accident that Great Britain, the United States, New Zealand, Australia, and Canada initially opposed the United Nations Declaration on the Rights of Indigenous Peoples in 2007. Great Britain spoke for many when it objected to the "groupism" of the declaration and foregrounded the individualism of human rights: "The United Kingdom fully supported the provisions in the Declaration which recognized that indigenous individuals were entitled to the full protection of their human rights and fundamental freedoms in international law, on an equal basis to all other individuals. Human rights were universal and equal to all. The United Kingdom did not accept that some groups in society should benefit from human rights that were not available to others."[111] The inability to recognize settler colonialism's foundational violence and enduring logic of elimination is mirrored in the controversy over the museum's physical foundation. Built at the junction of the Red and Assiniboine Rivers known as The Forks, the museum sits atop what might be Manitoba's richest archaeological site of Indigenous heritage. According to local archaeologists, the CMHR's mitigation and excavation procedures adhered at best to minimal rather than exacting standards and did not sufficiently engage with Indigenous communities. For years now, the museum has not released a major report on this matter. The lack of transparency about the procedures has frustrated experts and community leaders; it is a metaphor for the museum's operations over a decade and for the logic of elimination: one building was erected on the remains of previous communities, just as one society replaced another.[112]

What, then, are the prospects for a happy ending to this tale? Federal Minister of Heritage James Moore is on record as telling the museum "many times" that "this museum is *not* going to be—*cannot* be—a source of division in this country; because taxpayers are not going to pump in $21 million per year to operate this museum if they see it as a perpetual source of division for the people of Winnipeg, the people of Manitoba and the people of Canada."[113] Unanimity is difficult to foresee when the CGF pleads for equality of genocides—excepting the Indigenous one—and thinks that any other outcome is racist; when the UCC complains about the underrepresentation of Ukrainian suffering; and when the CJC and Friends of the CMHR insist that the Holocaust remain at the museum's core and consider it anti-Semitic if it does not. Indigenous leaders threatened to withdraw their million-dollar donation, and, with a straight face, the museum told them that they cannot "buy" the "genocide" label, accurately sensing that most Canadians are behind the museum on this point; these Indigenous expectations have been met with incredulity and resentment by columnists and bloggers.[114] Fearing a dilution of the museum's Holocaust focus that he co-conceptualized, David Matas, currently the senior legal counsel for B'nai B'rith, insisted that the museum include the establishment of Israel in 1948, "since to come to grips with the human rights lessons of the Holocaust means addressing the establishment of the State of Israel": it became a home for Jewish refugees, while, conveniently, Palestinian refugees were somehow victims of anti-Zionists rather than Israelis.[115]

The CMHR is too Jewish for some and not Jewish enough for others. Depending on your allegiance, it contains insufficient anti-communism, inadequate anti–anti-Semitism, or too much attention to Indigenous peoples even lacking the "genocide" label. No one is completely happy with the museum's changes over the past number of years. As might be expected, those whose campaigns failed to change the museum's contents protested at the opening ceremony. A journalist noted that "a loud and angry crowd of protesters was already raging against abortion, pipelines, colonialism, pollution, and even the very idea of this unusual museum." Some Indigenous groups, Palestinian Canadians, and others made clear their sense of injustice and exclusion.[116] The CMHR is in danger of becoming at once tragedy and farce, eliciting rancour and cynicism instead of the social catharsis and noble idealism envisaged by its founder.

Yet there are also signs that the museum just meets the threshold of satisfaction to appease key stakeholders. During the debates in 2012, Gail Asper reassured Jewish readers that the museum would send the atonement message that Irving Abella had urged in 1998 while also reiterating the danger of anti-Semitism.[117] A year later Myron Love at the *Canadian Jewish News* sounded a similarly upbeat note, announcing that "Shoah Education [Was] Still Key for [the] Human Rights Museum."[118] When questioned by Catherine Chatterley about the new focus, Clint Curle stressed that the Holocaust was being presented as an end itself: "The exhibits are focused on the Holocaust, and allow the visitors themselves to draw the connection to contemporary human rights. As such, the exhibits avoid reducing the Holocaust to a series of human rights lessons."[119] And, sure enough, soon after the museum (partially) opened on 19 September 2014, the Asper Foundation announced that it had signed a memorandum of agreement with the CMHR to bring students from all over Canada for its Human Rights and Holocaust Studies Program—as originally envisaged by Izzy Asper.[120]

For their part, Armenian community leaders, who had "been closely collaborating with the CMHR for over 10 years to ensure that the Armenian Genocide is properly represented in the museum," were delighted by the outcome. As Shahen Mirakian, who attended the opening ceremony for the Armenian National Committee of Canada along with the Armenian ambassador to Canada, related, "[t]o imagine that there would be a permanent exhibit on the Armenian Genocide in such a unique architectural marvel was truly moving."[121] This was the experience that the UCC and UCCLA wanted to share; it remains a possibility given that the Breaking the Silence gallery contains a small theatre showing a documentary about the Holodomor.[122]

Communal advocacy continues as before. Mirakian told a community newspaper that "we would like to see a more prominent role for the Armenian Genocide as a prototype for all the genocides which followed and as an example of the consequences when justice is not served for a genocide. We will work with the CMHR to make sure this happens."[123] He is not the only one with such an ambition. As the museum's opening brought to a close another round of the memory wars, waged since the 1990s about the genocide and human rights in Canadian history, it opened a new one. No longer an idea but now bricks and mortar, the CMHR serves as a site for compassionate Canadians to negotiate the meaning of their responsibility to protect.

NOTES

1   Catherine Chatterley, "The War against the Holocaust," *Winnipeg Free Press,* 2 April 2011.

2   The popular Black Rod blogger exemplifies this interpretation: http://blackrod.blogspot.com.

3   My own first take on the subject tended in the direction of the parable. See A. Dirk Moses, "The Canadian Museum for Human Rights: The 'Uniqueness of the Holocaust' and the Question of Genocide," *Journal of Genocide Research* 14, 2 (2012): 215–38.

4   Whatever the lessons learned from the linguistic turn of the previous generation, I take it that this point was made much earlier by Marx in "'The Eighteenth Brumaire of Louis Napoleon": "Men make their own history, but they do not make it as they please; they do not make it under self-selected circumstances, but under circumstances existing already, given and transmitted from the past." Karl Marx, "The Eighteenth Brumaire of Louis Napoleon" in *Karl Marx/Friedrich Engels Collected Works,* Vol 2. (New York: International Publishers, 1979), 103.

5   http://museumforhumanrights.ca/about-museum.

6   Speech delivered by President and CEO Stuart Murray at the CMHR's first Annual Public Meeting, 6 December 2011, http://museumforhumanrights.ca/about-museum/speeches-our-museum-leaders/speech-delivered-president-and-ceo-stuart-murray-cmhrs.

7   Clint Curle, "Education for Inclusive Pluralism: The Capacity of Museums and Sites of Conscience to Promote Human Rights," paper presented at the Ryerson University Conference on Prevention of Mass Atrocities, http://iid.kislenko.com/wp-content/uploads/2013/02/Documents.pdf and http://www.ryerson.ca/news/media/General_Public/20130205_atrocitiesconference.html.

8   http://migs.concordia.ca/W2I/home.htm; Frank Chalk, Kyle Matthews, and Carla
      Barqueiro, *Mobilizing the Will to Intervene: Leadership to Prevent Mass Atrocities* (Mon-
      treal: McGill-Queen's University Press, 2010).

9   International Commission on Intervention and State Sovereignty, *The Responsibility to
      Protect* (Ottawa: International Development Research Centre, 2001); Jennifer Welsh,
      ed., *Humanitarian Intervention and International Relations* (Oxford: Oxford University
      Press, 2004).

10   John Humphrey, *Human Rights and the United Nations: A Great Adventure* (Dobbs Ferry,
      NY: Transnational, 1984); Clint Curle, *Humanité: John Humphrey's Alternative Account
      of Human Rights* (Toronto: University of Toronto Press, 2007); Humphrey exhibit at the
      CMHR, http://humanrightsmuseum.ca/exhibits/jph/.

11   John Hucker, "Antidiscrimination Laws in Canada: Human Rights Commissions and the
      Search for Equality," *Human Rights Quarterly* 19, 3 (1997): 547–71; Michael Ignatieff, *The
      Rights Revolution*, 2nd ed. (Toronto: Anansi, 2007).

12   Rhoda E. Howard-Hassmann, *Compassionate Canadians: Civic Leaders Discuss Hu-
      man Rights* (Toronto: University of Toronto Press, 2003); Ross Lamberton, *Repression
      and Resistance: Canadian Human Rights Activists, 1930–1960* (Toronto: University of
      Toronto Press, 2005). A critical view is Sherene H. Razack, "Stealing the Pain of Others:
      Reflections on Canadian Humanitarian Responses," *Review of Education, Pedagogy, and
      Cultural Studies* 27, 4 (2007): 375–94.

13   Robert O. Matthews, "Sudan's Humanitarian Disaster: Will Canada Live Up to Its Re-
      sponsibility to Protect?," *International Journal* 60, 4 (2005): 1049–64.

14   Olivia Ward, "Canada Gets Human Rights Failing Grade from Amnesty International,"
      Toronto Star, 19 December 2012.

15   Minister of Foreign Affairs, *Human Security in Sudan: The Report of a Canadian Assess-
      ment Mission* (Ottawa: Ministry of Foreign Affairs, 2000), http://www.ecosonline.org/
      reports/2000/Human%20Security%20in%20Sudan.pdf.

16   Maude Barlow, "Harper Sells Canadian Human Rights to China," *Huffington Post,* 8 Feb-
      ruary 2012, http://www.huffingtonpost.ca/maude-barlow/harper-china-oil_b_1263034.
      html; S. James Anaya and Robert A. Williams, "The Protection of Indigenous Peoples'
      Rights over Lands and Natural Resources under the Inter-American Human Rights Sys-
      tem," *Harvard Human Rights Journal* 14 (2001): 33–86.

17   CBC News, "Ottawa Fights Charge It Discriminates against Aboriginal Kids," 25 February
      2013, http://www.cbc.ca/news/politics/story/2013/02/24/pol-canadian-human-rights-
      tribunal-hearings-first-nations-children.html. See also the court decision in *First Nations
      Child and Family Caring Society of Canada et al. v. Attorney General of Canada (for the
      Minister of Indian and Northern Affairs Canada)*, 2012 CHRT 17 (CanLII), http://canlii.
      ca/en/ca/chrt/doc/2012/2012chrt17/2012chrt17.html.

18   On global order and the West, see Mark Mazower, *Governing the World: The History of
      an Idea* (New York: Penguin, 2012). Liberalism's blindness to its intolerance of alterity in
      settler colonies is explored in Elizabeth Povinelli, *The Cunning of Recognition: Indigenous
      Alterities and the Making of Australian Multiculturalism* (Durham, NC: Duke University
      Press, 2002).

19   Andrew Woolford, Jeff Benvenuto, and Alexander Laban Hinton, eds., *Colonial Genocide
      and Indigenous North America* (Durham, NC: Duke University Press, 2014); A. Dirk
      Moses, ed., *Empire, Colony, Genocide: Conquest, Occupation, and Subaltern Resistance in
      World History* (New York: Berghahn Books, 2008); A. Dirk Moses, ed., *Genocide and Set-*

tler Society: Frontier Violence and Stolen Indigenous Children in Australian History (New York: Berghahn Books, 2004).

20   Patrick Wolfe, "Settler Colonialism and the Elimination of the Native," *Journal of Genocide Research* 8, 4 (2006): 387–410; A. Dirk Moses, "Conceptual Blockages and Definitional Dilemmas in the Racial Century: Genocide of Indigenous Peoples and the Holocaust," *Patterns of Prejudice* 36, 4 (2002): 7–36. On settler colonialism more generally, see Lorenzo Veracini, *Settler Colonialism: A Theoretical Overview* (Houndmills, UK: Palgrave Macmillan, 2010).

21   Christopher Powell, "Sinclair Is Correct: It Was Genocide," *Winnipeg Free Press,* 24 February 2012; David B. MacDonald and Graham Hudson, "The Genocide Question and Indian Residential Schools in Canada," *Canadian Journal of Political Science* 45, 2 (2012): 427–49; Andrew Woolford, "Ontological Destruction: Genocide and Aboriginal Peoples in Canada," *Genocide Studies and Prevention* 4, 1 (2009): 81–97. On issues of redress for and reconciliation with Indigenous Canadians, see Jennifer Henderson and Pauline Wakeham, eds., *Reconciling Canada: Critical Perspectives on the Culture of Redress* (Toronto: University of Toronto Press, 2013).

22   Clint Curle, "Raising Awareness of Armenian Genocide," 2 April 2013, http://museumforhumanrights.ca/explore/blog/raising-awareness-armenian-genocide; Carol Sanders, "CMHR Won't Flip on Armenian Genocide," *Winnipeg Free Press,* 8 April 2013. The Armenians were pleased with the outcome; see "Canadian Museum for Human Rights to Open Exhibit on Armenian Genocide," *PanArmenian.Net,* 10 April 2013. The Zoryan Institute is a Canadian-Armenian organization that promotes education and research on the Armenian genocide, human rights, and "diaspora-homeland relations"; see http://www.zoryaninstitute.org.

23   Rhonda Spivak, "CISA Announces Its First Year of Programming," *Winnipeg Jewish Review,* 2 October 2011; Bob Hepburn, "Canadian Anti-Semitism Institute Aims to Fill Worldwide Void," *Toronto Star,* 9 May 2012.

24   Oksana Bashuk Hepburn, "Canadian Museum for Human Rights: Right the Wrong," *Hill Times,* 16 April 2012.

25   Bernie Farber, "No Dogs and Jews Allowed," *Huffington Post,* 13 May 2012, http://www.huffingtonpost.ca/bernie-farber/human-rights-canada_b_1510399.html.

26   Details for this paragraph can be found in A. Dirk Moses, "Does the Holocaust Reveal or Conceal Other Genocides? The Canadian Museum of Human Rights and Grievable Suffering," in *Hidden Genocides: Power, Knowledge, and Memory,* ed. Doug Irvin, Alexander Hinton, and Tom LaPointe (New Brunswick, NJ: Rutgers University Press, 2013), 21–51. Regarding the Simon Wiesenthal Center, see its campus outreach division, which includes, among its missions, the following: "By exposing the truth behind anti-Semitism, hate and terrorism, by promoting human rights and dignity, by standing firmly with Israel, and by celebrating our unique identity as Jews, campus outreach is creating a strong and effective presence on campuses nationwide and giving a voice to the next generation of global human rights activists." http://iact.wiesenthal.org/site/c.khLQK1PCLmF/b.4416629/k.575E/About_Campus_Outreach.htm (accessed 30 November 2014).

27   The Holocaust Memorial Day Act, http://web2.gov.mb.ca/laws/statutes/ccsm/h068e.php.

28   David Matas, "The Struggle for Justice: Nazi War Criminals in Canada, from Immigration to Integration," in *The Canadian Jewish Experience: A Millennium Edition,* ed. Ruth Klein and Frank Dimant (Toronto: Institute for International Affairs B'nai B'rith Canada, 2001); Harold Troper and Morton Weinfield, *Old Wounds: Jews, Ukrainians, and the Hunt for Nazi War Criminals in Canada* (Chapel Hill: University of North Carolina Press, 1989).

29   David Matas, "Remembering the Holocaust Can Prevent Future Genocides," in *Geno-cide,* ed. William Dudley (San Diego: Greenhaven Press, 2001), 119–23. Excerpted from "Remembering the Holocaust," in *Genocide Watch,* ed. Helen Fein (New Haven, CT: Yale University Press, 1992). Yom ha-Shoah Holocaust Memorial Day Teacher's Guide, http://www.bnaibrith.ca/league/hh-teachers/guide00.html.

30   Norman Hillmer, "The Canadian War Museum and the Military Identity of an Unmili-tary People," *Canadian Military History* 19, 3 (2010): 19–27.

31   Irving Abella and Harold Troper, *None Is Too Many: Canada and the Jews of Europe 1933–1948* (Toronto: Lester and Orpen Dennys, 1983).

32   David Monod, "'Who Owns History Anyway?': The Political Assault on North American History," *Ahornblätter: Marburger Beiträge zur Kanada-Forschung* 90 (1999), http://archiv.ub.uni-marburg.de/sum/90/sum90-5.html.

33   Kelly Cryderman, "Jewish Groups Want Museum to Focus on Holocaust," *Ottawa Citizen,* 8 June 2000; Paul Samyn, "Asper-Led Museum Sets Off Alarm Bells: View of Genocide Said Too Exclusive," *Winnipeg Free Press,* 27 February 2003. Further details are found in Moses, "The Canadian Museum for Human Rights." Kafieh is a former president of the Canadian Arab Federation and later the legal counsel for the Canadian Islamic Congress.

34   Paul Samyn, "$125-M Holocaust Museum for City?," *Winnipeg Free Press,* 3 April 2002.

35   Dan Lett, "Conflict Is a Certainty: Museum's Challenge Is to Embrace Debate, Reject Hate," *Winnipeg Free Press,* 27 November 2010.

36   Paul Samyn, "Museum Price Tag May Hit $200M," *Winnipeg Free Press,* 4 April 2002.

37   A detailed and critical analysis of the Ukrainian Canadian associations and their relation-ship to the museum is Karyn Ball and Per Anders Rudling, "The Underbelly of Canadian Multiculturalism: Holocaust Obfuscation in the Debate about the Canadian Museum for Human Rights," *Holocaust Studies: A Journal of Culture and History* 20, 1 (2014): 33–80.

38   A copy of the letter, addressed to Paul M. Grod and Andrew Hladyshevsky of the UCC, is attached to the UCCLA submission to the Content Advisory Committee of the CMHR. See "The Canadian Museum for Human Rights: A Canadian Ukrainian Perspective," 11 June 2009, http://www.uccla.ca/CMHR_11June09.pdf.

39   David O'Brien, "Museum to Respect Ukrainian Rights," *Winnipeg Free Press,* 1 December 2003.

40   George Shirinian, "Canadian Museum for Human Rights and the Armenian Commu-nity," *Asbarez Armenian News,* 21 February 2012.

41   O'Brien, "Museum to Respect Ukrainian Rights."

42   "Heritage Minister James Moore Visits News Café," *Winnipeg Free Press,* 11 September 2012, http://www.winnipegfreepress.com/breakingnews/Heritage-Minister-James-Moore-dropping-into-News-Cafe-Wednesday-169332836.html.

43   Kim Stanton, "Canada's Truth and Reconciliation Commission: Settling the Past?," *International Indigenous Policy Journal* 2, 3 (2011), http://ir.lib.uwo.ca/iipj/v012/iss3/2; Statement of Reconciliation, http://www.edu.gov.mb.ca/k12/cur/socstud/foundation_gr9/blms/9-1-4e.pdf; Indian Residential Schools Settlement—Official Court Website, http://www.residentialschoolsettlement.ca/english.html; Truth and Reconciliation Commission, http://www.trc.ca.

44   Paul Samyn, "Aspers Got Grant for Lobbyist," *Winnipeg Free Press,* 22 November 2004. Angela Cassie was then the Heritage Canada spokeswoman who commented on possible irregularities with the grant awarding to Fontaine. Now she is the director of communica-tions and external relations at the CMHR.

45 Paul Barnsley, "We Can Do Better—Jewish Leader to Chiefs," *Windspeaker,* 1 August 2005.

46 Chris Cobb, "Fontaine Praises Bond of Jews and First Nations," *Winnipeg Free Press,* 23 June 2008.

47 Asper Foundation, "Irael [sic] Asper Announces Plans to Create Canadian Museum for Human Rights," 17 April 2003, http://www.friendsofcmhr.com/news_room/news_releases/index.cfm?id=23.

48 Rhonda Spivak, "Tanenbaum Donates $1 Million to Rights Museum," *Canadian Jewish News,* 13 March 2008.

49 Paul Samyn, "Rights Museum Faces Cash Crunch," *Winnipeg Free Press,* 3 January 2005.

50 *Report to the Minister of Canadian Heritage on the Canadian Museum for Human Rights* (Ottawa: Library and Archives Canada, 2008).

51 Ibid., "Table 7: Selected Topics or Issues Suggested by Respondents for the CMHR," 35.

52 Colin Campbell, "Controversy over National Museum of Human Rights in Winnipeg," *Maclean's,* 27 March 2006, http://www.thecanadianencyclopedia.com/index.cfm?PgNm=TCE&Params=M1ARTM0012931.

53 Legislative Summary, LS-57E, Bill C-42, An Act to Amend the Museums Act and to Make Consequential Amendments to Other Acts, 22 February 2008 (Library of Parliament: Parliamentary Record and Information Service, 2008), 4–5.

54 "Prime Minister Harper Receives Saul Hayes Human Rights Award," 31 May 2009, http://www.pm.gc.ca/eng/media.asp?id=2603.

55 CMHR, *Contents Committee Advisory Report* (Ottawa: Library and Archives Canada, 2010), 3, 74, http://humanrightsmuseum.ca/programs-and-events/programs/content-advisory-committee-final-report. Although journalist and museum supporter Dan Lett, "Conflict Is a Certainty," calls the committee "blue ribbon," Ira Basen writes that its recommendations were "predictable"; see Ira Basen, "Memory Becomes a Minefield at Canada's Museum for Human Rights," *Globe and Mail,* 20 August 2011.

56 http://www.bnaibrith.ca/files/211009.pdf. Their views were given airplay by boosters in the mainstream press. See David O'Brien, "Jewish Suffering Is Unique in History," *Winnipeg Free Press,* 22 April 2009.

57 Lord Cultural Services—CMHR, http://en.lordculture.com/projects/962/Canadian_Museum_for_Human_Rights.htm.

58 CMHR, *Content Committee Advisory Report,* 74, 43. Ken Norman was a member as well; see his chapter in this volume.

59 Ibid., 43, 75n62. The papers are cited as David Matas, "The Holocaust and the Canadian Museum for Human Rights," 8 March 2010; and David Matas, "The Holocaust Lens," 1 May 2010, "on deposit at the Museum."

60 Lett, "Conflict Is a Certainty"; emphasis added.

61 Samyn, "Asper-Led Museum Sets Off Alarm Bells"; Lubomyr Luciuk, "All Genocide Victims Must Be Hallowed," *Ukrainian Weekly,* 7 March 2004.

62 Basen, "Memory Becomes a Minefield."

63 Aldo Santin, "Most Oppose Separate Holocaust Gallery: Boosts Those Pushing Museum to Change Genocide Treatment," *Winnipeg Free Press,* 24 March 2011; Charles Lewis, "Controversial Poll Flashpoint in Rights Museum Debate," *National Post,* 30 March 2011; CJC coverage, http://www.cic.gc.ca/english/resources/por/june2011/index.asp.

64   Speech delivered by President and CEO Stuart Murray at the Memorial in Commemora-
      tion of Famines' Victims in Ukraine, 3 July 2012, Kyiv, Ukraine, http://museumforhu-
      manrights.ca/about-museum/speeches-our-museum-leaders/speech-delivered-president-
      and-ceo-stuart-murray-memorial; "CMHR Shines Light on 'Stalin's Secret Files' from
      Ukrainian Genocide," 15 November 2012, http://museumforhumanrights.ca/about-muse-
      um/news/cmhr-shines-light-"stalin's-secret-files"-ukrainian-genocide.

65   "UCC Welcomes Appointment of Dr. Lindy Ledohowski to Human Rights Museum
      Board," press release, 18 March 2011, http://www.ucc.ca/2011/03/18/ucc-welcomes-
      appointment-of-dr-lindy-ledohowski-to-human-rights-museum-board.

66   Samuel Moyn, *The Last Utopia: The Holocaust in History* (Cambridge, MA: Harvard Uni-
      versity Press, 2010); Marco Duranti, "The Human Rights Revolution and the Holocaust:
      Revisiting the Foundation Myth," *Journal of Genocide Research* 14, 2 (2012): 159–86.
      Moyn met with Clint Curle and Canadian academics, among them Michael Marrus, in
      a roundtable at the Faculty of Law, University of Toronto, on 11 November 2011. He in-
      formed his listeners that the "human rights revolution" was not based on Holocaust mem-
      ory—as Marrus had told the CMHR long before. See Charles Lewis, "Rights Museum
      Needs a Rethink, Academic Says," *National Post,* 5 April 2011. The museum thereupon
      changed its pitch. Samuel Moyn, "Remarks on Canadian Human Rights Museum," paper
      in possession of the author.

67   "Dr. Catherine Chatterley Interviews CMHR about Contents of Holocaust Gallery,"
      Winnipeg Jewish Review, 3 April 2013. In 2010, the CMHR commissioned me to write a
      memorandum on Raphael Lemkin's conception of genocide. I do not know whether or
      how it was used in the formulation and construction of the Lemkin exhibit.

68   Bernie Bellan, "What's Happening with the Holocaust Gallery in the New Canadian
      Museum for Human Rights?," *Jewish Post and News,* 17 November 2010; Myron Love,
      "Ukrainian Groups Oppose Museum's Holocaust Exhibit," *Canadian Jewish News,* 20
      January 2011.

69   Rhonda Spivak, "Open Letter to Lubomyr Luciuk, Director of Research, Ukrainian
      Civil Liberties Association, Re: CMHR," *Winnipeg Jewish Review,* 31 March 2011. Yude
      Henteleff likewise expressed alarm at the prospect of the Holocaust's decentring: "If this
      ['position of the Holocaust separate zone'] is in any way diminished it will significantly
      impair the museum in carrying out its stated objectives as noted in its enabling legisla-
      tion." Yude Henteleff, "Critical Conversations with Canadians: The Work of the Content
      Advisory Committee," University of Manitoba, 5 January 2012, http://law.robsonhall.ca/
      the-distinguished-visitors-lecture-series/now-playing/753-yude-henteleff-critical-conver-
      sations-with-canadians-the-work-of-the-content-advisory-committee.

70   "Dr. Catherine Chatterley Interviews CMHR."

71   Sharon Chisvin, "Local Institute to Combat Anti-Semitism," *Winnipeg Free Press,* 26
      March 2011; Rhonda Spivak, "CISA Announces Its First Year of Programming," *Winnipeg
      Jewish Review,* 2 October 2011; Irwin Cotler, "Universal Lessons of the Holocaust," *Times
      of Israel,* 5 April 2013, http://blogs.timesofisrael.com/the-holocaust-and-human-rights-
      universal-lessons-for-our-times.

72   Bob Hepburn, "Canadian Anti-Semitism Institute Aims to Fill Worldwide Void," *Toronto
      Star,* 9 May 2012.

73   "Editorial: Shoah's Uniqueness," *Jewish Independent,* 16 December 2011; emphasis added.

74   Quoted in Chisvin, "Local Institute to Combat Anti-Semitism."

75   Lionel Steiman, "Muller Advances a Conception of the Holocaust Different from that
      Recognized by Most Other Scholars," *Winnipeg Jewish Review,* 5 April 2012; Adam Muller,

"Holocaust Was Not Primarily an Antisemitic Experience," *Winnipeg Jewish Review,* 7 April 2012.

76 Bryan Schwartz, "Centrality of Antisemitism in Producing the Holocaust Is Known and Settled," *Winnipeg Jewish Review,* 24 April 2012.

77 Quoted in Lett, "Conflict Is a Certainty." Chatterley seems to share these views. See Catherine Chatterley, "A History of Israeli Apartheid Week," *National Post,* 3 March 2011.

78 Lett, "Conflict Is a Certainty." The term "strident" is Lett's.

79 Jenny Ford, "Memo on Holodomor Fails to Quell Concern: Ukrainians Worry about Museum Space," *Winnipeg Free Press,* 10 July 2012.

80 "UCC Concerned over Content of Canadian Museum for Human Rights," 6 April 2013, http://www.ucc.ca/2013/04/06/ucc-concerned-over-content-of-canadian-museum-for-human-rights.

81 Quoted in Joanne Pursaga, "Plans for Human Rights Museum Galleries Revealed," *Winnipeg Sun,* 4 March 2013.

82 Ruane Remy, "Human Rights Museum in the Wrong, Say Ukrainians," *Catholic Register,* 24 May 2013; Tessa Vanderhart, "Genocide Exhibit Too Close to Bathroom: Ukrainians," *Winnipeg Sun,* 29 March 2013.

83 Steve Andrusiak, letter to the editor, *Windsor Star,* 25 April 2013. On history and psychic dispersion, see A. Dirk Moses, "Genocide and the Terror of History," *Parallax* 17, 4 (2011): 90–108.

84 Rhonda Hinther university homepage, http://umanitoba.ca/faculties/arts/departments/womens_studies/members/3165.html.

85 "Heritage Minister James Moore Visits News Café"; "Dr. Catherine Chatterley Interviews CMHR." So far, the museum has related Guatemala as a human rights violation, showing the caprice of such categorizations. Bernice Pontanilla, "Guatemalan Partnership to 'Break Long Silence,' Says CMHR President," *Metro News,* 20 June 2013.

86 Tribute to Liberty, "About Us," http://www.tributetoliberty.ca/aboutus.html; Per Anders Rudling, "Multiculturalism, Memory, and Ritualization: Ukrainian Nationalist Monuments in Edmonton, Alberta," *Nationalities Papers* 39, 5 (2011): 733–68.

87 Quoted in Ryan Hicks, "Palestinian-Canadians Feel Ignored in Human Rights Museum," CBC News, 4 March 2013, http://www.cbc.ca/news/canada/manitoba/story/2013/03/04/mb-human-rights-museum-documents-winnipeg.html.

88 Pursaga, "Plans for Human Rights Museum Galleries Revealed."

89 James Kafieh and Canadians for Genocide Education, submission to the CMHR, roundtable discussion, Ottawa, 11 June 2009, 3-4, http://instituteforgenocide.org/en/wp-content/uploads/2012/03/CMHR-Submission-Nov-20-2009-2.pdf.

90 Ibid., 2.

91 Shari Narine, "Missing and Dead Residential School Children," *Windspeaker* 30, 4 (2012): 24; Colin Perkel, "At Least 3,000 Native Children Died in Residential Schools: Research," *Globe and Mail,* 18 February 2013; Judy Byington, "Is There Government Cover-Up of Child Genocide and Mass Graves?" *Examiner,* 18 December 2013, http://www.examiner.com/article/is-there-government-cover-up-of-child-genocide-and-mass-graves.

92 Phil Fontaine, Michael Dan, and Bernie M. Faber, "A Canadian Genocide in Search of a Name," *Toronto Star,* 19 July 2013. On this episode, see Ian Mosby, "Administering Colonial Science: Nutrition Research and Human Biomedical Experimentation in Aboriginal Communities and Residential Schools, 1942–1952," *Histoire sociale/Social History* 46, 91

(2013): 145–72; Bob Weber, "Atleo Calls on PM to Acknowledge 'Horrors' of Nutrition Tests on Native Children," *Globe and Mail,* 17 July 2013; James Daschuk, "When Canada Used Hunger to Clear the West," *Globe and Mail,* 19 July 2013.

93   Mary Agnes Welch, "CMHR Rejects 'Genocide' for Native Policies," *Winnipeg Free Press,* 27 July 2013; Stuart Murray, letter to the editor, "'Genocide' Will Have Its Place," *Winnipeg Free Press,* 28 July 2013; Dan Lett, "CMHR Flap Shows Perils of Being Linked to Ottawa," *Winnipeg Free Press,* 29 July 2013; Gloria Galloway, "Critics Press Ottawa to Recognize Wrongs against First Nations as Genocide," *Globe and Mail,* 30 July 2013.

94   David MacDonald, "Genocide Is as Genocide Does," *Winnipeg Free Press,* 25 September 2014.

95   Pursaga, "Plans for Human Rights Museum Galleries Revealed."

96   Avishai Margalit, *Ethics of Memory* (Cambridge, MA: Harvard University Press, 2002), 80.

97   CMHR Gallery Profiles, September 2012, 30.

98   CBC News, "Human Rights Museum Board behind Push for 'Positive' Stories: Canadian Museum Manager's Letter Indicates Desire for 'Optimistic Tone' for Peace Gallery," 3 December 2012.

99   CBC News, "Human Rights Museum Seeks Child Welfare Materials: Canadian Museum for Human Rights Calls for Materials from First Nations on 'Sixties Scoop,'" 7 May 2013, http://www.cbc.ca/news/canada/manitoba/story/2013/05/07/mb-cmhr-sixties-scoop-call-winnipeg.html.

100   Bartley Kives, "Canadian Museum for Human Rights Staff Exodus Tied to Content Change: Ex-Workers Blame Decision on 'Positive Stories,'" *Winnipeg Free Press,* 1 December 2012.

101   Matas, "Remembering the Holocaust."

102   Michael Dan, "Seeking the Right Word for a History of Suffering," *Ottawa Citizen,* 9 April 2014; Michael Dan, "My Hope for the Canadian Museum for Human Rights," *Canadian Jewish News,* 1 October 2014.

103   Phil Fontaine and Bernie Faber, "What Canada Committed against First Nations Was Genocide: The UN Should Recognize It," *Globe and Mail,* 14 October 2013.

104   "Dr. Catherine Chatterley Interviews CMHR"; Standing Committee on Canadian Heritage, Minutes-Evidence, 7 June 2000, para. 1630.

105   Charles Tilly, "War Making and State Making as Organized Crime," in *Bringing the State Back In,* ed. Peter Evans, Dietrich Rueschemeyer, and Theda Skocpol (Cambridge, UK: Cambridge University Press, 1985), 169–91; Janice E. Thomson, *Mercenaries, Pirates, and Sovereigns: State-Building and Extraterritorial Violence in Early Modern Europe* (Princeton, NJ: Princeton University Press, 1994); Chris Powell, *Barbaric Civilization: A Critical Sociology of Genocide* (Montreal: McGill-Queen's University Press, 2011); A. Dirk Moses, "*Das römische Gespräch* in a New Key: Hannah Arendt, Genocide, and the Defense of Republican Civilization," *Journal of Modern History* 85, 4 (2013): 867–913.

106   Tony Barta, "Relations of Genocide: Land and Lives in the Colonization of Australia," in *Genocide and the Modern Age: Etiology and Case Studies of Mass Death,* ed. Isidor Wallimann and Michael Dobkowski (New York: Greenwood Press, 1987), 237–52.

107   Cf. Anne Orford, *Reading Humanitarian Intervention* (Cambridge, UK: Cambridge University Press, 2003).

108 CBC News, "Human Rights Museum Sparks Debate over Term 'Genocide,'" 26 July 2013, http://www.cbc.ca/news/canada/manitoba/story/2013/07/26/mb-cmhr-aboriginal-genocide-debate-winnipeg.html.

109 Larry Krotz, "A Canadian Genocide?," *United Church Observer,* 23 March 2014.

110 Doug Saunders, "A Fight over the Word 'Genocide' Is No Way to End the Aboriginal Crisis," *Globe and Mail,* 19 October 2013.

111 United Nations General Assembly, GA/10612, press release on the declaration, http://www.un.org/News/Press/docs/2007/ga10612.doc.htm.

112 See the correspondence between archaeologists and the museum at http://www.assocmanarch.com/resources/CMHR+Letter.pdf and http://www.assocmanarch.com/resources/CMHR+response.pdf. See also Carol Sanders and Nick Martin, "Archeologists Dig for Information: 'Buried' Findings at Forks Excavation Site," *Winnipeg Free Press,* 16 December 2011; and Kimlee Wong, "Searching for Human Rights at the Canadian Museum for Human Rights," *rabble.ca,* 19 September 2014, http://rabble.ca/blogs/bloggers/views-expressed/2014/09/searching-human-rights-canadian-museum-human-rights.

113 "Heritage Minister James Moore Visits News Café."

114 Alexandra Paul, "It's the Million-Dollar Question: Manitoba Chiefs Say Donation Gives Them a Say on 'Genocide,'" *Winnipeg Free Press,* 6 August 2013; Alexandra Paul, "Donations Won't Sway Content, CMHR Declares," *Winnipeg Free Press,* 8 August 2013; Alexandra Paul, "Genocide Never Debated: Chief," *Winnipeg Free Press,* 10 August 2013; Susan Martinkuk, "Native Leaders' Talk of Genocide Just Fuels Anger," *Calgary Herald,* 9 August 2013; Black Rod, "The CMHR Stirs Up Hatred and Divisiveness. And It's Not Even Open," 8 August 2013, http://blackrod.blogspot.com.au.

115 B'nai B'rith, "Creation of Israel Must Be Included in New Museum," 7 August 2013, http://www.bnaibrith.ca/creation of israel-must-be-included-in-new-museum-says-bnai-brith-canada.

116 Joseph Brean, "Canadian Museum for Human Rights Opens amidst Controversy and Protests," *National Post,* 19 September 2014; Wong, "Searching for Human Rights." An exasperated response is Jonathan Kay, "Every Identity-Politics Activist Known to Humanity Is Attacking Canada's Human Rights Museum," *National Post,* 21 September 2014.

117 Gail Asper, "Lead by Example: A Family Motto and the Canadian Museum for Human Rights," *Think: The Lola Stein Institute Journal* 12 (2012): 14–15.

118 Myron Love, "Shoah Education Still Key for Human Rights Museum," *Canadian Jewish News,* 28 March 2013.

119 "Dr. Catherine Chatterley Interviews CMHR."

120 CBC News, "Human Rights Museum, Asper Foundation to Bring Thousands of Students to Winnipeg," 7 October 2014, http://www.cbc.ca/news/canada/manitoba/human-rights-museum-asper-foundation-to-bring-thousands-of-students-to-winnipeg-1.2790136.

121 Quoted in "Armenian Genocide Immortalized in Canadian Museum of Human Rights," *Asbarez Armenian News,* 9 October 2014, http://asbarez.com/127776/armenian-genocide-immortalized-in-canadian-museum-of-human-rights.

122 James Adams, "Inside the Canadian Museum for Human Rights, the Labyrinth of Conscience," *Globe and Mail,* 19 September 2014.

123 Quoted in "Armenian Genocide Immortalized."

TOWARD RADICAL TRANSPARENCY AT THE CANADIAN MUSEUM FOR HUMAN RIGHTS: LESSONS FROM MEDIA COVERAGE DURING CONSTRUCTION

CHAPTER 3

Helen Fallding

Judging by mass-media coverage, the striking building towering over The Forks in Winnipeg should be called the Ice Palace of Competing European Genocides or perhaps Our Lady of Perpetual Fundraising. The Canadian Museum for Human Rights is an unaffordable perpetuator of conflict among the descendants of immigrants, which hardly anyone will visit anyway, according to some of the main sources of information for Canadians who collectively own the new museum.

At least 275 Canadian news stories about the national museum were published or broadcast in the four years from 1 August 2008—the month that the museum's first board of trustees was appointed—to 31 July 2012.[1] The 2008 appointments completed the handover of the proposed museum's operations from Winnipeg's Asper family to the Canadian government.

More than half of the news stories focused primarily on the museum's finances or its anticipated exhibits.[2] In a human rights museum, every exhibit has the potential to generate controversy, yet almost two-thirds of the news stories about the CMHR's content were preoccupied with a single theme: did the museum's creators grant the Holocaust undue prominence compared with the Ukrainian famine known as the Holodomor?

By the time the Holodomor debate hit the news in late 2010, it was getting late to rethink the museum's plan to dedicate one of twelve inaugural galleries to the Holocaust. In early 2008, a government document had stated that the museum would "house the largest museum gallery in Canada devoted to the subject of the Holocaust,"[3] and fundraising had proceeded on that basis. Public debate about the justification for treating the Holocaust as unique was intense but not necessarily well informed. An insightful analysis of this issue by genocide scholar Dirk Moses[4] received no mainstream media coverage, demonstrating how the ponderous pace of academic publishing and the cost of accessing journal articles limit the impact of scholarly writing on public debate.

Museum staff worn out by the Holodomor conflict might be tempted to review future draft exhibits alongside only a few hand-picked advisors. However, sharing information with all interested Canadians might turn out to be a healthier option that aligns with the CMHR's official mandate. As the museum's statement of values notes, "the museum's status as a national institution also confers a set of principles including accountability and transparency."[5] Citizens who can see through the museum's glass walls and observe its inner workings will be best equipped to tackle what some scholars refer to as "difficult knowledge" and to fulfill the vision of a museum "for" rather than just "of" human rights.[6]

THE CASE OF THE MISSING CONTROVERSIES

If news column inches were square feet, then the Canadian Museum for Human Rights would have two giant galleries—one devoted to the Holocaust and the other to a few other European genocides. Off in the wings might be some minor exhibits on Chinese Canadian history, citizenship rights, children, refugees, and women.

In fact, the museum's twelve inaugural galleries address a huge range of topics, including potentially touchy Canadian content related to migrant workers, murdered women, Aboriginal rights, bath house raids, persecution of the Roma, religious freedom, queer resistance to oppression, and the notorious Morgentaler abortion rights case. None of these subjects, though controversial in other contexts, seems to have generated mainstream news stories in the four years analyzed for this chapter.

Perhaps other minorities should have followed the example of some Ukrainian Canadians who launched a relentless campaign in 2010 for greater prominence for their community's stories in the museum. They succeeded in grabbing both local and national attention, with forty-three stories published on the topic. Eighteen of thirty-one articles about the Canadian Museum for Human Rights in national publications (*Globe and Mail, National Post, Ottawa Citizen,* and *Maclean's*) were preoccupied with the Holodomor debate. Angela Cassie, the museum's director of communications and external relations, says that a prominent 2011 *Globe and Mail* article cemented misconceptions that the museum would be devoted primarily to genocide commemoration.[7] She called that a big step backward for efforts to explain the museum's broader focus on human rights action across a wide range of themes beyond genocide.[8]

To media consumers in Winnipeg, it felt as if tensions between a previous generation of Ukrainian and Jewish immigrants in the city's North End were playing themselves out: Canadian Jews had campaigned for the prosecution of Ukrainian immigrants who had served the Nazis, while some Ukrainian Canadians thought that Jewish immigrants viewed as having collaborated with communist oppressors were unfairly let off the hook.[9] Other established ethnic groups, such as the Armenian and Chinese communities, opted for a more polite dialogue with the museum,[10] resulting in minor news coverage of their concerns.[11] Newcomers to Canada escaping from ongoing atrocities in their homelands do not have the resources or lobbying clout of such established immigrant groups, and their voices have barely registered in news stories.

"Different communities are in different stages of grief and mourning," Cassie said. For the most vocal Ukrainian Canadians, that stage is apparently anger after their community finally won Canadian government recognition in 2008 of the Holodomor as genocide. Anger is pretty much guaranteed to generate more mass-media coverage than the kind of thoughtful dialogue that museum staff promoted in cross-Canada consultations in 2009 and 2010, before exhibits were designed by newly hired curators. Conspicuous controversy is more likely than nuanced discussion to sustain the attention of readers, viewers, and listeners. Some journalists admit privately that they should not have let a handful of Ukrainian Canadian activists set the agenda for their stories, but few reporters have time for independent investigation in a world in which media companies are struggling for financial survival.

As Cassie mentioned, other communities across Canada watched carefully to see how the CMHR resolved the Holodomor dispute. Acquiescing to all of the Ukrainian protesters' demands would have sent a message that the best way to influence museum content is to make noise. "I think that we've held firm," she said. However, the Ukrainian lobby did secure from the museum a speaking tour and guarantees for a commissioned film and content in seven exhibits.[12] These plans were still judged insufficient by many of those dissatisfied with the institution's treatment of Ukrainian suffering.[13]

One reason few other groups complained publicly is that little information was available concerning exhibits planned for ten of the twelve galleries. The museum went to great lengths to seek public input before designing its exhibits[14] but then shared draft plans with select experts and advocates rather than the general public. As a result, public concerns have coalesced around only partial awareness of the museum's plans.

The museum's website was deliberately unspecific[15] during the design phase, and gallery descriptions prepared for the museum's first annual meeting in December 2011 were not posted online. Plans for exhibits remained a mystery until the CBC posted online in March 2013 the results of an Access to Information request.[16] Even then the exhibit list was six months out of date and partially excised. Meanwhile, minutes from a March 2012 meeting, at which board members recommended drastic changes to the Forum gallery, remained impossible to access until 2014, following a complaint to Canada's information commissioner. When the minutes were finally released, all references to the relevant discussion had been excised.[17]

The CMHR's reluctance to name Indigenous genocide[18] came to light only after an unrelated revelation about experimentation on Indian residential school children led reporters to pose questions. Cassie justified shielding the museum's content plans from the public on the ground that museum staff wanted visitors to discover the exhibits for themselves when the new building opened rather than showing up with preconceived ideas of what they would find. Under Canada's Access to Information law, government institutions can refuse disclosure of plans not yet in operation if the consequences of the disclosure outweigh the public interest in disclosure.[19] Cassie was also wary of discussing specific exhibits since doing so inevitably raised questions about whether another issue close to someone's heart would be featured in a display. Notwithstanding this reluctance, in the face of continuing pressure about the Holodomor issue, the museum released details of its Ukrainian Canadian content to the public in December 2012.[20] Following the Indigenous genocide controversy,[21] the design for the museum's Indigenous Perspectives theatre was revealed at the final annual meeting before opening day.[22] As the museum's communications team expanded and the opening date neared, its approach to public disclosure evolved to include whetting the public's appetite rather than just relying on secrecy to build anticipation. Short descriptions of all the galleries were released seven months before opening,[23] and one month before opening media previewed ten stories to be highlighted in exhibits.[24] However, family members of museum staff invited to tour the museum one week before opening day as a "dress rehearsal" were required to sign a witnessed 750-word confidentiality agreement in which they vowed not to describe the museum's exhibits, galleries, content, information, design, or even architecture to anyone before opening day. These volunteers were required to acknowledge and agree that any breach of that promise "will result in irreparable harm and damage to CMHR for which there would be no adequate monetary remedy."[25] The dress rehearsal was cancelled in the end because the exhibits were not quite ready.

Some of the museum's curators are eager to engage the general public in designing exhibits, as some of the world's most innovative museums are doing through social media. Doing so would require the CMHR to commit to radical transparency and allow its preliminary ideas and designs to be posted online so that the public could contribute to the passionate debates about content that curators regularly have among themselves. This open and interactive approach would allow many Canadians who might never make it to Winnipeg in person to sign up as content development volunteers, and it might inspire more people to visit the museum since they would be stakeholders in its design. Such widespread public involvement could enrich exhibits, but the success of such a project would require more clarity about the museum's content approval process. Groups consulted by curators on some inaugural exhibits might have felt misled by the museum when galleries changed direction after exhibits had already passed peer review.[26]

Intriguing models of the dynamic exchange between museums and their users are available, and they highlight the merits of this approach to curation in the digital age. The Liberty Science Center in New Jersey, for example, encouraged the public to co-create exhibition content through a project website on which staff posted all "notes, ideas, meeting times, papers and other aspects of the exhibition development and design process."[27] Public co-curators commented online but were also welcome to participate in meetings by phone, and some eventually became involved in grant applications. Likewise, the Australian Museum has used a blog and Facebook to involve the public in exhibit development—including asking the public to help identify potential exhibit themes—without generating "inappropriate comments" online.[28]

Although the Australian curators did not specify what kinds of inappropriate comments they feared, racist diatribes and domination of the online discussion by single-issue advocates are realistic fears for the CMHR in any unmoderated forum. "If you're not going to carefully manage [the public's response] and monitor it, and people start attacking, and you're not nipping it in the bud, it ends up moving away from the objective," Cassie said. Archivists practising similar "distributed curation"—in which collections are created and organized collaboratively via the Internet—argue for "radical trust" that appropriate safeguards can be developed.[29] Mass-media stories can draw the public's attention to the launch of such co-creation initiatives, further promoting museums and widening their exposure to potential visitors.

The CMHR does host a web page inviting Canadians to upload their human rights stories,[30] but that information is not collected for the purpose of exhibit development. Tight timelines and a staff squeeze after money was redirected to help manage burgeoning building costs made gathering online exhibit input from the general public unrealistic while the CMHR was being built, Cassie noted. She pointed out that the innovations mentioned above were put into practice by established institutions.

Cassie acknowledged that there might be room for wider public input into exhibit design as the museum more fully incorporates human rights principles such as participatory decision making into its research approach. "Once we have a stronger foundation, we'll be in a better position to have those debates," she said in late 2012. The museum's subsequent calls for photos and stories on same-sex marriage and Aboriginal child welfare were a promising step.[31]

EMBRACING NEGATIVE COVERAGE

The media's obsession with the Holocaust and genocide galleries has skewed public perception of the CMHR, in which only about 20 percent of the content is focused on genocide. However, there is a silver lining to this distortion: Canadians largely unfamiliar with the Holodomor received a much-needed education about the Ukrainian famine when the issue of its representation came to dominate the debate about museum content. More than half of the stories mentioning the word *Holodomor* between 2009 and 2012 in Canada's main national newspaper, the *Globe and Mail*, related to the Canadian Museum for Human Rights.

Meanwhile, more recent controversies over whether the museum's government-appointed board is overly involved in decisions about exhibit content and design finally drew public attention to the Canadian human rights stories that will be the institution's primary focus.[32]

It might be in the museum's best interests to embrace conflict as a way of promoting human rights education. Doing so would be consistent with the CMHR's vision statement, which boldly declares that "the museum will not shy away from controversy; it will recognize and present the wide variety of legitimate perspectives on sensitive issues fairly and openly and will embrace constructive public debate."[33]

Unfortunately, such a sentiment might be at odds with the museum's communications objectives. A draft strategy on "representing the museum" from early 2012 suggests that all requests for presentations by employees—including expert researchers—should be vetted by communications staff and all speaking notes and PowerPoints screened for "the potential for controversy (negative)."[34] A plan by the museum's communications staff to monitor whether future media coverage is positive, negative, or neutral should, in keeping with the museum's mandate, be replaced by evaluation of whether the coverage promotes Canadians' understanding of human rights. Viewed according to this latter standard, the Holocaust-Holodomor debate can be seen as an educational opportunity rather than just a public relations problem for the museum.

Rather than further debate about which issues deserve more exhibit space, Cassie wanted to encourage visitors to look beyond their specific experiences of oppression toward a broader vision of human rights. "Not everyone is looking for a mirror," she said. Her comment brings to mind early architectural drawings of the CMHR that gave the impression that passersby would be able to see inside the building. In fact, the giant panes of glass installed have turned out to operate more like one-way mirrors during the daytime. Staff at their desks have a spectacular view of Winnipeg, but they remain invisible to outsiders. Similarly, opacity surrounding content development at the museum might be intended to deflect criticism, but instead it contributes to a kind of parochialism as critics focus only on the presence or absence of reflections of their own communities' stories.

FOLLOW THE MONEY

Had the CMHR been dubbed Our Lady of Perpetual Fundraising, the lady in question would be the indefatigable Gail Asper. She is the national campaign chair for the fundraising body Friends of the Canadian Museum for Human Rights, but some Canadians have the mistaken impression that she runs the museum itself.[35] The Jewish community's disproportionate generosity in funding a museum championed by one of its prominent families has fed the perception that museum content was designed to appease donors. That charge has led in turn to accusations that some of the museum's critics are guilty of anti-Semitism.[36]

The CMHR has an unconventional funding structure for a Crown corporation, with the government that owns it covering less than a third of the building's construction costs. The museum's precarious financial situation has attracted more media attention than any other topic, especially in Winnipeg, where fundraising efforts have been concentrated.

The city's newspaper of record, the *Winnipeg Free Press,* supported the museum with encouraging editorials and at least twenty stories promoting fundraising events and donations during the four-year period analyzed for this chapter. The newspaper owners' personal interest in the museum for business and philanthropic reasons likely played a role in shaping *Free Press* coverage of the CMHR, as Moses has pointed out,[37] but it is easy to overestimate the influence of owners on daily coverage. Many Winnipeg journalists have a soft spot for human rights issues because they or their children are members of disadvantaged groups or because they have a professional commitment to freedom of expression.

The smaller-circulation tabloid *Winnipeg Sun,* however, has painted the museum as an extravagant "rights palace" for the elite,[38] built at a time when the average Winnipegger might prefer that the city construct a water park.[39] The museum, for its part, has resorted to posting rebuttals on its website after the *Winnipeg Sun* declined to publish the museum's letters to the editor.[40] The difference between the *Sun* and *Free Press* was most stark when the competing newspapers managed to give the same poll results conflicting headlines: "CMHR Not Worth the Trip: Canadians"[41] versus "Canadians Support Museum."[42]

The *National Post* was a museum promoter during the years that the newspaper was controlled by the Asper family. That changed abruptly after the newspaper changed hands in 2010, culminating in a column suggesting that the museum building is doomed to be converted into a convention centre and casino.[43] Global television, also previously owned by the Aspers, broke a story about museum T-shirts made in countries with poor workers' rights,[44] but otherwise it mainly regurgitated stories from wire services. CTV Winnipeg, a local affiliate of the national broadcaster, has shown more ongoing interest in the museum.

As a private-public hybrid, the Canadian Museum for Human Rights is vulnerable to accusations of both donor and political interference. The

8. Spoof conversion of the museum into a water park.

CMHR and the new Museum of Immigration in Halifax are the only national museums in Canada in which the first CEO is appointed by the heritage minister rather than by the museum's board.[45] The CMHR's chief executive officer and first two board chairs had no expertise in either museums or human rights prior to joining the museum, but they do know something about money and politics. CEO Stuart Murray and inaugural board chair Arni Thorsteinson were fundraisers with strong ties to the Progressive Conservative Party of Manitoba, and replacement board chair Eric Hughes is an oil company accountant who helped Prime Minister Stephen Harper with his political campaigns.

Museum boosters argue that, during the construction phase, fundraising talent was more important than human rights expertise, but the political appointments backfired when they came to media attention. Former party leader Murray came under fire for his history of voting against equal rights for same-sex couples,[46] while Hughes has been accused of overruling the judgment of the museum's expert curators in his push for more Canadian content.[47] In response to his concerns, some exhibits on contemporary international issues were replaced by Canadian stories described by the museum's New York–based designers as "didactic-light."[48] Bullying, Armenian orphans, and francophone and Sikh rights in Canada are scheduled to take the place of exhibits formerly committed to the representation of transitional justice efforts in Northern Ireland, Darfur, and the slums of India.

No media outlet appears to have pointed out the incongruity of appointing Thorsteinson, whose connection to a notorious 1995 Manitoba election vote-rigging plot ought to have undermined his credibility as a spokesperson for democratic rights.[49] Some media organizations made internal decisions that his past was no longer relevant to their coverage of his current activities,[50] while in other cases the omission might have been due to a failure of institutional memory.

Differences in vision between staff with human rights expertise and the CEO and board members have driven away at least one museum researcher. Six of the original team of eight researchers and curators hired in 2010 had left by the end of 2013, before the museum opened. However, in response to criticisms of the museum's working environment, Cassie argued that much of the general staff turnover that has attracted media attention[51] can be more properly attributed to the museum's funding crunch. Faced with the museum's financial struggles, she argued, some staff wanted more job security and the larger budgets that they had originally been led to expect. Before governments stepped in with loans and cash advances in mid-2012, layoffs and delays to the museum's opening until at least 2017 were on the table.

A week before the museum opened in September 2014, fears of political interference resurfaced when Minister of Heritage Shelly Glover asked to review all content that mentioned the Canadian government.[52]

CHANGE BEGINS HERE

The CMHR will have a different meaning, of course, for foreigners immune to such parochially Canadian concerns. In the four years assessed for this study, there was little international coverage of the museum. The *New York Times* referred in passing to the original architectural competition, and the *Washington Post* recommended perimeter tours of the construction site to visitors to Winnipeg.[53] Across the Atlantic, Britain's *Independent* noticed the museum when the Queen showed up to unveil the cornerstone.[54] Beyond this, international coverage remained thin.

Cassie was looking forward to seeing how the tenor of Canadian news coverage might change after the CMHR opened and staff members had time to deliver more museum programming across the country. A national story on a museum-sponsored tour by Holodomor experts offers a glimpse of how future news coverage might be more educational.[55] Cassie has been reassured by her colleagues at Pier 21—Canada's new immigration museum in Halifax—that reporters' obsession with location, size, and money dissipates once a museum opens.

Media coverage is likely to develop greater depth if the Canadian Museum for Human Rights allows curators to become the public faces of the enterprise, as Canada's other national museums do. In 2013, the websites of both the Canadian War Museum and the soon-to-be-renamed Canadian Museum of Civilization actively invited reporters to schedule interviews with curators.[56] In contrast, a communications protocol presented to the CMHR board in September 2012 identified the director of research as an approved spokesperson but not other curators.[57] It remains to be seen how free experts working at the Winnipeg museum will be to speak about contemporary human rights issues without being controlled by managers more interested in branding a "new product."[58] The museum's defence of naming the Armenian genocide in the face of pressure by Turkey is a hopeful sign,[59] as was having a panel of staff experts take questions at the museum's 2013 annual meeting[60] and including curators among those interviewed by reporters on opening day.

However, the museum's deletion of a commissioned International Women's Day blog post that included one sentence critical of the Conservative government[61] again raised suspicions of political interference or at least timidity. The museum subsequently issued a statement that it preferred blog posts to be "anecdotal accounts of personal experiences."[62]

The draft strategy document on representing the museum refers to the need to deliver "the right communication messages" to "the right audiences at the right time."[63] Controlling the message is standard practice in the corporate world and an alarming trend across government departments, where it increasingly stifles Canadian government researchers.[64] I would argue that the right time to share information about a public institution is as soon as any citizen asks for it—unless the requested information is subject to exemptions included in Canada's Access to Information law.

The museum's Code of Conduct,[65] which staff were required to sign in 2013, notes that one of the CMHR's organizational values is "cultivating a human rights culture that promotes dignity, encourages self-expression and values diverse experiences and multiple perspectives." However, it appears that some self-expression can occur only in private. The code notes that "employees of the CMHR are expected to refrain from making public comment that is critical of CMHR policies, programs or management. Such comments could subject the CMHR to reputational damage." Staff are encouraged to report, confidentially, suspected breaches of the code by their peers, creating a chill on open discussion of how the museum could improve. The code makes no reference to academic freedom for its researchers.

In the Main Street offices where CMHR staff toiled before moving to their spectacular new building, meeting rooms were named after freedoms protected in Canada. I would like to see the words *Freedom of Information* painted across a wall in the museum's new communications office. If the museum develops a reputation for openness, then it will save staff time responding to formal information requests, which in turn will save interested members of the public from waiting six months or more for answers. Secrecy surrounding the museum's exhibit plans bred suspicion of political interference, a suspicion that might be allayed through more easily accessible information.

A human rights museum should model the transparency that we expect from our governments and that underpins the security of many of our other rights. Openness is as important to the museum's credibility as are its environmentally friendly design[66] and sourcing of T-shirts from manufacturers that respect workers' rights. I would love to see the museum's blog invite readers to weigh in on tricky internal debates, such as whether or not planned exhibits are too negative and what role donors and governments should play in decisions about content. Public submissions could also be invited for topics to highlight in the museum's temporary exhibit space. "You can help us change the world," we are reminded by fundraising ads from Friends of the Canadian Museum for Human Rights. Canadians will be better able to act for change if the museum's policies and content plans are widely available for public debate, including through the media.

NOTES

1 The stories were identified through a ProQuest search of the Canadian Newsstand Major Dailies and Canadian Business and Current Affairs Complete databases, supplemented by a search of websites for the Canadian Broadcasting Corporation, the *Winnipeg Sun,* CTV Winnipeg, Global Winnipeg television, and CJOB radio. Letters to the editor were not included, and duplicates were eliminated when a story was published in a local paper and then sent out across the country over wire services. Broadcast stories were not included if at least partial transcripts were not readily available.

2 The following is a breakdown of the articles by dominant theme, evaluated by review-ing the headline, lead, nut paragraph, and subject to which the largest proportion of the article was devoted:

Budget (88 stories): fundraising efforts (23), government funding struggles (23), donations (20), budget shortfall (10), controversial spending (6), property tax tussle (4), and a spoof (2).

Content (67): Holodomor controversy (43), national consultations (7), virtual exhibits (5), Chinese issues (3), citizenship rights (2), and one story each on museum art, children's rights, the Holocaust, the Irish famine, refugees, women, and lessons from the Vancouver riots.

Building (27): construction progress (14), archaeology (3), environmental sustainability (3), security (3), and one each for architecture, cost, delays, and Aboriginal ceremony related to laying the foundation.

Staffing (21): appointments (9), turnover (5), hiring (4), unionization (2), and a profile of the CEO.

Formalities (19): Queen's visit (10), sod turning (7), and the Governor General's visit (2).

Vision (13): Asper family (5), education (2), ideas (2), Winnipeg as the new Geneva (2), and other museums as models (2).

Economic impact (12): tourism (10) and construction (2).

Governance (11): board members (6), annual meeting (2), board chair resignation (2), and the board's role (1).

Neighbourhood (8): Gandhi statue and proposed avenue (5) and proposed water park (3).

Collaboration (7): with Winnipeg universities (5), Library and Archives Canada (1), and the Netherlands (1).

Public support (2): poll results.

3   Mark Mahabir, "Bill C-42: An Act to Amend the Museums Act and to Make Consequen-
      tial Amendments to Other Acts," 22 February 2008, www.parl.gc.ca/About/Parliament/
      LegislativeSummaries/bills_ls.asp?lang=E&ls=c42&Parl=39&Ses=2&source=library_prb.

4   A. Dirk Moses, "The Canadian Museum for Human Rights: The 'Uniqueness of the Holo-
      caust' and the Question of Genocide," *Journal of Genocide Research* 14, 2 (2012): 215–38.

5   Canadian Museum for Human Rights, "Annual Report 2008–9," https://humanrights.ca/
      sites/default/files/2008_09_Annual_Report_English.pdf.

6   See the chapter by Angela Failler and Roger Simon in this volume.

7   Ira Basen, "A $310 M Battlefield/Rights and Wrongs," *Globe and Mail,* 20 August 2011, F1.

8   Angela Cassie, interview with Helen Fallding, Canadian Museum for Human Rights of-
      fices, 12 December 2012. All subsequent references to Cassie are from this interview.

9   Moses, "Canadian Museum," 225.

10   Zoryan Institute, "How Will the Canadian Museum for Human Rights Represent Geno-
      cide?," 17 February 2010, www.zoryaninstitute.org/Announcements/How%20Will%20
      the%20Canadian%20Museum%20for%20Human%20Rights%20Represent%20Genocide.
      pdf.

11   Geoff Kirbyson, "Content Focus of Rights Museum," *Winnipeg Free Press,* 27 November
      2011, A4.

12   Canadian Museum for Human Rights, "CMHR to Commission Inaugural Film on Ukrai-
      nian Genocide," news release, 20 December 2012, https://humanrights.ca/about-museum/
      news/cmhr-commission-inaugural-film-ukrainian-genocide.

13   Kevin Rollason, "Discontent Remains on CMHR, Holodomor," *Winnipeg Free Press,* 9
      April 2013, A5.

14   See the chapter by Ken Norman in this volume.

15   Canadian Museum for Human Rights, "The Canadian Museum for Human Rights
      Responds to Misconceptions in the Media," news release, 6 January 2011, https://human-
      rights.ca/about-museum/news/canadian-museum-human-rights-responds-misconcep-
      tions-media.

16   Ryan Hicks, "Palestinian-Canadians Feel Ignored in Human Rights Museum," CBC News,
      4 March 2013, www.cbc.ca/news/canada/manitoba/story/2013/03/04/mb-human-rights-
      museum-documents-winnipeg.html.

17   Canadian Museum for Human Rights, "Minutes of the Board of Trustees Meeting #28
      Held March 20th and 21st, 2012."

18   Mary Agnes Welch, "CMHR Rejects 'Genocide' for Native Policies," *Winnipeg Free Press,*
      26 July 2013, B1.

19   Office of the Information Commissioner of Canada, "Section 21—Advice/Recommenda-
      tions," in *Investigators Guide to Interpreting the ATIA,* 2006, http://www.oic-ci.gc.ca/eng/
      inv_inv-gui-ati_gui-inv-ati_section_21.aspx.

20   Canadian Museum for Human Rights, "CMHR to Commission Inaugural Film on Ukrai-
      nian Genocide."

21   Welch, "CMHR Rejects 'Genocide' for Native Policies."

22   Canadian Museum for Human Rights, "Unique CMHR Theatre to Feature Immersive
      'Surround' Technology," 10 December 2013, https://humanrights.ca/about-museum/news/
      unique-cmhr-theatre-feature-immersive-surround-technology.

23 "Human Rights Museum Exhibits Revealed," Global News, 20 February 2014, globalnews. ca/news/1161291/human-rights-museum-to-feature-11-galleries.

24 Geoff Kirbyson, "Museum Provokes Mixed Emotions: CMHR Preview Inspiring and Heart-Wrenching for Viewers and Storytellers Alike," Winnipeg Free Press, 14 August 2014, A9.

25 Canadian Museum for Human Rights, confidentiality agreement, distributed 5 September 2014.

26 "Human Rights Museum Pushes 'Positive' Stories," CBC News, 3 December 2012, www. cbc.ca/player/Embedded-Only/News/Canada/Manitoba/ID/2312327648/.

27 Wayne Labar, "Can Social Media Transform the Exhibition Development Process? Cooking: The Exhibition—An Ongoing Case Study," in Museums and the Web 2010: Proceedings, ed. J. Trant and D. Bearman (Toronto: Archives and Museum Informatics, 2010), www.archimuse.com/mw2010/papers/labar/labar.html.

28 Lynda Kelly, "The Impact of Social Media on Museum Practice," paper presented at the National Palace Museum, Taipei, 20 October 2009, australianmuseum.net.au/Uploads/ Documents/9307/impact%20of%20social%20media%20on%20museum%20practice.pdf.

29 Elizabeth Yakel, "Who Represents the Past? Archives, Records, and the Social Web," in Controlling the Past: Documenting Society and Institutions (Essays in Honor of Helen Willa Samuels), ed. Terry Cook (Chicago: Society of American Archivists, 2011), 257-278.

30 https://humanrights.ca/act/share-your-story.

31 Canadian Museum for Human Rights, "Response to same-sex marriage call exciting for CMHR researchers," 27 February 2013, https://humanrights.ca/blog/response-same-sex-marriage-call-exciting-cmhr-researchers, and "CMHR Issues Call for Photos, Stories on Aboriginal Child Welfare," 7 May 2013, https://humanrights.ca/about-museum/news/ cmhr-issues-call-photos-stories-aboriginal-child-welfare.

32 "Human Rights Museum Pushes 'Positive' Stories," CBC News.

33 Canadian Museum for Human Rights, "Annual Report 2008–9."

34 Canadian Museum for Human Rights, "CMHR Representing the Museum Strategy," 14 February 2012 draft.

35 David Asper, "CMHR Critics Should Back Off Gail," Winnipeg Sun, 11 April 2012, www. winnipegsun.com/2012/04/11/gail-not-demon-of-cmhr-asper.

36 Catherine Chatterley, "The War against the Holocaust," Winnipeg Free Press, 2 April 2011, A16; Dan Bitonti, "German-Canadian Group Assails Holocaust Exhibit; 'Saddens' CJC Head," National Post, 18 December 2010, A2.

37 Moses, "The Canadian Museum for Human Rights," 227.

38 Tom Brodbeck, "Bills Soaring at Rights Palace," Winnipeg Sun, 28 February 2011, www. winnipegsun.com/news/columnists/tom_brodbeck/2011/02/28/17446421.html.

39 April Fool's spoof attributed to the fictitious Hugh Manatee, "Cash-Strapped Rights Museum to Be Converted to Water Park," Winnipeg Sun, 31 March 2012, www.winnipegsun. com/2012/03/31/cash-strapped-rights-museum-to-be-converted-to-water-park.

40 Angela Cassie, "Letter to the Editor of the Winnipeg Sun," 10 January 2012, https://humanrights.ca/about-museum/news/letter-editor-winnipeg-sun.

41 Paul Turenne, "CMHR Not Worth the Trip: Canadians," Winnipeg Sun, 31 January 2012, www.winnipegsun.com/2012/01/31/cmhr-not-worth-the-trip-canadians.

42 Editorial, "Canadians Support Museum," Winnipeg Free Press, 3 February 2012, A10.

43   Jonathan Kay, "Build It, and They Won't Come," *National Post,* 22 December 2011, A17.

44   "Rights Museum Facing Heat over Foreign Goods," Global News, 24 October 2012, www.globalwinnipeg.com/exclusive+rights+museum+facing+heat+over+foreign+goo ds/6442740366/story.html.

45   Mahabir, "Bill C-42."

46   Caroline Vesely and Carol Sanders, "New Museum Head under Fire," *Winnipeg Free Press,* 19 September 2009, B1.

47   "Human Rights Museum Pushes 'Positive' Stories," CBC News.

48   Ralph Appelbaum Associates, "Steering Committee Decision Register: L3Z4—Canadians Making a Difference," 17 December 2012.

49   "Vote-Rigging Scandal Emerges in Manitoba," CBC Digital Archives, www.cbc.ca/ar-chives/vote-rigging-scandal-emerges-in-manitoba.

50   As a *Winnipeg Free Press* editor, I participated in these discussions, though my opinion did not prevail.

51   Bartley Kives, "Canadian Museum for Human Rights Staff Exodus Tied to Content Change," *Winnipeg Free Press,* 1 December 2012, A5.

52   Mary Agnes Welch, "Tories Seek Museum Content: Want List of All Exhibits that Refer to Federal Government," *Winnipeg Free Press,* 16 September 2014, A3.

53   Andrea Sachs, "The Spirit of Manitoba, Canada's Mystery Province," *Washington Post,* 3 August 2012, www.washingtonpost.com/lifestyle/travel/the-spirit-of-manito-ba/2012/08/02/gJQAduVZUX_story.html.

54   "Queen Unveils 'Magna Carta' Cornerstone for Canada Museum," *Independent,* 5 July 2010, www.independent.co.uk/arts-entertainment/art/queen-unveils-magna-carta-cor-nerstone-for-canada-museum-2019238.html.

55   Paul Waldie, "A Ukrainian Quest to Shed Light on Horror Soviets Kept in the Dark," *Globe and Mail,* 18 November 2012, www.theglobeandmail.com/news/world/a-ukraini-an-quest-to-shed-light-on-horror-soviets-kept-in-the-dark/article5414086.

56   Canadian War Museum media page: www.warmuseum.ca/media.

57   Canadian Museum for Human Rights, "Message and Meaning: Strategic Communica-tions," September 2012.

58   Stuart Murray, "Speech Delivered by CMHR President and CEO Stuart Murray at the CMHR's 2012 Annual Public Meeting," 6 December 2012, https://humanrights.ca/about-museum/news/speech-delivered-cmhr-president-and-ceo-stuart-murray-cmhrs-2012-annual-public.

59   Carol Sanders, "CMHR Won't Flip on Armenian Genocide," *Winnipeg Free Press,* 8 April 2013, A6.

60   Canadian Museum for Human Rights, "2013 Annual Public Meeting," 10 December 2013, https://humanrights.ca/about/governance-and-corporate-reports/annual-public-meetings/past-annual-public-meetings.

61   Bartley Kives, "Censorship by CMHR Alleged: Blogger's Words about Tory Record on Women's Issues Pulled from Site," *Winnipeg Free Press,* 11 March 2014, www.winnipeg-freepress.com/local/censorship-by-cmhr-alleged-249390631.html.

62   Canadian Museum for Human Rights, "Statement from the Canadian Museum for Human Rights (CMHR) in relation to Dr. Strong-Boag Blog on International Women's

Day," 11 March 2014, www.humanrights.ca/about-museum/news/statement-canadian-museum-human-rights-cmhr-relation-dr-strong-boag-blog#.U6iqX_ldV8E.

63   Canadian Museum for Human Rights, "CMHR Representing the Museum Strategy."

64   Clayton Greenwood, "Muzzling Civil Servants: A Threat to Democracy," Environ-mental Law Clinic, University of Victoria, 20 February 2013, www.elc.uvic.ca/press/documents/2012-03-04-Democracy-Watch_OIPLtr_Feb20.13-with-attachment.pdf; Library and Archives Canada, "Code of Conduct: Values and Ethics," March 2013, www.clagov.wordpress.com/2013/03/15/lac-canada-code-of-conduct.

65   Canadian Museum for Human Rights, "Code of Conduct," 1 March 2013.

66   "Rights Museum Will Be 'Green': Spokeswoman," *Winnipeg Free Press,* 13 November 2008, A6.

ILLUSION AND THE HUMAN RIGHTS MUSEUM

CHAPTER 4

David Petrasek

Past decades have witnessed the proliferation of so-called idea museums. These public buildings exist primarily not to display artifacts or art or objects with either some intrinsic value or value derived from their historical use or importance. Rather, though they might include artifacts, the goal is to showcase and win interest in and support for ideas that have some transcendent moral appeal—tolerance or peace, for example. Within this broader trend, a growing number of museums are devoted to the topic of human rights or closely related themes such as specific denials of human rights (slavery or genocide).

Some see a difference between the human rights museum that takes a historical approach—for example, explaining a particular example of genocide, such as the Holocaust—and one that focuses on the idea of human rights, which would perhaps result in a more forward-looking narrative. In truth, however, it is difficult to imagine both a general human rights museum that does not include historical accounts of human rights abuses and a museum devoted to a particular past atrocity that does not say something about its present and continuing relevance.[1] "Ideas and history remain intertwined," as another contribution to this book makes clear, nowhere more so than in the context of human rights, in which there is a strong urge to use the past as a warning and the lessons of past human rights abuses as a means of educating the visitor to be part of a better and more tolerant future.

The most prominent new addition to the list of human rights museums is the Canadian Museum for Human Rights (CMHR), which opened in

September 2014. The towering building that houses this museum stands prominently on the eastern edge of Winnipeg's skyline. Even before the museum opened, however, there was much evidence that it struggled with this problem of the past, present, and future of human rights. Although its directors have been at pains to argue that it is not a "genocide museum" or a museum of the history of human rights abuses in Canada, precisely how it treats those issues has led to a great deal of controversy. There has been a rancorous debate, in particular, over the nature and scope of its planned galleries devoted to the Holocaust and other significant genocides or historical incidents of mass atrocity.[2] Moreover, even as some debate the specific content of the CMHR, there is continuing unease about the very idea of a human rights museum, as a number of contributions to this book make clear.

Some fear that such a museum will be controlled by special and powerful interests to present particular (and incomplete) human rights narratives with particular (and biased) accounts of their recognition and denial. This is perhaps a greater risk in countries under authoritarian rule. But even in democracies such as Canada, questions of funding and management structure might have undue influence on curatorial decisions. Indeed, there are allegations that the CMHR has come under such pressure.[3]

Linked to this fear of partiality is the view that a human rights museum will tend toward a "top-down" presentation of human rights, as gifts granted through law, treaty, and recognition by states rather than as the concrete outcomes of struggles by the powerless.[4] By moving human rights from the clamour of the street into the quiet of the gallery, they risk becoming, in this view, depoliticized—not in the sense of manipulation but delinked from the real struggles that validate them. To avoid controversy, there will be significant pressure on any human rights museum to be wary of presentations of actual and ongoing human rights struggles or at least struggles that implicate nearby victims or perpetrators or their kin or supporters. In a country as ethnically diverse as Canada, this might—for the risk averse—rule out a large number of topics. This fear is not groundless. Press reports suggest that curatorial staff have been urged to focus on "good news," and planned presentations on how poverty in present-day Canada might raise human rights concerns were reportedly shelved because of such pressure, allegedly from the CMHR board.[5]

Linked to the fear of sanitizing rights is the fear that a museum will gloss over the inherently competing, and occasionally contradictory, claims embraced within the concept of human rights. A human rights museum will feel pressure to position itself around points of consensus rather

than conflict. The result leaves visitors with the impression of having encountered "received wisdom," ignoring the deep divides and ambiguities
that bedevil both the idea of human rights and the movement supposedly
united in their defence. And it is only through an honest exposure of these
debates and dialogue around them that an idea of human rights can remain relevant and compelling and gain new adherents.[6]

All of which prompts questions. Should we welcome the growing number of human rights museums? Is the advancement of respect for human
rights well served by such projects? These questions go beyond the CMHR.
Museums of any sort can perpetuate the interests of the powerful, misrep-
resent history, privilege certain stories over others, and perpetuate stereotypes. However, if human rights museums fall into the same trap, then it is
especially damaging. The very idea of human rights is to challenge power
and liberate the oppressed. If a museum devoted to the topic reinforces oppression and marginalization, then it is likely to breed cynicism not just for
the particular project but also for the idea of human rights itself.

The short answer is that, where the risks of manipulation are too
high, and the promise of curatorial independence and courage too low, we
should be sceptical about the value of a human rights museum. But even
assuming scrupulous impartiality, and curatorial decisions deeply attuned
to issues of inclusion, there are still significant risks attached to the notion
of a human rights museum.

Three such risks arise even in well-intentioned efforts to "tell the
story" of human rights. Without intending to downplay the more obvious
fears noted above, the remainder of this chapter explores these three risks,
which can arise even when there is curatorial independence and freedom.
Such risks seem to be inherent in the ambiguities of presenting an "idea"
that has a past, present, and future.

The first risk arises from the urge to use representations and accounts
of historical atrocities to teach lessons about preventing future ones.
Conventional wisdom holds that one can build respect for human rights
today by learning of the abuse of these rights in the past. But it is not clear
that the knowledge of past human rights abuses prevents their reoccur-
rence. Such historical understanding might be overrated as a method of
inculcating respect for human rights for the simple reason that the past is
an unreliable source of lessons when it comes to identifying current—or
predicting future—human rights abuses.

The second risk inherent in a museum of human rights is the urge to
locate the story of human rights within a narrative of progress. The need to

"tell the story" almost inevitably leads to an account that moves the visitor from barbarism to enlightenment, from a world where rights were routinely denied to one where they are increasingly recognized and respected. There might be grounds to justify such a narrative regarding particular rights in particular contexts, but it is certainly misleading as a general account.

The third risk, related to the illusion of progress, is the illusion of permanence—the suggestion that human rights discourse has triumphed and is here to stay. The establishment of a "museum" for human rights is proof of this conceit, that human rights are and will remain the dominant global framework for understanding justice and human dignity in a tumultuous and unequal world. Coupled with the illusion of progress, this notion of permanence invites complacency about both the present and the future.

THE ILLUSION OF UNDERSTANDING

In the museum context, portrayals of past human rights abuse almost necessarily go beyond memorializing to expose some deeper truths. The starting point is the premise that, when presented with examples of the denial of human rights, visitors will understand better the need to protect them. The idea is that this understanding will turn visitors into agents for change: by exposing them to the atrocities of the past, they are better equipped to oppose them in the present and future. But does exposing the bigotry of past generations lead to a rigorous scrutiny of our own? Or does it, because of the distance provided by time and space, lead the visitor to see the perpetrators as having almost alien qualities? "How could *they* have done these things?" And this "otherness" or "outside" quality of those who abused human rights—an easily assumed perspective because it is so reassuring—will do little to encourage the visitor to look "inside" or at today's world for contemporary parallels.

President Clinton's opening of the Holocaust Museum in Washington in April 1993 led to renewed commitment to the promise of "never again." But just one year later, in April 1994, the same president (and his administration), in the same city, played a key role in demanding the withdrawal of UN peacekeepers from Rwanda as the genocidal attacks against Tutsis began. US opposition was a major reason why the United Nations failed for several weeks to send further troops, even when the scale of the massacres became clear.[7]

History does not always teach us the right lesson or in any case the lesson that we need to react appropriately to current human rights abuses. Indeed, new insights in psychology should lead us to be wary of placing too much weight on the so-called lessons of history, particularly as applied to understanding the human passions and politics, bigotries, deep hatreds, and paranoia that underlie systematic human rights abuses. Daniel Kahneman, the Nobel Prize–winning Harvard psychologist, refers to the "illusion of understanding," by which he means that our intuitive, "fast" system for thinking (in contrast to our reason-based, "slow" system) relies too heavily on drawing lessons from the past.[8] As Kahneman puts it, everything makes sense in hindsight: why risky lending practices, mounting debt, and inadequate regulation led to the financial collapse of 2008; why the Versailles Treaty sowed the seeds for a new war in Europe; why denying Tamil rights led to a civil war in Sri Lanka; and so on. But because it all makes sense as we look back, we jump to the conclusion that what makes sense in hindsight today was predictable yesterday. In Kahneman's words, "the illusion that we understand the past fosters over-confidence in our ability to predict the future."

This is an especially relevant observation with respect to the teaching of human rights. We look back—at the rise of Hitler, at the Khmer Rouge seizure of power, at the pre-genocide tensions in Rwanda—and the chain of events leading to mass atrocity seems to be clear. We think that we know what to look for and how to guard against it. But every genocide unfolds in its own unique and uniquely horrible ways. The truth is that a deep understanding of the Holocaust provides few parallels that would aid in understanding the events leading up to, for example, the genocidal *anfal* against the Kurds of Iraq in 1988 (other than the banal lesson that dictators cannot be trusted).

Of course, this is not an argument against teaching the history of the Holocaust or other incidents of mass atrocity. They must be taught in order to commemorate and bear witness to the suffering of the victims, to ensure that the historical record is clear, and to expose the criminality and immorality of the perpetrators. These are all valid and essential objectives. But if a human rights museum is to push us to understand and act against *present and future* human rights abuses, then it should be wary of relying too much on the historical approach.

Consider an example close to home. Canadian history has recorded the colonial-era abuses against the First Nations, Métis, and Inuit people of Canada. Such abuses, and the continuing overt discrimination that these groups suffered well past Confederation and into the twentieth century, were well known. Yet, though "official" history acknowledged past discrimination and injustice, the Indian residential school system persisted into the 1990s, and its injustice—widely acknowledged today—was not part of the teaching of this history. Human rights abuse, even of the kind that destroys lives, communities, and cultures, is not always obvious or even apparent to those who do not experience it, even if they feel equipped by history to spot it.

THE ILLUSION OF PROGRESS

A second reason for rejecting an overly historical orientation for a human rights museum is that the historical approach is imbued with biases of the present. Today's bias with respect to human rights is a narrative of progress: that support for human rights is steadily advancing; that with every passing year we spot and legislate against further indignities; that we are better able than previous generations to identify intolerance. It is almost inevitable that a human rights museum that takes visitors on a journey from the past to the present will follow such a narrative line. Indeed, the very architecture of the museum in Winnipeg might encourage such a narrative, since visitors enter from below and proceed in spirals upward through galleries to an ascending Tower of Hope. This ascension will leave visitors with the unshakable conviction that things are improving.

Of course, viewed narrowly from the Canadian perspective, this is a compelling narrative. There is no doubt that, for the most part, human rights are better respected today in Canada than they were in the past. Even if that is so, however, it is no guarantee for the future. But, more importantly, can we credibly sustain such a narrative on a global scale?

This question of whether humans are in fact treating each other better has been the subject of a good deal of debate in recent months, prompted by the publication of a book by another Harvard professor. In *Better Angels of Our Nature: The Decline of Violence in History and Its Causes,* Stephen Pinker argues that we live in an era of unprecedented peace and safety.[9] Although we are fed a steady diet of mayhem and madness by the media ("if it bleeds, it leads"), the fact is that humans today are safer than ever before from war and violence of all kinds. Why is this so? According to Pinker, "the reason so many violent institutions succumbed within so short a span of time was that the arguments that slew them belong to a coherent philosophy that emerged during the Age of Reason and the Enlightenment … a worldview that we can call *Enlightenment humanism.*" Pinker makes it clear that the "rights revolution" is a key part of such a philosophy.

Pinker produces a wealth of statistics to make his point that violence is on the decline and that people are being treated better. He has his critics, however. Some challenge the reliability of his data on violent death in the Middle Ages and much earlier eras (data that are essential to his point about the relative security of our era). Others argue that his definition of violence is too narrow, pointing to "structural violence" that leads to impoverishment and famine. In reviewing Pinker's book, the English philosopher John Gray argues that it is an "illusion" that liberal humanism will create a better world.[10] In his view, progress is possible in science but not ethics or morality. This is an inescapable conclusion, as he sees it, if one accepts Darwin's account of our animal origins and evolution. The application of reason to human affairs and politics need not inevitably result in more humane policies. Although progress in science brings advances to the quality of human life, it equally enhances our ability and capacity to destroy human life; think of global warming or the nuclear bomb.

Many believe that Pinker is right. One can certainly discern a "rights revolution," inasmuch as international law and institutions have steadily advanced in this area, especially in the past twenty years. Furthermore, attempts to measure the impacts of civil wars have similarly pointed to a more or less steady decline over the past two to three decades in the lethality of war.[11] Yet, though Gray's pessimism regarding human nature might seem overblown, we would be wise to be cautious before heralding a more peaceful world.

Why? Because trends regarding violent death need to be set against other worrying indicators. A short list of them would include the widening global inequalities between and within countries; very uneven poverty reduction efforts, with over a billion still living in extreme poverty and slum populations rising exponentially; severe environmental stress in dozens of countries; shortages of key resources, including arable land, water, and food; and increasing risks regarding the spread of nuclear and biological weapons. If one considers too that global institutions seem generally ill equipped to marshal the will and resources to tackle these challenges, then one would hardly be assured about a less violent future.[12]

Ours is not the first generation to imagine that it stands on the cusp of a Kantian "perpetual peace." The Peace Palace is in The Hague, Netherlands. This building, built in a neo-Renaissance style, has a tall and graceful tower, boasts a rich, marbled interior, and evokes memories of a gilded age of European diplomacy. It was the inspiration of a transnational group of peace activists who dreamed of a building to house the newly created international Permanent Court of Arbitration. The building would be a monument to the peace that it was hoped this court would ensure but also, with its international law library, a practical resource for those dedicated to peace. This was not a utopian project, at least not deliberately so. When the Peace Palace was conceived, Europe was living through a peaceful age, with no major war having been fought on the continent for almost forty years. The Dutch government donated land, and the Peace Palace was built with money raised from philanthropists. This "museum," the modern world's first international statement against war, opened on 28 August 1913—just less than a year before the outbreak of the First World War, a devastating conflict that ushered in the deadly twentieth century.

THE ILLUSION OF PERMANENCE

We need idealism. Almost every human endeavour would seem less interesting if we did not think that it could be improved. But a human rights museum should present the topic in a manner that assumes neither continued progress nor permanence. The future of the idea of human rights is by no means assured—a fact often obscured by casually linking this idea to Enlightenment thinking and thereby bestowing it with a pedigree of several centuries.[13]

"Human rights" are not the same as "citizen rights." A human right is held by virtue of being human. Much of Enlightenment thinking about rights and liberty took as its starting point the nation-state; rights proclaimed were those held by the citizens of those states. Notwithstanding the "universal" language of the French Declaration of the Rights of Man or the American Declaration of Independence, in proclaiming rights to life and liberty, the authors of these texts assumed the rights holders to be a limited class. Slaves, Indigenous people, colonial subjects, and in some cases women and those without property were not considered holders of the same "natural" rights.

Today the term "human rights," at least in Canada, captures two related but different ideas: (1) that the Charter of Rights and Freedoms grants to Canadians and those subject to the government's jurisdiction a set of guarantees; (2) that there is a universal standard, agreed to in international law, of individual human rights held by all human beings. Of course, there is considerable overlap between these sets of rights, but it is by no means a perfect fit. There are substantive differences. Canada, for example, has ratified international human rights treaties on economic and social rights, but they are not in the charter. Differences also exist with respect to whom governments owe the duty to respect, protect, and fulfill rights. Under the charter, for the most part, such duties are owed to Canadian citizens or persons in Canada; it is less clear, however, that all universal human rights treaties to which Canada is bound are so limited. In specific cases, obligations under international human rights treaties can give rise to duties that extend beyond borders. Issues such as climate change, global poverty, the arms trade, human trafficking, access to essential medicines, and many others are increasingly pointing to moral and sometimes legal obligations that cross borders, and this will be the terrain of many future human rights struggles. These are contentious issues, and it is not at all certain that the struggles will be resolved in line with the understanding of "human rights" in its universal sense.

The fact is that the "rights revolution" is of recent origin. The civil and political rights proclaimed by Enlightenment scholars might enjoy a long history, and it is fair to say that they are firmly entrenched in a shared vision of the liberal state (at least in Canada and other established democracies). But the same is not the case for human rights understood in their broader, international, and universal sense; this is an idea of recent vintage and currency. Samuel Moyne's recent book *The Last Utopia: Human Rights in History*[14] makes this abundantly clear. Moyne convincingly shows that the popularity of human rights in its universal sense really took off only in the 1970s, before which it was a rather marginal issue of international affairs and foreign policy. His explanation is grounded in the failure of other utopian projects and the adoption by progressive forces of a kind of anti-politics in the face of communist repression and socialist failure. Whatever the reason for the recent popularity of human rights, Moyne notes, continuing popularity is by no means assured.

Although the past two decades in particular have seen enormous strides in cementing the enforcement of international human rights in international law, we should not assume that this will be lasting. As with the Peace Palace, events can unravel quickly. Global power balances are shifting. Can we be certain that emerging powers such as China will place continuing importance on human rights in international affairs? Will a future UN secretary general say (as Kofi Annan did in 2005) that human rights are the third pillar of the United Nations, along with peace and development?

Many ideas have travelled along the road from being the next big thing to being the last big thing. Global struggles for justice are hardly new. The language that frames these struggles has changed over time. Today, the discourse of human rights is prominent in such struggles, but it need not remain so. Indeed, its very prominence is bound to invite critique, already emerging. Grassroots activists and all who distrust courts complain of the legalism of such an approach,[15] communitarians and religious thinkers find the individualism of human rights claims disruptive,[16] and many outside Europe and North America distrust the "Western" language of human rights, recalling the fact that many of these rights were defined while their countries lived under colonial rule.[17] Those who are impatient for reform might find that political mobilization, not rights adjudication, offers a quicker path to social justice.

Recognition of individual human rights and freedoms is one path, but not the only one, to building more just societies. Many believe that it has proven its worth. But one must respect the critique of human rights: not the disingenuous one that would justify torture or atrocity but the one that would assert different paths to human dignity and flourishing. The struggle to win human rights can succeed only if the idea of universal rights is received not as dogma but via dialogue—and such dialogue needs to treat seriously the critique of the existing international human rights framework.

The Canadian Museum for Human Rights has set itself the right objective: to challenge and equip all who visit it to take action to promote human freedom and well-being. However, if it is to do so successfully, then it should pay much more attention to how it depicts the present and future than the past, and it must find a way to promote human rights without proselytizing them.

NOTES

* This is a revised version of a lecture delivered on 19 January 2012 at the annual conference of the Canadian Political Science Students' Association, held at the University of Manitoba. It was part of a series of lectures co-sponsored by the university and the Canadian Museum for Human Rights on the idea of a human rights museum. I am grateful to Natalie Brender for her comments on an earlier version of this chapter.

1   See Stephan Jaeger's chapter in this volume.

2   Paul Waldie and Daniel Leblanc, "Canadian Human Rights Museum Dogged by Controversy," *Globe and Mail,* 20 December 2011, http://www.theglobeandmail.com/news/politics/canadian-human-rights-museum-dogged-by-controversy/article2278785/.

3   "Human Rights Museum Staff Leave Amid Interference Allegations," CBC News, 30 November 2012, http://www.cbc.ca/news/canada/manitoba/human-rights-museum-staff-leave-amid-interference-allegations-1.1131274.

4   See Christopher Powell's chapter in this volume.

5   Dan Lett, "No Political Interference Here: Chairman," *Winnipeg Free Press,* 6 December 2012, http://www.winnipegfreepress.com/opinion/columnists/no-political-interference-here-chairman-182324661.html.

6   See Ken Norman's chapter in this volume.

7   Jared Cohen, *One Hundred Days of Silence: America and the Rwanda Genocide* (Lanham, MD: Rowman and Littlefield, 2007).

8   Daniel Kahneman, *Thinking Fast and Slow* (New York: Doubleday, 2011).

9   Stephen Pinker, *Better Angels of Our Nature: The Decline of Violence in History and Its Causes* (New York: Viking, 2011).

10 John Gray, "Delusions of Peace," review of *Better Angels of Our Nature: The Decline of Violence in History and Its Causes*, by Stephen Pinker, *Prospect*, 21 September 2011, http://www.prospectmagazine.co.uk/2011/09/john-gray-steven-pinker-violence-review/.

11 See, for example, *Human Security Report 2009/2010: The Causes of Peace and the Shrinking Costs of War*, http://www.hsrgroup.org/human-security-reports/20092010/overview.aspx.

12 National Intelligence Council, "Global Trends 2030: Alternative Worlds," 12 December 2012, http://publicintelligence.net/global-trends-2030/.

13 Samuel Moyne, *The Last Utopia: Human Rights in History* (Cambridge, MA: Harvard University Press, 2010).

14 Ibid.

15 Michael Mandel, *The Charter of Rights and the Legalization of Politics in Canada* (Toronto: Thompson Educational Publishers, 1994).

16 A good summary of various communitarian critiques can be found in Rhoda E. Howard, "Human Rights and the Search for Community," *Journal of Peace Research* 32, 1 (1995): 1.

17 Makau Mutua, *Human Rights: A Political and Cultural Critique* (Philadelphia: University of Pennsylvania Press, 2002).

SPATIALIZATION AND DESIGN

PROCESS IMAGES: DESIGNING THE CANADIAN MUSEUM FOR HUMAN RIGHTS

Text by Adam Muller

"There is a realm of translation from research to the project[, and] you can't explain how it happens—it's kind of supernatural," Antoine Predock admits. "You want to leave it alone and not try to rationalize, but it has an aura of magic and alchemy."[1]

The following five images map the visual evolution of the Canadian Museum for Human Rights from the perspective of its architect, Antoine Predock, as he worked through his design process. As might be expected, this process began with a rough sketch and then moved through a variety of conceptual stages as his idea of the museum began to come into focus. The images show how each iteration of the structure's design adds a layer of detail, nuance, and texture, until finally a three-dimensional model (Image 5), which includes roughed-in interior volumes (Image 4), can be produced. Interestingly, Predock uses clay as a design aid as part of his creative process (see Image 3). He describes the clay as serving to further his exploration of the building's form but in a way that is more explicitly anchored in the reality of its physical details than are his earlier—what he calls "anticipatory"—drawings (Images 1 and 2). The clay also mirrors the rich, wet ground into which the CMHR is sunk, anchored by its four spiralling "roots."

Attention to the particulars of place is one of Predock's calling cards as an architect. His buildings are strikingly attuned to the light, weather, and soil conditions of the locations where they are built. Predock has said that, before an architect gets down to drawing, he must experience the building site with his body in order to properly gauge its temperament. Indeed, with reference specifically to the CMHR, he observed in an interview in May 2014 that "this is a love-hate building. You have to experience it with your mind and your body. Take it on and see what happens to you."[2]

NOTES

1   Quoted in Peter C. Newman and Allan Levine, "An Outlaw's Vision for the Museum for Human Rights," *Maclean's*, 11 August 2014, http://www.macleans.ca/culture/an-outlaws-vision-for-the-canadian-museum-for-human-rights/.

2   Dan Lett, "'You'll Realize It's Another World. It Will Be an Adventure': Public Invited to let CMHR Speak to Them," *Winnipeg Free Press*, 30 May 2014, http://www.winnipegfree-press.com/opinion/columnists/public-invited-to-let-cmhr-speak-to-them-261203931.html.

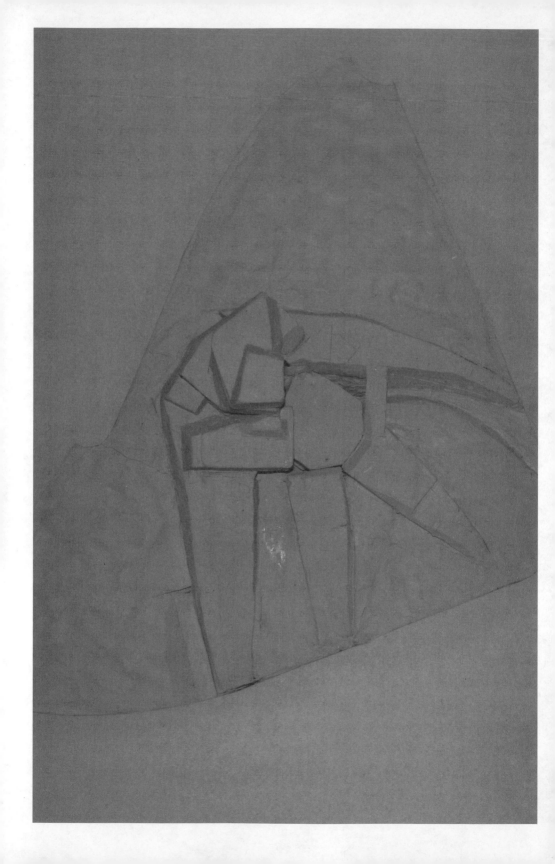

CHANGE OF PLANS: CONCEPTUALIZING INAUGURAL EXHIBITS AT THE CANADIAN MUSEUM FOR HUMAN RIGHTS

CHAPTER 5
Karen Busby

This chapter introduces readers to the inaugural exhibits of the Canadian Museum for Human Rights (CMHR) and provides a glimpse of the inner workings of the museum with respect to exhibit conceptualization. These exhibits are described in iterative, high-level summary documents prepared by museum staff called Gallery Profiles.[1] My main focus is on the differences between the September 2012 and September 2013 Gallery Profiles. Although a comprehensive review of the exhibits is not the focus of this chapter, I do reference some of the inaugural exhibits as presented once all of the exhibits were fully opened in November 2014. (Some exhibits opened to the public in September 2014, but most of the exhibits opened two months later.) I conclude the chapter by offering some thoughts on future areas of research on exhibit content processes.

The Gallery Profiles briefly describe the elements of the ten permanent galleries, including exhibits, objectives, main messages (what the visitor will know), and visitor experiences (what the visitor will do). Most of the profiles also include information such as a description of text content, but the panel texts and other exhibit details—such as artifacts to be used—are not set out in most of the profiles. Some of the information in the 2012 Gallery Profiles, obtained pursuant to an Access to Information request, was

redacted. The justification asserted for withholding information in most
cases is an exercise of the access officer's discretionary power to redact
information about plans not yet put into operation.[2] The same Access to
Information request also sought information related to gallery and exhibit
designs from the Content and Audit Committees and board meetings. The
request resulted in hundreds of pages of material, but since most of it was
redacted it is not referred to in this chapter.

BEGINNING THE TOUR

Most visitors to the CMHR will begin the tour in Buhler Hall, a cavernous,
multifunctional space. The 2012 Gallery Profiles for Buhler Hall note that
"messaging will convey that the territory the museum occupies is a meeting
place and a crisscrossing of First Nations (several First Nations) and Métis
territory."[3] This message is missing from the 2013 profiles. Nonetheless,
the inaugural exhibit in Buhler Hall powerfully acknowledges Indigenous
presence. A beautifully lit copper cast of 750-year-old footprints, human
and bison, unearthed during the archaeological dig undertaken before the
museum was built remind visitors of the long Indigenous presence in the
territory. A video projected on a massive wall also welcomes visitors in
numerous languages, including the local Indigenous languages.

The first gallery, What Are Human Rights?, begins with an immersive
multimedia experience in which visitors can listen to human rights stories
and see images appear and disappear on a large screen. They can also study
a timeline that considers the question "Where did human rights come
from?" and inquires into the broad concept of "human rights" throughout
history and around the world. Both the 2012 and the 2013 Gallery Profiles
state that this gallery "sets the foundation for building the knowledge, attitudes and skills that visitors will develop during their visit to the museum,
with the ultimate goal of inspiring them to action."[4]

The CMHR uses lived experiences as the starting points for most of its
exhibits. As Jodi Giesbrecht and Clint Curle observe in their contribution
to this volume, abstract concepts such as justice and dignity become more
broadly accessible when they are illustrated through a lived experience.
They go on to note that "the contradictory, open-ended, and ambiguous
nature of lived experience required us to deliberately eschew a preconceived narrative framework in the hope that these rich stories would be
able to speak for themselves." The inaugural exhibit, What Are Human
Rights?, which features many voices, demonstrates how successful this

approach can be. The storytellers, even as they present complex and at times contradictory answers to the question, are engaging and compelling.

INDIGENOUS PERSPECTIVES GALLERY

The typical visitor then enters the Indigenous Perspectives gallery. The objectives of this gallery include conveying Indigenous concepts of rights and responsibilities, appreciating the diversity of Indigenous peoples (with a specific focus on Indigenous languages), and understanding a holistic view of rights. This gallery includes a theatre in the round, a smudging terrace, commissioned artwork, and an exhibit on the museum's special geographical location. There are several significant differences between the 2012 and 2013 profiles for this gallery.

The name of the gallery has changed from Aboriginal Peoples of Canada (2012) to Indigenous Perspectives (2013). This change reflects a growing preference for use of the word *Indigenous* over *Aboriginal,* especially since the United Nations Declaration on the Rights of Indigenous Peoples was adopted by the General Assembly in 2007. However, the two words are used interchangeably in both profiles for descriptions of exhibits in other galleries.

In 2012, the main message for one exhibit in this gallery was to have been "Aboriginal concepts of humanity honour all living and nonliving entities, and are kept alive by oral tradition."[5] By 2013, this message had become "First Nations, Métis and Inuit have possessed throughout time, and continue to maintain today, their own concepts of rights, responsibilities and humanity."[6] A text panel in the inaugural exhibit states, in large typeface, that "First Nations, Métis and Inuit peoples have concepts of rights and responsibilities based on worldviews in which everyone and everything is interrelated."

Similarly, the 2012 main message for another exhibit was to show that communities have their "own distinctive language and words expressing human values."[7] In 2013, this was changed to "own distinctive language, words and symbols expressing human rights and responsibilities."[8]

A narrow focus on storytelling has been expanded to include the broader and more complex notion that "Indigenous peoples articulate their rights through the use of traditional knowledge, oral histories and ceremonies."[9]

Observe that the 2013 iteration of the message in each of these examples presents Indigenous laws as coherent, dynamic, and enforceable. This message is reinforced in the Protecting Rights in Canada gallery in the Canada's Legal Traditions exhibit, which acknowledges the French, British, and Indigenous systems on which Canada's legal system has been built.

The 2012 profiles contemplated an outdoor terrace with plants that visitors could touch. That space is described in the 2013 profiles as a smudging terrace or space for spiritual ceremonies. Smudging is an Indigenous purification ceremony that involves burning herbs and other plants. Inclusion of a space for smudging is important because many Indigenous elders and knowledge keepers are reluctant to participate in knowledge sharing unless they have first smudged.

Indigenous peoples' claims to land and land use in Canada are highly contested. Thus, the narratives used and messages conveyed in the Indigenous Perspectives gallery and other exhibits (e.g., the *Marshall* case treatment in the Debate Table exhibit in the Protecting Rights Canada gallery) to describe Indigenous peoples' land interests are worth closer examination to reveal whether or not conflicts have been minimized. In this short chapter, I can briefly examine one exhibit on land rights.

One exhibit in the Indigenous Perspectives gallery is designed to convey the special significance of the museum's site, especially for First Nations and Métis people. The museum is located on land ceded by Treaty One near where the Assiniboine River flows into the Red River, and a large window in this gallery overlooks this land. Under this window is a panel on this land. The message contained in the 2012 profile for this exhibit was that, "historically and today, Aboriginal peoples have struggled to assert their rights in the face of violations" and that the "interpretation will specifically highlight the connections to the land and water and the Forks and the stories of how various First Nations and Métis have lived and interacted here. [Next sentence redacted.]"[10] This message of struggle and violation is not repeated in the 2013 profile; rather, the "main message" simply notes that this area has been "a meeting place for thousands of years, with First Nations, Métis, fur traders and settlers converging in this special place."[11] The window exhibit was the only exhibit in the Indigenous Perspectives gallery not completed when the museum officially opened in September 2014. The text panel under the window provides the following information:

An Ancient Meeting Place

This museum stands at The Forks, a traditional meeting place
of great significance for First Nations and Métis peoples.
For more than 6,000 years, Indigenous groups travelled long
distances to the site where the Red and Assiniboine Rivers

meet. They gathered here to trade, forge alliances and hold ceremonies.

Generations of Métis families also lived and worked along these rivers. When newcomers began claiming the land, it sparked a Métis uprising that erupted in 1869. Louis Riel led this resistance movement to defend Métis rights and culture. Riel's grave now lies near St. Boniface Cathedral, on the far side of the Red River.

Indigenous Ties to the Land

To know who you are, you must also know where you come from. This means understanding the relationship you have with the territory of your people.

Map tracing the Red and Assiniboine Rivers, 1817. First Nations chiefs signed a treaty with Lord Selkirk granting use of the land around the rivers for Scottish and other settlers.

Indigenous camp near the Red River, 1866. Aboriginal peoples have been a constant presence in this river region since ancient times.

Louis Riel, around 1878, was one of the several leaders who defended land and cultural rights for the Métis—a people of mixed First Nations and European ancestry.

Surprising in their absence from this panel are references to Treaty One, signed in 1871 between the Canadian government and the Anishinaabe and Swampy Cree chiefs, or to profound disagreements that still exist over interpretation of this treaty. In contrast, for example, an exhibit on Treaty One at Lower Fort Garry, the federal national historic site where the treaty was signed, acknowledges that the signatories disagree over how it should be interpreted today. And, as presaged by Gallery Profile changes between 2012 and 2013, there is no mention of contemporary violations and struggles. Since the federal government is engaged in litigation with Treaty One signatories and Métis people over land rights, these omissions are problematic.

Given the persistence of settler colonialism in Canada, the museum faces real challenges concerning how to present Indigenous content. As Ruth Phillips notes in this volume, in the past museums have been tied to colonial practices of cultural appropriation and misrepresentation. Museums, in her view, must now confront the violence and trauma associated with Canada's treatment of Indigenous peoples, contemplate redress, and express calls to action.

The CMHR's Indigenous Perspectives exhibits make a conscious effort to focus on survivance rather than suffering. Gallery personnel repeatedly stated prior to opening that there would be Indigenous content in every gallery in the museum, and, according to the Gallery Profiles, suffering and loss will be dealt with in complex ways. The Canadian Journeys gallery includes exhibits on Métis rights, violence against Aboriginal women, Indian residential schools, and cultural displacement in the North. Another gallery has a small exhibit that focuses on actions to address water infrastructure in First Nations communities, and another invites conversations on whether or not the Indian residential school program in Canada meets the definition of the word *genocide*. The iterative conceptualization and instantiation of inaugural exhibits concerned with Indigenous issues, with the notable exception of the window exhibit on land rights, demonstrate that the museum has gone some distance in moving away from practices of appropriation and misrepresentation, and toward confronting violence and trauma, considering redress, and expressing the required call for action. Yet Tricia Logan, a former CMHR Indigenous curator in a much more complex review of the decision-making on these exhibits has written that the museum "is accepting a model of complacency and promotion of the status quo."[12]

CANADIAN STORIES

The Canadian Journeys gallery is the largest in the museum and is described as an essential destination for school groups. Here, according to both the 2012 and the 2013 Gallery Profiles, visitors should "gain a deeper understanding of Canada's complex and, at times, contradictory history as it relates to social justice and human rights and the factors that make Canada's human rights culture special" and "appreciate the need for ongoing vigilance in Canada to ensure the continued protection of our human rights."[13] This gallery also presents Quebec's unique perspective on human rights in order to reflect its distinct history, language, and legal traditions.

This gallery includes a digital canvas referencing six different stories and an image grid referencing close to thirty stories. Its main attraction is the eighteen story niches that cover topics as diverse as cultural dispossession in the North, the 1970 October Crisis, and the experiences of migrant workers in Canada. Images and stories for the Canadian Journeys gallery were selected based on various criteria: identified as important during various consultation processes, associated with a significant turning point, indicative of the constitutional architecture of Canada, reflective of the diversity of Canada, or capable of galvanizing debate, reflection, dialogue, and action.

The lists of topics for the image grid and digital canvas were redacted from the 2012 Gallery Profiles but included in the 2013 version. Thus, a comparison of the two texts is not possible. Little of the information for the eighteen story niches was redacted, so some of the evolution of curatorial decision making for these exhibits can be traced. For example, a positive story on the Underground Railway (a network that helped American slaves to escape) was added in 2013, but Queer Resistance no longer has a story niche and is now just an image on the image grid. (Queer activism is also explored in other galleries.) Some of the objectives for and main messages of the story niches also changed significantly.

What can we discern about changes between 2012 and 2013 to the Canadian Journeys story niches from taking a closer look at the information? The following changes are worth noting.

The objective of the Indian Residential Schools niche in 2012 was to draw similarities between the residential school system and the current child welfare system. The 2013 objective is to tell the story of the residential schools and their lasting impacts on Aboriginal children, families, and communities. The 2013 message, unlike the 2012 message, acknowledges (using language from the official apology delivered by the prime minister) that "the residential school system was extremely destructive ... with tragic intergenerational consequences."[14] Note that much more detailed material on this topic is included in the Study Table exhibit in the Breaking the Silence gallery.

The Stolen Sisters niche, far more developed in the 2013 Gallery Profiles than in the 2012 iteration, has as its objective "to bring awareness to the ongoing problem of violence against Aboriginal women."[15] With this imperative in view, Jamie Black created an art installation titled REDress, a series of empty red dresses hung in front of a stark woodland backdrop. The Gallery Profile for this exhibit, unlike the profiles for many others, also describes the text to be used in the panels. Because the name changed from Stolen Sisters (a political campaign name used by Amnesty International) to From Sorrow to Strength: Aboriginal Women and the Right to Security and Justice, and profile information[16] is somewhat different from the text panels that appeared in the inaugural exhibit, a comparison of these texts is worth noting:

2013 GALLERY PROFILE: STOLEN SISTERS: MISSING AND MURDERED ABORIGINAL WOMEN	INAUGURAL EXHIBIT TEXT: FROM SORROW TO STRENGTH: ABORIGINAL WOMEN AND THE RIGHT TO SECURITY AND JUSTICE
Aboriginal women are disproportionately represented in the number of persons who are missing or murdered in Canada every year and much needs to be done to correct this human rights tragedy.	Aboriginal women and girls—sisters, mothers, daughters—go missing with disturbing frequency in Canada. Their disappearances tend to receive little mainstream attention.
The long-standing pattern of discrimination, impoverishment, and perceived police inaction are considered to be major factors that put Aboriginal women in jeopardy.	First Nations, Inuit and Métis women are three times more likely to experience violence than other Canadian women. They are overrepresented as homicide victims. Many of their murders remain unsolved. Their fundamental rights to safety and justice are at stake.
Initiatives, many Native-led, have been created to address the health and safety of Aboriginal women.	Aboriginal women and supporters are addressing the causes of this tragic pattern of violence and indifference. They are targeting poverty, racism and sexism, as well as bias in the media and the justice system. Voices are calling for every woman to be treated with dignity.

The main message for the refugees story niche in 2012 was that "refugees who escape threatening situations to come to Canada have little control over their acceptance and the way they are portrayed in the media, despite the UN Convention on the Rights of Refugees."[17] The 2013 message that "Canada is recognized around the world as a safe haven for refugees" is surprising given recent shifts in refugee policy.[18] The text in the inaugural exhibit is similar to the 2013 message, but it adds the question "do you think Canada is doing enough for refugees?"

The main message in 2012 for the story niche on racial segregation was "the incident of Viola Desmond's arrest happened in a wider context of racial segregation that existed in many parts of Canada."[19] But in 2013 this message became "in 1947, Viola Desmond, a black Nova Scotian, was arrested and charged for what appeared to be a racially motivated reason."[20] The 2013 iteration decontextualizes this story and, inexplicably, contests the motivation for Desmond's arrest, thereby undermining the message. The text in the inaugural exhibit stated that, "at Desmond's trial, no one admitted that race was behind her arrest.... Her story is a reminder that although Canada had no formal system of racial segregation, colour barriers were tolerated as recently as 1940."[21]

The main message for the Right to Vote story niche in 2012 was "in Canada's past, the right to vote was frequently given to or taken away from various categories of people for political reasons."[22] In 2013, the message changed to "the democratic right to vote in elections was not available to all Canadians until 2002."[23] It is unclear why this story was depoliticized by rinsing out the reasons for and the ways in which governments denied people the right to vote. The inaugural exhibit stated that "Canadians have not always had equal access to the ballot box." Examples of excluded groups were included, as was an example of the manipulation. The text stated that, "in 1917, a wartime federal election showed how voting rights could be manipulated. Prime Minister Robert Borden wanted to prevent people who opposed compulsory military service from voting against him. So his government stripped the vote for some from some groups, such as pacifist Mennonites. It granted the right to vote to groups supportive of the war effort, including military nurses."

The main message for the same-sex marriage story niche in 2012 was "some same-sex couples have fought hard to have their unions recognized in law, while other 'queer' people question the institution of marriage itself."[24] The 2013 message is quite different: "In 2005, Canada became the fourth country in the world to legalize same-sex marriage."[25] It is unclear why this story was depoliticized: that is, leaving the impression that the government moved of its own accord—rather than in response to years of agitation—to address this issue. Elimination of the Queer Resistance story niche aggravates this depoliticization. It is also disappointing that the exhibit loses the richness of engagement with the question on the institution of marriage. The inaugural exhibit acknowledged that "not all couples want to marry. But thanks to activists who led the way down the aisle, all have the choice."[26]

The main message for the Religious Oppression niche was redacted from the 2012 profiles. The 2013 profiles state that the main message is that "freedom of religion is protected in Canada today, but this was not always the case, and groups such as the Jehovah's Witnesses and other Canadians have been instrumental in ensuring religious rights."[27] The 2011 Ralph Appelbaum Associates *Content Outline* lists potential case studies as including Jehovah's Witnesses, Mennonites, Doukhobors, and Indigenous peoples and describes the story as "many groups and individuals have been persecuted because of their religious beliefs. Many responded by fighting back, secretly practicing ceremonies, engaging in court challenges, and mobilizing communities."[28] Since questions remain about the degree to which freedom of religion is protected in Canada today (e.g., consider the debate in Quebec over whether Muslim women who wear headscarves can access government services and employment), the 2013 message might be optimistic. Again, the language of a political fight has been watered down.

Christopher Powell, in his contribution to this volume, expresses concern over whether the museum's exhibits will talk about bottom-up struggles for social change. Jennifer Carter similarly exhorts us to ask whether human rights museums are used by governments as political instruments to promote the interests of the state or as fora for dialogue to enrich civil society. Some observations can be made about the examples outlined above. Some examples suggest that the story of struggle might be omitted, at least some of the time. As well, matters currently in the political arena—such as religious oppression, treatment of refugees, and violence against Indigenous women—might be presented in a way that minimizes government actors' roles in terms of rights violations.

The Protecting Rights in Canada gallery (called Canada's Challenge in 2012) focuses on how individuals and groups achieve change through work at the judicial or political level. One of the smallest galleries in the museum, its exhibits emphasize Canada's distinctive legal system and animating doctrines (e.g., the "living tree" doctrine), the different legal traditions that have influenced it, including British common law, French civil law, and Indigenous legal regimes, and, via an interactive Debate Table, the importance of engaged debate on human rights issues.

The 2013 Gallery Profiles contain much fuller treatments of the cases (mostly Charter cases) to be explored through interactive videos at the Debate Table exhibit. But in what appears to be a last-minute decision, two cases referenced in the 2013 Gallery Profiles—*Rodriguez* (on assisted suicide) and *Morgenthaler* (on abortion)—were removed from the Debate Table. The *Morgenthaler* video was featured at an event held for journalists ten days before the CMHR opened.[29]

Two other significant differences between the 2012 and 2013 profiles for the Protecting Rights in Canada gallery include the 2013 addition of information on the Charter and an exhibit on mobilization. Surprisingly, there were no specific references in the 2012 profiles to what many would call Canada's most important rights document, the 1982 Canadian Charter of Rights and Freedoms, and there were only passing references to the Charter in exhibits in other galleries. The new mobilization exhibit, Voices of Inclusion, has an objective that is somewhat similar to the Collective Initiatives exhibit that was to be included in the Rights Today gallery. The latter exhibit was eliminated from the profiles between 2012 and 2013.

GENOCIDES AND OTHER MASS ATROCITIES

The Examining the Holocaust gallery is described in both the 2012 and the 2013 Gallery Profiles as "a unique addition to the worldwide body of Holocaust-related exhibit experiences.... The Museum's approach to the Holocaust is not memorial, but deliberately analytical. The gallery as a whole poses two questions: *how?* and *why?* and addresses them through three distinct but related themes ... Abuse of State Power, Spreading Fear and Hatred, and War and Genocide.... Visitors learn what happened in the Holocaust and consider aspects of the Holocaust with broad relevance to human rights struggles today."[30]

The 2013 profiles contain far more detail about this gallery's exhibits than do the 2012 profiles. While part of the Examining the Holocaust exhibit focuses on the larger question of how social and political conditions evolved so that the systematic destruction of human rights became possible, the objective of most of the other exhibits is to make visitors understand the importance of personal vigilance and responsibility.

The main message in 2012 for visitors viewing a documentary film on the Holocaust and Canada's response was that "there were surprising and disturbing similarities between the rise of Nazism in Germany and attitudes in Canada in the 1930s." This message was repeated in 2013, but the following text was added: "We need to reflect our values and avoid being bystanders to human rights violations today."[31]

The Complicit in Genocide exhibit is intended to underscore the impact of personal responsibility; individuals do the actual work necessary for mass killing to occur. It features objects that show or imply a human hand or involvement, such as architects' drawings, surgical instruments, and an unopened gas canister.

The objective of the Defining Genocide exhibit (formerly called Lemkin's Techniques of Genocide) is to enable a deeper understanding of the dynamics of genocide. Whereas the focus in 2012 was solely on the Holocaust, the 2013 profiles expand this exhibit to include other genocides and mass atrocities, including the Armenian genocide, the Holodomor, "the

Spanish colonization of America's indigenous peoples," and "the British colonization of Tasmanian aboriginals."[32]

The Turning Points for Humanity exhibit (formerly called Hope and Hard Work) is designed to be bright and open following the difficult experience provided by the Holocaust gallery. The lofty principles of the Universal Declaration of Human Rights are projected high on a large screen while interactive exhibits demonstrate how a number of people use ground-level activism to transform the world by advocating together. Among those featured are human rights activists who have been bestowed with honorary Canadian citizenship in recognition of their work in promoting human rights. The Gallery Profiles assert that the exhibit's objectives are to inspire hope and challenge people to action.

The next gallery, Breaking the Silence, provides a quiet, respectful space wherein visitors can learn about genocides and other mass atrocities with a view to helping them understand that terrible human rights violations continue to occur. Visitors are encouraged to recognize the importance of resisting denial and minimization. Undoubtedly, this gallery will draw more attention—praise and criticism—than any of the other galleries.

One exhibit in this gallery, Canada Speaks Out, according to the 2013 profiles, will "acknowledge the role played by diasporic Canadian communities and by Parliament in officially recognizing five genocides: the Armenian genocide, Holodomor, Holocaust, Rwandan genocide and Srebrenica genocide."[33] A subtle shift perhaps, but it is worth noting that the 2012 iteration spoke to "breaking the silence about" rather than "officially recognizing" these particular genocides.[34] Stuart Murray, surprised to learn shortly after the opening of the CMHR that his contract as CEO would not be renewed, seemed to eschew the notion of official recognition by governments. On his last day in office, he published an editorial jointly written with Chief Commissioner Murray Sinclair of the Truth and Reconciliation Commission stating that it was the role of properly constituted courts, and not others such as the museum or commission, to determine whether particular events constitute an act of genocide.[35]

The Breaking the Silence gallery also houses a massive study table containing a world map with an animated interface, graphics, text, photos, and captions, allowing for the study of sixteen atrocities, including Canada's Indian residential schools, the partition of India, the Mayan genocide in Guatemala, and Japanese "comfort" women. (The list of atrocities under consideration for inclusion in this exhibit was redacted from the 2012 document, so consideration of the evolution of this exhibit is not possible.) It also contains study carrels where visitors can view short videos of survivors and those close to them telling their stories. As noted earlier, Giesbrecht and Curle tell us in their contribution that the museum's aspiration to use "the contradictory, open-ended, and ambiguous nature of lived experience requires us to deliberately eschew a preconceived narrative framework in the hope that these rich stories would be able to speak for themselves." The survivors' videos powerfully demonstrate the effectiveness of this approach.

Giesbrecht and Curle assert in their afterword to this volume that, "while museums do not have the prerogative to adjudicate crimes, be they homicide or genocide, they do have the responsibility to host difficult, sustained, public conversations on these issues." The text and other materials used in the Breaking the Silence gallery, and especially the study table, will need to be handled sensitively if the museum is to achieve its intention of encouraging debate on issues such as "when does a mass atrocity become a genocide?"[36] But the granularity of information provided in this gallery's exhibits—on five genocides, the study table, and the video carrels—is impressive. That density, and the difficult decisions about which atrocities to include in the inaugural exhibits and which to leave out, at least initially, are bound to draw both praise and criticism.

INSPIRING ACTION

The difficult Breaking the Silence gallery leads to the youth-focused Actions Count gallery. Among other things, the Canadian Stories exhibit in this gallery features positive and hopeful stories about how "Canadian individuals and groups are actively involved in promoting and maintaining human rights."[37] Once again, the 2012 list of stories was redacted, and therefore no comparison is possible.

The 2011 Ralph Appelbaum Associates *Content Outline* document describes a very different set of exhibits in the space now occupied by the Actions Count gallery. A planned gallery titled Pathways to Peace was to include a series of exhibits focusing on conflict resolution and cultural change in various countries. It was eliminated between 2011 and 2012. According to media reports,[38] the board thought that there was not enough Canadian content in the museum and recommended that this space be used to feature contemporary Canada as a safe haven for new Canadians where rights are recognized and respected.

The Rights Today gallery exposes visitors to contemporary global human rights struggles. The gallery conveys the idea that the struggle for human rights is pressing and ongoing around the world. The Everyday Objects exhibit uses common products such as coffee beans, cooking oil, and water to demonstrate how consumer choices have significant impacts on human rights. Another exhibit, an interactive world map, tells stories related to children's rights, Indigenous rights, women's rights, health rights, and labour rights. The Media Literacy Theatre encourages critical thinking, and another exhibit examines how music contributes to an awareness of human rights issues. The Human Rights Defenders exhibit introduces visitors to twelve people from around the world and eight Canadians who defend human rights in their work every day. The Collective Initiatives exhibit designed "to present recent issues and stories about people's collective efforts" and reinforce that "the struggles of asserting human rights require joint, interdependent efforts"[39] was eliminated by 2013. This content might now be included in other galleries, such as Turning Points for Humanity.

The final gallery, Inspiring Change (known as the Take Action gallery in the 2012 profiles), encourages visitors to move from awareness through engagement and interaction to contributions to positive social change. For example, the 2013 Gallery Profile states that visitors can fill out a card committing them to engage in some kind of human rights–related activity, and if they wish they can mount the cards on the Imagine Wall for others to see. In November 2014, facilitators were present in the gallery to encourage conversations on how to "take action" and to encourage visitors to fill in cards completing the sentence "I imagine…." Or visitors can listen to music that inspired support for human rights campaigns. It is interesting to note the change in the main message for one of the exhibits in this gallery: in 2012, the message was "each person's thoughts and opinions are valued"; in 2013, the message was much more active: "Advances in human rights come from imagining a better future and taking action."[40]

SOME THOUGHTS ON FUTURE RESEARCH

This short overview suggests possibilities for numerous lines of subsequent research on the influences and choices comprising curatorial decision making for the CMHR's inaugural exhibits. Questions include the following:

> Do the exhibits focus too much on top-down approaches to
> human rights? Given the focus on lived experiences as the
> starting point for all exhibits, do the exhibits feature individual
> human rights defenders but downplay collective actions?

How do the exhibits deal with difficult and politically charged issues such as Indigenous claims to land and land use in Canada or whether the label "genocide" should be used to describe the effects of colonization on Indigenous peoples?

Is the Canadian government's role as a human rights violator watered down and its role as a human rights champion exaggerated? Are positive stories told at the expense of dealing with hard truths?

Was the museum justified in redacting information on some of the exhibits under consideration in the 2012 Gallery Profiles? Will researchers be able to interview museum staff, past and present, contracted researchers, and Advisory Committee members? Will they be able to obtain materials such as minutes of curatorial process meetings and board meetings, annual reports, approach papers, peer-review reports, and communications with the architect and exhibit designers, or will such access be blocked?

How did the museum's vision, mission, mandate, or guiding principles, as reported in its corporate plans, change in the four years before the official opening? For example, why was the museum's explicit advocacy mandate, expressed as late as the 2010 corporate report,[41] eliminated? What were the forces behind changes to corporate plans?

How was the Board of Governors involved in curatorial decision making? Were board members under any pressure from the federal government, and if so, what was the nature of this direction?

ACKNOWLEDGEMENTS

I would like to acknowledge the research assistance of Danielle Barchyn, Jared Wheeler, and Diana King; support from the University of Manitoba's Centre for Human Rights Research, Legal Research Institute, and Undergraduate Student Summer Research Award; and the helpful comments that I received on earlier versions of this chapter from Helen Fallding, Aimée Craft, Adam Muller, Andrew Woolford, Jill McConkey, and an anonymous reviewer.

NOTES

1   Canadian Museum for Human Rights, 2012 Gallery Profiles, 12 September 2012 (hereafter "2012 Profiles"); Canadian Museum for Human Rights, 2013 Gallery Profiles, 19 September 2013 (hereafter "2013 Profiles"). Copies of these documents are in my possession. I also refer to the Content Outline document prepared by Ralph Appelbaum Associates, consultants working with the museum, in February 2011.

2   For the most part, content was redacted under Section 21(1)(d) of the Access to Information Act, which gives a government institution the discretionary power to withhold plans not yet put into operation. However, as Helen Fallding describes in her chapter, the access officer should also assess whether the consequences of disclosure outweigh the public interest in disclosure.

3   2012 Profiles, 6.

4   Ibid., 8; 2013 Profiles, 7.

5   2012 Profiles, 16.

6   2013 Profiles, 14.

7   2012 Profiles, 17.

8   2013 Profiles, 16.

9   Ibid., 20.

10   2012 Profiles, 18.

11   2013 Profiles, 19.

12   Tricia Logan, "National Memory and Museums: Remebering Settler Colonial Genocide of Indigenous Peoples in Canada" in *Remembering Genocide*, ed. Nigel Eltringham and Pam MacLean (New York: Routledge, 2014), 125.

13   2012 Profiles, 19; 2013 Profiles, 21.

14   2013 Profiles, 33.

15   Ibid., 51.

16   Ibid.

17   2012 Profiles, 40.

18   2013 Profiles, 47. See, for example, *Canadian Doctors for Refugee Care v Canada*, 2014 FC 651, in which the Federal Court of Canada struck down a federal law restricting access to health care by refugee claimants.

19   2012 Profiles, 41.

20   2013 Profiles, 48.

21   2012 Profiles, 41.

22   Ibid., 38.

23   2013 Profiles, 43.

24   2012 Profiles, 45.

25   2013 Profiles, 52.

26   2012 Profiles, 45.

27   2013 Profiles, 55.

28   Ralph Appelbaum Associates, *Content Outline*, 15 February 2015, 12. This document was obtained pursuant to an Access to Information request. It is in my possession.

29   Two journalists reported on the *Morgenthaler* video: Dan Lett, "True to Izzy's Vision: Museum Raises Challenging Questions, with Complex Answers," *Winnipeg Free Press,* 19 September 2014, http://www.winnipegfreepress.com/canada/winnipeg-human-rights-museum-will-examine-why-did-it-happen-ceo-275707591.html; Steve Lambert, "Rights Museum Opening Draws Protests: CEO Says That's What It Is Supposed to Do," *Winnipeg Free Press,* 19 September 2014, http://www.winnipegfreepress.com/canada/winnipeg-human-rights-museum-will-examine-why-did-it-happen-ceo-275707591.html.

30   2012 Profiles, 54; 2013 Profiles, 65.

31   2012 Profiles, 56; 2013 Profiles, 67.

32   2013 Profiles, 71.

33   Ibid., 84.

34   2012 Profiles, 71.

35   Murray Sinclair and Stuart Murray, "Canada Must Confront the Truth," *Winnipeg Free Press,* 11 November 2014, http://www.winnipegfreepress.com/opinion/analysis/canada-must-confront-the-truth-281166292.html.

36   Clint Curle, in answer to a question at a plenary session on the CMHR at the International Association of Genocide Scholars annual conference held in Winnipeg in July 2014, stated that the museum's role is to facilitate discussion on the issue of when a mass atrocity can be classified as a genocide.

37   2013 Profiles, 88.

38   Canadian Broadcasting Corporation, "Human Rights Museum Board behind Push for 'Positive' Stories: Canadian Museum Manager's Letter Indicates Desire for 'Optimistic Tone' for Peace Gallery," 3 December 2012, http://www.cbc.ca/news/canada/manitoba/human-rights-museum-board-behind-push-for-positive-stories-1.1205264. See also Bartley Kives, "Canadian Museum for Human Rights Staff Exodus Tied to Content Change," *Winnipeg Free Press,* 1 December 2012, A5.

39   2012 Profiles, 84.

40   Ibid., 105; 2013 Profiles, 87.

41   Corporate reporting documents for the CMHR, including corporate plans and budgets, are available at http://humanrights.ca/sites/default/files/corporate_plan_2010-2011_to_2014-2015_en.pdf .

TRANSCENDENCE OR STRUGGLE? TOP-DOWN AND BOTTOM-UP NARRATIVES OF HUMAN RIGHTS

CHAPTER 6

Christopher Powell

> If governments make human rights the structure and the very framework of their political action, that is well and good. But human rights are, above all, that which one confronts governments with.
> —Michel Foucault, "Confronting Governments: Human Rights"[1]

The journey begins in the earth, in darkness and savagery, and proceeds up into the sky and light and hope. Not officially; I have added the word *savagery.* The website of the Canadian Museum for Human Rights (CMHR) states that the "architectural design creates a path for the visitor from darkness to light."[2] The first permanent exhibit on this path, down in the earth, is the Indigenous Perspectives gallery. In Western imagery, darkness is associated with evil, sin, and suffering; light with good, redemption, and joy. The architect writes that "the journey begins with a descent into the earth, a symbolic recognition of the earth as the spiritual center for many indigenous cultures."[3] But the far end of that journey is the Tower of Hope, "an illuminated beacon symbolizing the brightness of enlightenment: the goal of the human-rights journey."[4] The word *savage* derives from classical

Latin *silvaticus,* which means "woodland, wild." It acquired its connotation with violence and brutality by the early nineteenth century,[5] that is, sometime during the long age of European imperialism. The Indigenous peoples who met at The Forks where the museum now stands were not especially violent or brutal, but they were woodland peoples. The museum will not describe Canada's policies toward Indigenous peoples as genocide,[6] although it should.

INTRODUCTION

One of the most important stories that the CMHR will tell concerns not any one particular atrocity or human rights violation, or any one particular human rights success, but the question of what human rights are and where they come from. The museum has already begun to answer this question in its architectural form. When visitors enter the gallery, in a presumed state of ignorance, they enter at ground level and ascend through a spiral of educational galleries, arriving, enlightened, in the gleaming spire that connotes transcendence. This architectural form is conducive to what I call the "top-down" narrative of human rights, in which human rights descend, as if from the heavens, and we rise to meet them. But the actual exhibits and other informational elements of the museum will ultimately determine the overall narrative presented to visitors. Every exhibit, whatever its specific subject matter, will contribute to an overall narrative enabling the visitor to imagine what human rights are and, by extension, how he or she can relate to them.

In this chapter, I argue for a narrative framework in which human rights appear as social constructions:[7] that is, things made by people. In particular, human rights appear to me as tools forged in the heat of struggles against oppression, tools that are always culturally specific, historically contingent, dynamic, and unfinished. I argue that this way of narrating what human rights are and where they come from offers the fullest, most radical, and most subversive available expression of the demands of the human rights movement. I also argue that this narrative, which I call the "bottom-up" narrative, will necessarily work against the grain of another top-down narrative, in which human rights appear as ahistorical essential truths discovered by enlightened people and implemented with varying degrees of success by hegemonic social institutions, especially the state. This top-down narrative is bound to be preferred by those social elites who comprise the dominant stakeholders in the Canadian Museum for Human Rights, the Canadian state and its allies among the economic elite. Finally, I propose that, despite the resistance that the bottom-up narrative inevitably encounters, the struggle to articulate it both in external critique of the CMHR and in internal curating practice (as in the Agricultural Migrant Workers exhibit; see Armando Perla's contribution to this volume) is a worthwhile form of human rights activism.

In making this argument, I must cast aside the mantle typically assumed by social scientists who comment on public institutions, that of the disinterested observer who speaks with the authoritative voice of purely objective reason. I write as an interested party. I have been inspired for all of my adult life by, and occasionally involved in, the human rights movement: not as an idealist but as one engaged in a concrete struggle for a radically egalitarian, inclusive, and emancipated society. This inspiration has led me into the role of an academic social scientist. And, though my argument draws on social scientific theories that have been developed through rigorous argument in close dialogue with systematic empirical studies, the ultimate basis of my contentions lies in an intuition: that the most valid purpose of human rights is not to establish a legitimate form of domination but to challenge all possible forms of domination in the name of a shared human freedom. This intuition does not amount to a claim that my position rests on self-evident ethical truths; rather, it serves as the point of entry from which my inarticulate, embodied social being can become articulate, at this time and under these conditions.

TWO NARRATIVES

Meaning is negotiated. The meaning of any given assemblage of information (or "text") is constructed by the person who views it (the "reader") through an active process of interpretation.[8] In the CMHR, the active interpretive involvement of visitors will be all the more pronounced in the many electronic exhibits enabling them to choose which documents they view and in which order, or navigate virtual spaces, or otherwise shape their individual experiences. Nevertheless, even a non-linear text shapes the possible interpretations available to the reader. Even without seeming to do so, a museum exhibit can provide the viewer with crucial framing assumptions that anchor his or her interpretations to particular meanings.[9] In part, these assumptions come from outside the text entirely, from its cultural context. It is this connotative meaning that translates the CMHR's architecture into a narrative of transcendence, for instance.[10] In Canadian society, the predominant story about rights, and about social truths in particular, is the top-down one, and the museum's exhibits will tend to rely on and reinforce this narrative unless they actively disrupt it.

What do I mean by top-down and bottom-up narratives? First, these are ideal types. Max Weber defined ideal types as hypothetical constructs, based on empirical observation, that distill the complexity of social action into a pattern defined by a singular logic of motivation.[11] One rarely observes a pure type in the field, only actions that conform to it more or less closely. My pure type of the top-down narrative has several defining features. First, it construes human rights, or their basis, in terms of theological or metaphysical essences. Essences exist beyond human agency and beyond historical change. Second, as essences, they exist primarily as ideas; although they are applied in practice, the idea comes first. Third, as essences, human rights are sacred, and therefore they are authoritative; in the top-down view, it is difficult to imagine how human rights could have any authority if they were merely constructed. Fourth, as essences, human rights are discovered, not made. Fifth, human rights constitute a norm to which we can conform more or less closely and which, despite their transcendent origins, must be enforced like other social norms. And sixth, the implications of these assumptions tend toward elitism. The discovery of human rights appears as a mark of superior cultural achievement, conveyed by terms such as "Enlightenment" (though, to moderate the chauvinism of this idea, we might acknowledge that every culture has some rudimentary form of human rights or human rights precursors). Elaboration of the contents of human rights is best achieved by experts: legal scholars, political philosophers, and so forth. And the implementation of human rights is best achieved through law, that is, through the exercise of state power.

In the bottom-up narrative, human rights appear as social constructions—as things made by people. First, they are therefore culturally specific and historically variable. Second, they exist as practices, as ways of doing things, and emerge out of practical situations. Ideas about human rights emerge as responses or solutions to practical dilemmas. Third, how sacred or authoritative they are is a practical social achievement, not an expression of their "nature." Human rights emerge out of politics at its most profane, out of struggles over power. Their status as truths or otherwise depends on the outcome of power struggles, especially struggles of oppressed groups against dominant groups in society. Fourth, human rights are "discovered" only in the sense that one discovers how to do something or how to make something—a kind of discovery always driven by practical exigencies. Human rights are made, not found; they are tools long before they can become truths. Fifth, the normative quality of human rights is secondary to their pragmatic political function. This function is to push social relations in the direction of fundamental human equality and freedom. The universalism of human rights activism is pragmatic, because freedom for any particular group of human beings depends on freedom for all. The propagation of human rights norms, and the implementation of declarations and laws, are political tactics; they mark the points of compromise between human rights and state power, the shapes to which human rights adapt themselves in order to wrestle with state power, rather than the ultimate expression of essential truths.

Finally, then, the implication of these assumptions is egalitarianism. The discovery of human rights appears not as a mark of superior cultural achievement but as the invention of a way of doing things in response to particular historical circumstances and material conditions. Their universalization is the universalization of practices or of the concrete social relations that those practices engender. The true "experts" on human rights are those who use them in practical social struggles, hence those who alter their meanings, who deploy them selectively and opportunistically to suit the needs of particular struggles. Thus, the contents of human rights vary, from one situation to another as well as over time, and this variation is not a corruption of pristine essence but a mark of the diversity and vitality of human rights struggles and of the complexity and variability of forms of injustice and oppression. And the implementation of human rights norms in national and international laws is only a means to an end, not the end of the human rights movement. States might use human rights to provide themselves with legitimacy,[12] parties or factions within states might use human rights to gain political capital (as did the administration of President Jimmy Carter), and human rights activists might benefit from this opportunism in the short to medium term. But in the long term, the legitimation of political domination[13] is incompatible with the practical transformations toward which the human rights movement tends. The complete realization of human rights requires the fundamental transformation of state power into a more radical democracy than currently exists.

HUMAN RIGHTS AS SOCIAL CONSTRUCTIONS

What does it mean to treat human rights as social constructions? First I must abolish the common misconception that calling something a social construction means saying that it is not real. This might represent a philosophical notion of constructionism[14] but not a sociological one. Part of the groundwork for the sociological understanding of social construction was laid by Emile Durkheim, who observed that fundamental categories of perception—time, space, number, causality, substance, and personality—are established through social practice.[15] Not only are the units of measurement of time a social artifact, but also the quality of time—whether it passes according to the flow of events or the regularity of a clock, for instance[16]—is structured by social interactions. For Durkheim, this did not make time any less objective, because social practices are objective in their relations to individuals.[17] The objectivity of time, therefore, is a social objectivity, one produced and maintained through the objective persistence of group practices.

Peter Berger and Thomas Luckmann build on Durkheim's account to present social construction as a dialectical process in which individual human action and the external, objective reality of social institutions continually and dynamically condition one another.[18] A social practice developed through intentional social action, through repeated use, comes to confront social actors as an external, objective thing; actors therefore treat the practice as having a reality of its own and incorporate that reality into their knowledge of the world and into their own conduct.[19] This reality is neither essential, since it emerges from intentional social action, nor fictive, since once established it cannot be willed away by individuals. It requires sustained collective effort to produce social constructions and sustained collective effort to abolish them. In this way, a social construction is a thing built by people, much as a house—or a museum—is a thing built by people.

Contemporary sociology of scientific knowledge treats scientific truths as social constructions in just this sense.[20] Starting from the observation that, in the first instance, scientific knowledge is a product of human beings interacting with material objects and with each other, sociologists of scientific knowledge follow a rule of symmetry[21] stating that both true and false accounts of nature must be explicable in terms of the same analytic concepts. This makes it inadmissible to explain false beliefs as the products of social factors such as ideologies or political interests but then to explain true beliefs as the products of some entirely different set of factors, some direct contact with non-social reality unmediated by social practices. Applying the same rule of symmetry to human rights would mean that, if we understand oppression in terms of power relations, for example, we must also account for the power relations involved in making human rights an effective reality in people's lives. Importantly, understanding human rights as social constructions does not make them false, any more than treating scientific truths as social constructions somehow invalidates them. Rather, both types of truths appear as practical solutions to practical dilemmas. Scientists work to produce explanations of the natural world, explanations that inspire general agreement and facilitate further scientific inquiry. But these explanations emerge out of, and feed back into, practical attempts to control—exert power over—particular parts of the natural world. Human rights activists work to produce normative claims that inspire general agreement and facilitate further human rights struggle, and they do so in the context of practical attempts to secure a measure of emancipation, enfranchisement, or inclusion for particular oppressed subjects. To "discover" a scientific truth or a truth about human rights is to discover an effective way of accomplishing certain goals.

UNIVERSALIZING THE CONTINGENT

Understanding human rights in this way helps us to make sense of one of the fundamental dilemmas that bedevils human rights theorists: the de facto non-universality of human rights.[22] Although proponents might claim that rights are universal,[23] and indeed might be obliged to make this claim by the metaphysical assumptions of Western political discourse,[24] human rights are not universally observed in practice, nor are all struggles against oppression framed in terms of human rights. It is also not the case that all oppressed people are in a hurry to adopt human rights discourse enthusiastically once they are introduced to it. An essentialist account of human rights implies that all rational people should recognize the validity of human rights claims and obliges us to adopt ad hoc hypotheses, variations on the theme that people somehow do not understand what is good for them, which violates the spirit of universal egalitarianism. But if human rights are a practical solution to the dilemmas of a particular historical situation, then the difficulty of universalizing them immediately makes sense. To make human rights universal (or, to be precise, human-universal) would require either that the practical dilemmas for which they are a solution be made universal or, more realistically, that human rights be modified to address the diverse needs of people operating with different cultural histories and facing different forms of oppression. How to do that while preserving some sort of coherence to the human rights movement is, of course, a substantial practical and theoretical challenge.

It will be easier to overcome this challenge if we have a good grasp on the problems that human rights are intended to solve and of the social history of those problems. One crucial aspect of this history is the particular intensity of processes of individualization associated with Western modernity. Although human rights are not always and everywhere rights of the individual, the social enfranchisement of the individual and the protection of individuals from the superior power of the state and other collective institutions are two of the most common themes taken up by proponents of particular human rights. To understand both the appeal of human rights and the limitations of that appeal, it is useful to know that human beings are not always and everywhere individuals, at least not in the fullest sense of the term.

Karl Marx's writings on alienation provide a rudimentary account of the social construction of modern individuality.[25] Marx observes that the commodification of labour power creates a situation in which the individual worker experiences his or her material interests as separate from those of other workers or the human collectivity, because his or her own human creative capacities appear as a commodity, the sale of which entails an individual relation between the worker and capital. Durkheim also locates the root of what he calls "the cult of the individual" in the capitalist economy, in the division of labour that makes specialization of function the basis of human interdependence and social solidarity.[26] Norbert Elias adds to this the individualizing effects of the sovereign state's monopolization of military force, which removes direct physical force from the normal conduct of everyday life.[27] This monopolization undermines the direct authority of individual members of the warrior class and shifts the balance of power between those who control and those who do not control the means of force in favour of the latter. And Michel Foucault's work on disciplinary power supplements all of these accounts by mapping the individualization of the exercise of power.[28] Disciplinary power works to achieve greater power effects through a more economical exercise of force by cultivating knowledge about the characteristics of individuals and enmeshing them in normalizing discourses that arrange those characteristics in subtle hierarchies based on differential conformity to idealized norms. In Foucault's account, "right" appears as the naturalization of the claims to power of the sovereign,[29] and once those claims are naturalized they can be appropriated by those whom the sovereign governs—that is, by the "community of the governed"[30]—as part of the ongoing contestation of power relations.

We can thus understand human rights as one possible solution among others to the dilemmas of social actors subjected simultaneously to forces that individualize them and forces demanding their conformity to hierarchical institutions. Benjamin Gregg recognizes this when he argues that the creation of a "human rights state" requires the transformation of political community along lines that enhance the scope for the individuality of political subjects.[31] However, Gregg does not adequately address the potential losses associated with such a transformation. Enhancing individualization can undermine collective institutions necessary for the maintenance of collective identities. For instance, we can easily imagine conflicts between rights defined primarily in individual terms and the collective ownership of land that remains integral to many Indigenous cultures. Inasmuch as the right to one's cultural traditions is a human right, different human rights might conflict with one another because of the incomplete understanding of the collective dimensions of individual life by human rights theory. As Elias observes, all human subjectivity involves both individual identity and collective identity.[32] The reconciliation of the two constitutes another theoretical and practical challenge for the human rights movement.

HUMAN RIGHTS AND THE CONTRADICTIONS OF SOVEREIGNTY

The social construction of human rights is a historical process or, if you will, a historical labour. The development of modern individualism is a broad process, involving both large-scale structures such as the global capitalist economy and the sovereign state and small-scale transformations in how people relate to others and themselves. Of course, formation of the contemporary human rights movement involves many more factors; human rights are not simply an inevitable by-product of individualization. But the broad social processes that serve as backdrops for local struggles do provide enabling conditions and definite constraints that shape the forms of these struggles in concrete instances. My own work on genocide has enabled me to examine one important set of constraints bound to affect the content of the Canadian Museum for Human Rights. These constraints result from the dynamics of state sovereignty, specifically the contradictory tendencies inherent in sovereignty as an institution.

To explain genocide as a systematic product of the expansion of Western civilization, I have proposed a dialectical account of sovereign power.[33] This dialectic has its roots in Elias's conception of the modern Western civilizing process as a progressive transformation of social life on two levels, the "macro" level of state formation and the "micro" level of subjectivity. Elias defines the state as the organization claiming a monopoly on the use of military force in a given territory, and he dispenses with Weber's emphasis on legitimacy in favour of a closer examination of force relations. The progressive monopolization of force by sovereigns from the thirteenth century onward enforces a pacification of social life that constrains social actors to govern, display, and use their own bodies (including their emotions) in order not to offend one another, as a means of pursuing their own social advancement. My critique of this "civilizing process" begins with the observation that neither state formation nor this "social constraint to self-constraint" actually abolishes violence. State formation enables the construction of ever-greater military capacity by states, up to and including the capacity for global nuclear omnicide, while the social constraint to self-constraint enables the construction of normative codes that, among other things, separate insider from outsider in ways that make genocide possible on hitherto impossibly large scales, even within the confines of orderly society. At the same time, the pacification of everyday life observed by Elias does exist for many social actors, and the ideals of civilized conduct inspire genuine efforts toward universal social enfranchisement, including abolitionism and anti-colonialism, efforts to end genocide, and the human rights movement. The civilizing process is therefore neither simply pacifying nor simply violent but contradictory.

Specifically, this contradiction takes the form of an alienated relationship between the subject and object of sovereign power. Where sovereignty is not established or is disputed, social actors might struggle violently with one another. Losing combatants, in order to prevent their own annihilation, might offer to submit or *defer* to winning combatants. In so doing, the two parties establish a hierarchical *difference* between each other. This action also *defers* further violence without dispelling it, since the victor retains the means to destroy the loser. I coined the term "deferentiation" to refer to this triple process of deference/differentiation/deferral. Deferentiation can also take place in entirely symbolic terms, as in a verbal contest between two political candidates, a moment of sexual or racial harassment in the street, or a trivial dispute over etiquette at a dinner party. Deferentiation is a relation, and relations of deferentiation combine to form an overall network or figuration, with the (actual or symbolic) figure of the sovereign at the centre and disenfranchised, abject subjects at the periphery.

Deferentiation connects subjects to the sovereign while also separating them: in every concrete relationship, dominated actors have an interest in lessening the power differential between superior and inferior, while dominant actors have an interest in increasing this differential. This conflict of interest expresses the central contradiction of sovereign power; the substance of that contradiction is the reciprocal but unequal exchange of deference for the deferral of violence. Dominant actors have an interest in mitigating this contradiction by encouraging dominated subjects to identify with them: that is, to perceive an identity between their own subjectivity and that of the sovereign. Dominated actors might also have an interest in this identification inasmuch as it increases the value of their own deference and so makes the sovereign more dependent on them. This mitigation can never completely succeed, however, because it cannot, all on its own, abolish the practical contradiction between those who exercise power and those on whom power is exercised.

What does this mean for human rights and the Canadian Museum for Human Rights? I perceive the CMHR as caught on the horns of this contradiction. The top-down narrative of human rights expresses the interests of the sovereign and of social elites with the closest access to sovereign power. In concrete terms, this narrative would encourage Canadian citizens who visit the museum to perceive the Canadian state, Canadian society, and their own subjectivity as mutually identified and symbolically interchangeable and thereby to perceive human rights struggles with or within Canada as human rights "successes" or "challenges" belonging to this composite figure. This identification also encourages, of course, downplaying the human rights problems in Canada, emphasizing those aspects of Canadian history that can be presented as positive for human rights, and on the whole treating Canada as a society in which human rights abuses are exceptional rather than normal. This narrative implies that human rights can be fully implemented in Canada without a fundamental transformation of Canadian society or of institutions such as the Canadian state. The top-down narrative encourages visitors to perceive human rights in terms of abstract norms rather than concrete struggles, and to perceive their own relationships to human rights in essentially atomized terms, disconnected from their own involvement in the complex web of power relations that Patricia Hill Collins calls the "matrix of domination."[34] Finally, the top-down narrative would have a hard time avoiding the implication that the "discovery" of human rights is a demonstration of the cultural superiority of Western societies or ascribing human rights abuses around the world to the perverse reluctance of colonized or post-colonized Others to adopt Western values.

The bottom-up narrative, on the other hand, expresses the interest of dominated subjects in reducing (or, more radically, abolishing) the power differential between sovereign and subjects. As such, in the context of the CMHR, it encourages visitors to regard the Canadian state itself as a socially constructed institution, to question its motives, and to perceive their own relations to it not in terms of abstract norms but in terms of concrete power relations. It highlights both the human rights problems that exist in Canada, including those involved in construction of the museum itself, and the opportunities for non-state actors to advance human rights goals in everyday life in collective politics at the local, provincial, and national levels. It emphasizes the agency of oppressed peoples and critiques the myths of privileged subjects as saviours, contemporary versions of the "white man's burden"[35] and the like. It presents human rights in pragmatic rather than idealistic terms, emphasizing the practical social relations through which people assert, secure, and exercise their rights. Indeed, the bottom-up narrative would entail an education in power politics, in the exigencies and interests that motivate political actors, thereby disrupting the comforting assumption that society is normatively ordered. The bottom-up narrative provokes viewers to examine their own involvement in the matrix of domination, in which they might be simultaneously oppressed and oppressor, and it encourages them to perceive a human rights commitment as a practical expression of solidarity rather than an individualized commitment to a delocalized ethical principle. Finally, it emphasizes the fluidity and complexity of human rights, their rootedness in particular situations, thereby illuminating the practical challenges involved in disseminating human rights across all human cultures.

As I said before, these are ideal types. I expect that *both* narratives can be found in the CMHR's exhibits, even within any one exhibit. Which narrative tends to predominate will depend on the power relations within the museum and those in which it is embedded. So, for instance, in his contribution to this volume, Ken Norman chronicles the earnest efforts by the museum's Content Advisory Committee to seriously engage the Canadian public in a dialogue about the museum's design and content, its recommendation that dialogue continue over the long term and that efforts be made to include those who had not yet been included, and its hope that this dialogue would function as a form of human rights praxis in itself—but he also notes that "the jury is out on whether the CMHR will be brave enough to offer its researchers and curators the rewards and risks of such a stimulating continuing conversation with Canadians." He further notes that the museum's website does not feature any hyperlink to a human rights organization; "bluntly put," he says, "this is a clear signal to those interested in engagement in current events in human rights that the CMHR is not a kindred spirit." Also in this volume, Helen Fallding observes that "the CMHR's chief executive officer and first two board chairs had no expertise in either museums or human rights prior to joining the museum" and that "differences in vision between staff with human rights expertise and the CEO and board members have driven away at least one museum researcher." In his analysis of the politics of the museum's creation, Dirk Moses concludes that the museum's dependence on private donors compromises its potential as a platform for human rights activism because "the more that human rights are emphasized, the less the interest from the private donors whose generosity is essential to the museum's financial viability."[36] Therefore, the narrative framework that the museum presents to visitors will be an object of struggle, and the museum itself a site of struggle, for the foreseeable future.

Antonio Gramsci's concepts of cultural hegemony and war of position provide a useful framework for understanding this struggle.[37] To explain the persistence of capitalist exploitation in the face of collective efforts to abolish it, Gramsci proposes that cultural institutions in society actively cultivate ways of thinking that naturalize the social order, securing the cooperation of the oppressed by making any alternative seem unthinkable. Rather than abolish these institutions (through the "war of manoeuvre"), those who oppose this hegemony are frequently constrained to struggle within them, making schools, the media, political parties, and other normal institutions into sites of struggle (in the "war of position").

Human rights activists can translate the terms of this theory, which Gramsci formulated to apply to class struggle, into an understanding of human rights struggle. The Canadian Museum for Human Rights is and will be neither simply a resource for the propagation of human rights nor simply a vehicle for self-serving government propaganda. Rather, it is already, and will continue to be for the foreseeable future, a site of positional struggle between forces that seek to extend state power and those that seek to curtail that power.

CONCLUSION

Cultural narratives can shape actors' knowledge of their own relations to each other and to social institutions. This capacity invests narratives with concrete political effectiveness. In this chapter, I have worked to present a bottom-up narrative of human rights, characterized by a sociologically informed, practice-oriented, constructionist account of the genesis of those rights. This bottom-up narrative contrasts with top-down narratives with present human rights as ahistorical essences. Crucially, the bottom-up narrative presents human rights as tools forged in the context of struggles, tools that necessarily oppose and subvert relations of domination, whereas top-down narratives present human rights as normative truths that work to legitimate and naturalize particular relations of domination. These are ideal types, rarely encountered in their pure form, and the Canadian Museum for Human Rights will tend to present both types of narrative, often mixed together. By presenting these narratives as ideal types, I hope to offer human rights activists a simple and effective resource for critiquing the museum and for communicating a practically effective understanding of human rights to the museum's audience. Given the constellation of forces at work in the museum's formation,[38] it seems likely that top-down narratives will predominate. However, I hope that, even if bottom-up narratives can only be presented in the form of external critiques of the museum articulated by human rights organizations and disseminated through news stories about the institution and its controversies, these narratives can still advance the cause of human rights struggles. Politicization of the museum in this way can help to disrupt the comforting identification of Canadian subjects with the Canadian state and with the dominant groups in Canadian society, and foster solidarity among differing subjects who stand to benefit from the extension of human rights in practice. In this way, the museum might be able to function as a vehicle for the propagation of human rights, despite itself.

NOTES

1   Michel Foucault, "Confronting Governments: Human Rights," in *Power: Essential Works of Foucault 1954–1984, Volume 3,* ed. James D. Faubion (New York: New Press, 2000), 471.

2   Canadian Museum for Human Rights, "Planning the Museum," http://museumforhumanrights.ca/building-museum/planning-museum (accessed 14 February 2014).

3   Predock, Antoine, "Canadian Museum for Human Rights," http://www.predock.com/CMHR/CMHR.html (accessed 14 February 2014).

4   Canadian Museum for Human Rights, 2014b, "The tower of hope," http://museumforhumanrights.ca/content/tower-hope (accessed 14 February 2014).

5   Oxford English Dictionary, "Savage," http://www.oed.com (accessed 14 February 2014)

6   CBC News, "Human rights museum sparks debate over term 'genocide,'" 26 July 2013, http://www.cbc.ca/1.1400154 (accessed 14 February 2014).

7   The idea of human rights as social constructions has been discussed before; see Neil Stammers, "Social Movements and the Social Construction of Human Rights," *Human Rights Quarterly* 21, 4 (1999): 980–1008; Benjamin Gregg, *Human Rights as Social Constructions* (Cambridge, UK: Cambridge University Press, 2011); Jack Donnelly, "The Social Construction of International Human Rights," *Relaciones internacionales* 17 (2011): 1–30; and Rainer Forst, *The Right to Justification: Elements of a Constructivist Theory of Justice* (New York: Columbia University Press, 2012). However, the account of social construction in this chapter is based on my own reading of sociological theory and is derived, for better or for worse, independently of these sources.

8   Jonathan Culler, *On Deconstruction: Theory and Criticism after Structuralism* (Ithaca, NY: Cornell University Press, 1982), 31ff.; Roland Barthes, *Image, Music, Text,* trans. Stephen Heath (New York: Hill and Wang, 1977).

9   Arnold Harrichand Itwaru and Natasha Ksonzek, *Closed Entrances: Canadian Culture and Imperialism* (Toronto: TSAR Publications, 1994).

10   Stuart Hall, *Representation: Cultural Representations and Signifying Practice* (London: Sage Publications and Open University, 1997), 228; Roland Barthes, *Mythologies,* trans. Annette Lavers (New York: Hill and Wang, 1972), 109ff.

11   Max Weber, *Economy and Society, Volume 1* (Berkeley: University of California Press, 1978), 20–21, 57; Max Weber, "'Objectivity' in Social Science and Social Science Policy," in *The Methodology of the Social Sciences,* ed. Edward A. Shils and Henry A. Finch (Glencoe, IL: Free Press, 1949), 50–112.

12   For a critique, see Christopher Powell, "Crisis of Co-Optation: Human Rights Social Movements and Global Politics," *Alternate Routes* 15 (1999): 5–34.

13   For a conceptualization of domination, see Weber, *Economy and Society,* 31–33, 53–54.

14   Ian Hacking, *The Social Construction of What?* (Cambridge, MA: Harvard University Press, 1999).

15   Emile Durkheim, *The Elementary Forms of Religious Life,* trans. Karen E. Fields (New York: Free Press, 1995), 8–18.

16   See, for example, Robert V. Levine, *A Geography of Time: On Tempo, Culture, and the Pace of Life* (New York: Basic Books, 1998).

17   Emile Durkheim, "The Rules of Sociological Method," in *Durkheim: The Rules of Sociological Method and Selected Texts on Sociology and Its Method,* ed. Stephen Lukes (New York: Free Press, 1982), 31–166.

18   Peter Berger and Thomas Luckmann, *The Social Construction of Reality: A Treatise in the Sociology of Knowledge* (London: Penguin Books, 1966).

19   Berger and Luckmann's account of the reification of social institutions echoes and broadens Marx's account of the fetishization of commodities; see Karl Marx, *Capital: A Critique of Political Economy, Volume 1,* trans. Ben Fowkes (London: Penguin Books, 1976), 163–77.

20   Barry Barnes, David Bloor, and John Henry, *Scientific Knowledge: A Sociological Analysis* (Chicago: University of Chicago Press, 1996); David Bloor, *Knowledge and Social Imagery* (London: Routledge and Kegan Paul, 1976); Bruno Latour, *Reassembling the Social Sciences: An Introduction to Actor-Network Theory* (Oxford: Oxford University Press, 2005).

21   Bloor, *Knowledge,* 7.

22   See, for example, Arvind Sharma, *Are Human Rights Western? A Contribution to the Dialogue of Civilizations* (Oxford: Oxford University Press, 2006).

23   See, for example, Stephen James, *Universal Human Rights: Origins and Development* (New York: LFB Scholarly Publishing, 2007); Olivia Ball and Paul Gready, *The No-Nonsense Guide to Human Rights* (Oxford: New Internationalist Publications, 2006); Michael Freeman, *Human Rights: An Interdisciplinary Approach, Key Concepts* (Cambridge, UK: Polity, 2002); Jack Mahoney, *The Challenge of Human Rights: Origin, Development, and Significance* (Oxford: Blackwell Publishing, 2006); and Micheline R. Ishay, *The History of Human Rights: From Ancient Times to the Globalization Era* (Berkeley: University of California Press, 2008).

24   Lynn Hunt, *Inventing Human Rights: A History* (New York: W.W. Norton and Company, 2007).

25   Karl Marx, "Economic and Philosophical Manuscripts of 1844," in *Karl Marx Frederick Engels Collected Works Volume 3,* trans. Martin Milligan and Dirk J. Struik (New York: International Publishers, 1975), 229–348.

26   Emile Durkheim, *The Division of Labour in Society* (New York: Free Press, 1984); Emile Durkheim, *Professional Ethics and Civic Morals* (London: Routledge, 1992).

27   Norbert Elias, *The Civilizing Process: The History of Manners and State Formation and Civilization,* rev. ed., trans. Edmund Jephcott (Oxford: Blackwell, 2000); Norbert Elias, *The Society of Individuals* (New York: Continuum, 2001).

28   Michel Foucault, *The History of Sexuality, Volume 1: An Introduction,* trans. Robert Hurley (1976; New York: Vintage Books, 1990); Michel Foucault, *Discipline and Punish: The Birth of the Prison,* 2nd ed., trans. Alan Sheridan (New York: Vintage Books, 1995).

29   Michel Foucault, "Right of Death and Power over Life," in *The Foucault Reader,* ed. Paul Rabinow (New York: Pantheon Books, 1984), 258–72.

30   Foucault, "Confronting Governments: Human Rights," 474.

31   Benjamin Gregg, *Human Rights as Social Constructions* (Cambridge, UK: Cambridge University Press, 2011).

32   Norbert Elias, *Involvement and Detachment* (Oxford: Basil Blackwell, 1987), xii, xxxix, lxi, lxvi; Elias, *Society of Individuals,* 156, 196–205; Richard Jenkins, *Social Identity,* 3rd ed. (London: Routledge, 2008).

33   Christopher Powell, *Barbaric Civilization: A Critical Sociology of Genocide* (Montreal: McGill-Queen's University Press, 2011), 126–62. This radical critique was motivated by my reading of the histories of colonial genocides in Africa and the Americas, especially David E. Stannard, *American Holocaust: The Conquest of the New World* (Oxford: Oxford University Press, 1992), and Sven Lindqvist, *"Exterminate All the Brutes": One Man's Odyssey into the Heart of Darkness and the Origins of European Genocide* (New York: New Press, 1996). If one frames the study of genocide only in terms of physical extermination of ethnic minorities within a nation-state, then genocide can reasonably appear as a pathological exception to the normal workings of modern Western civilization—though even this is disputable. See Zygmunt Bauman, *Modernity and the Holocaust* (1989; reprinted, Ithaca, NY: Cornell University Press, 1991). However, if one expands one's gaze to include genocides of colonial others committed both through mass murder and through the forcible erasure of cultures, then genocide seems less like a pathology and more like an integral part of the global expansion of the European state system.

34   Patricia Hill Collins, *Black Feminist Thought: Knowledge, Consciousness, and the Politics of Empowerment* (London: Routledge, 2000), 18, 227ff.

35   "The White Man's Burden" is a poem by English poet Rudyard Kipling. Its first stanza
      reads thus:
      Take up the White Man's burden, Send forth the best ye breed
      Go bind your sons to exile, to serve your captives' need;
      To wait in heavy harness, On fluttered folk and wild—
      Your new-caught, sullen peoples, Half-devil and half-child.

      The remainder of the poem continues in this vein; see Rudyard Kipling, "The White
      Man's Burden," *McClure's Magazine* 12, 4 (February 1899): 290–291. More generally, the
      phrase refers to the belief expressed by the poem that European imperialism is morally
      justified and necessary as a means of bringing civilization to the inferior races of the
      Earth. See, for example, Anne McClintock, *Imperial Leather: Race, Gender, and Sexuality
      in the Colonial Contest* (London: Routledge, 1995), 32.

36   A. Dirk Moses, "The Canadian Museum for Human Rights: The 'Uniqueness of the Holo-
      caust' and the Question of Genocide," *Journal of Genocide Research* 13, 2 (2012): 215.

37   Antonio Gramsci, *Selections from the Prison Notebooks,* ed. and trans. Quintin Hoare and
      Geoffrey Nowell Smith (New York: International Publishers, 1971), 12–13, 235, 350.

38   See Moses, "Canadian Museum," and his chapter in this volume.

ENGAGING MACHINES: EXPERIENCE, EMPATHY, AND THE MODERN MUSEUM

CHAPTER 7

Adam Muller, Struan Sinclair, and Andrew Woolford

Since the advent in 2004 of what has been termed Web 2.0,[1] new technologies have continued to emerge that promise ever more refined capacity for promoting interpersonal engagement and understanding in a variety of contexts but especially in modern museums. In such spaces, it has become impossible to ignore technology's potential to foster knowledge and empathy, not merely for those wishing to express themselves, those in need of being recognized and understood, but also for others open to learning from such representations.[2] However, a number of fundamental questions concerning the efficacy of "digital curation" remain unanswered, one of which lies at the heart of a major collaborative and SSHRC-funded initiative that we have undertaken. Is it actually possible in museum contexts such as the Canadian Museum for Human Rights (CMHR) for new technologies to bring us into a closer and more morally and politically transformative relationship with the suffering experienced by others in a space such as a Canadian Indian residential school (IRS)?

Of particular interest to us is the possibility that new and emerging technologies offer for creating spaces conducive to the emergence of what we call "empathic communities." Such communities can be provisionally defined by their members' enhanced recognition of, and feeling of responsibility for, some specific other. As Susie Linfield and a broad range of other thinkers, including Sven Lindqvist, Hannah Arendt, Jean Améry, and

Martha Nussbaum, variously and rightly observe, without empathy "the politics of human rights devolve into abstraction, romantic foolishness, and cruelty."[3] The representation of experiences of suffering and atrocity is therefore crucial to both the theory and the practice of social justice. To quote Linfield again, "we cannot talk—at least in meaningful or realistic ways—about building a world of democracy, justice, and human rights without first understanding the experience of their negation."[4]

A usefully realistic and meaningful discussion of the negation of human rights, however, must involve more than just acquiring data—the facts, figures, and even stories and images of moral atrocity, what R.G. Collingwood famously described as the historical "chronicle."[5] In part, this is because such information can become debilitating, overwhelming its consumers regardless of the additional contextualization and "aesthetic distance" provided by museums, classrooms, or other sites devoted to the representation of traumatic experience. In addition, though, our collective memory already overflows with trauma narratives, large and small. We remain deeply immersed in (and shaped by) what cultural theorist E. Ann Kaplan has called a "trauma culture."[6] Hence the significance of Lindqvist's contention that "it is not knowledge that we lack. What is missing is the courage to understand what we know and draw conclusions."[7]

In what follows, we intend to marshal a preliminary and partial response to Lindqvist's challenge to make something useful out of what we know by examining whether or not a robust understanding of atrocity events is possible through interactions with novel representational technologies capable of creating powerfully motivational (immersive and reciprocally self-constituting) spaces comprising analogues of lived experience. More specifically, we discuss the theoretical rationale and some technological concerns underpinning the planned construction and evaluation of Embodying Empathy, a digital storyworld prototype that we are constructing with potential applications in museums, since one of its aims is to provide museumgoers with an enhanced experience of a historical environment derived from accounts of a specific locus of mass violence: a Canadian IRS. We begin by offering a brief description of how this storyworld will be built, including an assessment of some of its main challenges. We then discuss the storyworld's potential for communicating multivocal and community-based understandings of Indigenous experiences of residential school suffering, and we conclude by considering its possible limitations as a representational tool.

WHY USE EMERGENT DIGITAL TECHNOLOGIES
IN THE REPRESENTATION OF ATROCITY EVENTS?

Emergent digital technologies offer opportunities for further theoriza-
tion of the historical and ethical possibilities of representing atrocity and
mass violence in museum contexts.[8] In genocide, museum, and cultural
studies theoretical milieus, questions about responsibility and indifference have long animated debates, particularly concerning the mediating
agency of technology.

On one side of these debates are those for whom technology serves
to increase empathic distance rather than understanding, yielding novel
forms of human cruelty. Social psychologist Stanley Milgram's experiments
on obedience, for example, have been read as providing a cautionary tale
about a mediating technology's power to diminish our concern for others.
His imposing "shock"-generating machine, which required experimental
subjects to "harm" someone (actually an experimental "confederate")
hidden but audible behind a laboratory wall, functions on this view as a
distancing device allowing subjects to ignore the pleas of faceless sufferers
whose fates they remotely control.[9] Sociologist Zygmunt Bauman has since
expanded on Milgram's insights to argue that modernity's technological
sophistication constituted a necessary, though not a sufficient, cause of the
Holocaust, enabling "ordinary" men and women to become willing tortur-
ers and executioners.[10] For Bauman, contemporary technologies such as
radio, film, train systems, gas chambers, and bureaucratic modes of organization were among several factors that forestalled Germans' empathy
for their Jewish neighbours and made possible the efficient manufacture
of death through the concentration camp system.[11] Moreover, specifically
with respect to representational technologies, a large and growing body of
work has documented the negative psycho-social effects of representations
of violence in media domains such as contemporary television, film, and
gaming, and it notes in particular the tendency of these media to diminish
empathic identification through the proliferation of atrocity representations, creating what legal theorist Cass Sunstein has termed "moral numb-
ness."[12] For example, a study of adolescent behaviour by Mirjana Bajovic,
a doctoral student at Brock University, made headlines early in 2014 when
it was reported that her evidence showed how exposure to video game violence weakened gamers' ability to empathize with others' suffering. More
than this, Bajovic argued that prolonged exposure to violent games risked
causing young people to lose their ability to distinguish right from wrong.[13]

Some scholars, however, are beginning to take issue with blanket scepticism concerning the moral potential of emerging representational technologies. Accordingly, Sophie Oliver bemoans the "chorus of moral sceptics who admonish completely the use of video games and simulation for social education or humanitarian activism," concluding that the "digital sphere may be no more problematic than other representational modes when it comes to remembering and talking about human suffering—activities themselves wracked with controversies and limitations, but that we must nonetheless not abandon."[14] Garry Young and Monica Whitty's work on psychological parity and contiguity between actual and virtual domains suggests that there exists a more permeable membrane than is often supposed to exist between on- and offline behaviours, including those associated with values such as empathy and solidarity.[15] Aylish Wood points out that the use of new technology and social media in museums "opens up new ways to be attentive to diverse audiences and draw them into a discussion as ethical actors themselves."[16] Alison Landsberg likewise hypothesizes that immersive experiences available in the "transferential spaces" comprising the museum yield what she calls "prosthetic memories," embodied experiences of others' suffering capable of becoming part of a personal memory archive and "informing not only one's subjectivity, but one's relationship to the present and future tenses."[17]

Among its several overlapping objectives, our project's methodology is intended to contribute empirical evidence to what has heretofore been largely confined to a theoretical debate in order to open up consideration of the *specific* ways in which technology can or cannot play an affirmative role in connecting us with often distant and unknown others. To that end, we plan to develop a digital storyworld, or "virtual IRS," an environment informed by a diverse set of experiences acquired through our use of a "participatory design" strategy adapted from computer engineering protocols. Participatory design refers to the practice of integrating users into the design process itself and thus viewing them less as the objects or consumers of technology and more as active collaborators, helping to determine the nature and scope of technological innovation. According to Ole Sejer Iversen, Kim Halskov, and Tuck W. Leong, participatory design "empowers stakeholders and allows them to feel connected to the design process."[18] By inviting participants to immerse themselves experientially in a storyworld importantly of their own making, we intend to answer the following questions: (1) Can immersive technology, carefully designed and implemented, produce a nuanced encounter that improves on static exhibits when it comes to intensifying museumgoers' empathic engagements with experiences of atrocity? (2) What can we expect in terms of the strength and retention of these empathic responses, with specific concern for their capacity to influence subsequent education and social action in a manner that encourages active and sustained engagement with decolonizing practices?

ACTUAL AND VIRTUAL: THE EMBODYING EMPATHY PROTOTYPE

Reframing discussion of these important and long-standing questions, this chapter introduces the Embodying Empathy prototype, a digital installation in which participants can explore particular experiences of Canada's IRS survivors. Our prototype draws on recent developments in augmented reality (AR) and virtual reality (VR) in order to provide a rich, flexible, and fully interactive environment conducive to users' engagement with the agents, events, and experiences represented. AR and VR are terms denoting points on what Paul Milgram and Fumio Kishino identified nearly twenty years ago as a "virtuality continuum,"[19] with actual reality and complete virtuality lying at each of its extremes. AR offers perspectives on the real world enhanced or supplemented by computer-generated sensory input (sounds, images, textures, and so on), while VR consists of virtual (i.e., computer-generated) landscapes into which real-world agents, objects, and activities can be inserted.

Both AR and VR technologies provide opportunities for new forms of interaction with, and (ideally) understanding of, the real world.[20] Their implications for museums are clear. As Matthias Krauss and Manfred Bogen have argued, AR is particularly relevant to the curatorial work being undertaken by museums "since a virtual augmentation substitutes for breakable or dangerous elements. In addition, since virtual augmentations are not strictly bound to physical laws, they may expose or exaggerate aspects that could otherwise not be seen and understood."[21] At the National Museum of Nature and Science in Tokyo, for example, information sent to a visitor's cell phone can provide an AR rendering of a dinosaur, overlaying in real time the actual fossilized remains of the animal with (virtual) muscular tissue, viscera, and skin as the phone's camera travels the length of the fossil's frame. Similarly, innovative uses of AR can be found at the Bilbao Guggenheim, the Allard Pierson Museum in Amsterdam, and the Deutsches Museum in Munich.[22] According to Krauss and Bogen, and their view seems to be widely shared among the curatorial community, "Augmented Reality seems to be the next great thing for museums."[23]

To ensure that our storyworld conforms to Tri-Council guidelines concerning research involving Aboriginal peoples, as well as OCAP (ownership, control, access, and possession) principles as sanctioned by the First Nations Information Governance Committee of the Assembly of First Nations, Indigenous and community involvement has been cultivated from the beginning of our project.[24] When completed, our prototype exhibit will be indebted to our direct experiences of related installations but more profoundly to our extensive and ongoing consultations with survivors, intergenerational survivors, elders, and Indigenous representatives, as well as curators, technical directors, and other staff at a number of leading organizations devoted to the representation of Canada's IRS history and legacy, including our partners the National Research Centre for Truth and Reconciliation (NRC), the Legacy of Hope Foundation (LHF), and the Shingwauk Residential School Centre. We are fortunate in that the NRC will be permanently hosted at the University of Manitoba following the successful submission of a bid to do so in 2012 and the signing of an agreement with the Truth and Reconciliation Commission that took place in June 2013.

Our design process itself has been configured to respond to the representational and decolonizing demands of Indigenous knowledge transmission.[25] In order to facilitate straightforward adoption of and integration with existing and future projects by our partners and other individuals and institutions, our design aims include simplicity, modularity, and scalability across media platforms, so that versions of our storyworld prototype can be deployed in a variety of spaces, including museums, galleries, and challenging rural and urban environments, either as structured installations or as free-standing, self-contained environments (e.g., using wearable technology to layer a virtual IRS environment over an existing space or ruin). The fallibility of our "participatory design" strategy,[26] which revolves around trial-and-error innovation through regular stakeholder consultations that draw on Indigenous methodologies such as the sharing circle,[27] means that we cannot know in advance what our precise software and hardware requirements will be; they will be arrived at dialogically to best suit end-user needs. We envision three kinds of primary end users: (1) IRS survivors, whose knowledge will shape the virtual IRS world, as well as commemorative and educational agencies that have as their mission making this history accessible to all Canadians—our goal is not to elicit testimony of residential school experiences but to gain feedback on the technologies and representations used; (2) Indigenous elders, considered end users of our project because of their central role as preservers and sharers of Indigenous knowledge; and (3) intergenerational survivors and naive users (those with no direct connection to and little knowledge of residential schools), who potentially have the most to learn about the IRS experience from the virtual world.

The design of our IRS storyworld will enable us to access the effects of immersive technologies[28] on a wide range of users' empathic responses, where empathy is provisionally operationalized in three ways: (1) within the storyworld, as an "empathy score" calculated from two objective parameters, amplitude and duration (i.e., the proximity between a user and agents and objects in the virtual world and the length of time that a user spends with each object, person, and task);[29] (2) via survey-based self-assessments and interviews guided by our working definition of empathy as "our ability to access the life of the mind of others in their bodily and behavioral expression; an ability that moreover can improve with familiarity, learning, and salience";[30] and (3) through open-ended qualitative interviews with participants that probe the variety and complexity of engagement with the virtual IRS and the range of experiences represented therein. In particular, these interviews will interrogate the ways in which participants engage in making meanings within the virtual world, examining the extent to which any empathy felt can be distinguished from the easy and vicarious identification with the suffering of others. To this extent, immersion in the virtual IRS should ideally enter the participant into a relationship with knowledge that reflects what Angela Failler and Roger Simon refer to in this volume as "learning from" rather than "learning about" residential schools (indeed, given the temporal flexibility of the storyworld and its capacity for personalizing in-world experiences, it might be possible to "learn along with" virtual agents). Through the analysis of experiencers' engagements with Embodying Empathy, we will be able to evaluate the potential of digital technologies to help forge empathic and ethically engaged communities from those who witness, interact with, and attempt to come to terms with museum-quality representations of suffering.

TECHNICAL CHALLENGES

Historically, one of the key technical challenges for immersive environments has been the transparency of the user interface, its effective invisibility and intuitiveness, allowing "the user to concentrate during his work on *what* he wants to do and not on *how* to do it [and] ... not interfering with the learning procedure [and guiding] the user through it by the use of proper metaphors and successful mapping to the real world, e.g., by providing him with the appropriate icons, correct labeling, exact phrasing, constructive feedback etc."[31] As we currently envision it, following our preliminary consultations with stakeholders, our prototype will be built within an open-source virtual environment.[32] All decisions concerning content and design, such as those related to perspective, location, and whether the school should be entered by a single character or selected characters (e.g., child, health or government inspector, or relative), will be made through our ongoing participatory design process, including sharing circles and interviews. However, there are several technologies that we foresee as being useful for ensuring an immersive experience. For example, the simulation might be run on a see-through display using a customized interface designed for maximum transparency. We envision wearable technology capable of mid-air and micro gestures (e.g., reaching out a hand to open a door or proffer an object), enabling hands-free navigation of the virtual terrain in order to minimize the intrusiveness of technology into the user's experience. The experience would thus be akin to a site visit but with the added flexibility provided by non-traditional movements (e.g., between times and places). Input devices and environment could work together to produce a highly dynamic and interactive landscape wherein users can explore a wide variety of exhibits and leave digital traces on these displays, adding their own particular responses to the layers stored by the program for others to experience, simultaneously as well as later. These combined traces, in addition to providing an uncommonly rich user experience, will potentially yield valuable information on how exhibits are experienced and understood.

Based on our initial consultations, we expect the storyworld to represent a broad cross-section of the experiences of Canadian Aboriginal children who attended Indian residential schools in the early twentieth century, as developed following a comprehensive inventory of contemporary and historical testimonies. Our program's user might choose, for example, to explore the school from the perspective of a child on her or his first day there, and in this way the user can experience uncertainty and confusion as nuns speak in an unfamiliar language or as children are physically punished or psychologically abused for speaking an Indigenous language. Users witnessing these experiences might choose to leave behind a message on a classroom slate for other users to see,[33] creating looping effects digitally transforming and enhancing the displays and optimally, depending on the uses to which subsequently generated information is put, serving to narrow the (inevitable) gap separating a world historical event, an actor, or a trauma from its secondary observer. The virtual IRS also provides an interface through which users can interact with Truth and Reconciliation Commission testimony and archives, for example by clicking on a tape recorder that then links to a survivor's spoken testimony or coming across IRS plans and documents within a staff member's office, and each "bundled" experience might then be separately archived within a visitor's virtual "basket" or "bookbag." Although in a space such as a museum our installation will require proprietary input devices and displays, the core storyworld is intended to be portable across venues and platforms: we will host a web-based version on our project server, and future instantiations may be accessed through inexpensive, widely available mobile devices equipped with the Embodying Empathy build or app, to be designed in house.

Our aim is to employ our participatory design strategy to develop a virtual world that is more than a simulation and less than a game, that offers a user interface that is maximally transparent, and that provides something like Rita Raley's "composed experience," a structured but flexible environment conducive to what Raley sees as "an interpretive gap between instruction and [action]. That gap is a sign of ambivalence, the uncertainty of meaning[,] and thus [it is] open to improvisation and experimentation."[34] The composed spaces of Embodying Empathy, we hypothesize, can serve as an effective venue of transmission of the difficult knowledge[35] that is one legacy of the Canadian IRS system. If this is the case, then what we are calling "proximal embodiment" might help to promote a complex, nuanced, and enduring awareness of (as well as an identification with) Aboriginal suffering, one that operates simultaneously on critical, emotional, historical, and ethical levels.

NEW TECHNOLOGIES IN THE CMHR

The Canadian Museum for Human Rights is intended to be a nontraditional "ideas museum" that introduces multiple narratives about human rights through its exhibits rather than simply offering a collection of artifacts framed by a linear history. In this manner, the museum seeks to be an "interactive" space within which visitors must engage with and interpret its displays. This goal will be accomplished, in part, through the museum's use of multimedia and digital technologies. As the *Report to the Minister of Canadian Heritage on the Canadian Museum for Human Rights* (2008) attests, "interactive exhibits may include personal audio recording tracks and devices (e.g., downloadable for iPods, cellular phones, etc.)

that allow the visitors to select their own tour of the museum at their own pacing, and in their preferred language. Web-based animations, which are capable of presenting pictorial and textual information in dynamic ways, can also be used on site or online with visitors who prefer more 'hands on' interactions. Video conferencing is another affordable means to attract both specialized and general audiences offsite."[36] By making use of these and other technologies, the CMHR hopes to encourage new forms of visitor engagement with suffering as well as moral and political achievements that mark crucial steps toward overcoming human rights violations. Additionally, the museum is still struggling to manage controversy surrounding which cases to include in its exhibitions as well as the amount of space that it can devote to each case. Augmented and virtual realities can assist in resolving such issues by creating "hybrid" spaces that extend physical space through computer-based manipulation.[37]

Thus far, however, it is unclear to what extent the CMHR will embrace new technologies and specifically how such technologies will be used to communicate human rights violations against Indigenous peoples in Canada, since the museum promises to be a dynamic space. We do know, however, that the museum features several displays related to the harms of settler colonialism in Canada. In particular, the treatment of residential schools is largely contained in two sections: Breaking the Silence, which explores the role of secrecy and denial in atrocity events, and Canadian Journeys, which covers Canada's history as both a defender of human rights and a perpetrator of human rights abuses. In Breaking the Silence, museum visitors interact with a digitized story table designed to educate them about the historical context of, specific violations within, denials and distortions of, and role of human rights language in promoting redress for residential school abuses. In the Canadian Journeys exhibit, residential schools are represented within a "niche" eight feet by eight feet, and connections are drawn between the IRS system, the "'60s Scoop," and contemporary child welfare practices. The main wall features a picture of residential school students sitting in their desks, staring out at museum visitors as they sit at one of two desks on which a video related to life within the schools is projected.

In this compact space, the desks offer the most immersive and emotive experience of residential schooling. It is problematic, however, that the experience is centred on the classroom, since it frames the residential school experience in terms of the pedagogical moment, even though the educational rigour of these schools was minimal. Indeed, students in residential schools spent only a small portion of their day in pursuit of academic learning, with as much, if not more, time committed to vocational and religious training.[38] But the small space allotted to the residential school display has forced its designers to make decisions that ultimately narrow the representation of these schools. It is in such instances that the "hybrid space" created by emergent digital technologies can make its greatest contribution to museum curation, since these technologies inherently allow for multiple and therefore less reductive representations of atrocity when space is at a premium.[39] There is thus the potential for emergent digital technologies to allow us to relate complex, "multivocal," and "community-based" stories that move beyond the epistemic violence of attempts to grapple with settler-Indigenous histories that reduce them to a single, oversimplified, settler-defined narrative.[40] The emphasis here on a "multivocal" and "community-based" approach is drawn from the work of Ruth Phillips, who uses Stephen Greenblatt's terminology to describe the spectrum of ways in which museums collaborate with Indigenous peoples in producing exhibits. The multivocal exhibit opens up multiple voices and perspectives, allowing no authoritative voice to determine content. Such exhibits, however, can be difficult for museumgoers to understand and interpret. The community-based exhibit, in contrast, places the curator as a resource for the community, enlisted to communicate their experiences and perspectives. Many contemporary efforts to decolonize museums, including the efforts of CMHR curators, combine these approaches. However, Embodying Empathy can enhance multivocal and community-based moments in its virtual storyworld as it works to fashion a space in which multiple experiences of residential schools might be represented while simultaneously placing authority over content firmly in the hands of primary end users: the community of survivors, intergenerational survivors, and elders.

The multivocal ambitions of the Canadian Museum for Human Rights are restricted by the museum's desire to have all explanatory text pitched at a Grade 9 reading level. No matter the quality of writing produced by museum staff, it remains exceedingly difficult to communicate the complexity of the residential school experience through overly simplified expositions. Problems associated with the CMHR's adherence to this language requirement erupted in a national controversy during the summer of 2013 when the public, and particularly Aboriginal stakeholders, became aware of the museum's decision not to use the title Settler-Colonial Genocide for an exhibit.[41] It finally emerged that the museum deemed this terminology unsuitable for less mature readers. In contrast, an immersive storyworld display that is not text dependent can communicate multiple experiences of, and perspectives on, residential schools. One can enter such a storyworld from different subject positions—student, relative, friend—and interact with this world and its characters from these standpoints. As well, the increased freedom of movement available to the experiencer means that she or he can be exposed to diverse experiences of the same world. From the student perspective, for example, a first experience might be that of being brought to a chair only to see hair clippings fall from one's head. But such moments of discipline and cultural erasure do not have to be reductively presented; they can also be accompanied by exposure to moments of beauty or pleasure—a look out a window at a stormy Manitoba sky, say, or a meaningful glance from a fellow student. An immersive storyworld creates opportunities for multivalent interactions organized around the experience of atrocity-as-lived.

In exactly this manner, the unevenness of colonialism might also be better conveyed through digitally mediated representations.[42] Residential schools were designed with the goal of eliminating Indigenous identities so that Aboriginal people would no longer be perceived as obstacles to land dispossession and the project of Canadian nation building. But this overarching policy found different expressions at particular schools.[43] Thus, all Indigenous persons, whether First Nations, Inuit, or Métis, did not live their boarding school days in the same ways. The fluid and adaptive potentials of emergent digital technologies hold promise for allowing region- and school-specific representations of residential schools rather than simply a replication of the colonial tendency to treat Indigenous groups as parts of an undifferentiated Aboriginal mass.

It is important to acknowledge, however, that efforts to represent the complexity of residential school history cannot simply subscribe to a liberal pluralism assuming that all voices deserve equal space in the discussion. Given the historical privileging of settler colonial voices on Canadian history, a project such as Embodying Empathy must be community based in the sense that Phillips discusses: the investigators are conduits for the community, facilitating delivery of the narratives and counternarratives that Indigenous stakeholders believe are most important for communicating their experiences of residential schooling. In this manner, consideration must be given to exactly how these technologies might be made to mesh with OCAP principles and more generally to make Embodying Empathy a space in which Indigenous peoples can assert control over how they are represented.[44] The hitherto unfortunate history of museological representations of Indigenous lives and cultures demands that one must approach such efforts with great humility and caution.[45] But the pliability and portability of digital technologies, coupled with our participatory design methodology, will, we trust, allow us to ensure that these principles are fundamental to the design and implementation of the digital storyworld and to change course when errors are made. As we have noted above, conforming to OCAP principles requires, among other things, early and continuous consultation with Aboriginal stakeholders. These consultations will help to ensure that the storyworld will meet the needs of Indigenous users in a variety of contexts, and offer an effective means of training and technology transfer capable of equipping survivor organizations and other interested parties with adaptable, amendable, and updatable versions of the IRS experience.

CONCLUSION

There are thus grounds for feeling some cautious optimism about the potential of emergent technologies to represent atrocities such as Canada's history of Indian residential schools both within and outside museum spaces. However, there are also several limitations and causes for concern that must be kept in mind when undertaking a project such as Embodying Empathy. The first is ensuring that the storyworld is immersive without being game-like, and therefore capable of providing more than a superficial and fleeting engagement with Canada's past. Most games operate by offering a series of increasing player rewards, triggering experiences of pleasure and satisfaction as the player moves through the game world. To avoid becoming game-like, the storyworld cannot be rewards based, since designing it around such a "pleasure principle" would lead to a number of pressing ethical issues related to the message that one should properly convey in any representation of residential school harms. But this raises a second challenge, since without such a reward structure how is one to draw in and immerse storyworld participants? Under such circumstances, filmic and literary modes of immersion might need to stand in for those more typical of virtual worlds—the stories comprising the storyworld must be sufficiently compelling and the world appropriately realized for an experiencer to get "lost" within its virtual horizons.

Such a storyworld, no matter how perfectly realized and multivocal, would obviously provide only a partial telling of any residential school tale, of woe or otherwise. And some of this incompleteness must be an imperative of our design. This is because, for the sake of not traumatizing participants, or indeed for fear of retraumatizing any survivors who might happen to visit the storyworld, some of the most powerfully destructive aspects of residential schools must not be digitally recreated. We mean here specifically the extreme physical and sexual violence that was rife within these institutions. However, there is still value in representing the culturally destructive *purpose* of Indian residential schools as well as the ways in which they sought to disorient and forcibly transform the lives and identities of Indigenous children. The Canadian public, though still woefully underinformed about residential schooling, has at least a vague knowledge of the abuses that occurred in the schools. These are the experiences most frequently discussed in newspapers and on radio and TV. They also formed the basis of the class action lawsuits and government and church apologies that began to appear in the 1990s. Given this baseline awareness of IRS violence, there is even more value in representing the destructive aspects of these schools that are often overshadowed by accounts of severe sexual and physical abuse.

Only a handful of residential schools remain standing to serve as venues of knowledge transmission about this critical period of Canadian history. With so few sites of consciousness available, and a dwindling number of survivors remaining to give testimony, new virtual technologies appear to hold promise for making Aboriginal peoples and settler Canadians more aware of the history of residential schools and their continuing impacts on our shared world. However, without further investigation of the efficacy and representational adequacy of such vehicles, commemorative and educational institutions such as museums are in danger of being seduced by technology without establishing clear empirical grounds to justify the expense of implementing virtual technologies and without having complete knowledge of the potential limitations of immersive and empathy-fostering representations of the past.

NOTES

1   The term designates the emergence of dynamic interactive technologies well suited to collaboration and thus to the composition of new forms of social solidarity.

2   See Lynda Kelly, "How Web 2.0 Is Changing the Nature of Museum Work," *Curator: The Museum Journal* 53, 4 (2010): 405–10; and Amelia Wong, "Ethical Issues of Social Media in Museums: A Case Study," *Museum Management and Curatorship* 26, 2 (2011): 97–112.

3   Susie Linfield, *The Cruel Radiance: Photography and Political Violence* (Chicago: University of Chicago Press, 2010). See also Allison Landsberg, *Prosthetic Memory: The Transformation of American Remembrance in the Age of Mass Culture* (New York: Columbia University Press, 2004); Alison Landsberg, "Memory, Empathy, and the Politics of Identification," *International Journal of Politics, Culture, and Society* 22 (2009): 221–29; and Tzvetan Todorov, "The Abuses of Memory," *Common Knowledge* 5 (1996): 6–26.

4   Linfield, *Cruel Radiance*, xv.

5   R.G. Collingwood, *The Idea of History* (Oxford: Oxford University Press, 1994).

6   See E. Ann Kaplan, *Trauma Culture: The Politics of Terror and Loss in Media and Literature* (New Brunswick, NJ: Rutgers University Press, 2005).

7   Sven Lindqvist, *Exterminate All the Brutes* (New York: New Press, 1996), 172.

8   For recent work on this nexus of concerns, see C. Greig Crysler, "Violence and Empathy: National Museums and the Spectacle of Society," *Traditional Dwellings and Settlements Review* 17, 2 (2006): 19–38; Joseph Nevins, "The Abuse of Memorialized Space and the Redefinition of Ground Zero," *Journal of Human Rights* 4 (2005): 267 82; and Julie Anne Taylor, "Teaching African American History through Museum Theatre," *The Councilor: The Journal of the Illinois Council for the Social Studies* 72, 2 (2011): 1–11.

9   Stanley Milgram, *Obedience to Authority: An Experimental View* (New York: HarperCollins, 1974). See also Herbert Kelman and Lee Hamilton, *Crimes of Obedience* (New Haven, CT: Yale University Press, 1989); James Waller, *Becoming Evil: How Ordinary People Commit Genocide and Mass Killing*, 2nd ed. (Oxford: Oxford University Press, 2007); and C. Haney, W.C. Banks, and P.G. Zimbardo, "Interpersonal Dynamics in a Simulated Prison," *International Journal of Criminology and Penology* 1 (1973): 69–97.

10 Zygmunt Bauman, *Modernity and the Holocaust* (Cambridge, UK: Polity, 1989). See also Hannah Arendt, *Eichmann in Jerusalem: A Report on the Banality of Evil* (New York: Viking, 1963).

11 See also Edwin Black, *IBM and the Holocaust: The Strategic Alliance between Nazi Germany and America's Most Powerful Corporation* (New York: Crown Publishers, 2001); Christopher Browning, *The Path to Genocide: Essays on Launching the Final Solution* (Cambridge, UK: Cambridge University Press, 1992); Stewart Clegg, "Bureaucracy, the Holocaust, and Techniques of Power at Work," *International Review of Management Studies* 20, 4 (2009): 326–47; and Raul Hilberg, *The Destruction of the European Jews* (Teaneck, NJ: Holmes and Meier, 1985).

12 Cass Sunstein, "Some Effects of Moral Indignation on Law," *Vermont Law Review* 33, 3 (2009): 408. For more on "empathy fatigue," see Carolyn Dean, "Empathy, Pornography, and Suffering," *Differences: A Journal of Feminist Cultural Studies* 14, 1 (2003): 88–124; Carolyn Dean, *The Fragility of Empathy after the Holocaust* (Ithaca, NY: Cornell University Press, 2004); Dominic LaCapra, *History and Its Limits: Human, Animal, Violence* (Ithaca, NY: Cornell University Press, 2009); and Sophie Oliver, "Simulating the Ethical Community: Interactive Game Media and Engaging Human Rights Claims," *Culture, Theory, and Critique* 51, 1 (2010): 93–108.

13   Mirjana Bajovic, "Violent Video Game Playing, Moral Reasoning, and Attitudes towards Violence in Adolescents: Is There a Connection?" (PhD diss., Brock University, 2012).

14   Oliver, "Simulating the Ethical Community," 106.

15   Gary Young and Monica Whitty, "Games without Frontiers: On the Moral and Psychological Implications of Violating Taboos within Multi-Player Virtual Spaces," *Computers in Human Behavior* 26, 6 (2010): 1228–36.

16   Aylish Wood, "Recursive Space: Play and Creating Space," *Games and Culture* 7 (2012): 98.

17   Landsberg, *Prosthetic Memory,* 66.

18   Ole Sejer Iversen, Kim Halskov, and Tuck W. Leong, "Values-Led Participatory Design," *CoDesign: International Journal of CoCreation in Design and the Arts* 8, 2–3 (2012): 87–103.

19   Paul Milgram and Fumio Kishino, "Taxonomy of Mixed Reality Visual Displays," *IEICE Transactions on Information and Systems* E77-D12 (1994): 1321.

20   See Lev Manovich, "The Poetics of Augmented Space," *Visual Communication* 5, 2 (2006): 219–40; and Awoniyi Stephen, "Intrinsic Information in the Making of Public Space: A Case Example of the Museum Space," *Space and Culture* 6, 3 (2003): 309–29.

21   Matthias Krauss and Manfred Bogen, "Conveying Cultural Heritage and Legacy with Innovative AR-Based Solutions," in *Museums and the Web 2010: Proceedings,* ed. J. Trant and D. Bearman (Toronto: Archives and Museum Informatics, 2010), n. pag.

22   Ibid. See also an account of the virtual site museum in K. Young-Seok, T. Kesavadas, and S.M. Paley, "The Virtual Site Museum: A Multi-Purpose, Authoritative, and Functional Virtual Heritage Resource," *Presence: Teleoperators and Virtual Environments* 15, 3 (2006): 245–61. As well, see a description of the augurscope in H. Schnädelbach et al., "The Augurscope: Redefining Its Design," *Presence: Teleoperators and Virtual Environments* 15, 3 (2006): 278–93.

23   Krauss and Bogen, "Conveying Cultural Heritage," n. pag.

24   See First Nations Centre, *OCAP: Ownership, Control, Access, and Possession,* sanctioned by the First Nations Information Governance Committee, Assembly of First Nations (Ottawa: National Aboriginal Health Organization, 2007). See also Chapter 9 of the second edition of the *Tri-Council Policy Statement: Ethical Conduct for Research Involving Humans* (Ottawa: Government of Canada, 2014).

25   Discussion of the decolonization of museums can be found in the work of scholars such as Ruth Phillips and Amy Lonetree. See Ruth Phillips, *Museum Pieces: Towards the Indigenization of Canadian Museums* (Montreal: McGill-Queen's University Press, 2011); and Amy Lonetree, *Decolonizing Museums: Representing Native America in National and Tribal Museums* (Chapel Hill: University of North Carolina Press, 2014). However, this project requires not only a concern for decolonizing the space of the museum but also a consideration of the need to decolonize our methodologies. For discussion of decolonizing methodologies, see Linda Tuhiwai Smith, *Decolonizing Methodologies: Research and Indigenous Peoples,* 2nd ed. (London: Zed Books, 2012); and Margaret Kovach, *Indigenous Methodologies: Characteristics, Conversations, and Contexts* (Toronto: University of Toronto Press, 2009). Finally, given that our team is composed of both settler and Indigenous scholars, those of us from the settler community have sought to unsettle our assumptions and expectations about the research process. See Paulette Regan, *Unsettling the Settler Within: Indian Residential Schools, Truth Telling, and Reconciliation in Canada* (Vancouver: UBC Press, 2011).

26   See Susanne Bødker and Ole Sejer Iversen, "Staging a Professional Participatory Design Practice: Moving beyond the Initial Fascination of User Involvement," in *Proceedings of*

the Second Nordic Conference on Human-Computer Interaction (New York: ACM Press, 2001), 11–18; Judith Gregory, "Scandinavian Approaches to Participatory Design," *International Journal of Engineering Education* 19, 1 (2003): 62–74; Finn Kensing and Jeanette Blomberg, "Participatory Design: Issues and Concerns," *Computer Supported Cooperative Work* 7 (1998): 167–85; Finn Kensing, Jesper Simonson, and Keld Bødker, "MUST: A Method for Participatory Design," in *Proceedings of the Fourth Biennial Conference on Participatory Design*, ed. J. Blomberg, F. Kensing, and E. Dykstra-Erickson(Palo Alto, CA: Computer Professionals for Social Responsibility, 1996), 129–40; and Elizabeth B.N. Sanders, "From User-Centred to Participatory Design Approaches," in *Design and Social Sciences*, ed. J. Frascera (London: Taylor and Francis Books, 2002), 1–8.

27 Kovach, *Indigenous Methodologies;* Lynn F. Lavallée, "Practical Application of an Indigenous Research Framework and Two Qualitative Indigenous Research Methods: Sharing Circles and Anishnaabe Symbol-Based Reflection," *International Journal of Qualitative Methods* 8, 1 (2009): 21–40.

28 Where immersion is typically described in terms of a movement between perceptual spaces, "passing through the surface of the image or picture to enter the very space depicted on the surface." M. Lister et al., *New Media: A Critical Introduction* (London: Routledge, 2008), 115.

29 See Marc Cavazza et al., "Intelligent Virtual Environments for Virtual Reality Art," *Computers and Graphics* 29 (2005): 852–61.

30 Dan Zahavi, "Simulation, Projection, and Empathy," *Consciousness and Cognition* 17 (2008): 522.

31 Athanasis Karoulis and Andreas Pombortsis, "Heuristic Evaluation of Web-Based ODL Programs," in *Usability Evaluation of Online Learning Programs*, ed. Claude Ghaoui (Hershey, PA: Information Science Publishing, 2003), 91.

32 Researchers and artists working with AbTeC, or Aboriginal Territories in Cyberspace, have used Second Life and other gaming platforms as vehicles for exploring questions of identity and representation (among others) within Native and non-Native communities alike. See also Jason Lewis and Skawennati Tricia Fragnito, "Aboriginal Territories in Cyberspace," *Cultural Survival* 29, 2 (2005): 29–31.

33 Such messages and other traces would need to be regularly moderated to guard against insensitive and hurtful commentary.

34 Rita Raley, "Walk This Way: Mobile Narrative as Composed Experience," in *Beyond the Screen: Transformations of Literary Structures, Interfaces, and Genres*, ed. J. Schäfer and P. Gendolla (Bielefeld: Transcript Verlag, 2010), 313–14.

35 See Erica Lehrer, Cynthia E. Milton, and Monica E. Patterson, eds., *Curating Difficult Knowledge: Violent Pasts in Public Places* (Basingstoke, UK: Palgrave Macmillan, 2011).

36 Canada, Department of Canadian Heritage, *Report to the Minister of Canadian Heritage on the Canadian Museum for Human Rights* (Ottawa: Department of Canadian Heritage, 1998), Catalogue No. CH4-133/2008E-PDF, 30.

37 See Luigina Ciolfi and Liam Bannon, "Designing Hybrid Places: Merging Interaction Design, Ubiquitous Technologies, and Geographies of the Museum Space," *CoDesign: International Journal of CoCreation in Design and the Arts* 3, 3 (2007): 159–80; Adriana de Souza e Silva, "From Cyber to Hybrid: Mobile Technologies as Interfaces of Hybrid Spaces," *Space and Culture* 9, 3 (2006): 261–78; and Adriana de Souza e Silva and Girlie Delacruz, "Hybrid Reality Games Reframed: Potential Uses in Educational Contexts," *Games and Culture* 1, 3 (2006): 231–51.

38   See J.R. Miller, *Shingwauk's Vision: A History of Native Residential Schools* (Toronto: University of Toronto Press, 1996); and Truth and Reconciliation Commission, *They Came for the Children: Canada, Aboriginal Peoples, and Residential Schools* (Winnipeg: Truth and Reconciliation Commission of Canada, 2012).

39   See Ciolfi and Bannon, "Designing Hybrid Places"; de Souza e Silva, "From Cyber to Hybrid"; and de Souza e Silva and Delacruz, "Hybrid Reality Games Reframed."

40   See Ruth Phillips, "Community Collaboration in Exhibitions: Toward a Dialogic Paradigm," in *Museums and Source Communities: A Routledge Reader,* ed. L. Peers and A.K. Brown (London: Routledge, 2005), 155–70. As well, see Stephen Greenblatt, "Resonance and Wonder," in *Exhibiting Cultures: The Poetics and Politics of Museum Display,* ed. Ivan Karp and Steven Lavine (Washington, DC: Smithsonian Institution Press, 1991), 45–56. See also Amy Lonetree, ed., *The National Museum of the American Indian: Critical Conversations* (Lincoln: University of Nebraska Press, 2008); and Lonetree, *Decolonizing Museums.* On the notion of epistemic violence, see Gayatri Chakravorty Spivak, "Can the Subaltern Speak?," in *Marxism and the Interpretation of Culture,* ed. Cary Nelson and Lawrence Grossberg (London: Macmillan, 1988), 271–313.

41   Arguments related to the application of this term can be found in Andrew Woolford, Jeff Benvenuto, and Alexander Laban Hinton, eds., *Colonial Genocide in Indigenous North America* (Durham, NC: Duke University Press, 2014).

42   Examples of efforts to deal with the "unevenness of colonialism" can be found in the literature on colonial genocide. Such conceptualizations of colonial genocide have been particularly advanced through the work of Australian scholars. See, for example, Tony Barta, "Relations of Genocide: Land and Lives in the Colonization of Australia," in *Genocide and the Modern Age: Etiology and Case Studies of Mass Death,* ed. I. Wallimann and M.N. Dobkowski (Syracuse, NY: Syracuse University Press, 1987), 237–52; Ann Curthoys and John Docker, "Genocide: Definitions, Questions, Settler-Colonies," *Aboriginal History* 25 (2001): 1–15; A. Dirk Moses, "An Antipodean Genocide? The Origins of the Genocidal Moment in the Colonization of Australia," *Journal of Genocide Research* 2, 1 (2000): 89–106; A. Dirk Moses, "Genocide and Settler Society in Australian History," in *Genocide and Settler Society: Frontier Violence and Stolen Indigenous Children in Australian History,* ed. A. Dirk Moses (New York: Berghahn Books, 2004), 4–48; A. Dirk Moses, "Empire, Colony, Genocide: Keywords and the Philosophy of History," in *Empire, Colony, and Genocide: Conquest, Occupation, and Subaltern Resistance in World History,* ed. A. Dirk Moses (New York: Berghahn Books, 2008), 3–54; and Alison Palmer, *Colonial Genocide* (Adelaide: Crawford House, 2000).

43   This point has been more widely acknowledged in the context of American Indigenous boarding schools. See, for example, Brenda J. Child, *Boarding School Seasons: American Indian Families, 1900–1940* (Lincoln: University of Nebraska Press, 1998); Clyde Ellis, *To Change Them Forever: Indian Education at Rainy Mountain Boarding School, 1893–1920* (Norman: University of Oklahoma Press, 1996); K. Tsianna Lomawaima, *They Called It Prairie Light: The Story of Chilocco Indian School* (Lincoln: University of Nebraska Press, 1994); Scott Riney, *The Rapid City Indian School 1898–1933* (Norman: University of Oklahoma Press, 1999); and Robert A. Trennert, *The Phoenix Indian School: Forced Assimilation in Arizona, 1891–1935* (Norman: University of Oklahoma Press, 1988). For a call for more such work to be done in Canada, see James Miller and Edmund Danziger Jr., "'In the Care of Strangers': Walpole Island First Nation's Experiences with Residential Schools after the First World War," *Ontario History* 92, 2 (2000): 71–88.

44   On the potential for new technologies to enable Indigenous people's control of their representations, see Lewis and Fragnito, "Aboriginal Territories in Cyberspace."

45   See Phillips, *Museum Pieces.*

CURATORIAL
CHALLENGES

CURATORIAL PRACTICE AND LEARNING FROM DIFFICULT KNOWLEDGE

CHAPTER 8

*Angela Failler and Roger I. Simon**

There is still much debate over what constitutes a curatorial practice that does not reiterate the idea of the museum as an institution with privileged authority to prescribe and proscribe the content and significance of people's cultural heritage. Two interrelated questions are key to this consideration. First, how can exhibitions enact a pedagogy or structure dynamics of teaching and learning in a way that does not presume to inform "uninformed" visitors about the museum's expertise or moralize about how they should think and feel? Second, how might exhibitions enhance the interweaving of thought, feeling, and judgment regarding issues that matter to people without determining in advance the desired substance of visitor responses? Although the provision of information is an important function of any museum, it is not the only significant pedagogy at work in its interactions with museumgoers. Curatorial staff must also devise frameworks that assemble people so that, through interactions with exhibits and each other, they deepen their awareness of their situations in the world and elaborate not only their own viewpoints or those of the museum but also a collective vision of a more just society.

---

*I, Angela Failler, have developed this chapter from a proposed abstract, recent conference papers, and other writings by Roger I. Simon, who was professor emeritus at the Ontario Institute for Studies in Education at the University of Toronto. Roger died on 17 September 2012 before he could carry out a draft of the chapter himself. He entrusted these materials to me with the hope that his ideas would yet contribute to meaningful conversation on the prospect of a human rights museum. Undoubtedly, they already do. Roger was an eminent scholar whose provocative inquiries into ethics, pedagogy, remembrance, and social justice have influenced

In order to foster this kind of interaction, museums have begun, in the spirit of "new museology," to resist the stultifying intent to "cancel the distance between the ignorant person and knowledge"[1] and instead encourage visitors and "the public" to act as participants in self-directed meaning making.[2] One strategy toward achieving this goal has been to turn to the gathering and incorporation of personal stories as part of the exhibition *mise-en-scène*.[3] The Canadian Museum for Human Rights, for instance, made story gathering central not only to its pre-inaugural community consultation process but also to its content development and display.[4] This "turn" can be seen most obviously in its Share Your Story niche within the Canadian Journey's gallery, and on the museum's website, which features a collection of first-person narratives and an invitation for online visitors to submit their own stories by uploading audio, video, photographic, and/or written material.[5] The narratives featured here reference histories of human rights abuse and subsequent economic and social marginalization as well as individual triumphs and collective resistance to different forms of subjection. But the curatorial challenge inherent to this turn requires going beyond simply providing a forum for various people to tell their stories. Storytelling has to be framed as an invitation to participate in establishing new relations between words and things as well as between objects and their meanings. That is, such stories need to help sketch possibilities for new configurations between what can be seen, said, and thought about human rights abuses, the human rights movement, and even what is implied by pairing the concepts "human" and "rights" in a world in which to be human is to be connected to the suffering of others.[6]

This chapter raises three issues that curatorial practice must attend to in order to support learning not just *about* but also *from* the stories and histories represented at a human rights museum. First, there is a problematic tendency toward narcissism when visitors use museums as sites of self-affirmation to confirm what they already know, particularly in the

---

educators, curators, artists, and cultural critics alike, those committed to thinking through the difficulties of bearing witness to violent pasts in the present. To be sure, his legacy has touched other contributors to and readers of this book.

The key questions and terms that Roger outlined in his original abstract form the basis of this chapter. The extensions that I have made to flesh out and cohere the discussion reflect my own interpretations of his work, our overlapping research interests, and preliminary conversations that he and I had about the (then) forthcoming Canadian Museum for Human Rights (CMHR). I have completed this chapter from my residence in Winnipeg, which allows me proximity not only to the museum but also to local debates and emergent publics and coun-

face of "difficult knowledge." We encounter such knowledge in moments when narratives or images seem to be disturbingly foreign or inconceivable, bringing us up against the limits of what we are able or willing to understand.[7] What such moments imply for curatorial practice at a human rights museum needs further thought and discussion. Second, given that the narratives and images featured by a human rights museum are likely to provoke intense affective responses as well as inchoate thoughts, we need a better understanding of how curatorial practice can support (without determining) the potential insights generated in and through these experiences. Third, needed is a discussion of curatorial practices that will support analogical thinking in order to foster connections across histories of diverse lives and differing events without reducing these singularities to equivalent forms. In other words, the histories exhibited at a human rights museum must illuminate the present and future as much as they re-present the past while mitigating the tendency to make straightforward comparisons or emblematic interpretations that render specific histories substitutable by or for others. Considering how these concerns might be addressed within a human rights museum will open a critical conversation about curatorial practices at the CMHR and beyond. This is a conversation that the museum deserves, and we too deserve it if we are to expand our understanding of how museums and galleries can contribute to the vitality of Canadian civic life.

Prior to opening, the CMHR garnered significant attention for being embroiled in controversies over the relative status and space that it was expected to accord certain historical events. Well publicized, for example, was the Ukrainian Canadian Congress's challenge (supported by other organizations representing people of Eastern European heritage) to alter the decision to devote a main gallery in the museum to the Holocaust (the Nazi attempt to eradicate European Jews), while a narrative detailing Stalin's policies that resulted in the Holodomor (the mass starvation of

terpublics as they form around this new institution. I have also undertaken this work with the support of the Cultural Studies Research Group at the University of Winnipeg. Together we are considering the challenges faced by the CMHR and its staff in being charged with the task of representing human rights issues. We are centrally concerned with how narratives and images of human violation, suffering, and resilience can be used to foster a better understanding of the conditions necessary for promoting social justice. Roger's advocacy for the role of curatorial practice toward this aim focuses our attention on encounters between museum visitors and exhibitions. This chapter, in particular, theorizes the facilitation of visitor experience through curatorial frameworks as key to the potential for a human rights museum to serve as a productive site of public dialogue, pedagogical engagement, and social transformation.

Ukrainians) was to be placed in a gallery that would jointly display other events of mass violence and systemic discrimination.[8] As interesting as this controversy was to those of us concerned with the interrelation of public history, museums, and memory studies, changing the substance of the conversation about the CMHR is crucial here. We need to shift the expectations and interests that people might have regarding the museum away from sectarian disputes and toward its importance for the civil fabric of our society, including international efforts to secure a more just and peaceful world. Competitive victimization is surely a limited dynamic within which to undertake the crucial work of "remembrance-learning" in Canada.[9] Yet, in order to make this shift, it is also necessary to grasp the current controversies as symptomatic of deeper issues affecting the framework within which the CMHR is predominantly being discussed.

Controversies over the allotment of museum space are grounded in the notion that cultural practices can serve as a means of conferring or gaining social recognition. Hence, when an institution with some perceived status begins to structure these practices, it becomes an arena of contestation over the distribution/redistribution of what counts in the formation of the historical perspective of a society. This is especially true for cultural institutions understood to be state sanctioned, as the CMHR is, by virtue not only of being state funded but also of having official status as a national museum established through amendments made by Parliament to the Museums Act.[10] In such a case, the museum, through its circulation of specific narratives and representations, confirms acceptable forms and images of social activity and individual identity by which social recognition is also thereby conferred.[11] Canadian museums, for instance, operate within a symbolic environment constituted through a history of state "statements" informed by an evolving policy of multiculturalism that has distributed social recognition on the basis of certain stories, images, and performances deemed markers of "cultural difference" or "diversity." Not only does recognition by museums then become a factor in the identification of certain individuals and groups as entitled to rights, protection, and representation, but also it is a way of acknowledging the social worth of specific aspects of a culture and its associated history.[12] Institutional valuation carried out in this manner underscores recognition as a distributed good, a good that presupposes a capacity to measure and/or judge the relative worth of a culture's history for practices of national or transnational memory. On such terms, the museum-based strategy of making visible particular histories and memories is rendered an extension of the state's multicultural logic.[13]

But can this strategy transform the larger, historically formed context in which human rights struggles and abuses take place? That is, how might the CMHR be seen as doing something more than regulating competing claims for space, and what might be the role of curatorial practice in this?

Before exploring this question further, a lexical observation should be made. The new national museum in Winnipeg is not the Canadian Museum *of* Human Rights (a name perhaps presupposing a mandate limited to historiography) but the Canadian Museum *for* Human Rights. In other words, it has been established not only to record and display but also to elaborate, defend, and advocate for the importance of human rights. Setting out the terms through which this mission is to be accomplished, the CMHR has described its approach as "not based on things" but as instituting the concept of an "ideas museum." During a set of public speeches in 2009, the museum's former chief operating officer, Patrick O'Reilly,[14] explained it this way: "Rather than exhibiting artefacts and complementing them with a story, the focus is on telling the story enriched with artefacts."[15] However, to do the work that they do, museums must already be ideas driven. Posing a fundamental difference between starting an exhibition design with an idea or a story as opposed to an artifact is to ignore this reality. More important here is the realization that, despite the economics that have impelled museums toward "edutainment," it is the commitment to an engagement with ideas and an understanding of their complexity and civic importance that must be preserved as the heart of museum work in Canada. And, while dialogue regarding which or *whose* ideas and histories are represented within Canadian museums will inevitably remain a focus, serious discussion is still needed on *how* the presentation of ideas and histories can be enacted and for what purpose.

In this regard, there are several ways in which an ideas museum might function. One conventional notion is that a museum is a public outlet for the ideas of selected experts, ideas informed by their specialized knowledge and training in judgment about what constitutes a significant historical narrative or excellence in aesthetic expression. At such a museum, the purpose of offering ideas is to enact a pedagogical relationship in which curatorial judgments are made so that, through a process of transmission, the distance between the knowledge of experts and the presumed "inexperienced" views of museum visitors is suppressed or at least narrowed. In other words, curation here is designed to compensate for the visitor's "lack" of the museum's endowments. Yet, whether in museums, schools, or popular education, attempts to reduce this distance or lack only reinstate it since the successful transmission of predetermined ideas in this formulation relies on reiterating the authority of experts and the incapacity of museumgoers, or students, to think, judge, or know for themselves.[16]

A variant of this pedagogy is an ideas museum that operates as an authoritative resource bank through which visitors encounter an impressive array of views on a restricted number of predetermined themes. Here curatorial judgments are made to underscore the notion that ideas that matter are often contentious and that it is important to be informed of the existing range of different perspectives on an issue. Patrick O'Reilly illustrates this approach (in the same speech cited above) when he states that "an ideas museum necessitates that we demonstrate multiple perspectives, based on sound research and scholarship by multiple parties, providing visitors with a comprehensive range of perspectives.... Our objective is to foster a better understanding of human rights and to advance that knowledge through a better understanding of others' points of view."[17] However, this approach fails to significantly shift the pedagogical relations mentioned above, for it still presumes that experts will simply inform a relatively uninformed set of museum visitors about a range of perspectives on a given topic or issue. Moreover, it leaves museum staff to confront the considerable challenge of how to provide a substantive narrative or interpretive framework that makes divergent views grounded in radically different epistemologies commensurable.

Besides these two notions of ideas museums, two more proceed from the intent to influence visitors to adopt a mode of engagement in which they stop being "just spectators" (whether of expert knowledge or of stories about the experiences of others) and become agents of social change. Hence, a third notion regarding how an ideas museum might function is rooted in curatorial judgments that attempt to instigate the presentation of ideas as an impetus to action. The supposition here is that something will be felt or understood as a result of visiting a museum that impels people to help make the world a better place in which to live. In other words, the hope is that, by engaging with exhibits and programming, people will come to know what has to be done to address the realities of violation and violence beyond the confines of the museum.[18] The CMHR president and chief executive officer subsequent to O'Reilly, Stuart Murray, made this intention clear in a speech delivered as part of a speaker series at the University of Manitoba in 2011: "We [the CMHR] must become a centre of excellence for learning, teaching and scholarship. But we must also empower our visitors, and provide outlets for their knowledge, and encourage and provoke the kinds of actions that can together topple the barriers that still stand in the way of universal rights."[19] Yet this curatorial pedagogy persists in maintaining a distance between those responsible for curation and museum visitors, this time an assumed opposition between a commitment to the desirability of action and a passivity (or disempowerment) that needs to be undone.

What is shared by the above three museological frameworks is that each remains grounded in a specific "distribution of the sensible" (to borrow another phrase from Rancière), wherein a priori experts possess valuable knowledge (or desire for change) that others do not.[20] A fourth framework, then, as an alternative to the three outlined above, differs in that it is neither rooted in such presumed inequalities nor focused on the selection and effective transmission of predetermined knowledge and insights certified through institutional authority and expertise. The curatorial pedagogies appropriate to this fourth framework suggest that the distance the museumgoer has to cover is not that between her or his ignorance and expert knowledge but that between what one already knows and what one still does not know but has begun to learn.[21] This movement of learning does not emanate from a curatorial cause and effect in which one simply receives or absorbs the knowledge imparted by the museum. Following Rancière again, the point of such learning is not to "occupy the position of the scholar," or the museum expert in this case, but to better practise translating for oneself the expressive world beyond one's experience, putting one's experience into words for others, and subjecting one's words to the test of verification.[22] This is a movement of learning that the museum and its staff cannot comprehensively know or determine in advance. The exhibitions and supplementary programming of a museum premised on this kind of framework are designed to create a "third term" between curatorial expertise and the knowledge and interests of museum visitors in which ideas can be generated and tested.[23] In this context, no one owns the meanings of exhibitions.

Put slightly differently, this framework aims to foster forms of relating and participating that enact a redistribution of the sensible beginning with the assumption that museums aspiring to transform the societal context in which they participate must recognize their *mise-en-scène* as sites of what Rancière also calls "dissensus." In dissensus, there is not a "single regime of presentation and interpretation of the given imposing its obviousness on all. [Dissensus] means that every situation can be cracked open from the inside, reconfigured in a different regime of perception and signification."[24] The intent of a museum premised on a framework of dissensus is not to be the bearer or revealer of pre-established perspectives or truths but to open possibilities for the exploration of disparate yet mutually implicated lines of thought regarding a world held in common, one that can be considered, debated, and worked through. Such a museum presumably would not aim to earn itself or Winnipeg the designation as "the new capital for human rights"[25] but find ways to decapitalize, decentre, and decolonize authorial claims to knowledge as a basis for exchange and activism. Such a museum might begin, for instance, by acknowledging its own implication in ongoing legacies of settler colonialism (having established itself on Indigenous land in the name of "human rights") as a seeming contradiction to its *raison d'être*. That is, such a museum would not only tolerate exposure of its internal contradictions but also actively resist its own concretization by welcoming others to use and challenge its representations and interpretative frameworks for the sake of grappling with and learning from difficult knowledge.

The role of curation is central to the potential and feasibility of facilitating this kind of learning. Curators are responsible for different aspects of museum practice with varying levels of autonomy depending on the scale and nature of their institutional contexts. They serve as content specialists who research, publish, and lecture in particular subject areas. They make choices about how museum collections are acquired and how exhibitions are developed out of those collections. They work with other staff to render exhibitions as events not solely defined through their content or form but also defined through the ways in which exhibits are materialized and enacted through judgments about *how* content and form are to be shown and arranged in museum spaces, including the "discursive environment" that inscribes these spaces and the materials inside it (signage, image labels, explanatory text, exhibition guides). Although educational staff might be more directly responsible for delivering programming to the public, in all of the ways mentioned above curatorial decisions contribute directly to the pedagogical frameworks of exhibitions, shaping the potential for visitors to learn not just about but also from the histories on display.

In *Lost Subjects, Contested Objects: Toward a Psychoanalytic Inquiry of Learning,* Deborah Britzman elaborates on a distinction between "learning about" and "learning from" first articulated by Sigmund Freud in his paper "On the Teaching of Psycho-Analysis in Universities."[26] According to Britzman, "whereas learning about an event or experience focuses upon the acquisition of qualities, attributes, and facts, so that it presupposes a distance (or, one might even say, a detachment) between the learner and what is to be learned, learning from an event or experience is of a different order, that of insight.... Learning from requires the learner's attachment to, and implication in, knowledge."[27] In other words, the distinction between learning about and learning from has to do both with the ontological status given to knowledge and with the learner's imagined proximity to that knowledge. In learning about, knowledge is taken to be an object separate from or outside of the self that can nevertheless be acquired, owned, or mastered; in learning from, knowledge is understood as a relation contingent on a willingness to recognize one's connectedness to an event or experience that might well be "separate" in the sense of belonging to another time, place, or people but that can nevertheless be seen for its enmeshment with the structures, privileges, and constraints of one's own life.[28] For instance, I might not have been directly involved in or witness to the deployment of Indian residential schools in Canada, but I might still recognize ways in which my own privilege, as someone who passes as white, has been secured by this history and the ongoing ways in which the racist and colonialist ideologies that justified the schools during their existence continue to produce Indigenous peoples as needing either civilizing or annihilation. But more than just recognizing or seeing these kinds of connections—that is, in addition to adopting a "spectatorial sensibility" in this way—learning from also requires a "summoned sensibility" whereby we allow ourselves to feel compelled to respond, as well as be *response-able,* to the experiences and histories of others beyond our own memories (or to the memories of others beyond our own experiences and histories).[29] That is, though a spectatorial sensibility might allow me to "see" connections between systemic violence carried out against Indigenous peoples and my own relative security in a white settler society, I must also learn to translate this seeing into an ability to *respond* to the conditions out of which such inequality, violence, and oppression arise. Learning from, in other words, is about more than recognizing the other's difference. Learning from involves learning to take the experiences and memories of others into our own lives and to live and act as though they mattered.[30]

Perhaps it is expected that curators at a human rights museum work to cultivate a spectatorial sensibility among visitors by bringing into presence (making visible) certain events and experiences that might otherwise be absent from or beyond our historical purview, thereby expanding our knowledge *about* a diversity of issues and perspectives on human rights. But how might curators also help to develop visitors' capacities to learn *from* these events and experiences? That is, how might curatorial decisions be made to contribute to our summoned sensibilities and response-abilities to those histories and experiences that we tend to imagine as "not ours" or, even more defensively, "not our fault"? In plainer language, how might curators at a human rights museum help us to face the real and daunting question, "What am I supposed to *do* with the stories of others, in particular stories of widespread suffering and trauma?"[31] Indeed, learning from is especially challenging in the face of difficult knowledge emerging in response to histories of violence, abuse, and genocidal practices, past and present. What is difficult about difficult knowledge in these instances is not just becoming aware of the "terrible facts" but also, more precisely, figuring out what to do with such knowledge and imagining how to learn from it, especially when it triggers our fears, defensiveness, aggression, or feelings of hopelessness, threatening to undo our fundamental frameworks for making sense of ourselves and the world around us.[32]

Given these challenges, we tend to resist difficult knowledge and the implication that learning from (it) demands. In her contribution to this volume, curator Mary Reid offers an apt example of such resistance as the tendency of museum visitors encountering representations of traumatic events to position the traumatic experience as something that is other: "Although I can empathize with the trauma, it still happened to someone else, at some other time, in some other part of the world." What the museum visitor's response suggests here is that, even when, as spectators, we are willing and able to recognize particular traumatic histories as sad or regrettable, we are still generally inclined to maintain a sense of them as "not mine" or, again, "not ours." Another example of resistance to learning from difficult knowledge is the tendency toward a narcissistic, vicarious identification with the suffering of others. In this case, empathy is enacted through a fantasy of acquiring or inhabiting the other's knowledge and experience. Such enactments are cultivated, for example, by curatorial designs inviting museum visitors to participate in simulations, role playing, or "immersive realities" ("imagine yourself in their shoes"). Although these designs are intended to evoke affective responses by involving visitors as more than "just spectators," they nevertheless limit the potential to learn from the histories on display by denying the radical alterity or non-replicability of experiences of human trauma. In other words, when witnessing is organized through a framework that encourages a sense of sameness or an identification with the memories or experiences of others, rather than a sense of epistemological humility, it becomes all the more difficult to see or imagine oneself as potentially implicated or participating in legacies of power and privilege entwined with the conditions of the other's suffering.

A third and related tendency in the face of difficult knowledge is to reduce singularities to equivalent or familiar forms. Here significant differences between events, experiences, or circumstances are collapsed so that one atrocity is made comparable to or emblematic of another.[33] Curatorial practices contribute to this collapsing when attempts are made to render the "foreign" intelligible by framing representations through already recognizable terms. The problem with such framing is that it risks not only foreclosing what is specific and non-replicable about a given history but also blocking the potential for new and unanticipated insights to be generated in the context of visitors' interactions with exhibits and each other. Mieke Bal describes this dilemma in terms of how to sustain the singular difficulty offered by a given image amid a proliferation of images of suffering exhibited alongside one another. In her commentary on Beautiful Suffering, an exhibition of photographs portraying various scenes of pain and death, Bal observes that, if we "put about one hundred such photographs together [in an exhibition], … the hardship vanishes. … An image of consequences of a famine here, a corpse lying about there, and a wounded figure and lots of blood just over there, [and] soon the turbulent emotions vanish."[34] In other words, for Bal, the curatorial challenge of exhibiting a large and diverse collection of difficult images is how to preserve rather than dilute their "punctum" or affect;[35] although the largeness and diversity of the collection might have been curated with the democratic intent to represent a range of experiences, the affective force is nullified if viewers experience the multitude of images blurring into one another in a way that results in desensitization or disconnection or provokes "vicarious traumatization," thereby hindering the viewer's ability to move beyond affect and begin critically thinking through.[36]

How the CMHR responds to these and related dilemmas will depend significantly on whether and how its curators are empowered to grapple with difficult knowledge and the challenges of learning from history. But of course this grappling does not belong to curators alone. The point, rather, is for the museum, its staff, and the public to collectively anticipate the CMHR and its exhibitions as sites of difficult knowledge worth encountering as such. These sites might indeed unsettle our established ways of knowing and being, our sense of certainty about the stories of our own lives and the lives of others, but through them we can also learn better how to expand our capacities to respond thoughtfully and effect change. Again, the role of curators here is not to determine in advance what these responses or changes should look like. Rather, curators must develop

museological frameworks that encourage, in the face of difficult knowledge, our "patience with the incommensurability of understanding and an
interest in tolerating the ways meaning becomes, for the learner, fractured,
broken, and lost, exceeding the affirmations of rationality, consciousness,
and consolation."[37] It is in supporting precisely such patience as a condition
for learning that curatorial practice at the CMHR can do more than regulate
the spaces of various histories in competitive terms. In other words, by
fostering a framework that exposes us to difficult knowledge, curatorial
practice at the museum might help to bring us into consciousness of what
we do not yet know but nevertheless have, in our own ways, begun to learn.

NOTES

1   This paraphrase comes from Jacques Rancière, critiquing not the pedagogical strategies
     of museums alone but the broader dynamics of teaching and learning in contexts of (art)
     spectatorship. See Jacques Rancière, *The Emancipated Spectator*, trans. Gregory Elliot
     (London: Verso, 2009), 8.

2   This is a widely made observation of museums at present. See, for example, Eilean Hooper-
     Greenhill, *Museums and the Shaping of Knowledge* (London: Routledge, 1992); and Jen-
     nifer Barrett, *Museums and the Public Sphere* (Malden, MA: Wiley-Blackwell, 2011).

3   The term "*mise-en-scène*" as used in this chapter is meant to describe the material-social
     practice of arranging exhibits within museum space, which structures how visitors
     encounter and engage with them and enables and/or limits certain forms of thought.

4   See the CMHR's *Content Advisory Committee Final Report to the Canadian Museum for
     Human Rights,* 25 May 2010, http://publications.gc.ca/collections/collection_2011/mcdp-
     cmhr/NM104-1-2010-eng.pdf.

5   See the CMHR's Share Your Story webpage, where "anyone can tell a story about human
     rights. It might be a personal experience or something that happened in your neighborhood
     or even a story from another part of the world. You can choose to share your own story by
     clicking Record your Story or listen to other people's stories about human rights by selecting
     View Stories." https://humanrights.ca/act/share-your-story (accessed 5 July 2013).

6   For a relevant discussion on the notion that being human is to be interconnected with the
     suffering of others, and thus a question of relationality and responsibility, see Emmanuel
     Levinas, "Useless Suffering," in *Entre Nous: Thinking of-the-Other,* trans. Michael B. Smith
     and Barbara Harshav (New York: Columbia University Press, 1998), 99–101.

7   The phrase "difficult knowledge" as used here comes from Alice Pitt and Deborah
     Britzman, "Speculations on Qualities of Difficult Knowledge in Teaching and Learning:
     An Experiment in Psychoanalytic Research," *International Journal of Qualitative Studies
     in Education* 16, 6 (2003): 755–76. See also Deborah P. Britzman, *Lost Subjects, Contested
     Objects: Toward a Psychoanalytic Inquiry of Learning* (Albany, NY: State University of New
     York Press, 1998); Erica Lehrer, Cynthia E. Milton, and Monica Eileen Patterson, eds.,
     Curating Difficult Knowledge: Violent Pasts in Public Places (Houndmills, UK: Palgrave
     Macmillan, 2011); and Roger I. Simon, "A Shock to Thought: Curatorial Judgment and
     the Public Exhibition of 'Difficult Knowledge,'" *Memory Studies* 4, 4 (2011): 432–49.

8   On the publicity of this controversy in print news media, see Helen Fallding's contribu-
     tion to this book. See also A. Dirk Moses's "The Canadian Museum for Human Rights:
     The 'Uniqueness of the Holocaust' and the Question of Genocide." *Journal of Genocide
     Research* 14 (2012): 215-238; A. Dirk Moses's "Does the Holocaust Reveal or Conceal
     Other Genocides?: The Canadian Museum for Human Rights and Grievable Suffering"
     in *Hidden Genocides: Power, Knowledge, Memory,* edited by Alexander Laban Hinton,
     Thomas La Pointe, and Douglas Irvin-Erickson, (New Brunswick, NJ: Rutgers University
     Press, 2014), 21-51; Karyn Ball and Per Anders Rudling's forthcoming "The Underbelly
     of Canadian Multiculturalism: Holocaust Envy and Obfuscation in the Debate about
     the Canadian Museum for Human Rights," *Journal of Holocaust Studies*; and Catherine
     Chatterley's forthcoming "Canada's Struggle with Holocaust Memorialization: The War
     Museum Controversy, Ethnic Identity Politics, and the Canadian Museum for Human
     Rights," *Holocaust and Genocide Studies* 29 (Spring 2015).

9   The phrase "remembrance-learning" here refers to an understanding of remembrance as
     "a means for an ethical learning that impels us to a confrontation and 'reckoning' not only
     with stories of the past but also with 'ourselves' as we 'are' (historically, existentially, ethi-
     cally) in the present. Remembrance thus is a reckoning that beckons us to the possibilities
     of the future, showing the possibilities of our own learning." See Roger I. Simon, Sharon
     Rosenberg, and Claudia Eppert, "Introduction: Between Hope and Despair: The Peda-
     gogical Encounter of Historical Remembrance," in *Between Hope and Despair: Pedagogy
     and the Remembrance of Historical Trauma,* ed. Roger I. Simon, Sharon Rosenberg, and
     Claudia Eppert (Lanham, MD: Rowman and Littlefield Publishers, 2000), 8. The signifi-
     cance of this understanding in relation to the CMHR is effectively elaborated through the
     remaining discussion of this chapter. On the limits of a competitive victimization frame-
     work in the context of the CMHR, see Olena Hankivsky and Rita Dhamoon, "Which
     Genocide Matters the Most? An Intersectionality Analysis of the Canadian Museum for
     Human Rights," *Canadian Journal of Political Science* 46 (2013): 899-920.

10   See Library of Parliament, Bill C-42: An Act to Amend the Museums Act and to Make
     Consequential Amendments to Other Acts (Legislative Summary-597E), 22 February
     2008, http://www.parl.gc.ca/About/Parliament/LegislativeSummaries/bills_ls.asp?lang=E
     &ls=c42&Parl=39&Ses=2&sour%20ce=library_prb.

11   See Philip Corrigan and Derek Sayer, *The Great Arch: English State Formation as Cultural
     Revolution* (Oxford: Basil Blackwell, 1985), 3.

12   See Charles Taylor, *Multiculturalism and "The Politics of Recognition": An Essay,* with com-
     mentary by Amy Gutmann, ed. (Princeton, NJ: Princeton University Press, 1992).

13   For a thorough critique of this logic (including Taylor's) beyond the context of museum
     practices but nonetheless relevant to the present discussion, see Rita Kaur Dhamoon,
     Identity/Difference Politics: How Difference Is Produced and Why It Matters (Vancouver:
     UBC Press, 2009). Dhamoon argues that official multiculturalism, as both a logic and a
     practice based on an economy of recognition-distribution, denies the force of racism and
     other relations of power as structuring how and for whom recognition is conferred. In
     other words, rather than acknowledging the ways in which individual and group iden-
     tifications are consolidated in and through relations of power and politically motivated
     inclusions/exclusions, official multiculturalism upholds identifications as expressions of
     naturalized "differences."

14   O'Reilly left this position on 28 February 2011. See Mia Rabson, "Chief Operating Officer
     Leaves Rights Museum," *Winnipeg Free Press,* 3 March 2011, http://www.winnipegfree-
     press.com/local/chief-operating-officer-leaves-rights-museum-117302453.html.

15   Patrick O'Reilly, "Speech Delivered by Mr. Patrick O'Reilly to the Rotary International
     District #5550 World Peace Partners on Tuesday, April 7, 2009," http://museumforhu-

manrights.ca/about-museum/speeches-our-museum-leaders/speech-delivered-mr-pat-
rick-o-reilly-rotary-international-d#.UoJ7L-L29Ew (accessed 5 January 2013).

16   See Rancière, *The Emancipated Spectator*, 8.

17   O'Reilly, "Speech."

18   This curatorial pedagogy and its focus on "taking action" have been promoted by the
      CMHR in various ways: through promotional videos; slogans used on signage near the
      museum building; the museum design itself, which features a Take Action gallery as the
      final destination of visitor tours; and the museum mission statement: "The Canadian
      Museum for Human Rights is envisioned to be a national and international destination,
      a centre of learning where Canadians and people from around the world can engage in
      discussion and commit to taking action against hate and oppression." For this mission
      statement, go to "About the Museum," http://museumforhumanrights.ca/about-museum#.
      UoJ8BOL29Ew (accessed 5 January 2013).

19   Stuart Murray, "Speech Delivered by President and CEO Stuart Murray to University of
      Manitoba 'Thinking about Ideas Museums' Speaker Series, September 9, 2011," http://mu-
      seumforhumanrights.ca/about-museum/speeches-our-museum-leaders/speech-delivered-
      president-and-ceo-stuart-murray-university#.UoJ3EOL29Ew (accessed 18 June 2013).

20   Rancière, *The Emancipated Spectator*, 12. See also Jacques Rancière, *Politics of Aesthetics:
      The Distribution of the Sensible*, trans. Gabriel Rockhill (London: Continuum, 2004).

21   See Rancière, *The Emancipated Spectator*, 10–11.

22   Ibid., 11.

23   "Third term" is also a phrase from Rancière, ibid., 14–15.

24   Ibid., 48–49.

25   Murray, "Speech."

26   Sigmund Freud, "On the Teaching of Psycho-Analysis in Universities," in *The Standard
      Edition of the Complete Psychological Works of Sigmund Freud*, Vol. 17, edited and trans-
      lated by James Strachey, in collaboration with Anna Freud, assisted by Alix Strachey and
      Alan Tyson, 171–173 (London: Hogarth Press and Institute for Psychoanalysis, (1995
      [1925]).

27   Deborah P. Britzman, *Lost Subjects, Contested Objects: Toward a Psychoanalytic Inquiry of
      Learning* (Albany: SUNY Press, 1998), 117.

28   See Roger I. Simon's discussion on memorial kinship in *The Touch of the Past: Remem-
      brance, Learning, and Ethics* (Houndmills, UK: Palgrave Macmillan, 2005), especially
      Chapter 5 on transactional public memory.

29   Ibid., 92–93.

30   What is described here as "learning from" has also been described in similar terms by
      Simon as "remembering otherwise." See ibid., 9.

31   Simon, Rosenberg, and Eppert, *Between Hope and Despair*, 17; emphasis added.

32   Pitt and Britzman, "Speculations," 755–76.

33   For instance, the 1985 Air India bombings have been sensationalized as "Canada's 9/11"
      or made analogous to 9/11 in popular, journalistic, and news media discourse. See, for
      example, Stewart Bell, *Cold Terror: How Canada Nurtures and Exports Terrorism around
      the World* (Toronto: John Wiley and Sons, 2004); and Tom Godfree, "Air India Flight 182
      Tragedy 'Canada's Own 9/11,'" *Ottawa Sun*, 30 September 2012, http://www.ottawasun.
      com/2012/09/30/air-india-flight-182-tragedy-canadas-own-911 (accessed 24 July 2014).

34   Mieke Bal, "The Pain of Images," in *Beautiful Suffering: Photography and the Traffic in Pain,* ed. M. Reinhardt, H. Edwards, and E. Duganne (Chicago: University of Chicago Press, 2007), 105.

35   "Punctum" is a term developed by Roland Barthes to describe the powerful force or affect that details of a photographic image can elicit in the person looking at it that exceeds the meaning or context of the image itself. See Roland Barthes, *Camera Lucida: Reflections on Photography,* trans. Richard Howard (1980; reprinted, New York: Hill and Wang, 1981).

36   I have borrowed the phrase "vicarious traumatization" from E. Ann Kaplan, who uses it to describe experiences of greater and lesser degrees, including everything from temporary discomfort to feeling overwhelmed, profoundly disturbed, shocked, numbed, or even "changed forever" by a second-hand encounter with trauma. See E. Ann Kaplan, *Trauma Culture: The Politics of Terror and Loss in Media and Literature* (New Brunswick, NJ: Rutgers University Press, 2005), 91. Adapting Martin L. Hoffman's (2000) research on trauma and empathic witnessing in the therapeutic context, Kaplan is interested in whether being vicariously traumatized in the context of media spectatorship—that is, as a spectator of mediated images—blocks the potential for empathic response or actually prompts empathic response in the form of "responsible witnessing": that is, witnessing motivated not simply by voyeuristic curiosity but also by a wish to better understand the conditions out of which trauma arises and a desire to act to change those conditions (see 22–23).

37   Britzman, *Lost Subjects* 118.

VIEWER DISCRETION: CURATORIAL STRATEGIES AND CONSEQUENCES OF EXHIBITION SIGNAGE

CHAPTER 9

Mary Reid

Exhibition signage plays a crucial role in making meaning. A prominent part of the visual identity of an exhibition, "signage" is a catch-all term that includes banner/title signage, object labels (more commonly referred to as tombstone labels), extended text labels, information panels that tend to be more weighted to factual data, didactic panels that tend to demonstrate a point of view such as a curatorial thesis, and advisory posters. When specifically linked to representing the unrepresentable (or "difficult knowledge," as referred to in other chapters in this volume) within the context of a museum dedicated to human rights, exhibition signage is paramount in terms of the construction and understanding of already highly fraught and sensitive issues. In other words, as I address in this chapter, exhibition signage manages and even holds the power to make meaning. This argument moves quickly through standard forms of exhibition signage and then focuses on a particular kind of meaning-making signage: the advisory label.

HOW DO YOU MAKE MEANING?

In his 1984 article "Museum, Managers of Consciousness," prominent German American artist and educator Hans Haacke (born 1936) writes that "consciousness is not a pure, independent, value-free entity, evolving according to internal, self-sufficient and universal rules. It is contingent, an open system, responsive to the crosscurrents of the environment. It is, in fact, a battleground of conflicting interests. Correspondingly, the products of consciousness represent interests and interpretations of the world that are potentially at odds with each other.... As they are shaped by their respective environments and social relations, they do in turn influence our view of the human condition."[1] Thirty years later this sentiment is still a prevailing reality that museums deconstruct and distill in an attempt to represent an accurate and unbiased retelling of history. Yet is this really possible? Can the curatorial and/or educational staff (also known as "interpreters") of a museum really present an unbiased perspective in the textual information that they draft, edit, and produce? After all, each of our decisions is biased to some degree because of our education, our cultural identity, and our working and living environments.

MAKING LABELS

Standard museum practice takes into consideration the various types of visitors, and a lot of care is taken to ensure that any information presented in an exhibition gallery is politically correct and non-offensive. However, drafting text that will become part of an exhibition is probably one of the most difficult and ideologically and emotionally charged aspects of the production of an exhibition, next only to (and sometimes on par with) selection of the objects themselves. A big reason that this kind of writing is challenging is the institutional reliance on "sound bites" (to borrow a term from news production) to provide an efficient medium for the transmission of information. This is one of the most significant hurdles to overcome when retelling history through the vehicle of an exhibition. This challenge is further complicated when applying a semiotic methodology to the understanding of which meanings and understandings textual information imparts both directly and indirectly to museum visitors. In her 1997 essay, anthropologist Pauline Turner Strong outlines succinctly how a semiotic approach to museum labels illuminates "a full range of messages and especially ... messages about the communicative events in which labels themselves function."[2] Drawing on C.S. Peirce's triad of semiotic theory (signs = icon, index, and/or symbol), Strong supports the conclusion that "museum labels function primarily as indexes.... As such they indicate a complex set of relations among displayed objects, the contexts and meanings attributed to them, and the knowledges, identities, expectations, and agendas of both museum professionals and the publics they serve."[3] Accordingly, seen as an extension of or support to the actual object, exhibition signage plays a vital role in not only managing but also producing consciousness.

In museum and gallery practice, exhibition signage is the first platform that the viewer engages with in the process of making meaning. This process moves back and forth both between the object and the viewer and between the past and the present, simultaneously, which in turn enables the continual checking and rechecking and reimagining of ideas.[4] And it is the reimagining of ideas that is particularly important within the context of a human rights museum committed "to taking action against hate and oppression."[5] In order to accomplish these goals, to take such action, ideas must be reconsidered, rethought, and possibly reimagined. Therefore, making meaning is a key component of this process of change.

One would normally expect that a viewer's reading of a label or information panel would occur after looking at the object on display, but in many cases the reverse is true. Many museum visitors never bother reading some or even any of the textual information provided for them. This is particularly the case in art galleries, where the artworks displayed are thought to be imbued with the power to speak "for themselves." In the case of museums, though, textual information becomes by default the "authoritative voice" for the object.

However, the onerous process of distilling an extraordinary amount of research to fit current standard museum and gallery guidelines in terms of word count and sentence length is never apparent to the visitor. Generally, textual information is drafted by the curator and then edited by an educator or interpreter skilled in streamlining text so that it is easily understandable as well as consistent and neutral in voice and tone. This refining process might require that the text go back and forth several times between curator and educator, and even a copy editor eventually weighs in. All in all, exhibition signage in a major museum is not taken lightly; text is carefully crafted and undergoes rigorous revision before it is finalized.

In an acknowledgement of the fact that reading is less efficient while standing, the standard word count for an exhibition information or didactic panel is between 100 and 250 words and for an object label between 50 and 100 words. Efforts to keep sentences short, jargon-free, and clear, and the voice active, aid the delivery of information.[6] As a result of the need to keep matters as straightforward as possible, though, a lot of information is left out of panels and labels, and hard decisions are made to justify privileging some facts and stories over others. These decisions in turn are largely what informs or directs a visitor's interpretations and thus experience of a museum; they create meaning and produce consciousness.

Object labels and their larger counterparts, information and didactic panels, stitch together the viewer, the display presented,[7] the view of history or perspective that the curator/educator/interpreter wants to tell, as well as the human relationships embedded in all of these aspects. Labels can direct looking but more importantly guide learning and understanding. Exhibition signage "is most effective when it focuses on what visitors can see, understand, and respond to based on their own experiences. People learn by relating new ideas, information, or experiences to old ones. At each stage in the learning process they need to feel a sense of satisfaction, accomplishment, and control before they can proceed."[8] It is this complex relationship of looping feedback that positions curatorial authority and the visitor's own agency in meaning making as crucial components that can be either in line or at odds with one another. However, it is precisely this unique structure, as set up by museums, that provides the potential for social change. It is from this position and using a framework of social work perspectives that museum studies specialist Lois H. Silverman has outlined how museums foster human relationships by "making meaning together."[9] Hence, the textual information that supports an exhibition is an important ingredient in this recipe of socially engaged discourse and exchange.

TRIGGER WARNING: THIS LABEL MIGHT OFFEND

Several excellent articles and other documents provide more details on best practices for label and information panel writing for museums and galleries.[10] However, one type of label or panel is little talked about or addressed in the existing literature. This is the "warning" or "viewer discretion" sign/poster. It is often overlooked, but it remains powerful in terms of its ability to make and shape meaning. Unlike the object labels and information or didactic panels placed within the exhibition display, warning signs are placed in locations designed to be encountered prior to entering a potentially offending exhibit. Sometimes they are even placed in the foyer of the museum. Similar to their counterparts that aid in interpretation and learning, these types of labels can predict and shape viewers' ideas about the content and message of an exhibition before it is viewed.[11] More often than not, a warning label might stop a visitor from entering an exhibition while simultaneously creating an opinion on something that the visitor has not yet seen. While supposedly introducing the idea that the concept the visitor is about to encounter is complex and perhaps challenging to understand, an advisory label, as Failler and Simon outline in their contribution to this volume, can effectively cut the visitor off from an opportunity to learn from the exhibit. Given this opportunity, visitors can assume the role of researcher and interpreter simultaneously, in the process creating a transformative experience of self-authoring, operating on multiple levels.

Unlike standard exhibition labels, very little has been written about the emergence of warning or advisory labels in museums and art galleries, though more recently their presence has been aligned in the media with the broader debate over the use of "trigger warnings."[12] It is unclear when and where these "special" labels originated, but they began to appear more frequently in the late 1980s and became more prevalent during the fervour of political correctness in the 1990s.[13] Standard phrases such as "mature/adult content" or "parental advisory" are commonly employed. Their application became more apparent in and around art exhibitions that featured explicit sexual content, the most notable being the deceased American photographer Robert Mapplethorpe's solo touring exhibition *A Perfect Moment*. His retrospective was exhibited at the Contemporary Arts Center in Cincinnati in 1989, and, even though an advisory label was placed at the entrance to the museum, the director of the museum, Dennis Barrie, was arrested and tried for obscenity for displaying five works featuring homoerotic sexual acts and two works depicting young children whose genitals were visible. Barrie was eventually found not guilty by a jury, but the process of his exoneration took years and absorbed hundreds of thousands of dollars in legal fees. All in all, the charges and very public court case were extremely damaging to the Contemporary Arts Center and to Barrie both professionally and personally. The use of warning labels hit a new level of due diligence with the *Sensation* art exhibition that toured during the late 1990s and included a health warning: "The contents of this exhibition may cause shock, vomiting, confusion, panic, euphoria, and anxiety. If you suffer from high blood pressure, a nervous disorder, or palpitations, you should consult your doctor before viewing this exhibition."[14] The exhibition featured work by several young British artists, notably Damien Hirst's tiger shark suspended in formaldehyde titled *The Physical Impossibility of Death in the Mind of Someone Living* and Chris Ofili's black Madonna, *The Holy Virgin Mary*, which incorporated pornographic images and elephant dung.

Unlike in the film world, in the museum world there is no official body or policy to govern the use of advisory labels. Instead, decisions about when and where to place them are made within individual museums, generally on a case-by-case basis. Notions of community standards and ideas about appeasing controversy or even anticipating it are generally part of these behind-the-scenes discussions. For the most part, it is understood that cautionary signs, instead of just providing warnings, can actually create, manage, and shape public and institutional behaviour. Their very presence constructs an idea of what is controversial and "disciplines" spaces by providing a means to distinguish between those that in some relevant sense are benign and those that are shameful or guilt inducing. In so doing, these cautionary practices pre-empt a visitor's ability to make her own decisions and create her own interpretations and understandings, and they prematurely foreclose on tough conversations and unanticipated responses. As manifestations of inevitable compromise, crude responses to censorship demands, and sometimes even signs of panic or fear, these warning labels stigmatize the exhibition space.[15]

Although warning signs are now considered a well-established museum practice, it might still be productive to ask how effective they are given what we know about cases such as the Mapplethorpe exhibition. Are they just a knee-jerk, cover-your-bum strategy? Or are they a necessary compromise, one that allows for the exhibition of representations that lie outside the norm? And who defines or decides what this "norm" finally is?[16] As mentioned earlier, the closed-door discussions of cautionary signage unfold in the absence of any real external and official standards governing their composition and use. It is therefore worth considering how the micromanaging of anxiety and prevalent cautionary strategies will play out in a museum dedicated to the subject of human rights, telling difficult stories of abuse, injustice, and trauma.

EXHIBITION CONTENT, ADVISORY LABELS, AND THE CMHR

Many adults as well as children will visit the recently opened Canadian Museum for Human Rights (CMHR) to experience a variety of attempts to represent material so abstract, painful, or horrific that it might be thought of as fundamentally unrepresentable. Accordingly, any display in the CMHR seems to be condemned never to get to the profound core of the matter under description, instead required by the complexity of the task at hand merely to rest at the surface. For example, how does one represent genocide? Certainly, documentary photographs and survivor testimonials provide obvious starting points, but even they do not quite get to the intangible essences, the emotional and psychological stress and suffering caused by this kind of trauma. This is because the mind will commonly dehumanize a traumatic observation to allow its mental capacities to move on.[17] Much as when presented with images and stories representing genocide, feelings provoked might include one of thankfulness that this did not happen to me. And, though I can empathize with the trauma on display, I am nevertheless aware that it happened to someone else, at some other time, in some other part of the world. It is not uncommon for an audience to want to dissociate from traumatic experience, to come to see it as something "other," anomalous, or personally irrelevant in order to obtain some means of moving past the trauma. Unfortunately, this dissociation from and externalization of trauma only limit one's understanding of human rights violations, for they are happening everywhere, even here in Canada, even in our own back-yards. However, the question must also be asked, what does it really mean to understand another's trauma, and how might one do so? Continuing the trajectory outlined in Failler and Simon's chapter, how does one learn from another's difficult knowledge? Even if one properly identifies with someone else's trauma, will doing so only cause more suffering and pain through the retraumatization of secondary witnesses? Any attempt to represent events such as the Holocaust in totality obviously runs the risk of triggering pain-ful and difficult feelings in any audience.

Our understanding of human rights is constantly shifting because of scholarly production and the proliferation of cases that test the limits of what we know. Human rights talk, partly as a result of these shifts and the real political consequences of our human rights consciousness, is regularly implicated in controversy, and this kind of disputatiousness does not lend itself to display in a blissfully secure environment such as the highly sani-tized space of a museum, within which the information presented has been vetted or edited to ensure a "comfortable" audience experience. But should a human rights museum aim to provide a comfortable experience? After all, change usually happens within what we can call zones of discomfort. The discussion of human rights within the context of a museum should not be comfortable or safe or clean. In exhibits of this nature, expressions of the personal impacts of human suffering remain paramount.[18] Hence, exhibition content is highly emotional and fraught with socio-political im-plications, which in regard to the CMHR have been played out extensively in the press (as outlined in the chapter in this volume by Helen Fallding).

Eilean Hooper-Greenhill, a leading scholar of museum studies, pro-poses that "we need to consider the museum as a communicator."[19] And, yes, selection and control of expressive meaning lie importantly with the com-municator, who becomes the power broker in this transaction.[20] But really how powerful is that control? How can the range and level of interpretations and reactions that will be elicited and evoked in a museum dedicated to hu-man rights be predicted? Where does communicative power *really* lie?

To consider this question of power, we need to look at the potential audience of the CMHR. Although recently several museums and art galler-ies have invested in conducting surveys to find out who their audiences are and why they visit these institutions, unfortunately more often than not the audience of exhibitions is conceived of as the catch-all "general public."[21] Largely because of financial and labour constraints, there has been very little research on the level of information that this general public brings with it into a museum, and to date there has been very little empirical investigation of the experiences had or sought by this abstracted mass visitor.[22] The decision to visit a museum, or the decision to stay away from it, is informed by meanings constructed from prior experiences or the anticipation of such meanings arising from future museum-going experiences.[23] These meanings can be adjusted and shifted (and regularly are), yet they remain for the most part completely intangible and unknowable to the museum curator and perhaps even to the visitor herself.

If we assume that at the CMHR the representation of culture and identity will yield sites of multiple meanings within which different histories, languages, experiences, and voices intermingle amid diverse relations of power and privilege, what might the role of the advisory label be? The question of whether such labels are needed or even applicable has already been decided by the CMHR. Under the "Parental Advisory" section of the museum's website is a simple statement: "Please note that certain photographs and other images in [the] Canadian Museum for Human Rights are graphic in nature and may not be suitable for everyone."[24] I find it curious that photographs are singled out from "other images" in this advisory notice and that the terms "graphic in nature" and "not suitable" are taken by the museum to provide sufficiently negative connotations that the amorphous mass of "everyone" is assumed to be suitably warned. This "Parental Advisory" touches on the point of contention at the heart of this chapter (namely, the work that such warnings are both intended to do and actually do), yet as a *fait accompli* it simultaneously circumvents the difficult discussion of how to represent profound trauma through sustained consideration of how this experience will affect the visitor.

As has been well documented elsewhere (not least in the contribution by Muller, Sinclair, and Woolford to this volume), the experience of observing trauma can trigger traumatic feelings or repressed memories in the viewer. And as I have explained above, a successful exhibition label allows its reader to connect what she has read to her own wider experience of the world, building on her knowledge base, expanding it, and linking it to the object or display presented. Ideally, the exhibition label facilitates what we might think of as a kind of conversation. As Hooper-Greenhill observes, "the process of constructing meaning is like holding a conversation. No interpretation is ever fully completed. There is always more to say, and what is said may always be changed."[25]

ART AND REPRESENTING THE UNREPRESENTABLE

Daniel Ariew concludes his thesis "Representing the Unrepresentable: The Traumatic Affect" with the claim that, "to properly represent trauma, to allow others to receive these events from an emotional standpoint, one must sacrifice the historical information at hand. To truly feel traumatic experience, one needs narrative and humanization to relate to something the primary observer cannot recount directly to his or her audience."[26] This statement is obviously problematic because it forsakes historical documentation for subjective interpretation and hence muddies the power relations at work in the reception and construction of meaning even further. However, Ariew's larger intention is to argue in defence of representing trauma not necessarily realistically but less directly through art. In his view, it remains too easy to become desensitized to, say, traumatic experience as it is conveyed to us through documentary photographs. The subjective power of creative art, however, can serve to transmit many of the intangible (and therefore cardinally unrepresentable) qualities of traumatic experience in ways that remain emotionally gripping.

Representations of human rights through art can create a bridge between that which is representable and that which is not. One such example of this connective power is the ten-foot-by-twenty-two-foot painting titled *Circus* (2002) by deceased Winnipeg artist Caroline Dukes. She was born in Budapest, Hungary, and lived there during the German military occupation and later during the Stalin era. In 1958, along with her husband and children, she emigrated to Canada, first to Toronto and then nine years later to Winnipeg. In the last ten years of her life, her work turned to her personal experiences of persecution, which resulted from her ethnic heritage and staunch religious beliefs (she was an observant Orthodox Jew). Given its encompassing scale, *Circus* places the viewer almost as a participant in the dimly lit arena depicted. Art historian Elizabeth Legge writes about this work that:

> *Circus* was Caroline Dukes' vast and ambitious last work. We
> look down on the fourth side, as if from the bleachers in a strange
> ancient amphitheatre, within a repetitive architecture from which
> we cannot exit, in an anxiety dream that goes on and on. Alone
> in the centre, an ambiguous bare solitary figure stands straight,
> hands at its side, facing us as some symbolically universal human,
> in a theatre of cruelty. Dukes imagined the painting accompanied
> by tape-recorded laughter alternating with applause: an

ambiguous alternation between what might be taken as ridicule
and approval…. She wanted us to know that even our looking
could be morally compromised, and the sounds of jeering would
certainly violate any too comfortable identification on our part
with the solitary figure…. We have to be reminded of our own
complicity in some form of persecution.[27]

Exhibited at the Winnipeg Art Gallery in conjunction with Dukes's
posthumous retrospective, *Circus* was viewed alongside several of her
powerful works that dealt with this difficult subject matter. However, it
is significant, given the claims advanced above concerning the function
of cautionary signage, that the gallery did not find it necessary to use an
advisory label at the exhibition's entrance.

Displaying contemporary artwork is an alternative curatorial strategy
for the presentation of trauma, but it does not resolve issues connected to
the presence of advisory labels in museums and galleries. How should any
museum dealing with human rights issues negotiate the policy governing its use of exhibition signage? Will such a policy seek to absolve the
institution of responsibility for the consequences of tapping into a visitor's
emotional psyche by using an advisory or warning label? Or will it attempt
to create spaces or structures for sharing and support that will further the
transmission of information and understanding?

CONCLUSION

In response to these questions, it might be productive to refer back to the
quotation from Haacke: "Consciousness is a battleground of conflicting
interests."[28] Accordingly, a museum that wishes to be successful at fostering
public engagement through meaning making needs to proceed on the assumption that communication must be a two-way process. To achieve meaningful dialogue, a museum must be a collaborative discussant with its public
and not just a manager of consciousness, and this collaborative impulse
must be reflected in its use of exhibition signage. A recent example of successful dialogue was at a 2012 exhibition at Winnipeg's Plug In Institute for
Contemporary Art,[29] featuring artwork with explicit sexual content prefaced
by the following statement: "WARNING: Viewers may be surprised, shocked,
pleased, intrigued, offended, indifferent, curious, horrified, thrilled, bored
or otherwise *affected*."[30] "To affect" in this context means to alter something,
though it can also refer to emotional states. As I have explained above, advisory labels do "affect" the viewer, but they are most truly "affective" when

14. Caroline Dukes, Canadian (1929–2003), *Circus, 200*

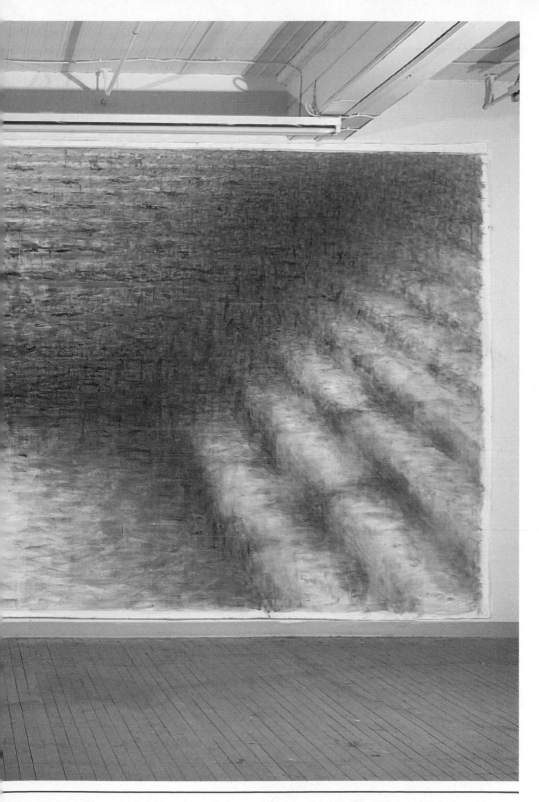

rylic, marble chips, and earth on canvas, 671 x 305 cm.

they can change a visitor's perspective. An alternative to this form of signage has been suggested by art historian Denis Longchamps, who thinks that a new type of warning label should be crafted specifically for the CMHR, one designed to challenge the museum's visitors but not immediately put them on the defensive. He proposes that a "new" advisory poster in the museum should read thus: "Entering this museum may have profound effects on you and may alter your way of thinking. You may find some images difficult, but it is in facing reality that we may change the future, your future."[31] That said, there are no clear answers or easy solutions to problems arising from museums' use of warning labels and really of all types of exhibition signage. What we need to remember is that such signs remain highly significant in terms of their power to make or constrain exhibit meanings or to produce audience consciousness. Consequently, curatorial strategies involving warning labels should be seen to have lasting consequences for museum environments as well as for the wider social world.

NOTES

1   Hans Haacke, "Museums, Managers of Consciousness," in *Institutional Critique: An Anthology of Artists' Writings*, ed. Alberro Alexander and Blake Stimson (Cambridge, MA: MIT Press, 2009), 280–81.

2   Pauline Turner Strong, "Exclusive Labels: Indexing the National 'We' in Commemorative and Oppositional Exhibitions," *Museum Anthropology* 21, 1 (1997): 42.

3   Ibid.

4   Eilean Hooper-Greenhill, "Changing Values in the Art Museum: Rethinking Communication and Learning," in *Museum Studies: An Anthology of Contexts*, ed. Bettina Messias Carbonell (Malden MA: Blackwell Publishing, 2004), 566.

5   Canadian Museum for Human Rights, http://humanrightsmuseum.ca/home.

6   Hooper-Greenhill, "Changing Values," 566.

7   Laura H. Hollengreen, "Space, Seam, Scenario: The Many Operations of the Museum Label," paper presented at the College Art Association Conference, Los Angeles, 24 June 2012.

8   The Minneapolis Institute of Arts, "Interpretation at the Minneapolis Institute of Arts: Policy and Practice," report prepared by the Interdivisional Committee on Interpretation, 2010, http://www.museum-ed.org/wp-content/uploads/2010/08/mia_interpretation_museum-ed.pdf, 38.

9   Lois H. Silverman, *The Social Work of Museums* (New York: Routledge, 2010).

10   Some of these include the following:

      The Minneapolis Institute of Arts, *Interpretation at the Minneapolis Institute of Arts: Policy and Practice*, report prepared by the Interdivisional Committee on Interpretation, 2010, http://www.museum-ed.org/wp-content/uploads/2010/08/mia_interpretation_museum-ed.pdf.

Museums Associations (London, UK), *Museum Practice: Signage,* http://www.museum-sassociation.org/museum-practice/signage.

Yves Jeanneret et al., "Written Signage and Reading Practices of the Public in a Major Fine Arts Museum," *Museum Management and Curatorship* 25, 1 (2010): 53–67.

Paulette M. McManus, "Oh Yes, They Do: How Museum Visitors Read Labels and Interact with Exhibit Texts," *Curator* 32, 3 (1989): 174–89.

Beverly Serrell, *Exhibit Labels: An Interpretive Approach* (Walnut Creek, CA: Altamira Press, division of Rowman and Littlefield Publishers, 1996).

11   See Jennifer Tyburczy, "Warning: Explicit Display in Museums," paper presented at the College Art Association Conference, Los Angeles, 24 June 2012.

12   Jenny Jarvie, "Trigger Happy: The 'Trigger Warning' Has Spread from Blogs to College Classes. Can It Be Stopped?," *New Republic,* 3 March 2014, http://www.newrepublic.com/article/116842/trigger-warnings-have-spreadblogs-college-classes-thats-bad.

13   Tyburczy, "Warning."

14   Tobin Siebers, "What Can Disability Studies Learn from the Culture Wars?," *Cultural Critique* 55 (2003): 191.

15   Ibid.

16   Relayed by Herb Enns, attributed to architect Neil Minuk, The Idea of a Human Rights Museum Workshop, Winnipeg, 1–2 February 2013.

17   Daniel Ariew, "Representing the Unrepresentable: The Traumatic Affect" (honours thesis, University of South Florida, 2011), 7, http://honors.usf.edu/documents/Thesis/U35202931.pdf.

18   Terence M. Dufy, "Museums of 'Human Suffering' and the Struggle for Human Rights," in *Museum Studies: An Anthology of Contexts,* ed. Bettina Messias Carbonell (Malden MA: Blackwell Publishing, 2004), 122.

19   Hooper-Greenhill, "Changing Values," 558.

20   Ibid., 561.

21   Ibid.

22   Ibid., 562.

23   Ibid.

24   Canadian Museum for Human Rights, 2013, http://museumforhumanrights.ca/parental-advisory.

25   Hooper-Greenhill, "Changing Values," 566.

26   Ariew, "Representing the Unrepresentable," 29.

27   Elizabeth Legge, "Caroline Dukes," in *Caroline Dukes: Concealed Memories* (Winnipeg: Winnipeg Art Gallery, 2008), 18–19.

28   Haacke, "Museums," 281.

29   *My Winnipeg Project,* chapter "Winter Kept Us Warm," curated by Noam Gonick, Plug In Institute for Contemporary Art, Winnipeg, 14 December 2012–1 February 2013.

30   Emphasis added. Thanks to Helen Fallding for providing this reference.

31   Email exchange with Denis Longchamps, Chief Curator, Art Gallery of Burlington, 11 March 2012.

REPRESENTING AGRICULTURAL MIGRANT WORKERS IN THE CANADIAN MUSEUM FOR HUMAN RIGHTS

CHAPTER 10

Armando Perla

Every year thousands of temporary agricultural workers travel to Canada to work in its fields. They arrive intending to provide better lives for their families back home. Sometimes they meet extraordinary Canadians who welcome them into their homes and lend a helping hand while they spend time as foreign workers in a strange land. However, sometimes their dreams and hopes are crushed in the fields, or on the roads, following a tragic accident. These workers' stories are full of accounts of courage, love, friendship, resilience, tears, loss, and hours of hard work spent under the Canadian sun. The Canadian Museum for Human Rights (CMHR) exhibit on Agricultural Migrant Workers reflects on the lives of these men and women who have made Canada their temporary home.

INTERNATIONAL FRAMEWORK

According to Article 2(1) of the International Convention on the Protection of the Rights of All Migrant Workers and Members of Their Families (CMW), a migrant worker is "a person … who is to be engaged, is engaged or has been engaged in a remunerated activity in a State of which he or she is not a national." This is by far the most comprehensive definition found in any international instrument dealing with migrant workers. There is no distinction between regular/documented or irregular/undocumented workers made in the definition. The convention acknowledges that documented migrant workers are entitled to claim more rights than undocumented migrant workers, but it also states that undocumented migrant workers must have their fundamental human rights respected, like all human beings. It emphasizes the connection between migration and human rights, which is increasingly becoming a crucial policy topic worldwide.

Moreover, by stating that a migrant worker is a person "to be engaged," the convention aims to protect migrant workers even before they have left their home countries. The convention does not create new rights for migrant workers; rather, its aim is to affirm for foreign workers the same rights that national workers already enjoy. The convention focuses on guaranteeing equality of treatment and the same working conditions for migrant and national workers. Some of the protections include freedom of discrimination in all aspects of work (art. 7); access to appropriate housing (art. 43(d)); access to health care (art. 28); access to educational institutions (art. 43(e)); freedom from arbitrary expulsion (art. 20); and protection from violence, physical injury, and threats of intimidation (art. 16).

WHY HASN'T CANADA RATIFIED THE CONVENTION?

The Canadian government has cited several obstacles in its justification for not ratifying the CMW. First, migration is often included with national sovereignty and taken to be the sole jurisdiction of the state. Canada, like many other states, values sovereignty in these matters on the ground that it might need to respond to perceived threats to national security posed by terrorism. Curtailing national freedom to make decisions about the treatment of migrant workers is viewed as potentially threatening.

Ratifying the CMW might seem to be unnecessary for their protection. Canada recognizes peremptory laws[1] such as the international principle of non-refoulement preventing victims of oppression from being returned to places where their lives or freedoms are threatened. These laws are already enshrined in conventions such as the one relating to the Status of Refugees and the Convention against Torture, so Canada does not see the necessity of agreeing to such protections in the convention.[2]

The spirit of the convention is different from that of Canada's immigration policies, which, in comparison with other nations with migrant workers, favour granting foreign workers access to citizenship. The movement behind the CMW originated to respond to the influx of workers migrating to Europe during the 1970s. Action Canada for Population and Development argues that, even when Canada was engaged in bringing in significant numbers of migrant ·workers during the same era,[3] national anxiety about how to handle the impacts of foreign workers was "negligible."[4] Canada has often argued that its immigration policy is open to and welcoming of newcomers; bringing foreigners to Canada is part of the nation-building effort. Therefore, the need for a convention to protect migrant workers' rights might be less urgent in this model society. Even if this argument has some force historically, recent statistics gathered by the United Food and Commercial Workers Canada (UFCW) show a shift from the nation-building model to a system of temporary migration more similar to those that initially inspired the CMW.[5]

Ratification of the CMW would force Canada to conduct a major revision of its current programs and legislation. Article 52 of the CMW specifies the rights of migrant workers to freely choose their remunerated activity. To meet this standard, Canada must alter migrant worker programs in order to provide workers with the freedom that they currently do not enjoy. Moreover, the Canadian government would have to oversee and guarantee the proper functioning of all migrant worker programs. At this time, with the exception of Mexico, where the Canadian government has minimum involvement in oversight, all migrant worker programs remain the responsibility of the employer rather than any government agency. Complying with the convention would therefore mean an increase in the costs to the government of keeping these programs functioning within the bounds of international human rights law.

Finally, human rights are already protected in Canada. The government's position is that ratifying the CMW and granting "special" rights to migrant workers are unnecessary because Canada is a state party to several other international human rights instruments.[6] At the domestic level, migrant workers are protected under the Canadian Charter of Rights and Freedoms. Do these multiple levels of protection make special protection for migrant workers redundant? Numerous reports, books, academic publications, and documentaries on the topic of migrant workers have shown that they are the victims of daily human rights violations in Canada. This evidence indicates that domestic legal measures have failed so far to adequately identify or protect migrant workers from systematic abuse.

MIGRANT WORKERS IN THE CANADIAN CONTEXT
Canada has a complex and varied system to classify its migrant workers. On its website, Human Resources and Skills Development Canada lists the different categories of migrant workers allowed in the country:

> Temporary Foreign Worker Program
>> Agricultural Workers: Seasonal Agricultural Workers Program (SAWP); Agricultural Stream; Stream for Lower-Skilled Occupations; and Stream for Higher-Skilled Occupations
>
> Live-In Caregivers
>
> Lower-Skilled Occupations
>
> Higher-Skilled Occupations
>
> Undocumented Workers[7]

This chapter focuses on an exhibit in the CMHR dedicated to workers classified as SAWP and Stream for Lower-Skilled Occupations. The thousands of agricultural workers travelling to Canada under these programs come from countries such as Jamaica, Mexico, Trinidad and Tobago, Barbados, Thailand, the Philippines, Guatemala, El Salvador, and others. They work in Canadian fields, orchards, and greenhouses, on crops from apples and asparagus to watermelon and zucchini. They also harvest grapes and tobacco. They care for roses and sod. They work in meat-processing plants and on dairy farms, yet they are almost invisible to Canadian society.

SEASONAL AGRICULTURAL WORKERS PROGRAM
Because of its dangerous, demeaning, dirty conditions, and low-paid, irregular, and long work hours, agricultural labour has proven to be one of the most challenging industries for which to recruit and maintain workers. These are the main reasons that Canadian farmers want to import workers who will accept worse conditions and lower pay than national workers and remain with their employers throughout the harvest period. Since Canadians cannot be forced to do work that they do not want to do, farmers demanded an offshore workforce that would be unable to freely change their employer and/or industry and thus be forced to remain working as long as needed. In 1966, SAWP came to fruition, and the first group of Jamaicans

arrived in Canada to work in its fields. At the same time, a system of pay withholding was put into place for the workers who joined the program. To this day, 25 percent of their wages is deducted from each payroll period (20 percent is given back to the worker at the end of the contract, and 5 percent is retained by the government as "administrative" costs).[8] This program is open only to countries from the Caribbean Commonwealth and Mexico and limited to the agricultural industry.[9] Participants have legal access to workers' compensation and provincial and/or private health care. However, there is a marked discrepancy between the law and actual practice. Workers can spend up to eight months at a time in the country, and there is no limit to the number of years that they can continue to return to Canada.[10] Even when workers have come back every year for over twenty-five years, there is no opportunity for them to gain permanent residence.[11] Spousal and family visas are not provided, so the worker must arrive alone, leaving behind his or her family. Workers also have to live on site in "adequate" housing facilities provided by their employers, for which from 7 to 10 percent can be subtracted from their wages.[12]

STREAM FOR THE LOWER-SKILLED OCCUPATIONS

This program started in 2002 as a "pilot project," and it has no restrictions on which countries can send workers to Canada. However, workers have to wait for three months before they can access provincial health care. During this time, their private health care is provided through their employers.[13] Under this program, workers can work up to twenty-four months consecutively, but their contracts are not renewable after four years.[14] In provinces other than Manitoba and British Columbia, this program offers no pathway to permanent residency either.[15] Like the SAWP, this program does not allow workers to travel with other members of their families.[16] "Suitable" housing is provided by the employer at a cost of thirty dollars per week. However, workers are not required to live on site.[17]

HUMAN RIGHTS ISSUES

The issues faced by agricultural migrant workers in Canada start with their inability to immigrate to Canada and their social exclusion while living temporarily here. Workers complain about being invisible in Canadian society. They feel isolated and often suffer from depression and other mental illnesses caused by the lack of family and community support. Such workers are forced to leave their families behind and have few opportunities to keep in touch while they are in Canada. Children back home grow up without mothers and fathers and often no longer recognize their parents when they return from working abroad. Marriages sometimes break up because of the challenges inherent in long-distance relationships.

Workers are often the victims of racism and discrimination. In 2005, the Quebec Human Rights Tribunal found that workers at Centre Maraîcher Guinois, one of Canada's largest commercial vegetable farms, had repeatedly been the victims of racist taunts and verbal abuse from farm owners. The tribunal also found that migrant workers were not allowed in the "white only" cafeteria, expected instead to eat in a dirty cabin with no running water or toilets.[18]

The living conditions of Canada's migrant workers are often deplorable. A great number live in overcrowded dwellings with little ventilation during the summer months, when inside temperatures rise well above forty degrees Celsius. It is not uncommon to find six grown men sharing one bedroom and one toilet per house.[19] Actual working conditions are not much better: the work is dirty, dangerous, and demeaning. Reports on the conditions of migrant workers testify to the poor working environments in which they toil, where accidents are common and fatalities occur.[20] On paper, workers formally have access to both private and public health care; however, accessibility proves to be a great challenge. Migrant workers do not have the right to receive language training while they are in Canada. Thus, the lack of interpreters in health-care institutions in regions with large concentrations of migrant workers virtually denies them access to health care.[21] Workers often do not seek medical attention for fear of being released from their contracts and sent back home if they are perceived as no longer being able to perform their work well.[22]

The Canadian government remains distant from the task of regulating and supervising the living and working conditions of the migrant workers whom it continues to allow into the country in order to keep its agricultural industry productive. Furthermore, as I have already explained, it refuses to sign and ratify the CMW under the pretence that migrant workers' rights are already protected under Canadian and other international laws. A recent report from the Metcalf Foundation titled *Made in Canada: How the Law Constructs Migrant Workers' Insecurity* states that "the evolution of these temporary migration programs shows a progressive stepping down in government's commitment to workers and government involvement and accountability in program administration."[23] The report also notes that, "while government creates the conditions which allow the migrant work relationships to be formed, the supervision of the relationship is increasingly privatized between employer and worker."[24] Ratifying the CMW would force the Canadian government to review its current position on the supervision of its programs for migrant workers.

AN INTERNATIONAL HUMAN RIGHTS COMPLAINT

In 2009, the UFCW filed a complaint against the Canadian government in front of the International Labour Organization (ILO), alleging that the Agricultural Employees Protection Act, 2002 (AEPA), of the Province of Ontario denies collective bargaining rights to all agricultural employees.[25] Canada has ratified the Freedom of Association and Protection of the Right to Organize Convention of 1948, but it has not ratified the Right to Organize and Collective Bargaining Convention of 1949. The government indicated that a case (*Fraser*[26]) on behalf of the UFCW was still pending resolution before the Supreme Court of Canada. This case had the same objective as the complaint in front of the ILO: namely, to declare the AEPA unconstitutional on the ground that it infringes section 2(d) of the Canadian Charter of Rights and Freedoms, which prohibits constraints on freedom of association. The government then proceeded to demand that the ILO defer its ruling on the case until *Fraser* was decided by the Supreme Court justices.[27] In November 2010, the ILO noted that, following the government's concerns, it had postponed its ruling until its next session in the hope that the Supreme Court would decide on *Fraser*. However, even though the case was first brought before the Supreme Court in 2004, the justices delayed reaching a decision.[28] In its interim report, the ILO found that the absence of appropriate mechanisms for "the promotion of collective bargaining of agricultural workers constitutes an impediment to one of the principal objectives of the guarantee of freedom of association: the forming of independent organizations capable of concluding collective agreements."[29] The ILO also requested that the government take appropriate measures for the promotion of collective bargaining in the agricultural sector.[30]

The *Fraser* case was finally decided in April 2011; the Supreme Court of Canada found that the AEPA did not infringe on freedom of association. The court stated that section 2(d) of the Canadian Charter of Rights and Freedoms only encompasses a duty to engage in meaningful and "good faith" efforts to arrive at a collective agreement and does not therefore protect any particular process.[31] However, in a dissenting opinion, Justice Rosalie Abella expressed the view that preventing agricultural workers from access to a process in order to protect family farms harms section 2(d) in its entirety.[32] In its follow-up report of March 2012, the ILO acknowledged the Supreme

Court's finding that "agricultural employers have the duty to consider employee representations in good faith" but nevertheless concluded "that this duty, whether implied or explicit, is insufficient to ensure the collective bargaining rights of agricultural workers under the principles of freedom of association."[33] As of January 2013, no efforts have been made by the Canadian and Ontario governments to comply with the recommendations made by the ILO. Ontario and Alberta remain the only two provinces where agricultural workers are not allowed to unionize in Canada.

MOBILIZATION

Although migrant workers are largely invisible to most Canadians, some of them have been able to reach out and speak about the issues that they face on a day-to-day basis. Civil society organizations and unions across the country have organized and mobilized to fight for the rights of this vulnerable group of workers.

In 2001, a labour dispute involving Mexican workers in Leamington—Ontario's greenhouse and tomato-growing capital—attracted the attention of labour and community groups. Twenty of the migrant worker leaders involved in the dispute were summarily dismissed and deported. In response to the situation, a Global Justice Caravan Project[34] was initiated to provide outreach and support to workers while investigating their concerns.[35] This mobilization drew the attention of several government officials at both provincial and federal levels. Work and research conducted by volunteers formed the basis of the 2001 report on migrant farm workers in Canada submitted by the Global Justice Caravan Project to the Minister of Labour. The clear and ongoing need for continued community organizing in rural Ontario led to the creation of Justicia for Migrant Workers, a social justice collective, in the summer of 2002.[36]

Also in 2002, the UFCW opened the first migrant worker support centre, in Leamington. Over the following decade, such centres were opened by the affiliated Agricultural Workers Alliance in Simcoe, Bradford, and Virgil, Ontario, as well as more recently in Portage la Prairie, Manitoba; Surrey, Kelowna, and Abbotsford, British Columbia; and Saint-Rémi, Quebec. These centres assist workers in claiming their benefits, educate them about their rights, provide general support, and advocate on their behalf.[37] In Ontario's Niagara Falls region, for example, a network entitled the Niagara Migrant Worker Interest Group combines health, social services, legal, community, and academic groups to collaboratively address these issues at the community level.[38] Many other volunteer organizations have assisted workers by offering transportation to medical appointments; providing information on health, safety, and rights; hosting social and religious events directed at migrant workers; and facilitating language training. For example, the Occupational Health Clinics for Ontario Workers (OHCOW), based in Hamilton, has been holding specialized occupational health clinics and training sessions for migrant workers in select rural centres for the past five years. Several groups, including OHCOW, put together a bilingual health and safety manual that was distributed to thousands of workers throughout the country.[39] Many other individuals volunteer their time teaching English or French or organizing special events, religious services, concerts, and other social gatherings to help integrate migrant workers during their time in Canada.[40]

MIGRANT WORKERS IN THE CMHR: DEVELOPING THE EXHIBIT

Exhibit development in the CMHR started even before the curatorial team came on board. As Ken Norman describes in his contribution to this volume, the first public engagement consultations started in the winter of 2009–10. CMHR officials travelled to twenty cities across the country and engaged in open discussions with over 1,700 members of Canadian society. During these roundtables, people contributed their own stories and those that they wanted to see included in the new museum. Soon after, in February 2010, the curatorial team arrived in Winnipeg from places such as Sweden, the United Kingdom, Montreal, and Ottawa. They brought with them expertise in anthropology, history, Indigenous and genocide studies, international and Canadian human rights law, journalism, and political science. In March 2010, the team started going through the many stories collected during the public engagement consultations and conducted a literature review to develop a theoretical framework to bring all of the stories together as part of a larger human rights narrative. The galleries were assigned to different members of the team according to their respective areas of expertise. That summer consultations with other academics from different regions of the country began to take place. The stories were fleshed out and further developed during these discussions. Shortly afterward, activists and other stakeholders were approached and consulted on the potential representations of the stories. Later, during the fall, field trips and visits to different farms and workers' homes were made in order to facilitate bringing the voices of actual migrants into the exhibit. Soon after this, oral histories with labour activists, community members, filmmakers, academics, artists, photographers, and members of the UFCW were conducted.

Janet McLaughlin[41] developed a content package for the CMHR on the situation of migrant workers. This material was later used to help develop an approach paper discussed during peer review of the Canadian Human Rights Journey gallery. The peer reviewers were Mary Eberts,[42] Pearl Eliadis,[43] and Ken Norman.[44] The peer review was attended by members of the curatorial team involved in this gallery, the interpretive planner, and the firm hired to develop the overall design of the CMHR, Ralph Appelbaum Associates (RAA). After the peer review was concluded and most of the stories in the gallery were approved, the approach paper was presented to different stakeholders, academics working with migrant workers, and other members of the community. The approach paper was then sent to the design firm for it to start developing a proposal. The first content elevation/rendering was received in June 2011, and the proposed design was discussed within the CMHR. Further consultations with stakeholders also took place before the exhibit design was finally approved.

In the winter of 2011, the first round of image selections took place. The curator of this exhibit and the image researcher at the CMHR established collaborative relationships with Vincenzo Pietropaolo,[45] the UFCW, activists, academics, and other stakeholders in order to provide RAA with a selection of images. While I was writing this chapter, RAA continued to work with these different stakeholders to create a database of images regularly presented to the CMHR team working on this exhibit. The role of the team was to ensure the accuracy and appropriateness of the images selected for the exhibit.

Up to this date, text writing saw several iterations and proved to be one of the most challenging steps in development of the exhibits. Artifact selection started in the winter of 2011–12. Based on the approach paper, RAA identified a bicycle as a possible artifact for inclusion in this exhibit. Bicycles are the main vehicle of transport used by migrant workers while in Canada, and several cases of migrant workers dying in accidents on the road have been reported. In cooperation with the UFCW, I was able to identify a bicycle that belonged to a migrant worker that could be donated to the CMHR. Because of the lack of appropriate storage space, it was held by the UFCW until the CMHR could properly acquire it.

The next step in development of the exhibit was to conduct oral history interviews with the migrant workers themselves in order to represent them in this space. This was by no means an easy task. Great care had to be taken to find migrant workers whose stories encompassed the variety of issues that had surfaced from the research process and the community engagement with migrant workers and activists. Ethical concerns also arise when conducting oral histories and human rights research.[46] Migrant workers are often vulnerable to coercion, and they fear retaliation if they speak up about the human rights violations that they experience while living in Canada. Extreme care had to be taken to ensure that no harm would occur to the contributors to and participants in these oral histories as a consequence of the exhibit.

PHYSICAL SPACE OF THE EXHIBIT

Trying to present the complexity of such a story, or collection of stories, in a CMHR exhibit was a great challenge. The space dedicated to agricultural migrant workers is located in the Canadian Journeys gallery. The exhibit consists of a "niche" of sixty-four square feet. In it, an introductory text panel briefly presents the topic of the exhibit to the visitor. Against the back wall, four cast figures representing migrant workers from different countries provide the focal point of the exhibit. Each figure holds a monitor-type screen representing a picture frame. The monitor has the capacity to reproduce segments of the oral histories discussed above. These media pieces can be activated by visitors and speak to the many issues experienced by migrant workers in their own words. When the monitors are not activated, they can display a still image representing the family members whom migrant workers have left behind.[47] A bicycle is also used as an artifact to represent issues related to the transport and safety of migrant workers.

CONCLUSION

As part of its mandate, the CMHR must "enhance the public's understanding of human rights, to promote respect for others, and to encourage reflection and dialogue."[48] That is why the museum cannot remain silent in the face of oppression. As an institution, the CMHR must enhance the public's understanding of migrant workers' rights and promote respect for them. Such a museum that fails to speak of the abusive treatment of migrant workers in Canada would be an accomplice to a government that does not believe in their rights.

Many people who visit this exhibit will be unfamiliar with its subject; indeed, their visit might be the first time that they face such issues. This exhibit exists to bring to light the injustices and other human rights violations to which migrant workers are subjected in Canada. It aims to make migrant workers' voices heard. This workforce that keeps the Canadian agricultural industry productive cannot remain invisible anymore.

Canadians need to know that migrant workers exist and that they are the constant victims of human rights violations. The government's inactivity has allowed the perpetuation of a system that discriminates against and exploits foreign workers without any accountability. Visitors should learn that remaining silent on this issue is not an option anymore. They can join many other Canadians who have mobilized and acted to defend the rights of migrant workers across the country.

NOTES

1   Peremptory laws are those from which no derogation is permitted; they are recognized by the international community as a whole as being fundamental to maintaining an international legal order.

2   Ryszard Cholewinski, Paul de Guchteneire, and Antoine Pecoud, eds., *Migration and Human Rights: The United Nations Convention on Migrant Worker's Rights* (Cambridge, UK: UNESCO and Cambridge University Press, 2009), 203.

3   Jamaica in 1966, Barbados and Trinidad and Tobago in 1967, Mexico in 1974, Antigua and Barbuda, Dominica, Grenada, Montserrat, St. Kitts-Nevis, St. Lucia, and St. Vincent and the Grenadines in 1976.

4   Cholewinski, Guchteneire, and Pecoud, *Migration and Human Rights*, 204.

5   UFCW Canada, *Report of the Status of Migrant Workers in Canada 2011* (Toronto: UFCW, 2011), 5.

6   International Covenant on Civil and Political Rights, International Covenant on Economic, Social, and Cultural Rights, International Convention on the Elimination of All Forms of Racial Discrimination, Convention against Torture, Convention of the Rights of the Child, Convention of the Rights of Persons with Disabilities.

7   Citizenship and Immigration Canada, www.cic.gc.ca/.

8   Citizenship and Immigration Canada, Agreement for the Employment in Canada of Commonwealth Caribbean Seasonal Agricultural Workers—2013, Section IV, http://www.hrsdc.gc.ca/eng/workplaceskills/foreign_workers/contracts-forms/sawpcc2013.shtml.

9   Human Resources and Skills Development Canada, http://www.hrsdc.gc.ca/eng/workplaceskills/foreign_workers/sawp/description.shtml.

10 Ibid.

11 Jenna Hennebry, *Permanently Temporary? Agricultural Migrant Workers and Their Integration in Canada*, http://www.irpp.org/pubs/IRPPstudy/IRPP_Study_no26.pdf.

12 Ibid.

13 Human Resources and Skills Development Canada, http://www.hrsdc.gc.ca/eng/workplaceskills/foreign_workers/sawp/description.shtml.

14 Ibid.

15 Hennebry, *Permanently Temporary?*

16 Ibid.

17 Ibid.

18 *Québec (Commission des droits de la personne et des droits de la jeunesse) v. Centre Maraî-cher Eugène Guinois JR Inc.*, 2005-779 (TDPQ).

19 I have visited workers' homes provided by employers in Quebec, Ontario, and British Columbia.

20 UFCW Canada, http://www.ufcw.ca/templates/ufcwcanada/images/awa/publications/ UFCW-Status_of_MF_Workers_2010-2011_EN.pdf; http://www.ufcw.ca/templates/ufcw-canada/images/Report-on-The-Status-of-Migrant-Workers-in-Canada-2011.pdf.

21 I have participated in meetings with community members and organizations trying to deal with this problem. A health-care bus with volunteer health-care providers that would travel between different farms was proposed by a community organization in the Niagara Falls region.

22 I have had several conversations with migrant workers and community activists who have expressed these views.

23 Metcalf Foundation, *Made in Canada: How the Law Constructs Migrant Workers' Insecu-rity*, http://metcalffoundation.com/wp-content/uploads/2012/09/Made-in-Canada-Full-Report.pdf.

24 Ibid.

25 Letter to ILO Director General Juan Somavia from UFCW Canada President Wayne Hanley, 23 March 2009, http://ufcw.ca/Theme/UFCW/files/ILO/ILO%20PDF/LTR_%20 J_%20Somavia_ILO%20re%20UFCW%20CAN%20vs_%20Ont_%20Govt_%20 03-09%20En.pdf.

26 *Fraser v. Ontario (Attorney General)*, 2011 SCC 20.

27 Case No. 2704, Interim Report by the Committee on Freedom of Association of the ILO, November 2010, http://oppenheimer.mcgill.ca/IMG/pdf/Report_ILO_CaseNo274_ UFCW_Canada_November_2010_1_.pdf.

28 Ibid.

29 Ibid.

30 Ibid.

31 *Fraser v. Ontario (Attorney General)*, 2011 SCC 20.

32 Ibid.

33 Report No. 363, March 2012, Case No. 2704 (Canada), http://www.ilo.org/dyn/normlex/ en/f?p=1000:50002:0::NO::P50002_COMPLAINT_TEXT_ID:3057155.

34 A number of volunteers drove around rural Ontario talking to migrant workers and ask-ing them to share their concerns.

35 Janet McLaughlin, "Those Who Construct, Care, and Cultivate: A Synopsis of Issues Fac-ing Past and Present Migrant Workers in Canada," prepared for the Canadian Museum for Human Rights, 2011.

36 Justice for Migrant Workers, http://www.justicia4migrantworkers.org/justicia_new.htm.

37 McLaughlin, "Those Who Construct."

38 Ibid.

39 Ibid.

40   Oral history interviews collected by A. Perla, J. Andres, V. Ayala, A. Diaz, and J. McLaughlin. I also had the opportunity to attend some of the welcoming events for migrant workers in the Niagara Falls region.

41   Janet McLaughlin is an assistant professor of health studies and a research associate of the International Migration Research Centre at Wilfrid Laurier University.

42   Mary Eberts holds the Ariel Sallows Chair in Human Rights in the Faculty of Law at the University of Saskatchewan and is a founding member of the Women's Legal Education Fund.

43   Pearl Eliadis is an internationally recognized human rights lawyer, author, and lecturer.

44   Ken Norman is a professor in the Faculty of Law at the University of Saskatchewan.

45   Vincenzo Pietropaolo has been an independent, internationally recognized, documentary photographer since 1971. Based in Toronto, he has completed major projects on Italian immigrant life in Canada, religious street rituals, migrant farm workers, health care, political protest, the labour movement, immigrant gardens, urban social issues, and architecture.

46   A research ethics policy framework was developed for the CMHR by the Canadian Centre for Ethics in Public Affairs in March 2011.

47   On several occasions when I approached migrant workers to talk about their experiences, they promptly took out family photographs that they wanted to share with me. One of the main reasons that migrant workers cited for coming to Canada was the opportunity to provide better lives for their families back home.

48   Museums Act, SC 1990, c. 3.

THE
MUSEOLOGY OF
HUMAN RIGHTS

CHAPTER 11
Jennifer Carter

Over the past few decades, and notably since the millennium, a new genre has evolved within the taxonomy of museums. Issues based, and human rights centred, these museums make human rights concepts, stories, and practices the core of their institutional mission, curatorial praxis, and exhibition and programming initiatives. There are now institutions, either newly inaugurated or in the planning stages, that self-identify as human rights museums in Chile, Paraguay, Belgium, Japan, Taiwan, South Korea, Pakistan, and Indonesia, in addition to a Federation of International Human Rights Museums (FIHRM) in Liverpool, United Kingdom, with an even broader membership base. Of these museums, one important example is the result of recommendations arising from a national Truth and Reconciliation Commission, and has been designed to facilitate greater social cohesion following human rights violations on national soil. Others, shaped by contemporary international social and political discourses, have evolved in light of a desire to promote and foster a human rights culture generally—though not in response to any single, specific human rights transgression. With its opening in 2014, the Canadian Museum for Human Rights (CMHR) in Winnipeg, Manitoba, is the newest museum of this latter kind.

Although the emergent phenomenon of human rights museums undoubtedly marks an important moment in the practices and bodies of research that shape, theorize, and probe critical museology and contemporary museological debates, it would be incorrect to suggest that museums as cultural institutions have only recently engaged in rights issues. There are many ways in which to interpret how concerns for rights have historically intersected with museum practices and cultural heritage, whether they were named as such or not. The first public museums were disciplinarian and ideological venues that reinforced for some and excluded others from dominant knowledge systems, essentialized discourses, and the preservation and valorization of intangible and tangible cultural heritage from which and through which these knowledge systems and discourses were largely constituted, publicized, and perpetuated. The new museology movement of the 1960s and 1970s, whether incarnated in the form of the first ecomuseums in France championed by Hugues de Varine and George-Henri Rivière, or the neighbourhood community museums of Anacostia in Washington, DC, and Casa del Museo in Mexico City, pioneered methods and philosophies that radically rethought the social purposes of museums while providing an important impetus for considering how museums could benefit the needs of their communities rather than the reverse—in contemporary parlance, these museological models sought to provide political, cultural, and social agency to their constituents. The very genealogy of museums provides fertile ground for tracing how different concepts of rights—mirroring broader rights transformations since the 1970s with the rise of human rights as a mass contemporary international social movement and inspiring transnational ideals—are negotiated in operational museology and articulated (or not), given agency (or not), and reconstituted (or not) within the collecting and exhibiting apparatus that is the museum and to what ends. As I will discuss further, some of what we might recognize of the more recent manifestation of "rights" in museological practice is already apparent in the work and ethos of memorial museums, a genre that emerged mainly in the 1980s. In the manner that museums, as Sandra Dudley and Kylie Message observe, are purveyors of the periods and localities from and in which they emerge, they are time capsules providing insight into the societal attitudes, political agendas, and social trends of their time and to which they are inextricably bound.[1] It is from this perspective that this chapter takes up the developing genre of human rights museums as one of many institutional trajectories in museological history responding to broader manifestations in political society.

This trajectory has seized in recent years on what Samuel Moyne has termed "the last utopia," the utopian program of world-reforming human rights. Moyne argues that, despite common conceptions that place them in the lineage of Enlightenment traditions, in their ideals and principles, human rights are a contemporary project, brought to bear on international society as a means of transcending national or state politics "amidst a crisis of utopianism": "When the history of human rights is told beyond myths of deep origins, it illustrates the persistence of the nation-state as the aspirational forum for humanity until recently. The state was the incubator for rights claims, both in the rise of the absolutist state, with its well-disciplined interior order and colonialist exterior expansion, then in the creation of the modern nation, in which citizenship and rights, identification and contestation, were always bound up with each other."[2] Yet, as Moyne goes on to argue, the concept of human rights as a transnational project came into its own not, as one might expect, in the 1940s following the UN Declaration of Human Rights, after which they remained (surprisingly) largely peripheral to political agendas, nor in the wake of a longer historical trajectory as an evolution of Enlightenment natural law, but at a moment of crisis in political orders, at the end of the glorious 1930s, and in the shadows of other utopian projects gone awry. And this, coupled with the shift from a morality program to a political one in the 1980s, with the proliferation of NGOs and the concept's more general vernacularization at grassroots levels, has imbued human rights with—borrowing again from Moyne—"a profound dilemma" as they assume "the burden of addressing all global ills."[3] When taken up as a museum project, this tension becomes all the more pronounced within museum discourses. Institutions of the state, and funded by publics, museums have engaged wholeheartedly in the human rights crusade. But to what effects? To what ends?

The recent "turn" in museum practices, from human rights grounded largely in the work of memorial museums to human rights assuming a wider focus within the purview of museological activities, merits critical attention, perhaps less for the similarities than for the differences (and their attendant political implications) arising between them. While some human rights museums, like many memorial museums before them, are dedicated to researching, archiving, memorializing, and generally promoting meaningful understanding and public awareness of human atrocities and traumatic pasts, others focus on the present and bring to greater public attention emergent rights issues, such as access to water and children's rights, or ongoing and insidious forms of human rights abuse, such as those arising from social discrimination on the basis of sexual orientation, disability, and ethnic or national origin. Bringing these stories to light museologically, like those that define the work of Liberty Osaka in Japan, constitutes for some individuals their first public sharing of an intensely difficult personal experience that might subject them to further discrimination. Because of the nature and diversity of the themes addressed by this newer form of human rights museum, and its focus on contemporary issues, it can be subject to specific local, political, and social tensions in ways that profoundly challenge or impede its work. For some, government pressures that restrict or censor content, impose funding cuts, or limit budgets are constant threats undermining the vital purpose served by these social and cultural institutions, both for their direct constituents (communities of mourners, peoples of discrimination, and those who have shared their personal stories, experiences, and artifacts) and for broader publics and communities of practice.

The institutional mandate that human rights museums have adopted by their pursuit of a social justice agenda assumes a key role for museums in contemporary society, one that is informed by, and informs about, human rights and social activism. It follows that, because of the centrality of human rights issues to these museums' institutional mission, a new generation of museums is collectively engaging in a profound rethinking of the traditional social and cultural functions of museums, functions largely focused on the core activities of collection and preservation; education, exhibition, and communication; and research. In their attempts to invest visitors with the knowledge and tools to become greater human rights advocates and defenders, human rights museums are inaugurating new pedagogies and programming initiatives informed by the larger intellectual and cultural practices of the fields of human rights and social justice.[4]

Although this first generation of human rights museums might seem to cohere through their common aim to make human rights—and can one presume the concept of "universal human rights"?—a museological phenomenon, the nature of the institution's investment in the subject is anything but universal. These museums have been established alternately as national and civic institutions, with widely divergent approaches and outcomes to communicating narratives about human rights and, perhaps more significantly, differing points of origins, uses of collections, funding structures, and social roles. Some have been founded in the aftermath of gross human rights abuses on national soil, as was the privately operated Museo de las Memorias: Dictadura y Derechos Humanos in Asunción, Paraguay, and the highly symbolic national initiative of the Museo de la Memoria y Los Derechos Humanos in Santiago, Chile. Following two national Truth and Reconciliation Commissions originating in Chile in 1990 and 2003, respectively,[5] the Museo de la Memoria y Los Derechos Humanos in Santiago focuses on repairing past injustices while enabling social reconciliation by making public "the systematic violations of human rights by the state of Chile between the years 1973–1990" and offering an "ethical reflection on memory, solidarity and the importance of human rights" in Chilean society with a never again mantra.[6] Others, like the Canadian Museum for Human Rights in Winnipeg, Manitoba, and the Children's Museum for Peace and Human Rights in Karachi, Pakistan (still in the planning stages), intend to nurture a socially just world by providing "socially relevant educational experiences" designed not only to sensitize publics about social intolerance[7] but also to alter public behaviour to have positive impacts on social values in relation to human rights in years to come.[8] Yet, unlike the museums in South America, these latter examples do not redress a single specific event in national history. Rather, at the CMHR, several thematic zones structure the visitor's itinerary synchronically and diachronically through a diversity of historical and contemporary human rights stories that highlight both the potential challenges to and the benefits of museums engaging meaningfully in human rights work.

The spectrum of museographical approaches undertaken by these institutions is both evolving and, to a certain extent, culturally specific. For these reasons, it is important to critically engage this new museum type by asking how human rights museums have interpreted a larger human rights turn in society and how they operate within different national frameworks and political agendas. Is this new generation of museums deployed as a political instrument to promote the interests of the state or as a forum for dialogue to enrich civil society? To what extent can these museums assume a leadership role in global practices dedicated to advancing human rights; conversely, to what extent are they stymied by the political entities that fund them in their attempts to present just accounts of human rights issues? These are essential questions as a growing number of human rights museums open their doors to the public in countries throughout Asia, Europe, North America, and South America.

In light of these questions, this chapter examines the emergent museological genre of human rights museums and considers how it models practices shaped not only by the discourses and pedagogies of the fields of human rights and activist museology but also by national, transnational, and political discourses. The chapter further investigates how human rights museums are addressing this important responsibility in their work. An inquiry into the ethical and pedagogical frameworks of human rights museums identifies issues inherent in the very concept of a human rights museum that affect questions of pedagogy and purpose, hinging as the institution does on the transgression from an inherited representational framework to one that models activist practices. The intention is to question the terms of an appropriate framework for a museum dedicated to taking up invariably contentious issues associated with human rights culture.

FROM SOCIAL TO SOCIAL JUSTICE AGENCY

Since the turn of the millennium, scholars and museum professionals alike have argued for a renewed sense of the social and political agency of museums at large.[9] In his important writing on the topic, Richard Sandell has challenged the exclusionary practices of museums by exploring how they can act as agents of social change, by overcoming forms of inequality too often reinforced in the traditional practices of museum work and institutional structures, and thereby encourage greater diversity of representation. Within a decade of his groundbreaking *Museums, Society, Inequality,* Sandell and Eithne Nightingale could claim in their introduction to the first anthology dedicated to the phenomenon of museums and social justice, *Museums, Equality and Social Justice,* that concerns for human rights, equality, diversity, and social justice generally have indeed moved from the margins to the core of museum practices, policies, and programs. Along similar lines, Robert Janes articulates in rather alarming terms the need for museums to renew themselves by championing contemporary issues in his provocative manifesto *Museums in a Troubled World: Renewal, Irrelevance or Collapse?* Fiona Cameron and Lynda Kelly's call to take up "hot topics" such as racial violence, terrorism, and climate change as part of museological culture has also significantly challenged institutional inertia with ideas for new modes of practice.[10] Viewed in this light, the commitment that a number of museums have displayed to advancing social justice awareness and education demonstrates that these cultural institutions have played—and continue to play—an important role in the arena of human rights. At the same time, with the rise of human rights museums modelling new and different ideas about what museums are designed to do and how they should interact with different publics, a number of new critical practices and concerns are surfacing from the need to reconcile the museum's traditional representational function with the specific ideals of a human rights culture.

The idea that museums—key institutions in civil society and widely considered influential in their representations of contemporary issues—engage in the arena of human rights is fruitful in several important ways. As sites of informal education, museums provide important public venues for discussion and debate about contentious topics that define contemporary discourse and enable deeper engagement than many other forms of public media (e.g., print and broadcast) because of the particular manner in which these institutions mediate these subjects with their diverse publics in exhibition galleries and programming. In this latter regard, museums are not only social spaces that permit dialogic engagement among visitors; their very spatiality, an essential feature of exhibitions, as Raymond Montpetit has well observed, means that visitors simultaneously engage physically, conceptually, and phenomenologically with the museum exhibition medium. These multiple modes of experience can deepen the visitor's engagement with museal space and its messages.[11] It can be argued that the very combination of the topic of human rights with museological practice provides museums with the timely challenge of renewing their commitment to improving the cultural health and well-being of the communities that host them by engaging in human rights not only as a subject of representation but equally as one of self-reflexivity on how the practice of human rights is institutionalized by museums themselves (in relation to collections, exhibitions, and human resources). One would fully expect, for example, a human rights museum to incorporate a heightened attention to human rights not only as a subject but also *as a practice,* such as by developing an appropriate policy for repatriation, by ensuring that minority views are not excluded from exhibitions, and by ensuring job equity.

MEMORIAL MUSEUMS AND THE HUMAN RIGHTS TURN

Museums that self-identify as human rights museums—that is, those that bear the term "human rights" in their names—are undoubtedly a recent occurrence in the museum world. What is so interesting about this development is that they are appearing around the globe, in dramatically different geopolitical contexts, and that they are addressing a wide range of local and global issues in ways specific to the human rights field. With the remarkable exception of Japan, where five city human rights museums were founded throughout the 1980s and 1990s, the appearance of the human rights museum is largely a post-millennial phenomenon.[12] Outside Japan, several museums have been inaugurated in the past decade, including those in Seoul, South Korea, in 2012; Malines, Belgium, in 2012; Banda Aceh, Indonesia, in 2011; and Santiago, Chile, in 2010. There are two human rights museums in Paraguay's capital, Asunción: the first was established as an itinerant museum in 2002 and has occupied its current permanent location in a former detention centre since late 2005; the second, housed at the capital's archives and national courthouse, was inaugurated in 2008.[13] The Canadian Museum for Human Rights in Winnipeg opened in September 2014 after several delays occasioned by funding challenges; a national human rights museum is scheduled to open within the Jingmei Human Rights Memorial and Cultural Park (created in 2009) in Taiwan; it has been announced that the Green Island Human Rights Park, in Taitung County, Taiwan, which has a human rights monument, will also open a national museum; and the Children's Museum for Peace and Human Rights (CMPHR), in Karachi, Pakistan, has launched a capital campaign to begin work on a museum specifically geared to sensitizing children to the values of peace, social justice, and human rights. Significantly, this museum follows a fifteen-year initiative by the Human Rights Education Program (HREP) in Pakistan (now renamed CMPHR), which has routinely specialized in teaching children about issues related to citizenship and human rights by providing hundreds of schools and schoolchildren with programming on activism, campaign projects, thematic workshops, and a youth network group (Right On Network).[14]

While such museums are a recent and still evolving phenomenon, there is a far larger group of museums all over the world that have addressed, for several decades already, human rights issues through their exhibitions and programming. The District Six Museum in Cape Town, South Africa, and the Memorial Museum of Dominican Resistance in Santo Domingo, Dominican Republic, are two very different museums whose fundamental *raison d'être* is defending basic human rights, such as protecting against displacements and forced removals of citizens from their homes and communities or against dictatorial abuses of power. The efforts of museums such as District Six and the Memorial Museum of Dominican Resistance were formalized in the Torreon Declaration of Museum Responsibility to Promote Human Rights, signed at the annual meeting of INTERCOM[15] in Mexico in 2009. Proclaiming that it is "a fundamental responsibility of museums, wherever possible, to be active in promoting diversity and human rights, respect and equality for people of all origins, beliefs and background," this declaration underscores the importance of all museological institutions to make human rights central to their practices. It does so broadly, such that one might understand the heightened attention to human rights to become manifest in the choice of exhibition content, in the approaches to programming (e.g., adopting multicultural educational pedagogy), and in institutional and human resource policies.

A conceptual museological trajectory also exists, linking self-identifying human rights museums with the wave of memorial museums that began to appear in large numbers throughout the 1980s and that address historical human rights transgressions. Consider, as a precursor to and early example of this genre, the Hiroshima Peace Memorial Museum, inaugurated in Japan in 1955, the first of several memorial museums to follow, including the Maison des Esclaves on Gorée Island in Senegal, which opened in 1978; the Tuol Sleng Museum of Genocidal Crimes in Phnom Penh, Vietnam, inaugurated in 1980; the Apartheid Museum in Johannesburg, South Africa, opened in 2001; and the Terroháza in Budapest, inaugurated in 2002. These museums are just a sampling of what Paul Williams has theorized as "a global institutional development."[16] He was the first to chart the then underanalyzed growth of memorial museums in his 2007 monograph *Memorial Museums: The Global Rush to Commemorate Atrocities,* describing museums of this evolving phenomenon as "a specific kind of museum dedicated to a historic event commemorating mass suffering of some kind."[17] Williams was quick to identify the inherent paradox in the confluence of a structure conceived both as a commemorative (the memorial) and as a contextual (the museum) domain. In the coming together of these two conceptual fields, he argued, was a new kind of social institution that provides both a "moral framework" surrounding sensitive historical events and far greater contextual information in the museographical treatment of these events. Although the pendulum might shift between these two extremes in any given memorial museum, the genre's global appearance and remit nevertheless attest to changing and wide-ranging attitudes toward the role and potential contribution of such museums to contemporary society. Despite how politicized the individual results might be, collectively memorial museums have responded to the growing social need to represent sensitive histories such as genocide, slavery, terrorism, and political oppression within the public forum of the museum to both local and global audiences and to give an important public voice to those victimized by massive abuses of political power and authority.

Some examples of human rights museums are indeed directly related to this lineage and bear the telltale traits of memorial museums identified by Williams. In their subject matter, these museums often focus on civilian victims who have died unnatural deaths related to abuses of power by perpetrators who might still be at large. And, unlike traditional history museums where museographical conventions dictate a concern for contextualization and a "neutral" representational method, in the memorial museum a number of shared characteristics have emerged. According to Williams,

> their site is usually integral to their institutional identity;
> they often maintain a clientele who have a special relationship
> to the museum (such as former members of a resistance,
> or the families of victims of persecution); they regularly
> hold politically significant special events (such as memorial
> days); they often function as research centers geared towards
> identifying victims and providing material to aid the
> prosecution of perpetrators; they are frequently aligned with
> truth and reconciliation commissions and human rights
> organizations; they have an especially strong pedagogic
> mission that often includes a psychosocial component in their
> work with survivors; educational work is stimulated by moral
> considerations and draws ties to issues in contemporary
> society in a way that is uncommon in standard museum
> presentations of history.[18]

The traits that Williams has identified in relation to memorial museums are equally pertinent to several human rights museums, with the important distinction that the latter museums have shifted the focal point of their metadiscourses from memorialization to social justice. This shift is not confined to nomenclature and semantics alone. In addition to highlighting the place of human rights discourses within the museographic paradigm, this new generation of museums has deployed a number of strategies that encourage visitors to go beyond the position of witness to the crimes on display by engaging in active practices to stem future abuses of power. Initiatives such as the US Holocaust Memorial Museum's Committee on Conscience are important to keep in mind as early examples of museums engaging proactively in contemporary crime prevention. In this regard, the pedagogy of the future CMPHR is instructive in that it intends to continue in the tradition of the HREP by promoting to generations of Pakistani children respect for the social values of justice and peace in addition to teaching them campaigning knowledge and skills.

The Museo de la Memoria y los Derechos Humanos in Santiago
has already done this in its programming and outreach activities. The
idea of equipping students with the knowledge of how a range of media
techniques (visual, spoken, and written) has been used to campaign on
behalf of different issues is at the core of its programming. Designed to
provide Chilean youth with the ability to express themselves and the
knowledge to identify the mechanisms of transgressions of power, the
museum's programs entail skills-based workshops that equip youth with
the creative and artistic means to engage in rights-based movements.[19]
Students are introduced to the concepts and mechanisms of discrimination, and, in skills-based workshops designed to teach about how to
use media (e.g., videos or comics), they are encouraged to tell their own
stories about human rights—whether lived or inspired by historical
precedents. This approach to educational and outreach programming
has the twofold significance of encouraging participants to reflect on the
values of human rights education (defined by UNESCO as equality, justice,
non-violence, and respect for human dignity) while also providing for a
broader investigation of the concept of right.[20] In the context of Chile,
education on Indigenous rights, especially concerning Chile's Mapuchi
population, is an important example.

Scholar Andreas Huyssen has characterized the pervasive need to
remember that defines not only our contemporary moment but also the
surge of museums founded since the 1980s as a central project of postmodern culture. As a form of media, the museum within this memory-
representation matrix is a prime site for exploring the limits of a social
phenomenon that has found expression alternately through the contrasting modes of evoking an experience and merely representing it.[21] In the
particular instance of memorial museums, this dichotomy is especially
significant for obvious reasons. Difficult histories have at times translated museographically in analogical terms, in such a manner that visitors
are immersed in reconstructed environments that emphasize a sensorial
connection with the past, without the benefit of also including critical
and contextual tools to better understand the complexity of this past.
Within these sites, providing nuanced and multivocal interpretations
is secondary to recreating universes of simulation intended to bring the
past forward but without the benefit of escaping a logic of victimhood.
It is thus important to consider the effects of representation and how
these sites can promote both individual and collective responsibility
in relation to the respect for human rights through a museographical

approach that opens up remembering and intergenerational and inter-cultural dialogue.

It is not surprising that in the past decade a number of memorial museums have begun to incorporate new strategies into their exhibition and programming initiatives that challenge this paradigm. It is perhaps here that the newer genre of the human rights museum aligns with what can be viewed as its precursor, insofar as the human rights museum and the memorial museum now find common ground in their intent not only to represent particular issues but also to develop ways for visitors to take concrete actions and to transcend the commemorative parameters within which memorial museums have traditionally operated. Important examples include the From Memory to Action gallery at the US Holocaust Memorial Museum in Washington, opened in 2009, and the Campaign Zone at the International Slavery Museum in Liverpool, both of which address these museums' respective historical subjects—the Holocaust and the international slave trade—in terms of their contemporary resonances. Both have experimented with techniques intended to elicit diverse forms of action from visitors, and both conceived these galleries well after the completion of their principal and permanent exhibitions. As such, these newer galleries are designed to take up the themes of genocide and slavery and to demonstrate how they continue to exist in contemporary and in-ternational contexts.

Two chapters in this volume are important references for my discus-sion, notably in regard to the roles of visitors and curators in relation to representations of suffering and atrocity that constitute one aspect of hu-man rights museums. In their chapter, "Engaging Machines: Experience, Empathy, and the Modern Museum," Adam Muller, Struan Sinclair, and Andrew Woolford premise their research on the notion that empathy is crucial to understanding human suffering—the suffering of others—a con-cept that underlies many muscological attempts to represent difficult his-tories. Their research considers modes of immersive engagement that can have impacts on subsequent forms of social action undertaken by visitors, in particular the potential for online initiatives to enable the development of "empathetic communities" through the creation of a digital storyworld prototype of a Canadian Indian residential school (Embodying Empathy). The thoughtful chapter by Angela Failler and Roger Simon provides an al-ternative viewpoint from which to consider a curatorial practice that does not, in their words, "reiterate the museum as a disciplinarian institution with a privileged authority to prescribe and proscribe … people's cultural heritage" but enables visitors to learn from the stories and histories of others in a deeply meaningful and constructive way in order to respond in an appropriate manner.

It is within this museological perspective that we can begin to situate the development of the human rights museum, a genre that might seem, on initial inspection, to arise from a larger and growing human rights culture that has manifested itself in several recent popular political movements such as the Arab Spring, Idle No More, and Occupy Wall Street. The emergence of a significant number of human rights museums over the past decade has coincided with an evolving social consciousness and increased awareness of the need for citizen engagement in obtaining and upholding democratic forms of government. This in itself provides new modes and models of practice for museum programming in the areas of citizen action. Imparting the tools and the know-how for new forms of civic engagement can be a key component of a human rights museum's objectives, and highly successful models of this practice already exist both in history and in ideas museums around the globe. Yet these museums are also products of their particular historical moment, responsive to the evolving social and cultural fabric of society and in support of social realities such as changing demographics, the impact of technology, and a growing participatory culture. In sum, what we are witnessing with the development of human rights museums is the potential for a hybridization of museological practices.

MUSEUM PRACTICES AND HUMAN RIGHTS EDUCATION

One example of the hybridization of human rights and museology has occurred in relation to the use of human rights education, which instructs on a range of advocacy methods and critical concepts that relate the theoretical foundations of human rights to concrete actions for their actualization. Message development, public outreach, mobilization, lobbying, and negotiation are some of the core elements of human rights education and training. The goal is to impart some of the skills of human rights practices, both to achieve these rights in societies where they are not widely respected, and to actively defend them where their vitality is imperilled. Some memorial museums have already begun to apply some of the tenets of the international field of human rights education and rights-based programming to their own practices. At the US Holocaust Memorial Museum (USHMM) in Washington, the From Memory to Action gallery models some of these practices within a suite of galleries curated by Bridget Conley-Zilkic in order to explicitly examine the contemporary legacies of genocide. The name is the first indication that the museum's traditional representational function has been recalibrated in order to compel a more active response to the material on display. Several museographical components encourage visitors to become active participants in seeking change, such as the Take Action! cards distributed at the entrance to the gallery. Visitors are invited to pledge their own forms of action against genocide, pledges that might ultimately become public once they have been posted on the giant Pledge Wall and electronic world map that archives the global reach of a growing number of visitor promises. The card doubles as a recording device when used in an interactive table within the same gallery, enabling visitors to stay connected with the USHMM by accessing from home information that they read while at the museum.

Like the USHMM, the International Slavery Museum (ISM) in Liverpool has also recently inaugurated a small gallery space dedicated to examining the contemporary legacies of slavery—an important counterpart to the main chronological narrative that chronicles the transatlantic slave trade begun in the mid-fifteenth century. The ISM is home to the Federation of International Human Rights Museums (FIHRM) and a self-proclaimed campaigning museum, and it regularly partners with NGOs such as the Environmental Justice Foundation and Anti-Slavery International in order to produce exhibitions and outreach programs that instruct on campaign techniques, notably for young audiences. This follows on the heels of heritage consultant and project manager Ali Bodley's efforts to promote active citizenship through the highly successful Campaign! Make an Impact! initiative that provides free cross-curricular school programs designed by the Museums, Libraries and Archives Council in the United Kingdom and that teaches young people how to mount their own campaigns on issues of significance to them (begun in 2009).[22]

HUMAN RIGHTS MUSEUMS AS SITES OF RECONCILIATION AND REPARATION

There is another way in which current human rights museums are responding to wider social and societal needs, and Chile's Museo de la Memoria y Los Derechos Humanos again provides an example. In a number of transitional societies around the world, Truth and Reconciliation Commissions (TRCS) are actively seeking to document human rights abuses on national soil and to recommend methods of symbolic collective reparation. In some cases, they can take the form of memorials; in others, as is the case in Chile, a museum. The difficulty of the TRC as a truth-seeking process is that its public mandate does not always result in criminal prosecutions of former persecutors identified by the commissions—rather, its opposite, political amnesty, can be the case—and its role must be understood within the political context of a society and the mandate given to the particular commission. Is the mandate designed to facilitate victim and social healing, or justice, or some measure of the two? It is literally, as Chilean human rights lawyer and advocate José Zalaquett has observed, a question of establishing a fine balance between "ethical imperatives and political constraints."[23]

Chile's own investment in two different commissions designed to investigate the atrocities of General Augusto Pinochet's military regime (1973–90) between 1990 and 2005 provides an interesting case study of a post-dictatorship transition within the larger context of continental neighbours undergoing much the same process. Yet, in the case of Argentina and Uruguay, the goals of the TRCs were not the same. Would Chile emphasize truth telling (like Argentina) or reparation (like Uruguay)? Moreover, how would these findings manifest themselves museographically in the very museum that was to provide the divided nation with a symbol of a new order—a reclaimed democratic past? The Museo de la Memoria took its cues from the second of Chile's commissions, the Comisión Nacional Sobre Prisón Politica y Tortura (September 2003 to June 2005), specifically mandated with the task of documenting human rights transgressions of torture and civil rights abuses and with identifying victims, not perpetrators, as a means of constructing a shared memory from the past. As Zalaquett would remark, "the unity of a nation depends on a shared identity, which, in turn, depends largely on a shared memory. The truth also brings a measure of social catharsis and helps to prevent the past from reoccurring. In addition, bringing the facts to light is, to some extent, a form of punishment, albeit mild, in that it provokes social censure against the perpetrators or the institutions or groups they belonged to."[24]

The Museo de la Memoria's museographical approach has been to concretize this mission, first through the institutional program, whose foundations literally rest on the museum's Documentation Centre, housing a collection of publicly accessible community human rights archives spanning 1973–90, and second through a permanent exhibition that provides a national and chronological account of General Pinochet's coup on 11 September 1973 and traces the junta's seventeen-year military rule through the stories of victims, their defenders and families, the mobilization of community organizations, and the forms of political resistance and activism that took shape in artwork, the news media, music, and other popular media of the period. It will be important to assess what place Canada's own active Truth and Reconciliation Commission on Residential Schools will occupy at the Canadian Museum for Human Rights.

CONCLUSION

It would be wrong to understand the idea of the human rights museum solely as a product of the human rights turn in society in recent decades. In certain ways, and depending on scale and political context, some human rights museums remain rooted in the practices of classical functions and typologies of museology: collections-centred history museums. There are also those that have combined a focus on a particular type of history or memorial museum—the Holocaust museum—with human rights, such as the Museum on Holocaust and Human Rights in the Kazerne Dossin in Mechelen near Brussels (discussed by Stephan Jaeger in this volume), opened in December 2012. A different approach has been taken by those museums that also form part of the Peace Network, such as a cluster of human rights museums in Japan, that share yet another conceptual foundation.

There are several notable and preliminary observations to be made in regard to Japanese human rights museums: they are not national in scale or narrative but city museums, and they are all members of a network of museums for peace, distinguishing themselves from war and military museums by the role that they play in promoting peace education and peace making. One scholar estimates that, of the almost 100 peace museums in the world, almost half exist in Japan.[25] These museums approach the theme of human rights differently, at Sakai largely through the framework of the horrors of war (the museum was established under the banners of the Declaration of the Protection of Human Rights and the Abolition of Nuclear Weapons), at Osaka through the lens of social discrimination.[26]

Without the obvious challenges of a museum of national stature whose operations are dependent on state funding, these city museums might well be in a better position to engage in the kind of human rights practices that arise from community initiatives rather than the top-down approaches of state-sponsored institutions. The Osaka Human Rights Museum (now known as Liberty Osaka), for example, was founded with the intention of addressing specifically local human rights issues, such as the social discrimination faced by several different communities in the city and beyond, including the Buraku, people living with physical disabilities, and different ethnic groups, and it has reached out to these communities accordingly. Yet the museum has recently faced very significant budget cuts, prompting concerns about how human rights museums can continue their important work. In all cases, it is crucial to be vigilant regarding the extent to which human rights museums are likely to remain independent in their choice of exhibition subject matter, narratives, and general institutional orientation.

As the Canadian Museum for Human Rights wrestles with the content and museographical approaches of its exhibition halls, I wish to conclude with some thoughts on the significant role that human rights museums can play in the important arena of social justice. As institutions, museums house collections—of material objects, intangible heritage, oral histories—while providing valued intellectual context for and interpretation of these collections through research, community consultation, and exhibitions. As public sites of informal learning, human rights museums have not only the distinct opportunity to embrace progressive museographical practices—highlighting, broadcasting, and informing on issues of human rights on any number of platforms (web, social media, exhibition halls, programming) as these issues unfold around the globe—but also the ability to reach a diversity of audiences in the kind of prose that facilitates multigenerational and multidisciplinary dialogue to occur. Once they venture into the realm of human rights, these museums can initiate visitors not only into the theories that ground human rights but also into the field's practices, with the hope that the human community will engage, in local and transnational contexts, in justice. Yet, for this to happen, it is crucial for museums and their leaders to recognize that they have an equally significant moral obligation to model engaged pedagogy in which critical thinking, radical openness, and responsible citizenship are not only upheld as core principles but also actively taught—in exhibition halls and well beyond them.

NOTES

1   Sandra Dudley and Kylie Message, "Editorial," *Museum Worlds: Advances in Research* 1 (2013): 1–6.

2   Samuel Moyne, *The Last Utopia: Human Rights in History* (Cambridge, MA: Belknap Press of Harvard University Press, 2010), 212.

3   Ibid., 214.

4   There is understandable overlap between the related concepts of social justice and human rights as well as different definitions given to each concept. Social justice as understood in this chapter implies justice in society and its requisite principles, such as equality and fairness, in distinction to mechanisms of inequality, discrimination, and prejudice that hin-

der a socially just society. Striving for social justice necessarily entails mitigating between individual and collective rights with the well-being of society in mind. As observed by the National Pro Bono Resource Centre at the University of New South Wales, "the concept of social justice involves finding the optimum balance between our joint responsibilities as a society and our responsibilities as individuals to contribute to a just society." National Pro Bono Resource Centre, "What Is Social Justice?," Occasional Paper 1, University of New South Wales, October 2011, https://wic041u.server-secure.com/vs155205_secure/CMS/files_cms/Occ_1_What%20is%20Social%20Justice_FINAL.pdf, 2. See also Eithne Nightingale and Richard Sandell, "Introduction," in *Museums, Equality and Social Justice*, ed. Richard Sandell and Eithne Nightingale (London: Routledge, 2012), 3. The concept of human rights has both legal and cultural definitions, and as used in this chapter it refers to those "inalienable rights of all members of the human family" that are "the foundation of freedom, justice and peace in the world," as proclaimed in UNESCO's Universal Declaration of Human Rights drafted in 1948. This important document protects individual rights "to life, liberty and security of person." UNESCO, Universal Declaration of Human Rights, http://www.un.org/en/documents/udhr/. The concepts of social justice and human rights share an understanding of equality as the foundation of a just society.

5   These are the Comisión Nacional de Verdad y Reconciliación (the Rettig Commission) that operated for nine months from May 1990 to February 1991 and the Comisión Nacional Sobre Prisón Política y Tortura (the Valech Commission) that operated for twenty-one months from September 2003 to June 2005.

6   Museo de la Memoria y Los Derechos Humanos, Definiciones Estratégicas, http://www.museodelamemoria.cl/el-museo/sobre-el-museo/definiciones-estrategicas-2/. Translation by Google.

7   The mandate of the CMHR, for example, is to "enhance the public's understanding of human rights, to promote respect for others, and to encourage dialogue and reflection." CMHR, Mandate and Values, http://museumforhumanrights.ca/about-museum/mandate-and-values. Promoting respect for cultural differences with an aim to overcoming social prejudice and discrimination is one important way that museums can sensitize publics to forms of intolerance manifest in societal relations.

8   Children's Museum for Peace and Human Rights, "Our Vision," http://www.cmphr.org/ourvision.html.

9   For some examples of this literature, see Richard Sandell, *Museums, Society, Inequality* (London: Routledge, 2002); Robert R. Janes, *Museums in a Troubled World: Renewal, Irrelevance or Collapse?* (New York: Routledge, 2009); David Fleming, "The Role of Human Rights Museums," paper presented at the inaugural conference of the Federation of International Human Rights Museums, Liverpool, UK, 15–16 September 2010; and Lois Silverman, *The Social Work of Museums* (New York: Routledge, 2010).

10   Fiona Cameron and Lynda Kelly, eds., *Hot Topics, Public Culture, Museums* (Newcastle-upon-Tyne: Cambridge Scholars, 2010).

11   Raymond Montpetit, "Making Sense of Space," *Museum International* 47, 1 (1995): 41.

12   These five Japanese museums are Osaka Human Rights Museum (Liberty Osaka), 1985; Kochi Liberty and People's Rights Museum, 1990; Human Rights and Peace Museum Fukuyama City, 1994; Sakai City Peace and Human Rights Museum, 1994; and Henomatsu Human Rights History Museum in Sakai (no founding date located). I am compiling a growing list of self-identified human rights museums around the globe and to date have located a dozen such institutions.

13   The Museo de la Justicia, Centro de Documentación y Archivo para la Defensa de los Derechos Humanos in Asunción, Paraguay, houses the Archives of Terror, a collection

detailing the atrocities committed under dictator General Alberto Stroessner's thirty-five-year regime (from 1954 to 1989, when Stroessner was forced from power in a military coup and into exile in Brazil), discovered by Martin Almeda in 1992. The centre also houses a modest exhibition space that provides a historical overview of human rights abuses in Paraguay as early as the sixteenth century, through the country's complicity in colonialism and slavery and infringement of local Guarani rights.

14   Children's Museum for Peace and Human Rights, "Background," http://www.cmphr.org/background2.html; Right On Network, http://www.cmphr.org/rightonnetwork.html.

15   The acronym stands for International Committee on Management, a subcommittee of the International Council of Museums (ICOM).

16   Paul Williams, *Memorial Museums: The Global Rush to Commemorate Atrocities* (Oxford: Berg, 2007), 9.

17   Ibid., 8.

18   Ibid., 20–21.

19   I have written on this museum and its programming initiatives in "Human Rights Museums and Pedagogies of Practice: The Museo de la Memoria y los Derechos Humanos," *Museum Management and Curatorship* 28, 3 (2013): 324–41.

20   UNESCO, Education, "Human Rights Education," http://www.unesco.org/new/en/education/themes/leading-the-international-agenda/human-rights-education/.

21   Andreas Huyssen, *Twilight Memories: Marking Time in a Culture of Amnesia* (New York: Routledge, 1995).

22   Campaign! Make an Impact!, http://www.bl.uk/campaign.

23   José Zalaquett, "Balancing Ethical Imperatives and Political Constraints: The Dilemma of New Democracies Confronting Past Human Rights Violations," *Hastings Law Journal* 43, 6 (1992): 1425, http://heinonline.org/HOL/Page?handle=hein.journals/hastlj43&div=55&g_sent=1&collection=journals.

24   José Zalaquett, "Introduction to the English Edition," in *Report of the Chilean National Commission on Truth and Reconciliation* (Notre Dame, IN: University of Notre Dame Press, 1993), 6–17, posted by the United States Peace Institute Library, www.usip.org, 4 October 2002. See also United States Institute of Peace, *Commission of Inquiry: Chile 03*, Truth Commissions Digital Collection, http://www.usip.org/publications/commission-inquiry-chile-03; and United States Institute of Peace, *Truth Commission: Chile 90*, Truth Commissions Digital Collection, http://www.usip.org/publications/truth-commission-chile-90. I have written more extensively about this subject in "Human Rights Museums and Pedagogies of Practice," *Museum Management and Curatorship* 28, 3 (2013): 324–41.

25   K. Yamane, "Peace Education through Peace Museums," *International Security, Peace, Development and Environment* 2 (n.d.): 2, http://www.eolss.net/Sample-Chapters/C14/E1-39B-21-00.pdf.

26   See Eika Tai, "Local and Global Efforts for Human Rights Education: A Case from the Osaka Human Rights Museum," *International Journal of Human Rights* 14, 5 (2010): 771–88.

PARALLELS
AND OBLIGATIONS

TEMPORALIZING HISTORY TOWARD THE FUTURE: REPRESENTING VIOLENCE AND HUMAN RIGHTS VIOLATIONS IN THE MILITARY HISTORY MUSEUM IN DRESDEN

CHAPTER 12
Stephan Jaeger

"IDEAS MUSEUM" VERSUS HISTORY MUSEUM[1]

Ideas museums are devoted to representing human rights, tolerance, peace, anti-war sentiment, and justice, among other concepts. The negative counterparts of these concepts—such as human rights violations, war, violence, atrocities, and genocide—are not typically represented in ideas museums in the twenty-first-century museum landscape. Instead, they are typically housed in historical museums about specific historical events or periods that often serve related memorial functions[2] and are linked to sites of commemorative significance (i.e., the museum is embedded in an authentic space wherein past atrocities have taken place).[3] Positive ideas museums tend to focus primarily on the present and future; they emphasize the idea of learning about the past in order to influence future behaviour and action.[4] Human violence and atrocities museums, in contrast, tend more toward documenting or experiencing aspects of the past.[5] Despite this striking difference, neither can an ideas museum simply abandon the representation of the past, nor can a history museum eliminate the expression of futurity, when educating audiences and expressing hope in and beyond the past. Ideas and history remain inseparably intertwined.[6]

This chapter argues that one of the biggest challenges for an ideas museum lies in how it deals with the relationship between past, present, and future.[7] Past, present, and future are inseparably intertwined, and their representation can be most effectively done by temporalizing instead of isolating their mutual relationship. The effect of such a temporalization[8] will be demonstrated through an analysis of the new permanent exhibition of the Military History Museum (MHM) of the German Armed Forces (Militärhistorisches Museum der Bundeswehr) in Dresden. This museum serves as the case study of a state-sponsored military history or war museum that at first glance would not be easily categorized as an ideas museum. Yet in practice it is not only more a cultural history than a military history museum but also represents violence and warfare as universal concepts (this universality is then challenged again in specific historical and cultural contexts). Consequently, the MHM, and particularly its representation of the Second World War, the Holocaust, and mass atrocities generally, serves as an ideal case both for analyzing the interaction of ideas and history in a twenty-first-century museum and for considering whether its exhibits are primarily either historical or the expression of a concept that utilizes the past, or whether a balance can be struck between cultural and historical specificity and abstract ideas, specifically between the past and the future. The chapter concludes with a brief reflection on the representational challenges and possibilities that emerge from this case study for ideas museums in general and the Canadian Museum for Human Rights in particular.

IDEAS AND THEMES VERSUS CHRONOLOGICAL HISTORY

For the past two decades, German history museums have struggled intensely with the idea of how to represent the history of the Second World War and the Holocaust. They usually follow a documentary mode typical of the tradition of German academic historiography and dominant in the state-sponsored German museum landscape. Accordingly, visitors are kept at a representational distance: they generally know that they are confronted with historical objects that document the past instead of being primarily immersed in a constructed experience of the past. For example, the German Historical Museum (Deutsches Historisches Museum) in Berlin highlights objects and images in general that are displayed and commented on, or the Topography of Terror (Topographie des Terrors), also in Berlin, emphasizes photography. They are organized in a structural-chronological way; the visitor learns about the past and encounters historical objects, but always with cognitive distance maintained, aware that the museum organizes the past in particular structural patterns. On the one hand, the new permanent exhibition of the Military History Museum in Dresden continues this German tradition of documentary distantiation. It bases its exhibits in particular on original objects and images and mostly avoids evoking empathy in the visitor in its pursuit of historical distance. On the other hand, the concepts at the heart of the MHM invite a discussion of temporality and futurity in ways not present or fully available in the traditional documentary approach characteristic of German museum historiography.

The MHM reopened with an entirely new permanent exhibition, designed by HG Merz and Holzer Kobler, in a redesigned building on 15 October 2011. A wedge by architect Daniel Libeskind cuts into and disrupts the classicist arsenal building constructed in the nineteenth-century military quarter Albertstadt in order to fragment and complicate memory of the past. By interweaving military with political, social, and cultural history, as well as the history of what the French Annales historians termed various "*mentalités*," the museum claims to approach military exhibitions in a radically new way.[9] This approach, according to the museum makers, allows two distinct models of time to be expressed: first, the time of evolution, in which violence and force are inherent to human behaviour (here they display anthropological consistency for the human species within the time of evolution); second, the time of cultural change, in which violence depends on its cultural, historical, and social surroundings.[10] To fulfill its goal of representing the history and anthropology of violence, the MHM has chosen a twofold approach: first, it presents the traditional story of German warfare from 1300 to the present as a chronological exhibition in the original arsenal building; second, a thematic exhibition in Libeskind's wedge—in German called *Themenparcours*, literally a "tour" through different themes—confronts the visitor with the violent effects of war in a more abstract way, as ideas and themes.[11] To visit the different sections of the chronological exhibition, the visitor must walk through the thematic exhibition in the wedge; consequently, the architectural design creates the effect that the chronological and thematic exhibitions are necessarily intertwined.

On its five floors (numbered 4 to 0 from top to bottom), Libeskind's wedge houses a thematic tour of war and violence in twelve sections, starting at the top with the section entitled Dresden View, featuring three

15. Front facade of the Military History Museum in Dresden.

air-war attacks during the Second World War: the Luftwaffe (German Air Force) attack on the Polish city of Wielun on the first day of the war, the Nazi air raid of Rotterdam, and the Allied firebombing of Dresden. Visitors can enter the tip of the wedge, oriented skyward, on the fourth floor, leaving the inside of the museum through a glass door, which opens up an obstructed—through tilted slabs—view of Dresden's cityscape.

Below this, the wedge's third floor is entitled Memory; below that is a floor that addresses the relationship between society and violence/war in five sections: Politics and the Use of Force; Language and the Military; Fashion and the Military; Music and the Military; and War and Play. The visitor—unless using the elevator—will use the original stairwell of the arsenal building to enter the first and ground floors of the wedge. The first floor focuses on the mentality of war in the section entitled The Formations of the Body and on war's effects in the sections War and Suffering, and Animals and the Military. Finally, the ground floor is divided into the sections Protection and Destruction, and Technology and the Military; the latter again emphasizes the links between civil society and war.

In the wings of the old arsenal building, the MHM represents its chronological exhibition, the history of the German military in three temporally distinct sections: 1300–1914 (ground floor west), 1914–1945 (first floor west), and 1945–Present (first floor east). All three sections of the chronological exhibition are divided into three information layers: introductory symbolic display cases, for example the fragments of a German Panzer I tank, symbolizing the beginnings of mobile warfare in the Second World War; display cases for the main chronology; and in-depth sections or "knowledge chambers," in which structures or topics specific to a historical period are represented. Generally, the chronological exhibition uses traditional curatorial techniques that present most objects installed in glass display cases and medium-sized military equipment set on stages between cases. This approach is complemented by survey panels, educational experience stations, media stations, and short tabular biographies, arranged in contrasting pairs of two people who lived during the same period, but took divergent paths in the same decision situation, always showing contrasting paths through life.

REPRESENTING VIOLENCE
A war museum that opts to represent relevant ideas must first address the concept of "war" as such. War is conceptually multidimensional and can be understood as being comprised of sub-concepts such as force, violence,

suffering, destruction, protection, perpetratorship, victimhood, formation/ order, and so on. This multidimensionality is reflected in the representational strategies of the MHM. A closer look at the section entitled War and Suffering—and how it represents suffering as an idea—can show how the museum represents war conceptually instead of merely documenting its constitutive historical events.

War and Suffering is located at the intersection of the wedge and arsenal building on the first floor between the chronological sections on the world wars in the western wing and the section 1945–Present in the eastern wing, indicating that suffering and war did not disappear with the end of the Second World War. The section is mostly comprised of a dark-coloured walkable showcase with a felt surface. The visitor must enter the showcase to visit its three subsections, Death, Injury, and Remembrance. Within the narrow showcase, allowing a maximum of about five visitors at the same time, visitors can open sliding windows of parts of the display cases, out of reverence for the dead and victims, so that visitors must decide for themselves whether they want to see the objects of death and suffering.

At first glance, the exhibits feel like a mishmash of suffering, pain, horror, and mourning without much structure or narrative to give them sense. Grave crosses and stones, a list of dead generals, identification tags, the skull of a soldier who committed suicide, letters from mourning mothers and from soldiers to their families, diary entries and photo albums about war and genocide, and photographs of genocides are displayed next to each other. The objects range from the Wars of Liberation (the Napoleonic Wars, between 1813 and 1815) to the twenty-first-century War in Afghanistan. However, no actual chronology is provided. The museum objects interact to create impressions of suffering that indicate the manifold ways in which injury, death, mourning, individual and collective suffering, and commemoration always accompany war. They range from the death of the unknown soldier to the war of annihilation in Eastern Europe during the Second World War. They show the rituals of the perpetrators and confront the visitor with real human remains in order to express the horror of war. They intermingle representational layers of suffering and death, individual, collective, and state remembrance and mourning, death of and through soldiers, standard warfare, and war crimes.

If the museum were exclusively focused on themes and ideas, then one could argue that War and Suffering—despite containing some impressive individual exhibits—is not representationally successful since it cannot create a story or even a structure by itself. It seems to eliminate all traces of historical specificity and juxtaposes not easily compatible themes. How can one compare the pogrom in Lviv with a mourning mother who writes a letter to an already dead Wehrmacht (German army) soldier, a perforated steel helmet from the First World War, or a grave cross of an ss soldier with a swastika and runes? The section attaches death to many different motivations, different reasons for respect and honour for the dead and for condemnation of the deeds in war, and yet the visitor can begin to think about what these similarities of death, pain, and mourning as well as what their striking differences signify. The section provides an impression of the manifold appearances of death and suffering in war; it explicitly avoids specific historical answers. The visitor is left with the impression of this manifoldness. Thus, concrete answers to questions about its meaning or significance cannot be found solely in the section on suffering[12] but can only be developed if the visitor connects many more pieces of the museum exhibition that create a temporal structure that counterbalances the apparent universality or arbitrariness of death and mourning in the section on suffering.

An analysis of the chronological exhibition—apparently the historical antithesis of the ideas approach in the thematic exhibition—can demonstrate how intertwined all of the different sections and exhibits in the museum are. The Barbarossa cabinet in the subsection on the war of extermination against the Soviet Union serves as an excellent example of how the exhibition establishes a specific historicity, the sense of actual history, for the visitor. In front of the cabinet is a computer terminal that endlessly repeats (with tone[13]) a film clip, *Fahnenjunker* (officer candidate), from 1943, showing a Wehrmacht lesson, in which future officers learn that they will fight a *weltanschaulichen Krieg* (a war based on worldview and ideology). This film clip sets the overall tone for the Soviet Union cabinets in particular and for the Second World War exhibition more generally. The scene on the computer lasts for a minute and nineteen seconds and runs continuously; when the volume is not muted, the scene dominates the audio heard throughout most of the Second World War section. The actual display cabinet indicates a weak temporality, a development from the opening of Operation Barbarossa over its military affairs to the mass killings, mostly through sets of photographs and two displayed pages from a photo album. The first set of photographs marks the view of the war, destroyed Russian equipment, apparently quick advancement, and distant views of Leningrad. The photographs aim to present how the layers of war would have been seen from a German, partly propagandistic, perspective. Eventually, the images draw viewers more closely toward actual events and war's effects.

16. Operation Barbarossa, мнм, chronological exhibition 1914–1945.

Photos of exhausted, injured, dead, and mutilated Soviet prisoners of war are displayed before the cabinet narrative closes with another set of photos showing genocide images from Kiev and Babi Yar. Finally, a two-sided page of a photo album from the hanging of Jews in Zhytomyr by an ss mobile killing unit (Einsatzgruppe) displays the contrast in its selection of pictures that juxtaposes hanging corpses with beautiful amateur landscape photographs of the surrounding area. The visitor is confronted with different constructed perspectives (the photographs seem to be taken by German soldiers or ss men throughout). The exact relations between them are left open, but the cabinet narrates war scenes from the perspective of "the eye of the beholder," shifting between proximity and distance, thereby creating the idea of war as all encompassing: military advancement and destruction, victory, brutality, and genocide, all under the ideological umbrella of the war based on worldview and ideology. The visitor gets historical impressions of the advancement of the Wehrmacht, its successes, the shift from destroyed armour at the beginning of the campaign to slaughtered human beings and the human catastrophe as a result of the German advance. This arrangement leaves no doubt that war and genocide/the Holocaust were inseparable during the Second World War and that the war had been planned by the Nazis from the beginning as a war of worldviews. To an extent, the visitor perceives a narrative—in a spatial rather than strictly chronological sense—of the collective experience of the war for German soldiers, with the photographic gaze making the effects and complexities of the war more immediate and present. At the same time, the Barbarossa cabinet is not simply a traditional two-dimensional display cabinet that represents one historical episode from a distance, giving the visitor a structural overview of a historical phase and the opportunity to zoom in on specific artifacts or images. Instead, the cabinet interacts with the ideas of ideology, suffering, and atrocity throughout the museum, allowing the visitor to assign the pieces from the thematic suffering section with the required historical specificity. The museum does not provide an in-depth analysis or even evaluation of historical events. It chooses to present the events to the visitor so that he or she can be affected by the representation.[14] This approach enables the visitor to experience a temporalized museum space that risks not giving enough guidance but allows for the representation of ideas and history in close conjunction without implying that history merely exemplifies general statements about different concepts prevalent in war.

The in-depth section of the world war part of the chronological exhibition presents similar structural elements of war in the First and Second World Wars. Just a brief look at one example of Second World War representations attempted by the museum, depicting the German armament industry and economy, can help to demonstrate how the MHM moves from documentary representation to experientiality in the chronological exhibition. A Leuna gas pump, a small model of a Tiger tank, an instruction book that displays the gas mileage of such a tank, a complete register of companies working in the ghetto in Łódź, a report on completion of Crematorium III in Auschwitz-Birkenau, a cost estimate from Topf & Söhne for SS construction management in Auschwitz-Birkenau, and other original objects create a space linking the war effort, forced labour, the Holocaust, and the German economy, all housed in one small display cabinet. Although the cabinet does not present one individual person (whom a visitor might then be able to relate to empathetically), it expresses an abstract experience for the visitor of how war, mass murder in the concentration camps, economy, and civil life were closely connected. This is not the experience of a historical collective but a structural experience in space; the visitor must again individually engage with the installation and link it to other parts of the chronological and thematic exhibitions.[15] The cabinet, then, does not merely document the links between the economy, war, and Holocaust; rather, it makes them present. On the one hand, the visitor can have no doubt about the historical complicity of German society and industry in the Holocaust or about the fact that the Holocaust and German war effort are impossible to separate; on the other hand, this particular cabinet contributes to the general understanding of war and atrocity by letting the visitor experience the interwovenness of the different components that allow war to happen and sustain it. The approach employed in the MHM permits a comparative representation of violence. Instead of isolating one conflict, human violence through different historical periods, in different cultures, and from different perspectives can be connected.[16]

The museum displays more than a dozen commissioned art installations that intentionally are not fully integrated into the chronological or thematic exhibition. These art installations allow the visitor to reach a more abstract level in her or his understanding of violence. For example, the video *Der Koyote* (The Coyote) by Nancy Davenport in the memory section shows an awkward male protagonist on the construction site of the museum experimenting with explosives and weapons. He consistently fails in his violent ambitions and creates humorous incidents instead. The

17. Armament in World War Two, мнм, chronological exhibition 1914–1945.

video—in the tradition of an animated cartoon—provides some lighter entertainment within the more serious war memory section,[17] yet at the same time it artistically challenges the visitor/viewer to ascertain its function in the museum, thereby superseding any historical representation of war by triggering aesthetic and self-reflexive experiences oriented toward understanding the relationship between violence and aesthetic pleasure. Many of the art installations in the MHM seek to destabilize the border between historically or biographically specific representations and conceptual art installations.[18] For example, in the chronology section 1945–Present, the museum presents several photographs and stories from Lukas Einsele's project *One Step Beyond—the Mine Revisited*, which gives landmine victims in the wars in Afghanistan, Angola, Bosnia-Herzegovina, and Cambodia a voice to remember their own experiences and express the collective fate of landmine victims. It also, however, looks past the use of mines as a weapon and into the future beyond. Einsele's project clearly creates historical spaces representing conflicts from the past two decades, but it also represents the universal experience of violence and victimhood and points to the future of the individuals beyond stepping on landmines. Consequently, it creates temporality through interaction with the viewer. In the tradition of the predominant German documentary curatorial mode, the museum shies away from the simulation of real experience; it maintains a distance. The installations that create the experience of war do less to make one specific past present than to make a simulated effect of violence in abstract form present: so, for example, an artwork by Sissel Tolaas simulates the smell of war, somehow reminiscent of the smell of the trenches during the First World War. Nowhere does the museum try to create empathy in the historical sense of the visitor reliving the past, only in a conceptual one as simulating abstract effects of war,[19] so that it always strives for an aesthetic or cognitive distance, allowing for a meta-experience of concepts of violence instead of simply alluring the visitor to relive the past.[20]

FUTURITY AND HUMAN RIGHTS

The MHM seeks a balance between an ideas museum and a history museum that allows it to respond to a number of representational challenges in a German "war and military" museum whose institutional owner is the Bundeswehr (the German Armed Forces). On the one hand, German history of the twentieth century is so distorted by atrocities in its colonies, the First World War, the Second World War, and the Holocaust, as well as the subsequent history of postwar divided Germany, that the provision of any heroic approach to military history, whether it represents the glory of a collective army or nation or of individual soldiers, is impossible.[21] Germany's collective memory is clearly pacifist or at least anti-war, as the public debates about German soldiers engaged in humanitarian missions and "just wars" such as those in Kosovo and Afghanistan occurring since German reunification in 1990 confirm. On the other hand, a German museum owned by the Bundeswehr must find a way to show the role of the German Armed Forces in a twenty-first-century German society, and it must grapple with the question of which specific traditions and history today's German army can or should refer to. A mere ideas museum always runs the risk of overemphasizing either the side of tradition and the values needed to justify the military or else anti-war concepts. History then would be reduced to an exemplary, partly decontextualized status, such as an isolated reading of the pogrom photographs from Lviv would suggest. Similarly, the focus on death, suffering, and injury, as well as on humanitarian challenges in the present, could lead to the idea that the MHM functions merely as an anti-war museum, one incapable of representing German military traditions and future roles.[22] The museum falls into neither trap, however, because it follows a twofold approach and combines historical abstraction and anthropological universalization with historical documentation. This approach allows for the creation of a dynamic relationship among past, present, and future (at least as long as the visitor engages with the presentism of the presentation).[23] For example, the display cabinet on the German armament industry during the Second World War not only leaves no doubt about the historical role that German society and corporations played in the Holocaust, or about the inseparability of the Holocaust and German war effort, but also leads to a historical-structural experience that demonstrates the connectedness of industry and war effort as well as the mechanisms and costs of war.[24] The visitor is always drawn to the abstract, yet at the same time the historical German collective perspective is too present to relax in the abstract and forget about concrete history.

The MHM presents futurity on different levels. The abstract notion of death challenges the visitor to reflect on whether commemoration and mourning are historical or universal and on whether or not these modes of dealing with war and violence change according to circumstances or time, an issue that remains unresolved. The clash between the indoctrination of an ideological war in the East and the regular war effort in the West challenges the notion of how soldiers react in certain surroundings, again as a

structural experience that exceeds the limits of available historical documentation and points toward future conflicts. The last section, concluding
the chronological exhibition, Challenges in the Twenty-First Century, is
clearly future oriented. It asks questions about how the role of the military
changed after 9/11. Yet again the museum keeps its historiographical roots;
it displays objects related to early-twenty-first-century conflicts but shies
away from developing a futurity concept or even predicting the future.
The last section of the chronological exhibition expresses the complexity
of conflicts today and displays in the cabinet Conflict Management the
complexity of modern war and peace processes as well as of peace and
reconciliation research. The museum sticks, however, to its distant and
presentist approach. It presents objects connected to twenty-first-century
warfare and names reasons for and repercussions of armed conflicts occurring around the world, but it does not draw any conclusions from them.
For example, the last artifacts in the chronological exhibition are three ladders used by Africans to attempt to climb over the border fence to Melilla
and Ceuta, two Spanish cities on North African territory, and so to the
European Union (six people died there in 2005), and they are introduced
with the observation that, for the first time, there are more refugees in
the world because of ecological disasters than because of war. What this
all means for military conduct and human society, and the evolution of
violence, however, is left to the visitor to settle in light of his or her own
idea of the future.[25]

To summarize, the MHM creates a museum space that puts the visitor
in a temporalized situation, one that transcends the mode of documenting
war to understand past atrocities that is typical for many German museums, as seen above. The past must still be understood, and it becomes present in light of the museum's representation of its cultural impact on society, whereas the ideas model forces the visitor to reflect on the relationship
between violence/war and his or her own personal attitudes and actions as
well as the broader future goals of human society. It is guided by historical principles, but the ideas aspect of the presentation is so elaborate that
it offers insights into the kinds of representational strategies available to
ideas museums such as the Canadian Museum for Human Rights (CMHR).
The combination of thematic/abstract concepts and historicity in a temporalized setting offers a way of representing ideas with implications for
the future while maintaining their historical specificity. Such an approach
could allow a human rights museum, for example, to represent the evolution of human rights as much as educate about present and future actions

that need to be taken in the name of human rights. It could help ideas museums generally to meet the challenge of simply presenting structural examples of ideas, such as specific human rights questions and conflicts, since they would still affect the visitor in narrative and temporalized settings. The debate about whether a historical event such as the Holocaust is overrepresented in relation to other human rights violations[26] could be defused by the CMHR by embracing a temporal approach oscillating between universality and historicity in its curatorial strategy. The Holocaust and the contextualization of its historical relation to the evolution of human rights[27] might then lead to structural experiences of other human rights violations and support rereadings of earlier historical events such as the Holodomor as well as contribute to museumgoers' understanding of the evolution of human rights and their violations in general and post-1945 in particular. Since the museum visitor would be engaged through structural experiences, a documentary-temporalized approach could work here; at least this representational solution does not need to appeal to any more direct forms of historical experience.

AFTERTHOUGHT

An interesting recent approach to these issues can be seen on display in the Kazerne Dossin: Memorial, Museum, and Documentation Centre on Holocaust and Human Rights in Mechelen near Brussels, which opened a new museum on 1 December 2012. The museum is housed in a new pentagon-shaped building designed by architect bOb Van Reeth of AWG Architecten. It is situated next to the former army barracks, now hosting a memorial exhibition and a documentation centre. During World War II the barracks were used as an ss transit camp from which more than 25,000 Jews, Sinti, and Roma from Belgium and northern France were deported to Auschwitz-Birkenau. The museum, on the one hand, is a documentary museum of the Holocaust and more specifically of Belgium's role in the genocide. Through this documentary mode, the museum avoids the evocation of empathy in its visitors. On the other hand, it calls itself "Europe's First Museum of Human Rights."[28] Although—unlike the CMHR—its focus is the Holocaust and is clearly historical, the museum leads visitors to compare the roots of numerous past and present conflicts, especially in three separate exhibit sections along the inner side walls: Migration, Discrimination, and Extermination. This comparative effect is created for the visitor through the experience of the opening film and exposure to photographs, texts, and some artworks as well as through quotations from the Universal Declaration of Human Rights. The museum particularly emphasizes the idea of tolerance in its human rights exhibits. Unlike the Holocaust exhibition, the human rights exhibits take sides and challenge visitors to connect human rights issues in the Holocaust with other past, present, and possible future conflicts. The Kazerne Dossin does not interweave history and ideas as much as the Military History Museum in Dresden does, and it more obviously steers the visitor toward an unambiguous pro-human rights message rather than stages ambiguities and dissonances, but both museums exhibit an intriguing clash between history and ideas.

NOTES

1   I am grateful to Erin Johnston-Weiss, Amy Freier, the participants at the ideas museum workshop, and the editors of this volume for their helpful comments.

2   See the chapter in this volume by Jennifer Carter for the memorial function of human rights museums in general, the chapter by Dirk Moses for the Canadian Museum for Human Rights, and the chapter by Jorge Nállim for a specific analysis of memory spaces, by example of post-dictatorship Argentina.

3   In the German context, the concept of memorial places (Gedenkstätten) with documentation exhibitions is particularly present in relation to the Third Reich, the Second World War, and the Holocaust. Such memorials include, among many others, the Topography of Terror, the House of the Wannsee Conference, the Memorial to the German Resistance, all in Berlin, as well as the different concentration camp sites in Germany, such as Dachau, Bergen-Belsen, Buchenwald, and Sachsenhausen.

4   See also Angela Failler and Roger Simon's chapter in this volume, which discusses four curatorial practices at an ideas museum, especially involving the museum visitor in order to instigate action and with Rancière the notion of the "emancipated spectator" for whom learning is made possible by "translating for oneself the expressive world beyond one's experience."

5   The Museum of Tolerance in Los Angeles describes its mission as not merely documentary in representing the past through artifacts and documents but also as a reminder to the visitor in the present "to act": "This Museum should serve to prevent hatred and genocide from occurring to any group now and in the future." http://www.museumof-tolerance.com/site/c.tmL6KfNVLtH/b.4866027/k.88E8/Our_History_and_Vision.htm. The Canadian Museum for Human Rights in Winnipeg is envisioned "as a national and international destination," "a centre of learning where Canadians and people from around the world can engage in discussion and commit to taking action against hate and oppression." http://humanrightsmuseum.ca/about-museum.

6   Reinhart Koselleck, *Futures Past: On the Semantics of Historical Time,* trans. Keith Tribe (New York: Columbia University Press, 2004). Koselleck argues on pages 258–63 that, under the condition of accelerating temporality in modernity, the "space of experience" and the "horizon of expectation" redouble "past and future in an unequal manner" (263). For an application of Koselleck's concepts to the twenty-first-century museum, see Ker-

stin Barndt, "Layers of Time: Industrial Ruins and Exhibitionary Spaces," *PMLA* 125, 1 (2010): 134–41.

7   For futurity in the museum, see Hermann Lübbe, *Der Fortschritt und das Museum: Über den Grund unseres Vergnügens an historischen Gegenständen* (London: Institute of Germanic Studies, University of London, 1982); Michael Fehr, "Zur Konstruktion von Geschichte mit dem Museum—fünf Thesen," in *Die Magie der Geschichte: Geschichtskultur und Museum,* ed. Martina Padberg and Martin Schmidt (Bielefeld: transcript, 2010), 39–51; and Michael Fehr, "Art—Museum—Utopia: Five Themes on an Epistemological Construction Site," in *Thinking Utopia: Steps into Other Worlds,* ed. Jörn Rüsen, Michael Fehr, and Thomas W. Rieger (New York: Berghahn, 2005), 169–73. See also the chapter by David Petrasek in this volume for a discussion of the role of the future in human rights education, though his analysis seems to downplay the complex relationship of past, present, and future in favour of the latter and consequently underestimates the necessary impact of historical representation.

8   See Koselleck, *Futures Past,* 37.

9   See http://www.mhmbw.de/index.php/ausstellungen. See also the exhibition guide, Gorch Pieken and Matthias Rogg, eds., *The Bundeswehr Museum of Military History: Exhibition Guide* (Dresden: Sandstein, 2012), especially Gorch Pieken, "Concept and Structure of the Permanent Exhibition," 21–27; and Matthias Rogg, "The Architecture," 15–19.

10   See Pieken and Rogg, *Bundeswehr Museum,* especially 22.

11   It is important to note that the temporality effect of the MHM is based on the interweaving of chronological and structural/thematic representation throughout the exhibition. The chronological exhibition is not purely temporal, nor is the thematic exhibition purely conceptual.

12   The museum catalogue, like the text panels in the showcase, give some idea of changes to the concept of death during the history of warfare, for example the increasing casualties among civilians, the discovery of trauma, or advances in medical treatment. Pieken and Rogg, *Bundeswehr Museum,* 94–99.

13   Unfortunately, the museum had turned off the tone during my most recent visit (January 2013), reducing the performative quality of the whole exhibition section.

14   This relates to a paratactic representation. See Roger Simon, "The Terrible Gift: Museums and the Possibility of Hope without Consolation," *Museum Management and Curatorship* 21 (2006): 187–204. In this piece, Simon argues with reference to Adorno (200–01).

15   Michael Bernard-Donals, "Synecdochic Memory at the United States Holocaust Memorial Museum," *College English* 44, 5 (2012): 417–36. Bernard-Donals explains this through the trope of synecdoche that—unlike metonymy—works against the impression that history could be a simple retrieval of the past. Objects in the museum relate to one another and mark the distance from the past to the viewer's present (422–24).

16   For other comparative approaches to museums in representing violence, genocide, and human rights violations, see Thomas Thiemeyer, *Fortsetzung des Krieges mit anderen Mitteln: Die beiden Weltkriege im Museum* (Paderborn: Schöningh, 2010). In this volume, see especially the chapters by Amanda Grzyb and Jennifer Carter.

17   For such an oversimplification of the effect of art in the museum, see Susanne Altmann, "Militärhistorisches Museum Dresden: Kunst statt Militaria," *Art: Das Kunstmagazin,* 6 January 2012, http://www.art-magazin.de/kunst/47904/militaerhistorisches_museum_dresden/.

18   See the chapter by Ken Norman in this volume for the significant role of the arts as an expressive and reflective tool for human ideas, as seen by the Content Advisory Committee to the CMHR.

19   Alison Landsberg, "Memory, Empathy, and the Politics of Identification," *International Journal of Politics, Culture, and Society* 22 (2009): 222–23. See also the chapter by Struan Sinclair, Adam Muller, and Andrew Woolford in this volume.

20   See Mark Salber Phillips, "Distance and Historical Representation," *History Workshop Journal* 57 (2004): 123–41; and Bernard-Donals, "Synecdochic Memory," especially 424–26 for a rhetorical discussion of distancing the viewer from atrocities in museum representations in order to prevent overidentification with victims and perpetrators.

21   See also Susanne Vees-Gulani and Stephan Jaeger, "Introduction: Representations of German War Experiences and the Legacy of the Second World War," *Representations of War Experiences from the Eighteenth Century to the Present,* special issue of *Seminar: A Journal of Germanic Studies* 50, 1 (2014): 1–17, especially 6–8 for the significance of the German legacy of the Second World War for the representational choices by the MHM.

22   The MHM has been occasionally described as an anti-war museum; for example, though written before the opening, see Stefan Locke, "Das neue Antikriegsmuseum der Bundeswehr," *Frankfurter Allgemeine Zeitung,* 18 May 2011.

23   In practice, a one-time visitor might be overwhelmed by the sheer number of objects in the chronological exhibition, or merely focus on the thematic course, so that in part the interweaving effect that creates temporality would not be experienced.

24   For a similar tension, see Failler and Simon in this volume. They discuss the difference between "learning about" and "learning from." In the MHM, the temporalization, allowing for a dynamic relationship between distance and proximity, leads to the possibility of learning from the past beyond mere documentary representation.

25   Andreas Kilb, "Militärhistorisches Museum Dresden: Ein Minenschaf zieht in den Krieg" *Frankfurter Allgemeine Zeitung,* 13 October 2011, http://www.faz.net/aktuell/feuilleton/militaerhistorisches-museum-dresden-ein-minenschaf-zieht-in-den-krieg-11492151.html/. Kilb sees the permanent exhibition as a never-ending historical narrative, based on dissonances and ambiguities, that shapes the form of the museum.

26   For further information on the representation of genocide and the Holocaust in the CMHR, see the chapter by Moses.

27   See Marco Duranti, "The Holocaust, the Legacy of 1789, and the Birth of International Human Rights Law: Revisiting the Foundation Myth," *Journal of Genocide Research* 14, 22 (2012): 159–86. Duranti recontextualizes the place of the Holocaust and the French revolutionary tradition in the birth and evolution of international human rights law.

28   Visitor flyer as distributed on 15 December 2012. See also the exhibition catalogue by the Kazerne Dossin and Hermann Van Goethem, eds., *Holocaust and Human Rights: Exhibition Catalogue* (Ghent, 2012).

OVERCOMING ILLITERACY IN IDEA-DRIVEN MUSEUMS: A CURATORIAL CONUNDRUM

CHAPTER 13

George Jacob

In an increasingly complex world of strife and struggle, a new genre of museums focused on the idea of human rights has gained considerable footing, both in the developing world and in the developed world. Notwithstanding the increasing number of these institutions, however, museum curators have seldom explored the means, methods, and metrics able to engage the fifth of the world's population limited by their inability to read and write. The problem of literacy is especially acute for institutions located in the developing world.

This chapter highlights the example of a living heritage museum, the Khalsa Heritage Centre located in the city of Anandpur Sahib, in the state of Punjab, India. One of the largest idea-driven museums of its kind in the world, its exhibit experience has risen to the twin challenges of idea-induced intangible content development and unconventional interpretive content delivery mechanisms. Discussion of this site and its methods for meeting the needs of its public(s) will be contrasted with approaches taken to the representation of human rights adopted by several other heritage and "ideas" museums. The chapter concludes with some brief remarks concerning the value of these examples for curators and museum planners at the Canadian Museum for Human Rights (CMHR) in Winnipeg.

THE IDEAS MUSEUM

The definition of what constitutes a museum has been revised several times by the International Council of Museums (ICOM) since its inception in 1946. While museums remained object oriented and Eurocentric for many decades, UNESCO adopted a wide-ranging Convention for Safeguarding Intangible Heritage in 2003. The convention drew its authority directly from the Universal Declaration on Human Rights (UDHR)[1] of 1948, the International Covenant on Economic, Social, and Cultural Rights of 1966, and the International Covenant on Civil and Political Rights of 1966. It serves to recognize and protect Indigenous expressions, folklore, living traditions, oral histories, social practices, knowledge, and skills integral to the idea of culture. The latest version of this convention adopted at the ICOM 2007 Vienna Conference defines a museum as "a non-profit, permanent institution in the service of society and its development, open to the public, which acquires, conserves, researches, communicates and exhibits the tangible and intangible heritage of humanity and its environment for the purposes of education, study and enjoyment." The inclusion of "intangible heritage" is a significant development in the curatorial conscience. In that greater sense, every museum is a living repository of ideas, some with material manifestations, while others serve as enablers of thought in action.

Idea-driven museums such as the Newseum in Washington, DC, designed by the same exhibit designer who worked on the Canadian Museum for Human Rights,[2] deal directly with living and evolving content but often end up providing little more than mildly enhanced selections of digitized content widely available elsewhere. Unlike museums focusing on historical and cultural objects, information-oriented museums have no obvious claim to the uniqueness or superiority of their content or to the physical protection of this information. The experience, selection, organization, and ultimate appreciation of these ideas must instead provide a comparable mandate. On 3 April 2013, a new mixed-use ideas museum/library opened in North Carolina. Designed by Bethesda-based Gallagher Associates, the Institute for Emerging Issues (IEI) brings people together around complex issues in pursuit of the state's future economic competitiveness. IEI offers a different approach to public policy organization, engaging potential users in public policy decision-making processes with informed choices drawn from scenario-building simulated exhibits. Similar scenario-based exhibit experiences have been developed at the California Academy of Sciences and the National Academy of Sciences,[3] with many others drawing inspiration from Peter Schwartz, the futurist writer, scenario builder, policy thinker, and co-author of *The Long Boom: A Vision for the Coming Age of Prosperity*.[4] These exhibits allow visitors to influence and model the impacts of multiple outcomes based on their inputs. Visitors influence exhibit parameters and project future scenarios in ways that provide insightful learning with the potential to directly affect policy makers and communities. This is because highly complex scenario-building models are used by many countries to simulate the spread of infectious diseases, the impact of immigration, the supply and demand flows of global trade, transportation, urbanization patterns, and a variety of other societal transformations.

One challenge for these museums is to create effective exhibits that somehow transcend the web-enabled information platforms already widely available. Museums facing limited resources for constant technology upgrades and long lead times in vetting content risk losing timely relevance. A museum experience has to be distinctly different and, more importantly, current in its adaptations. Ideas museums with filtered content simply cannot afford to compete with the all-pervasive and ever-expanding World Wide Web. They therefore must seek exhibit-driven solutions that require the development and implementation of different metrics for creativity and measures of success.

Although museum researchers and curators can generate impeccable interpretive material, this knowledge must be translated into an engaging exhibit experience. One significant risk in this process of translation is information overload, a clutter of text and images and the white noise of graphics negatively impacting the flow of visitor traffic through gallery spaces. Imagine, for instance, 47,000 square feet of exhibit galleries with 8,000 colour and black-and-white layered images, 100 touch screen stations, and streaming videos as you traverse a vertigo-inducing ramp in a cavernous, disorienting building. How does one translate mere edited or unedited information into an actual exhibit? At what point does an adult visitor stop reading panel after panel of bilingual text and image captions? Children with shorter attention spans are even less likely to benefit from this volume of information overload and distracting images. Visitor fatigue enters yet another dimension if the subject matter is difficult, tragic, shocking, disturbing, and/or painful.[5] The careful selection of material for and skillful presentation of it in "consumable" bytes to audiences are crucial to creating a memorable visitor experience.

THE FAITH-BASED SECULAR LIVING MUSEUM:
FUNDAMENTAL QUESTIONS

Although freedom of religion for an individual or community is enshrined in Article 18 of the UDHR, it has seldom been given much thought in a classical taxpayer-funded museum setting.

The first step in museum planning can sometimes be the most difficult. It requires answering fundamental questions in order to firmly establish the institutional mandate. The following questions just begin to scratch the surface of queries that must be addressed while planning a human rights museum or another institution involving intangible heritage. The list is long, and deliberately so, in order to give readers some idea of the groundwork required to refine a museum's conception of content and its subsequent manifestation as an exhibit experience.

What gives credibility to a national museum in which the staff, executive, or members of its governing board lack direct human rights fieldwork, peer recognition, and/or museum experience? Is there a culture of dialogue, tolerance of differing points of view, and transparency within the museum's organizational culture? What gives a museum the power to decide what is relevant and allocate "proportionate" exhibit space? Should every memory related to its theme be kept alive in some form or other? Whose voice narrates the content? Where there is no one correct answer or approach, how do differing perspectives find a balance? Is "balance" even necessary? Can and must museums take a political, moral, nationalistic, or policy-induced stand?[6] What happens when researchers and curators or even members of the board of a museum harbour differences of opinion? How does a museum attract corporate and/or individual sponsors vis-à-vis their product lines and/or their business practices (as they pertain to human rights) without undue influence on content development? What are the terms of reference for stakeholder engagement, advisory board, and community outreach that feed directly into the content on display? Who "settles" or has the final say in the outcome of public presentation, on what basis, and with which credentials? If the museum takes years to crystallize content development and multilingual translations, then how does it stay relevant in rapidly evolving and devolving flash-points of human rights that might need appropriate and immediate corrections and/or additions to existing content? Is the museum to be a "temple" that takes a monolithic, government-endorsed view of these complex matters, or is an ideas museum a forum for hosting and encouraging multiple perspectives and ongoing discourse, debate, and even discord?[7]

The Khalsa Heritage Centre in India offers a unique approach to curatorial practice, content development, and exhibit design that celebrates a 500-year living tradition. It addresses three areas of human rights: the right to education, the right to pursue religion or faith, and the right to universal equality (as understood by the UDHR). Designed by Canadian architect Moshe Safdie, known for iconic institutions such as the Skirball Centre expansion, the National Gallery of Canada, the ArtScience Museum in Singapore, Yad Vashem in Israel, and the Crystal Bridges Museum of American Art in Arkansas, this 650,000-square-foot facility offers insights into ideas-based exhibit development. More will be said below about Safdie's design and the exhibit it houses, but consideration of the unique curatorial and design challenges of this complex suggests answers to some of the following additional (and no less important) questions. How does an institution curate faith-based content requiring clearances from the clergy yet still guarantee historical accuracy and objectivity? What allows an exhibit to link historical perspectives to issues relevant to contemporary civil societies? How does one create an exhibit narrative for an audience that might be primarily illiterate? How can an institution engage diverse audiences in an exhibit experience that is organic, visceral, poignant, and emotionally moving?

SIKH UNIVERSALISM

With over 25 million followers, Sikhism is the fifth largest organized religion in the world. Preaching equality and advocating the transfer of authority from kings and local rulers to the eternal scripture, the ten Sikh gurus (teachers) affected incremental social reform the ramifications of which continue to be felt today.

Born in 1469 near Lahore (Pakistan), the first guru, Nanak, grew up in a deeply divided society. While faith-based divides existed between Hindus and Muslims, Hindu society itself was a fractured amalgam of caste-based socio-cultural stratifications. With Muslim invaders arriving in waves from 1000 CE onward, forced conversions of Hindus and slavery created new concerns among the native Hindu population. Although Sufis adopted a more peaceful approach to conversion, preferring to attract prospective converts with meditative, musical mysticism, they too created subtle pressure on the people spread across the Indus and the plains of the Punjab.

Hindu society of the period grappled with four predominant castes with at least thirty-six social subcastes. With the exception of the higher castes of Brahmins (preachers) and Kshatriyas (warriors), the other members of society lived in abject poverty. The condition of the Shudras (untouchables) was outright inhumane. Women had little voice in this society and were considered by the Brahmin clergy's interpretation of the code of societal conduct to be born inferior; child marriage was widespread, and widows were condemned to an existence marked by degradation. Hindu Brahmins often imposed meaningless rituals on society and exacted draconian penance in order to redeem sins, using these tools to further oppress an estimated 500 million people across the Indian Subcontinent.

It was within this repressive, centuries-old, socio-religious context that Nanak, at the young age of thirty, proclaimed the incredible notions of gender equality, freedom, human rights, and equal dignity. He advocated shunning idol worship and embracing an omnipotent, omniscient, monotheistic, eternal almighty. He preached universalism and aided its practice through the provision of simple moral and spiritual guidelines for all, grounded in humanity, humility, and hope.

For the next twenty-four years, Guru Nanak travelled far and wide from Assam in the east to Baghdad and onward to Mecca and Medina (Saudi Arabia) in the west; from Sri Lanka in the south to Laddakh, Nepal, and Tibet in the north. In his call to overthrow oppressive regimes, he provided moral justification for the use of force if it was imperative to preserve the dignity of human life. These teachings later laid the foundations of the Khalsa (the Pure) under Guru Gobind. It is this living tradition that is integral to the interpretive content of the Khalsa Heritage Centre, one of the largest idea-driven museums in the world.

Nanak emphasized the moral responsibility of truthful living over more abstract conceptions of truth by promoting the cardinal virtues associated with hard work, selflessness, and sharing God's bounty. His teachings drew from folklore and had a musical metric woven into hymns based on renditions of Indian classical music. Advocating common kitchens as sites for congregation and discourse, as well as for serving the needy, he revolutionized social traditions and established an egalitarian social order. In so doing, Nanak conceived of Sikhism as a religion of learning conducive to leading an exemplary life.

For more than 400 years following Guru Nanak's death in 1549, the Sikh faith has been challenged and its prophets and gurus vilified and persecuted. In the nineteenth century, following the advent of British colonial rule, there occurred a series of Anglo-Sikh wars that succeeded in decisively undermining Sikh political and cultural autonomy, causing the Khalsa to reunite under the doctrine of Guru Gobind Singh. The challenges facing Sikhism evolved and became even more complex following India's independence in 1947.

The young Indian nation's democracy was founded explicitly on the principles of secularism, the basic assumptions of which, codified in places such as the Indian Penal Code and Constitution, remain in tension with any form of religious orthodoxy, Sikhism included. The demands of preserving Sikh heritage and culture confronted an uneducated, dogmatic mindset in the postindependence, postcolonial world. Struggling to overcome the tradition of the caste system and to promote inclusivity, India faced the massive challenge of integrating sixteen official languages and 4,000 spoken dialects into a common cultural framework capable of reconciling publics within formerly proudly independent and linguistically distinct states. In the face of these tensions and this diversity, the challenge of establishing a historically accurate narrative in a museum such as the Khalsa Heritage Centre, which aims to explain the origins of the Sikh religion as well as the Khalsa Panth (the community of initiated Sikhs), proved to be formidable. Yet by considering its example it becomes possible to gain profound insight into the value to museum planning and design of community engagement, curatorial conviction, and imaginative creativity.

The Khalsa Heritage Centre, which took thirteen years to build, is located in the holy town of Anandpur Sahib, near Chandigarh, the capital of the state of Punjab and Haryana. The Heritage Complex has two structural clusters connected by a quarter-kilometre-long pedestrian bridge spanning a seven-acre cascading reflecting pool. Phase 1 of the project comprises fifteen exhibit galleries and Phase 2 an additional ten exhibit galleries. The first set of galleries, shaped like petals and crescents, addresses events from the 1430s to the 1940s, arranged chronologically, and it is devoid of written interpretive text. The historical violence and injustices experienced by Sikhs are exhibited with a fluid simplicity and explained through a poetic audio rendition of interpretive content that condemns the taking of life, inhumane treatment of fellow beings, and the politics of power and prayer.

Phase 2 addresses the societal impacts and consequences of a divided Punjab, post-partition in 1947, statehood, the siege of the Golden Temple in 1984, the riots that subsequently targeted the Sikh community following Prime Minister Indira Gandhi's assassination by her Sikh bodyguards,[8] and other milestones in contemporary Sikh history, including the

18. Fifty-metre-tall, sandstone-clad, fort-like turrets of the Heritage Complex.

resilience and success of the Sikh diaspora in Canada, Africa, Australia, New Zealand, the United Kingdom, and the United States, allowing Sikhs in these places to preserve their faith and celebrate their traditions.

INTERPRETING FOR THE ILLITERATE

In our preoccupation with bilingualism, Canadians often forget that there are countries like India with sixteen official languages printed on their currencies and 4,000 dialects or that even within Canada underrepresented Indigenous voices and immigrant languages are creating new challenges for communicating messages true to their intent.[9]

With UN reports pointing to 793 million adults and 127 million adolescents as print illiterate, museums, with their increasing tendency to rely on the public's visual literacy, hold the key to making a significant contribution to overcoming asymmetries of knowledge in spaces beyond the classroom blackboard. Education, and therefore literacy, are human rights according to Article 26 of the UDHR. Literacy is a tool of personal empowerment and a means of economic and human development. It is essential for eradicating poverty, reducing child mortality, curbing population growth, achieving gender equality, and ensuring development, peace, democracy, and good international relations. With literacy providing access to continuing educational opportunities, literate communities are better geared to meet the challenges of global competitiveness.

Ongoing consultations with content experts, researchers, advisors, scholars, and the clergy enabled the exhibit design team to lay out three fundamental principles for creating meaningful exhibit experiences. First, recognizing the significance of the primarily rural locale of Anandpur Sahib, set in the Himalayan foothills amid open farmland, the content of the Khalsa Heritage Centre had to be designed for a primarily illiterate audience. Second, given the mammoth size of the facility, which sprawls over 100 acres, local communities needed to be engaged in the exhibit development process in order to create a sustained sense of ownership and continued resonance linking the museum to its stakeholders. Third, the exhibit experience needed to adopt a non-technology-based solution in order to avoid excessive and unnecessary operations, maintenance, training, implementation, and recurring upgrade costs.

Because conventional museums rely so much on interpretive text panels and labels, it took an experimental leap of creative imagination to eliminate text copy in the museum that would have led to an endless, time-consuming cycle of revisions, translations, reading levels, and debates over semantics and syntax. Appreciating and accepting that there is no one right way to effectively tell a story, and that museums have a responsibility to provide accessible interpretive content, it became evident that a text-driven approach would have unjustly excluded many in the rural demographic visitor base.

Given that the scriptures (taken from *Guru Granth Sahib,* the central religious text of Sikhism) were connected to renditions of classical Indian music delivered with a simplistic metric, it was decided that the Khalsa Complex, as an ideas museum devoid of material culture and collections, would maintain a similar non-artifactual flow, linked by a poetic metanarrative. Surjit Pattar, a Punjabi poet laureate, was engaged to use vernacular poetry to transmit parables and philosophy pegged to events and milestones in regional and national history. The intent was to communicate the premise of universalism within an accurate historical perspective. The resulting "narrative" explains the context of the emergence of universalism from the prevailing caste-based societal structure. The historical timeline spanning 500 years provides vignettes of milestones in Sikh heritage and history without delving into a faith-based discourse per se, keeping in line with the secular nature of the institution and its taxpayer public funding base.

Although Chinese dissident artist Ai Weiwei's Tate Modern–commissioned 150 tons of sunflower seeds attracted global critical attention, similar and often more complex initiatives in the museum realm have gone unnoticed. Each of Ai's porcelain seeds was painstakingly painted by hand by 1,600 female artisans in the ancient Chinese city of Jingdezhen, renowned for its more than 1,500-year-long tradition of ceramic making. The resulting exhibition provided an occasion for rich reflection on a range of themes, including the individual and society and the depersonalizing costs of mass production.[10] Yet the exhibit design at the Khalsa Heritage Centre was realized in an even more complex way, by engaging 600 artisans to produce traditional arts and crafts using embroidery, weaving, sculpting, masonry, painting, carving, woodwork, and metalwork. Community service is an integral element of Sikhism, with the religion's followers regularly volunteering time to cook, clean, and serve at temples and festivals. The exhibit production philosophy borrowed from this tradition while engaging diverse communities in an exercise of collectively creating fifteen sophisticated exhibit galleries, custom-fitting an enormous volumetric space, and preserving traditional crafts from the alienating pressures of mass production and commercial exploitation of labour.

Once there was consensus on the appropriate approach to exhibit planning, the next step in the exhibit design process was to examine the traditional arts, architecture, and crafts from the region that had evolved through centuries—both living crafts and those in need of revival. The reign of the Mughal Empire influenced the Indian Subcontinent from 1526 to 1857 and saw the rise of adaptive styles of relational aesthetics. Scriptures and historical compilations were produced under royal patronage, and commissions were assigned that gave rise to distinct styles of creativity, influencing works' materiality, drawing techniques, choices of colours, and presentation methods and protocols. The research process required to mount the museum's exhibitions involved examining primary and secondary sources and identifying traditional practitioners of these ancient crafts. The museum engaged local talent, master craftsmen, weavers, muralists, artists, and embroiderers via segmented exhibit development contracts that enabled the local crafts to be adapted to the museum's specific (and modern) exhibit design requirements and production standards.

Significantly, the museum building had already been designed by Moshe Safdie prior to the development of interpretive content and exhibit design. The building was designed to emulate giant petals and crescents gazing skyward, girding a coliseum-like cascading terrace overlooking the aforementioned reflecting pool. Gallery spaces in the Khalsa Heritage Centre soar more than seventy feet in cylindrical configurations like silos and the ramparts of a fort, adding to the acoustic and design challenges of custom exhibits intended to be developed with the aid of local craftsmen, artists, weavers, and artisans.Mapping the interpretive timeline from the birth of Guru Nanak to India's independence from British colonial rule in 1947, the stylistic rendition of folk art coupled with adaptations of Mughal and Rajputana-style miniature paintings and embroidery follows a synchronous path with the storyline as it progresses through history. Not only did the design and production process engage the wider community in exhibit creation, but also the style evolves through galleries in a way that provides a sense of historical progression, even as its primary story revolves around lives lived unwaveringly according to principles of egalitarian universalism.

The poetic audio narrative is enhanced by symbolism and metaphor, which add texture to and deepen the exhibit experience. The orientation gallery titled Panj Pani (Land of Five Rivers, or Punjab) holds the world's largest hand-painted layered mural, which ramps up three floors to provide an incredibly immersive experience, towering up from a seemingly bottomless pool. City and village life, festivals, ceremonies, local rituals, and decorative motifs drawn from across the region populate this massive

19. Director George Jacob at the Khalsa Heritage Centre during construction.

20. A Sikh guard stands vigil at the Khalsa Heritage Centre during construction.

mural in a configuration that represents the seasons and colours of the land and its people.

Murals, paper lanterns, exquisite weaving, embroidery, woodcuts, and stonework are woven into the story in a combination of metaphors and other communicative devices that intuitively suggests to audiences something about the concepts of enlightenment, the living word, monotheism, prayer, devotion, the temple within, karma, respect for fellow human beings, moral duty, humility, service to others, and faith.

By its very nature, the exhibit experience is hard to describe in words. It is visceral, emotive, and organic, and it promotes reflection, thereby helping to give visitors a sense of purpose. In their quest for accurate, information-driven "exhibits," museums often forget the difference between an information cluster and an exhibit in which content transcends a mere collection of fact-based information. Assessing the qualitative impact of summative evaluation is vital to the creation of a memorable exhibit experience.

The immensely diverse and unconventional variety of visual immersion in spatial environments also contributes to dissipating visitor fatigue. The curatorial decision to avoid text enables semantic flexibility, while the musical and poetic renditions, anchored in metrical regularity, encourage retention. The simplicity of the poignant imagery and messaging allows for the exhibit's interpretive content to be absorbed and appreciated by a diverse cross-section of audiences. It is thus especially well suited to its content and indigenous socio-cultural milieu.

FUTURE FORWARD

Museums are the collective souls of civil societies. They have an intrinsic responsibility to preserve our many pasts, and they herald our many futures shaped by thoughts and ideas that have transcended time and influenced generations. They have a moral obligation that hinges on professional competence and their unique ability to offer an educational experience distinct from other forms of cultural content. The museum conceived as a sterile amalgam of facts and figures, presented in predictable formats and requiring extended preparation, runs the danger of producing irrelevant content in an increasingly interconnected information age.

The challenges discussed in this chapter, if left unaddressed, can not only cost idea-driven museums in terms of time and materials but also affect the deliverables at stake and such institutions' organizational culture in more than one way. The Khalsa Heritage Centre is a grassroots-based community initiative on an unprecedented scale as well as a moving and informative contemporary museum. It provides insights into the advantages of an alternative method of delivering thought-provoking and emotive content in a museum setting without incurring enormous life-cycle costs of exhibits that rely heavily on technology, upgrades, maintenance, expert human resources, and expensive enterprise content management systems and other cloud-based technologies for data uploads and retrievals.

The CMHR, like many other idea-driven museums, has grappled with some of the challenges discussed here over the course of its design process, content development, and attempts at community outreach. These struggles are not new to anyone familiar with museum development more generally, and indeed they are often typical growing pains of new institutions. The CMHR, however, also promises to do more than just struggle with process and product; it aims to pioneer innovative approaches to exhibition content, making the story of human rights compelling for those who see Canada as a place of refuge and an unflinching champion of human dignity in times to come.

NOTES

1   UN General Assembly, Resolution 217 A (III), adopted and proclaimed the Universal Declaration of Human Rights on 10 December 1948.

2   Ralph Appelbaum Associates of New York is one of the world's leading experiential interpretive design firms known for its exemplary work at the US Holocaust Memorial Museum in Washington, DC, among other landmark institutions around the world.

3   The National Academies of Sciences funded the Infectious Diseases exhibit, which extensively uses scenario-building interactive methodology, at the Marion Koshland Science Museum (installed in 2008).

4   Peter Schwartz et al., *The Long Boom: A Vision for the Coming Age of Prosperity* (New York: HarperCollins, 1999).

5   Gareth Davey, "What Is Museum Fatigue?," *Visitor Studies Today* 8, 3 (2005): 17–21.

6   See, for example, "CMHR Stands Firm: Rejects Turkey's Threats, Insists Killing of Armenians Was a Genocide," *Winnipeg Free Press*, 8 April 2013.

7   D.F. Cameron, "The Museum: A Temple or the Forum?," *Curator* 14, 1 (1971): 11–24.

8   Between 31 October and 3 November 1984, following Prime Minister Indira Gandhi's assassination by her Sikh bodyguards, 11,000 Sikhs were killed (3,000 in New Delhi), according to *Human Rights Watch World Report: India,* 2011, http://www.hrw.org/world-report-2011/india.

9   With 7,000 spoken languages around the world, many are dying at an alarming rate. UNESCO estimated in 2012 that 2,724 are under threat of extinction in the coming decades. See Russ Rymer, "Saving Lost Languages: Vanishing Voices," *National Geographic,* July 2012, 67–93.

10   *Sunflower Seeds*, exhibit installation, Tate Modern, London, 2010; retrospective, Hirshorn Museum and Sculpture Garden, Smithsonian Institution, Washington, DC, 2012. Personifying the metaphor of a faceless drop merging into the ocean of Chinese consumerism, the community-induced commission seemed to draw on the 1956 call to let a "Hundred Flowers Bloom," signifying a revolution in China, perhaps a communal caricature of the individualistic intensity of Van Gogh's *Sunflowers*.

CURATING ACTION: COMPARATIVE GENOCIDE EXHIBITS AND THE "CALL TO ACTION" AT THE KIGALI MEMORIAL CENTRE, THE UNITED STATES HOLOCAUST MEMORIAL MUSEUM, AND THE MUSEO MEMORIA Y TOLERANCIA

CHAPTER 14

Amanda Grzyb

> It is not enough to ask whether or not our memorials
> remember the Holocaust, or even how they remember it.
> We should also ask to what ends we have remembered. That
> is, how do we respond to the current moment in light of
> our remembered past? This is to recognize that the shape of
> memory cannot be divorced from the actions taken in its
> behalf, and that memory without consequences contains the
> seeds of its own destruction.
> —James Young, *The Texture of Memory*[1]

Nestled in one of the Kigali Memorial Centre's memorial gardens, in the shadows of the museum exhibitions and the mass graves, is a clay pot depicting an elephant speaking into a mobile phone.[2] Unlike the other installations at the centre, the sculpture does not serve an explicitly pedagogical or commemorative function. According to museum guides, it signifies the transmission of genocide memory from the developing nation of Rwanda "to the entire world."[3] Rather than marking a particular historical event or remembering the dead, the sculpture is a meta-memorial that represents one of the primary purposes of the contemporary genocide memorial museum itself: the dissemination of an official narrative of perpetration and suffering and the "lessons" that this history purportedly teaches us.

It is significant that the metaphorical conduit for this process of dissemination is a mobile phone, an information-communication technology that proliferates in the everyday lives of Rwandans and a symbol of the Rwandan government's stated goal of transitioning from subsistence agriculture to a "knowledge-based, service oriented economy by 2020."[4] Unlike the radio—the other dominant tool for communication in Rwanda, one that was so deftly exploited by the extremists who broadcast anti-Tutsi propaganda prior to and during the 1994 genocide[5]—the cell phone suggests a *dialogue* between two individuals. What does the notion of dialogue signify in the context of global memorial traditions and a new generation of twenty-first-century memorial museums often built apart from historical massacre sites and killing centres?[6] First, it reflects a preference for interactivity and engagement with museum visitors, who are invited to become collaborators in the consolidation of privileged forms of national memory. Second, a two-way conversation suggests that one account of genocide (in this instance, the history of the Rwandan genocide as articulated by the elephant) could invite parallels to other traumatic national histories (articulated by the recipient of the call), opening a space for comparisons between historical cases of genocide, crimes against humanity, and other human rights violations. And third, if we assume that the recipient of the call is an individual who now bears the moral burden for the historical narrative that she or he has just heard, then the sculpture also reinforces ideas about "secondary witnessing,"[7] the role of the bystander, and taking individual action against various forms of perpetration, discrimination, and structural violence.

It is at the intersection of these three elements—interactivity, an overarching framework of comparative genocide, and the "call to action"—that I situate my discussion. There is a growing number of both permanent and temporary comparative genocide and human rights exhibitions around the world, many of which are bound to injunctions for action against hate, violence, intolerance, and indifference. Jennifer Carter suggests that these museums reflect "a new institutional mandate" that includes a common "social justice agenda" (see her chapter in this volume). In general, comparative genocide galleries are found in what Rachel Hughes calls "ex-locus" memorial museums,[8] those built at a distance from the physical spaces where the perpetrators committed their crimes. In former massacre sites such as Auschwitz (Poland), Choeung Ek (Cambodia), and Nyarubuye (Rwanda), exhibits focus on material evidence, artifacts, human remains, and details about the local site-specific killing process; comparative genocide galleries at these sites are rare. According to Piotr Cywinski, director of the Auschwitz-Birkenau State Museum, visitors travel thousands of kilometres to places such as Auschwitz not simply to obtain knowledge but also for what he calls a "deep, private, individual experience."[9] Nor does Cywinski see a need to incorporate any comparative galleries into the planned updates to Auschwitz, despite the significant number of genocides, mass atrocities, and crimes against humanity perpetrated across the globe since the site opened as a memorial museum in 1947. He suggests that such overt comparisons are unnecessary because Auschwitz alone is already a "symbol ... for understanding other sides of the Holocaust, all other genocides, other histories.... And this symbol helps people relate to their [own] experiences, their histories, their lives."[10]

Without the perceived authenticity of *lieux de mémoires* such as Auschwitz, ex-locus memorial museums tend to engage visitors in educational and commemorative activities that expand rather than restrict the memory terrain. In other words, the "deep, private, individual experience" and informal connections to "other genocides" that Cywinski identifies as endemic to primary massacre sites are formalized in deliberate ways at many ex-locus memorial museums. Often these museums include comparative genocide galleries and a call to action as the capstone of the visitor's experience, a representational approach that in reality is far more vexing than a simple call from a mobile phone. For example, in the case of the Canadian Museum for Human Rights (CMHR), A. Dirk Moses argues that the tension between "atrocity memorialization ... and human rights education/ activism" hinders the museum's financial viability because private donors want to see the implementation of particular "memory regimes" (see his chapter in this volume). For Christopher Powell, inevitable moments of contestation over content indicate that the CMHR itself is an important site of hegemonic struggle between "bottom-up" and "top-down" narratives about genocide and human rights (see his chapter in this volume).

The explicit focus on action in new comparative genocide exhibits leads to a host of important questions. Can the comparative depiction of historical atrocities and subsequent calls to action ever be separated from what James Young identifies as the "social and political forces underpinning national memory?"[11] Do comparative exhibitions disrupt or reinforce official/hegemonic discourses about memory and human rights? What is the relationship between intellectual engagement, affect, and—in the words of the CMHR Mission Statement—"taking action against hate and oppression"[12] in a museum context? What is the purpose of comparative galleries when they are situated as an addendum or a supplement to a large central exhibition featuring a particular case of genocide (often—but not always—the Holocaust)? Does an "awareness" of human rights violations and global atrocities actually prompt a different outcome for future victims, contribute to genocide prevention, change the course of would-be *génocidaires,* or influence foreign governments, the five permanent members of the UN Security Council, and the prosecutors of the International Criminal Court? Is it appropriate to make links among genocides, local forms of discrimination, bullying, civic engagement, and "citizenship education" vis-à-vis renewed discussions on the role of bystanders in our own communities? Do exhibitions that emphasize a neoliberal conceptualization of individual rights and responsibilities overlook or diminish collective struggles for political and social change? What is the relationship between state-funded memorial museums and social movements that seek to challenge the state on contemporary issues of genocide intervention, human rights violations, or structural violence? Can we move from history to memory to action in substantive and meaningful ways? Should we try to do so?

In this chapter, I begin to explore some of these questions in relation to three case studies: the Kigali Memorial Centre's permanent comparative genocide exhibit *Wasted Lives* (2004); the United States Holocaust Memorial Museum's long-term temporary installation on genocide and intervention *From Memory to Action: Meeting the Challenge of Genocide* (2009–present); and the Museo Memoria y Tolerancia's permanent exhibitions *Memory* and *Tolerance* (2010). I conclude that, though all three memorial museums provide similarly conceived overviews of historical instances of genocide as defined by the 1948 UN Genocide Convention and/or judicial proceedings, and though all three encourage some form of action, they do so for different audiences, with different ideological motivations, and with substantially different outcomes. Although facilitating visitor action sounds like an intrinsically positive—even noble—ambition for genocide memorial museums, it is far from a univocal concept. Nor is it universal in its implementation. Calls to action produce notable tensions between the pedagogical imperative of genocide studies and the unavoidably instrumental/political foundations of the memorial projects themselves.

THE KIGALI MEMORIAL CENTRE'S WASTED LIVES EXHIBIT

The Kigali Memorial Centre (KMC) opened in 2004 on the tenth anniversary of the Rwandan genocide as a "tribute to those who perished"
and "an educational tool for the next generation."[13] Originally developed
in a partnership between AEGIS Trust (a UK-based genocide prevention
organization) and the Kigali City Council, the KMC now operates under a
memorandum of understanding between AEGIS Trust and the Rwandan
government's National Commission for the Fight against Genocide (CNLG),
a federal commission housed within the Ministry of Sports and Culture.[14]
The CNLG oversees all aspects of national genocide commemoration,
memorials, education, and research; manages the storage (and eventually
the digitization) of the Gacaca files;[15] and offers support and advocacy for
genocide survivors. Although there are more than 500 genocide memorials
across Rwanda, the KMC is one of only six sites classified as national-level
memorials by the Rwandan government. Unlike the other five national sites
(Bisesero, Murambi, Ntarama, Nyamata, and Nyarubuye), the KMC is not
located at—or, in the case of Bisesero, adjacent to—a major massacre site;
yet, as home to the largest mass grave in the country and located in the
capital city, where perpetrators killed victims at intersections, compounds,
churches, and private homes, it qualifies as an ambiguously ex-locus memorial museum. Since the inception of the CNLG in 2010, the Rwandan government has exercised increasing control over the way in which the genocide
is represented; this oversight includes official approvals of all material
exhibits about the genocide (which, in some cases, are kept under lock and
key for years because of debates over language and content) and a controversial campaign to centralize Rwandan collective memory through a series
of exhumations at smaller local and family memorials and the physical
consolidation of human remains at district- and national-level memorials.[16]

The KMC consists of five distinct components: a large permanent exhibition, *Jenoside*, about the history of the 1994 Rwandan genocide;[17] a small
permanent comparative genocide exhibition called *Wasted Lives*; a permanent exhibition about child victims in the Rwandan genocide; a series of
memorial gardens; and a mass grave that contains the bodies of more than
250,000 genocide victims. Several scholars, including Jens Meierhenrich[18]
and Kristin Doughty,[19] suggest that the KMC caters mostly to international
tourists and dignitaries, but the museum's own statistics suggest a more
balanced distribution of visitors: in 2012, on average, 54 percent of visitors
were Rwandan, and 46 percent were international, with the majority of the
Rwandans visiting during the official genocide commemoration period

from April to June.[20] There is a striking difference, however, between the
KMC's slick text and photo panels, touch-screen videos, commemorative art
installations, glass-encased human remains, café (with free wi-fi), and gift
shop (all in keeping with both genocide memorial museum conventions
and artifact preservation standards of the global North) and the other
national memorial sites, where—with the exception of Murambi's small
historical museum[21]—there are no such adornments or barriers. At the
other memorials, guides lead visitors through stacks of skulls and bones,
lime-preserved corpses, piles of shoes and blood-stained clothing, weapons, shrapnel-damaged walls, and mass graves without the aid of photos,
text panels, videos, or—in some cases—electricity. Guides and visitors
handle artifacts, walk right through massacre sites, and stand inches away
from human remains, shoes, and clothing that have not been treated with
the sorts of preservative chemicals used at Auschwitz and Majdanek.

Action, in one sense, is the *raison d'être* for the KMC. Without funding and support from AEGIS Trust, a national genocide museum might
still be under construction in Kigali. The CNLG has only recently opened a
small exhibition at Murambi (also with the financial aid and expertise of
AEGIS Trust) and struggles to complete the construction of rudimentary
exhibits at Bisesero and Nyarubuye. Founded in 2000, AEGIS Trust itself is
anchored by an action-oriented mission: "to work towards the prediction,
prevention and ultimately the elimination of genocide primarily through
research, education and the dissemination of information and advice."[22]
In other words, AEGIS Trust sees a direct connection between genocide
education and genocide prevention. The main *Jenoside* exhibition at the
KMC emphasizes the lack of action by the international community during
the genocide, including poor media coverage, the refusal of international
leaders to call the massacres "genocide" despite irrefutable evidence, and
the impotence of the United Nations Assistance Mission in Rwanda (UN-
AMIR), all but completely withdrawn by the UN Security Council shortly
after the genocide began. Unsurprisingly, the exhibition's narrative is
firmly pro-RPF,[23] and the concluding panels implicitly invite support for
the government's goals of post-genocide unity, reconciliation, reconstruc-
tion, and development.

However, the clearest message about action resonates from the KMC's
permanent comparative genocide exhibit, *Wasted Lives*. Here the museum
connects the detailed narrative of the Rwandan genocide with five other
historical cases: the Herero genocide, the Armenian genocide, the Holocaust, the Cambodian genocide, and the Balkans.[24] According to Honoré

Gatera, director of visitor services at the KMC, the comparative approach of *Wasted Lives* helps visitors to understand what individual cases have in common. In a 2012 interview, he suggested that visitors need to understand how "the tools that Hitler used to measure the noses of Jewish people were packed in a box and brought to Rwanda [by Belgian colonists] to measure the noses of the Tutsi—the same techniques, the same ideologies."[25] Each of the five historical examples in *Wasted Lives* demonstrates the consequences of "genocide ideology" and the lack of international intervention, but the exhibition does not make any explicit links between genocide and the broader discourses of human rights, bullying, everyday violence, and individual civic responsibility. At the KMC, action is firmly situated in a top-down discourse of international intervention, complemented by a few examples in the main exhibit of individual Rwandan rescuers who hid Tutsi neighbours in their homes. The penultimate panel in *Wasted Lives* is both critical of the United Nation's tools for intervention and cautiously optimistic about future prospects for new modes of genocide prevention: "After the Holocaust, the United Nations introduced a Convention on the Prevention and Punishment of Genocide (1948). It was intended to deter the continuation of genocide, but it was difficult to enforce and largely ineffective. The failure of the international community to act in a timely and effective way in Rwanda and the Balkans has now renewed efforts to find more successful preventative measures."[26] The final panel articulates the KMC's primary call to action: "Genocide is likely to occur again. Learning about it is the first step to understanding it. Understanding it is imperative to responding to it. Responding to it is essential to save lives. Otherwise 'Never again!' will remain 'Again and Again...!'"[27] Here the exhibition identifies a pedagogical imperative embedded in the memorial museum itself, one that makes explicit links among learning, understanding, and acting without identifying particular atrocities or contemporary genocides to which we should respond. In other words, at the KMC, action is the answer to the *Jenoside* exhibit (the genocide happened, in part, because the international community failed to act in 1994) while, at the same time, it drives questions that emerge from the museum's primary mandate. How can we help Rwanda to recover? How can we educate visitors? How can we act to prevent future genocides using the international legal and legislative tools at hand?

THE UNITED STATES HOLOCAUST MEMORIAL
MUSEUM'S *FROM MEMORY TO ACTION* EXHIBIT

Like the Kigali Memorial Centre, the United States Holocaust Memorial Museum (USHMM) in Washington, DC, is an ex-locus state museum that focuses primarily on one case of genocide—the Holocaust—while housing a secondary comparative genocide exhibit that explicitly encourages visitors to act by "meeting the challenge of genocide today." The USHMM first opened in 1993, guided by the following mission: "to advance and disseminate knowledge about [the Holocaust]; to preserve the memory of those who suffered; and to encourage its visitors to reflect upon the moral and spiritual questions raised by the events of the Holocaust as well as their own responsibilities as citizens of a democracy."[28] At the one-year anniversary of its opening, in 1994, American government officials found themselves earnestly proclaiming "never again" at the moment when the Rwandan government and Interahamwe militia were slaughtering thousands of Tutsi civilians in the streets of Kigali.[29] A year later, in 1995, the USHMM established its Committee on Conscience (COC), thus formalizing the relationship between its permanent historical exhibition on the Holocaust and the "responsibilities [of Americans] as citizens of a democracy" to acknowledge and prevent contemporary cases of genocide and crimes against humanity.[30]

The COC provides a strong mandate for visitor action, and the long-term temporary installation (2009–present), *From Memory to Action: Meeting the Challenge of Genocide*, is not so much a place to contemplate what it might mean to act as a place, with its three contemporary case studies, to situate bystander action both as the installation's ontological centrepiece and as its ultimate objective. Although the USHMM hosts its share of international visitors, the founding director of the museum is clear that its target audience is American: "The Museum has been built to tell America and the world the factual story of this most terrible event in modern history and to illuminate the crucial moral lessons it entails."[31] The context of the installation's action directive is therefore filtered through the distinctively American framework established in the permanent Holocaust exhibition, which begins with a large photo of American troops liberating Ohrdruf concentration camp, makes periodic reference to American failures to act (referencing both the Jewish refugees of the MS *St. Louis* transatlantic liner that was turned away from American ports in June 1939 and the refusal of Americans to bomb the railway tracks leading to Auschwitz-Birkenau),[32] and concludes with the testimonies of survivors who emigrated to the United States after the war.[33]

From Memory to Action consists of a large room lined with three horizontal text/photo canvas strips that provide basic overviews of the Rwandan genocide, the Srebrenica genocide, and the crisis in Darfur. In the centre of the room, television monitors play looping interviews with scholars, activists, survivors, witnesses, and perpetrators above a large interactive "touch table" that invites visitors to expand digital stories and deposit them into an "online collection" using half of a perforated pledge card. On the other half of the card, visitors are encouraged to write a pledge in response to the following question: "TAKE ACTION! What will you do to help meet the challenge of genocide today?" After signing the card, the visitor inserts it through an electronic scanner into a glass box, and the pledge is projected—along with many others—onto a large screen.[34]

According to its curator, Bridget Conley-Zilkic, *From Memory to Action* provides a way for visitors "to transform what they learn about the Holocaust into meaningful action."[35] In other words, the installation *curates action*. I suggest that the teleological thrust of the installation renders the historical and factual information on the canvas panels secondary, a claim supported by factual errors and ambiguities in the historical cases on display. For instance, Nyarubuye, a major massacre site in eastern Rwanda that received prominent international media coverage in the immediate aftermath of the Rwandan genocide,[36] is misspelled Nayarabuye. A photo of Ntarama church, where the Interahamwe killed approximately 5,000 victims on 14–15 April 1994, has an ambiguous caption that obscures the actual death toll: "A UN team found the bodies of 400 Tutsi murdered by Hutu militiamen in this church at Ntarama on Sept 16, 1994." Although there are no notable errors in the depiction of Darfur, the static nature of the exhibit suggests that the crimes against humanity—which peaked there in 2003–05—continue to rage on today. An adjoining room with additional information about state violence in Sudan emphasizes the general feeling that the Darfur crisis has not subsided, while, in actuality, we can now relegate Darfur to the growing list of cases in which the international community failed to intervene effectively (by encouraging peace negotiations, facilitating diplomatic efforts, or protecting civilians through UNAMID). If accuracy and historical context are secondary interests, then we can surmise that the three case studies are used primarily to produce a general sense of affect in the visitor (the realization that "never again" is "again and again") and defer to the exhibit's main purpose: a call to action

21. A clay pot depicts an elephant speaking on a cell phone, Kigali Memorial Centre.

TAKE ACTION!

www.ushmm.org/take_action

Your online access code: 3280CF7

What will you do to help meet the challenge of genocide today?

_____

_____

_____ Sign
                                 here:

Add your pledge to the glass case.

22. Take Action! pledge card at the *From Memory to Action* exhibit, United States Holocaust Memorial Museum.

that does not "meet the challenge" of a particular case of genocide but of *genocide* itself. In 2012–13, this message was further complicated by the USHMM's action-oriented capital campaign slogan "Never Again Begins with You: Donate Now," which suggests that a donation to the museum is also a form of action vis-à-vis genocide education.

What purpose do the pledge cards actually serve, and do the visitors follow through by taking action once they leave the museum? In one of the first evaluations of its kind, Joy Sather-Wagstaff and Rebekah Sobel tracked visitor engagement in a longitudinal study to determine how effectively *From Memory to Action* created a "third space" for visitors to act and how the exhibit facilitated "ongoing individual transformation that enables social action-oriented effects."[37] In an analysis of 9,127 pledges, they identified two main categories of action: "internal, self-directed, reflective actions," which included "believe, respect, remember, promise," and "external actions directed towards others," which included "teach/educate, prevent, speak up, help, send money, pray."[38] They then conducted 348 follow-up interviews with visitors six months and twelve months after their visits to *From Memory to Action* in an attempt to trace longer-term forms of engagement with the exhibit's directive. In the follow-up interviews, visitors described "small yet deliberate actions in the mundane everyday,"[39] such as talking about museum content, refraining from particular phrases, confronting others about racist comments, speaking in favour of tolerance and genocide prevention, and so on. Although Sather-Wagstaff and Sobel hypothesize that these sorts of actions "can make as much of a difference over time, if not more, as much grander, one-time actions," the visitors do not actually tackle the "challenge of genocide today."[40] Indeed, the study indicates that there is a significant disjuncture between the kind of action promoted by the exhibit (addressing genocide on a global scale) and the kind of action actually inspired by it (everyday acts of tolerance on a local scale), generating significant questions about the limits of genocide prevention in the context of an educational museum. Visitors do act but not necessarily in the ways that the curator envisaged.

EL MUSEO MEMORIA Y TOLERANCIA

It is precisely at the intersection between comparative genocide studies and action-oriented education that Mexico City's new Museo Memoria y Tolerancia (MMyT) situates its curatorial project. Opened in 2010 and funded primarily by private and corporate donations, the museum caters predominantly to Mexican and Latin American visitors. Its stated mission is "to transmit to broad audiences the importance of tolerance and diversity. To create awareness through historical memory, focusing on genocides and other crimes. To warn about the dangers of indifference, discrimination and violence for generating, instead, responsibility, respect and awareness in each individual."[41] The museum is divided into two main exhibits, *Memory* and *Tolerance*. There is also an educational program space, a gallery for temporary exhibitions, and a small children's museum, La Isla Panwapa, where children aged four to twelve can participate in a series of guided *Sesame Street*–themed activities about tolerance, diversity, cooperation, and community. The *Memory* exhibit begins with an extensive history of the Holocaust, including fourteen chronological sections ranging from the Jews in prewar European society to the Nuremberg Trials. Compared with the USHMM or the Schindler Factory Museum in Krakow, the MMyT's aesthetic approach is clean and minimalist, with the significant incorporation of photomurals, film and audio clips, spare use of text panels, and several commemorative art installations. Clips of Mexican newspaper coverage of Jewish persecution are found throughout the galleries, and the penultimate exhibit, *Reconstructing Life*, focuses on Holocaust survivors who emigrated to Mexico after the war. Immediately after the Holocaust galleries are eight smaller galleries about the 1948 UN Genocide Convention, the Armenian genocide, the former Yugoslavia, the Rwandan genocide, the Cambodian genocide, the Guatemalan genocide, Darfur, and the International Criminal Court.[42]

Unlike the KMC's *Wasted Lives* exhibit (which characterizes action as education, large-scale prevention, and—in the main *Jenoside* exhibit—support for Rwandan recovery) and the USHMM's *From Memory to Action* exhibit (where visitors' individual, local actions to promote tolerance resonate with a larger institutional directive to "meet the challenge of genocide today"), the MMyT makes an explicit connection between the history of modern genocide and everyday forms of discrimination. Upon leaving the final genocide galleries, visitors enter the *Tolerance* exhibit, where they are encouraged to think conceptually about "the other and I," and the power of words, stereotyping, and discrimination in everyday Mexican contexts. A film installation illustrates scenes of domestic verbal abuse, struggles against racism, and dialogue, while other galleries explore the power of media to invoke and perpetuate stereotypes. Other galleries depict global human rights abuses, poverty and human trafficking, discrimination against Indigenous peoples in Mexico, and civil society organizations and NGOs working to alleviate these challenges. The final gallery in the museum, a video installation, leaves the visitor with a personal question: "What attitude are you going to take? Perpetrator? Indifferent? Or Committed?" The culmination of the visitor's experience, which moves from genocide to discrimination to social and economic inequality, does not focus on overt structural reforms, national or collective responsibilities, or tangible reforms to bodies such as the UN Security Council or UN Genocide Convention. Instead, there is a decidedly individual call to action.

Although the Holocaust and genocide galleries have remained fairly static since the museum opened in 2010, the *Tolerance* exhibit has been changed three times in two and a half years, and it will undergo another complete overhaul in 2014. In a 2013 interview, the MMyT's content director, Jacobo Dayán Askenazi, explains that the fluid nature of the permanent exhibit reflects the museum's desire to "figure out the best way of exhibiting action, conscience, stereotypes, and discrimination."[43] He suggests that Mexico is an entirely different context from Europe, Canada, or America:

> In places like Mexico, the reality outside is awful. The daily
> lives of many Mexicans are very difficult. Talking only about
> crimes that occur somewhere far from Mexico is not fair,
> so we have to include the Mexican reality in the exhibit:
> diversity in Mexico, discrimination in Mexico, human rights
> in Mexico. We have to make that bond, that connection in
> the exhibit, then call the people to act, to react, to feel angry
> about the daily lives of millions of Mexican people.... We
> have learned that we have to touch something in the people
> that is connected to their indignation, their outrage.... You
> have to feel touched—not something like seeing poor people
> in Africa, not sentimental—you have to feel some anger
> inside of you that pushes you to action. What action you're
> going to take is not the museum's problem. It is not our role
> to tell you that you have to do this, and this, and this.... Do
> whatever you want: change your school, your community,
> your city, your country, your world. But you have to move
> yourself. You cannot keep on watching what is going on
> comfortably in your house.[44]

The MMyT does not advocate a particular kind of action; instead, it curates a feeling of outrage that visitors can use to motivate action outside the walls of the museum. For Dayán Askenazi, this is not likely to mean taking action in contemporary cases of genocide or crimes against humanity: "It's very difficult for a Mexican kid of eighteen to be responsible for what's going on in Darfur. I think that is an American way of thinking. Here I am responsible for what's going on in my school, in my city, in my neighbourhood, in the place where I work, in the places related to me. If I change my reality and the places around me, if we are many people doing this, then we can change the country."[45] The affect provoked by the comparative genocide galleries is consciously directed toward shaping *individual* attitudes toward tolerance, civil rights, and altruism. In this sense, the MMyT animates the distinction that Angela Failler and Roger Simon make between "learning about" and "learning from." They write that, "in learning from, knowledge is understood to be a relation contingent on a willingness to recognize one's connectedness to an event or experience that might well be 'separate' in the sense of belonging to another time, place, or people but that can nevertheless be seen for its enmeshment with the structure, privileges, and constraints of one's own life" (see their chapter in this volume). The MMyT guides visitors from learning about historical . genocides in the *Memory* exhibit to learning from their own relationships to everyday discrimination in the *Tolerance* exhibit but without a top-down directive that prescribes a particular course of action.

CONCLUSION

In Kigali, action means recognizing the need for global genocide prevention and intervention and, less explicitly, supporting the Rwandan government's goals of unity, reconciliation, and development. In Washington, "taking action to end genocide" with an electronic pledge card is not tied to particularly rigorous histories of contemporary cases of genocide, and visitors are much more likely to act in everyday encounters with intolerance than in global genocide prevention. In Mexico City, action means translating the lessons of genocide history into a decidedly Mexican context and making a personal commitment to embrace everyday forms of tolerance while rejecting indifference. These three different articulations of action suggest that, while all comparative genocide exhibits produce affect, the museums' expectations for visitor action are strikingly divergent. The visitor's subjectivity as an "actor" in the face of contemporary genocide and discrimination is delineated through a process of interpellation bound to the museum as an apparatus of the state. Each comparative genocide exhibit reflects its own national character, its own political influences, and the hegemonic structures that bear down on it.

When is action something more than a rhetorical urn for the hopelessness that visitors feel after seeing exhibits that detail incomprehensible scales of mass atrocities? How should they act, through which means, and for what purposes? In the words of Failler and Simon, can memorial museums create spaces for "a collective vision of a more just society" without "determining in advance the desired substance of visitor responses" and visitor actions? If taking action against genocide or being a "committed person" is not a universal concept, then perhaps the most important role that memorial museums can play—beyond genocide education—is to consciously create new spaces for dialogue about *the nature of action itself* and the role of the museum as a space for hegemonic struggle, for affect and outrage, for collective solutions to violence and inequality, and for exhibits that open up spaces that might truly move us from learning about to learning from.

ACKNOWLEDGEMENTS

I am grateful for financial assistance from Western University's Faculty of Information and Media Studies, the office of Western's former vice-president of research, Ted Hewitt, and Western's International Curriculum Fund, which funded field research in Mexico City, Rwanda, Poland, and Washington, DC, between 2009 and 2013. I am extremely appreciative to the CNLG, Jean de Dieu Mucyo, and Dr. Jean-Damascene Gasanabo, director of CNLG's Genocide Research and Documentation Centre, for permission to conduct interviews and take photographs at Rwandan genocide memorial sites. I would also like to acknowledge the contributions of my independent interpreter, driver, and guide, Didier Odie Muvunyi, an invaluable partner in my Rwandan research. Likewise, I am grateful to my friend Emery Rutagoyna, a former KMC employee; Honoré Gatera, director of visitor services at KMC; and all of the memorial guides who shared their knowledge with me on four research trips to Rwanda between 2010 and 2013: Leon Muberuka, Stanley Mugabarigira, Bellanula Uwitonze, Gaspard Mukwiye, Gilbert Sezirahiga, Didaciènne Uwamahoro, and Illuminé. Thanks to Rafael Alarcón Medina for conducting initial fieldwork in Mexico City on my behalf in January 2013 and to Jacobo Dayán Askenazi, content director at the Museo Memoria y Tolerancia, for sharing his perspective on the museum's exhibits during an interview in July 2013. Thanks also to Piotr Cywinski, director of the Auschwitz State Museum, for an interview in May 2011; Krista Hegburg from the USHMM's Center for Advanced Holocaust Studies; and Rebekah Sobel, program evaluator at the USHMM. Finally, I am grateful to my excellent research assistants, Amal Mohammed Bhaalo and Kait Bida, who worked tirelessly to transcribe my interviews from Poland and Rwanda.

NOTES

1   James Young, *The Texture of Memory: Holocaust Memorials and Meaning* (New Haven, CT: Yale University Press, 1993), 15.

2   Until 2014, the clay pot depicted an ape speaking into a mobile phone, though tour guides and audio guides identified the animal as an elephant. In the months before the twentieth commemoration of the genocide, the ape was replaced with the elephant pictured in this chapter.

3   English-language audio-guided tour: "An elephant with a mobile phone is communicating internationally to pass on the lessons to the entire world." Kigali Memorial Centre, visited October 2010 and February 2013.

4   World Bank, "Rwanda," http://www.worldbank.org/en/country/rwanda/overview. See also Government of Rwanda, "Vision 2020," http://www.cdf.gov.rw/vup.html.

5   See Christine L. Kellow and Leslie Steeves, "The Role of Radio in the Rwandan Genocide," *Journal of Communication* (Summer 1998): 107–28; and Scott Straus, "What Is the Relationship between Hate Radio and Violence? Rethinking Rwanda's 'Radio Machete,'" *Politics and Society* 35 (2007): 609–37.

6   See Louis Bickford and Amy Sodaro, "Remembering Yesterday to Protect Tomorrow: The Internationalization of a New Commemorative Paradigm," in *Memory and the Future: Transnational Politics, Ethics, and Society,* ed. Yifat Gutman, Adam D. Brown, and Amy Sodaro (New York: Palgrave Macmillan, 2010), 72–78; Paul Williams, "Witnessing Genocide: Vigilance and Remembrance at Tuol Sleng and Choeung Ek," *Holocaust and Genocide Studies* 18 (2004): 234–55; Veronique Tadjo, "Genocide: The Changing Landscape of Memory in Kigali," *African Identities* 8 (2010): 379–88; and Terence Duffy, "Exhibiting Human Rights," *Peace Review* 12 (2000): 303–39.

7   Jens Andermann, "Returning to the Site of Horror: On the Reclaiming of Clandestine Concentration Camps in Argentina," *Theory, Culture, and Society* 29 (2012): 78.

8   Rachel Hughes, "The Abject Artefacts of Memory: Photographs from Cambodia's Genocide," *Media, Culture, and Society* 25 (2003): 23–43.

9   Piotr Cywinski, Auschwitz State Museum, interview with the author, June 2010.

10 Ibid.

11 Young, *The Texture of Memory,* xi.

12 Canadian Museum for Human Rights, "Mission Statement," www.humanrightsmuseum.ca/about-museum.

13 Kigali Memorial Centre, http://www.kigalimemorialcentre.org/old/centre/index.html.

14 CNLG, http://www.cnlg.gov.rw.

15   According to Jean-Damascéne Gasanabo, director of the CNLG's Centre for Genocide
     Research and Documentation, there are approximately 60 million documents associated
     with the Gacaca files that require digitization. Jean-Damascéne Gasanabo, conversation
     with the author, September 2012.

16   See Jens Meierhenrich, "The Transformation of *lieux de mémoire:* The Nyabarongo River
     in Rwanda, 1992–2009," *Anthropology Today* 25 (2009): 13–19; and Kristin Doughty,
     "Memorials, Human Rights, and Controversy in Post-Genocide Rwanda," *Anthropology
     News* (September 2011): 10–12.

17   Although the Rwandan government refers to the 1994 Genocide against the Tutsi in
     Rwanda (sometimes shortened to Genocide against Tutsi or Tutsi Genocide) in all official
     documents and museum contexts, I use the term "Rwandan genocide" both because it is
     the conventional name for this genocide in the international community and scholarly
     research and because it is a more inclusive term that also conventionally references the
     massacre of politically moderate Hutu.

18   Jens Meierhenrich, "Through a Glass Darkly: Genocide Memorials in Rwanda 1994–Pres-
     ent," www.genocidememorials.cga.harvard.edu.

19   Doughty, "Memorials."

20   Honoré Gatera, Kigali Memorial Centre, interview with the author, September 2012.

21   AEGIS Trust also constructed a small museum at the Murambi genocide memorial,
     which opened in 2011 after years of controversy over the exhibit's content. Gilbert Sezira-
     higa, director of the Murambi genocide memorial, interview with the author, September
     2012.

22   See Aegis Trust online, http://www.aegistrust.org/index.php/Who-we-are/about-us.html.

23   The RPF (Rwandan Patriotic Front) is the former Ugandan-based, mostly Tutsi rebels
     who effectively ended the genocide when they took control of Kigali. Led by former rebel
     leader Paul Kagame, the RPF is now the ruling party of Rwanda.

24   *Wasted Lives* is preceded by the following disclaimer: "The exhibition introduces several
     genocides and genocidal situations. It does not give examples of all genocidal massacres
     because of limited space. It can only illustrate a few examples, representing a tragic cross-
     section of a century of genocide."

25   Honoré Gatera, Kigali Memorial Centre, interview with the author, September 2012.

26   Panel from the *Wasted Lives* exhibit, Kigali Memorial Centre, viewed October 2010.

27   Ibid.

28   USHMM, "Mission Statement," http://www.ushmm.org/museum/mission/.

29   See Frontline, *Ghosts of Rwanda,* 2004.

30   See "About Committee on Conscience," http://www.ushmm.org/confront-genocide/
     about/committee-on-conscience-members

31   Jeshajahu Weinberg, "From the Founding Director," in *The World Must Know: The His-
     tory of the Holocaust as Told in the United States Holocaust Memorial Museum,* 2nd ed., ed.
     Michael Berenbaum (Washington, DC: USHMM, 2006), xvi.

32   USHMM, visited by the author, December 2012.

33   Young, *The Texture of Memory,* 336, notes similar justifications in President Jimmy
     Carter's address of 24 April 1979 supporting a national Holocaust memorial on the mall:
     liberation by American troops, immigration to America by survivors, lack of American
     intervention, and universal nature of human rights evoked by the history of the Holo-
     caust.

34   For a more detailed description of *From Memory to Action*, see Amanda Grzyb, "Mobility,
     Human Rights Activism, and International Intervention in Darfur," in *Mobilities, Knowl-
     edge, and Social Justice,* ed. Suzan Ilcan (Montreal: McGill-Queen's University Press, 2013),
     377–96.

35   USHMM, "United States Holocaust Memorial Museum's New Exhibit From Memory to
     Action: Meeting the Challenge of Genocide Engages Visitors in Genocide Prevention Ef-
     forts," press release, 18 May 2009, http://www.ushmm.org/museum/press/archives/detail.
     php?category=03-coc&content=2009-05-18.

36   BBC journalist Fergal Keane provided shocking footage from Nyarubuye, which he later
     detailed in a book, *Season of Blood.* Likewise, Philip Gourevitch opened his popular book
     about the genocide, *We Wish to Inform You ...* , with an account of his visit to Nyarubuye
     in 1995.

37   Joy Sather-Wagstaff and Rebekah Sobel, "From Memory to Action: Multisited Visitor
     Action at the United States Holocaust Memorial Museum," *Museums and Social Issues* 7
     (2012): 293–305.

38   Ibid., 300.

39   Ibid., 303.

40   Ibid, 303.

41   Museo Memoria y Tolerancia, http://www.myt.org.mx/MytIngles.pdf.

42   According to Jacobo Dayán Askenazi, content director at the MMyT, the Armenian geno-
     cide and the Holocaust were selected as inspirations for Raphael Lemkin's 1948 Genocide
     Convention, and the other five cases were selected based on national or international
     legal proceedings (either through tribunals or through the ICC) that made legal determi-
     nations of genocide. Interview with the author, 5 July 2013.

43   Jacobo Dayán Askenazi, content director at the MMyT, interview with the author, 2 July
     2013.

44   Ibid.

45   Ibid.

WHAT (AND HOW) TO REMEMBER? SPACES FOR MEMORY IN POST-DICTATORSHIP ARGENTINA

CHAPTER 15

Jorge A. Nállim

Construction of the Canadian Museum for Human Rights (CMHR) in Winnipeg, Manitoba, sparked a number of passionate discussions. Intense debates surrounded the project from its inception, from whether its futuristic architecture fits within the urban landscape to more fundamental questions regarding why such a museum is justified, what should be included—or not—in it, and how those contents should be displayed. Aboriginal, Jewish, and Ukrainian groups publicly contended over the relative merits and importance of spaces in the new museum that captured their specific experiences with human rights violations and genocide, and other communities from Africa, Asia, Latin America, and the Caribbean wondered whether their stories would be considered and in what manner (see the contributions by Dirk Moses and Helen Fallding in this volume). In the middle of conflicts regarding funding and staffing of the museum, articles in the local press called attention to alleged internal debates between managers and current and former employees about whether the museum should be centred on "darker" narratives about genocide or if it should emphasize more "positive" stories.[1]

The fractious debates over the museum are not surprising; as the arguments made evident, the idea of a museum of human rights is problematic, at its core, on two fundamental levels. The first level concerns *what* is going to be remembered, what constitutes a human right or not, and why specific historical and social experiences would fit into that definition and, eventually, in the museum. The second level concerns *how* those experiences will be displayed in such a museum. Inevitably, a museum of human rights is thus a site of the intersection of concepts of history and memory and public space, concepts and relations that by no means are static but dynamic and changing.

The questions that now surround the CMHR have been relevant for many other countries in the world. This is particularly the case with Argentina, which in 1983 emerged from a vicious military regime that, over a period of seven years, killed tens of thousands of its own citizens. In 2007, one of the most notorious sites for human rights violations during the military regime, the Navy School of Mechanics (ESMA, for its acronym in Spanish) in Buenos Aires, was inaugurated as the Space for Memory and Human Rights (Espacio Memoria y Derechos Humanos; ex-ESMA). This chapter provides an overview of the sinuous process that led to the creation of this space between 1983 and 2007, highlighting the changing historical circumstances informing the debate surrounding human rights violations in the country and, more precisely, how to remember that past in a public space by way of museums and other memorials.[2] As scholarship on the Argentine case has argued, those public spaces are linked to debates about memory and the past, in which, as Elizabeth Jelin has expressed, social memories "are built and established through practices and 'marks.' They are social practices that are installed as rituals, material marks in public spaces and symbolic representations, including calendars."[3] Memories are products of specific circumstances and struggles, and therefore they need to be historicized in order to understand the conflicts that surround them as well as the manner in which they are represented.[4] Similar to the process of "invention of traditions" described by Eric Hobsbawm and Terence Ranger, memories and commemorations are not rigid but dynamic and changing as they are reinterpreted in different historical contexts, elements that can be clearly perceived in the process that led to the foundation of the Space for Memory and Human Rights in Argentina.[5]

HUMAN RIGHTS JUSTICE AND MEMORY IN A DIFFICULT TRANSITION, 1983–EARLY 1990s

On 10 December 1983, Raúl Alfonsín was inaugurated as the first civilian president following the collapse of the military regime that had ruled Argentina since 24 March 1976. The new government, as well as the whole society, faced the terrible legacy left by the military rulers and their allied social sectors in the media, upper and middle classes, business groups, and Catholic Church. For more than seven years, the military regime, influenced by Cold War doctrines of national security, had sought to reshape the country's economic, political, and social structures.[6] The results could not have been more disastrous. Economically, the combination of freeing up the market, opening Argentina to international markets, and repressing labour destroyed the country's economy and left people in a weaker and more vulnerable situation. This situation worsened when the country entered a period of economic crisis and experienced high levels of inflation since it was hit hard by the effects of the Latin American debt crisis in 1982–83.

More seriously, in order to impose its authority and policies, the military regime had engaged in an active campaign of state terrorism to prevent any opposition to its power. Emerging out of decades of political and economic instability, military leaders were determined to use violence to eradicate what they saw as the intrinsic roots of Argentina's woes. Those roots were loosely identified with lower- and middle-class popular groups connected with the left, the Peronist party, and labour that had been mobilized in the years prior to the coup. However, state terror was eventually extended to the whole society, resulting in widespread violations of human rights that left between 9,000 and 30,000 Argentines "disappeared" or killed by the state,[7] thousands forced into exile, and a society fractured and traumatized by the effects of practices that included arbitrary detention and torture.

In this context, the early years of the post-military period were marked by attempts, first, to establish the extent of human rights violations committed under military rule and, second, to bring to justice those responsible for these violations. There was one initiative in these years, discussed among and supported by some human rights organizations in 1984, to establish a "House of the Disappeared," conceived as a place to gather and store documentation related to state terrorism.[8] However, it did not gain momentum, for the search for truth and justice eventually became the main goal of human rights organizations. Rather than establishing a museum, the whole struggle for human rights played out in the open public space of Argentinian society. Alfonsín's administration indeed made some progress. The government derogated the 1983 amnesty law that the military leaders had enacted to protect themselves before leaving power. It also established the National Commission on the Disappearance of People (CONADEP) to investigate human rights violations committed under the military, and it decreed the prosecution of members of the military juntas that had ruled the country as well as of top leaders of armed leftist groups. Despite CONADEP's limitations in terms of scope and mandate—the commission was created without subpoena powers, for example—its 1984 report, titled *Never Again*,[9] dramatically brought to public awareness the reality of widespread human rights violations. In 1985, the junta leaders were brought to trial and sentenced to different prison terms.[10]

Besides CONADEP's work and the trials of Argentina's military leaders, there were other indicators of progress, such as the creation of state offices and institutions to deal with human rights. Examples include the Under-Secretariat of Human Rights at the national Ministry of Interior and, later, the 1994 constitutional reform through which international conventions of human rights were incorporated into the Argentine constitution. Moreover, public mobilizations and demonstrations, as well as the appearance of a large number of books, articles, and films on the military regime and violations of human rights, contributed significantly to the construction of social memories of what had happened. These activities also helped to identify the features of Argentine politics and society that had allowed those violations to happen. In addition, the weekly rounds of the Mothers of Plaza de Mayo in front of the presidential palace in Buenos Aires continued to mark the public space as a powerful symbol of memory and justice for both the political establishment and civil society.[11]

However, the impetus behind the search for justice was also compromised by historical circumstances. Alfonsín was concerned with the stability of democracy since he was facing opposition from wide sectors of the military establishment that were unrepentant for what they still saw as their victorious struggle against leftist guerrilla groups, which included what they perceived to be, at worst, inevitable "excesses" that resulted in the deaths of Argentine citizens. The government was criticized by military officer organizations, faced disobedience from those called to testify, and, in April and December 1987 and January 1988, had to confront uprisings of dissatisfied mid-rank military officers, who demanded a political solution to the trials. This context must be taken into account in order to understand the limitations on CONADEP's work and the two laws passed by the National Congress: the Full Stop law (1986), which imposed a deadline for presenting cases to the courts regarding illegal repression, and the Due Obedience law (1987), which exempted mid- and lower-rank officers based on the idea that they were following orders and, therefore, could not be punished. The reversal of the initial impetus for justice and democracy reached its peak with the election of Argentina's next president, Carlos Menem (1989–99). Facing another military uprising and wanting to consolidate support from conservative social sectors—including the Catholic Church and the military—Menem supported an amnesty that, he argued, would contribute to national reconciliation. In that spirit, and to the outrage of human rights organizations and the overwhelming majority of Argentine society, Menem issued in July 1989 a presidential pardon for more than 270 individuals accused of committing human rights violations, and in late 1990 he issued another one for all remaining military officers.[12]

These processes had a negative impact on human rights organizations. Although media coverage in general contributed to public discussion regarding the period of military terror, sensational revelations in the press focused on torture and killing details in the early years of the democratic transition resulted in what Claudia Feld aptly labels "the horror show," which initially trivialized and obscured important elements of what had happened.[13] Besides, CONADEP's and the government's implicit characterization of those murdered and disappeared as mere "victims" of state terror produced an abstract image that, while reassuring for the broader society, erased the political participation and activism of many of those who were killed or disappeared.[14] Moreover, human rights organizations were further divided on whether to support or not the trials of the junta members, Alfonsín's Full Stop and Due Obedience laws, the exhumation of bodies, and state reparations for relatives of victims of state terror. On the one hand, there were those who had a more radical position on anything that could be seen as a compromise in their struggle and who sought to rescue the most militant political trajectories of their lost relatives and friends. On the other, there were those who decided to occupy the available spaces and collaborate with the government while still maintaining a critical perspective. In addition to personal differences, these disagreements in terms of goals and strategies were at the core of the schism experienced in 1986 by one of the earliest, most active, and better-known organizations, the aforementioned Mothers of Plaza de Mayo. Finally, Menem's presidential pardon did provoke massive demonstrations mobilized by human rights groups and other political and social sectors, though this collective action neither stopped the pardons nor generated an environment of sustained social mobilization.[15]

RENEWED HUMAN RIGHTS ACTIVISM AND DISCUSSIONS
ON COMMEMORATIONS AND MUSEUMS, 1990s–2000s

Retrospectively, the seeming loss of momentum experienced by human rights organizations in their search for truth and justice in Argentina was temporary. The 1990s would see them once again occupying an important place in the public arena. Their political pressure and activism, as well as changing historical circumstances, would bring important political and legal changes to end impunity for human rights violators and were linked to renewed forms of and discussions on memorialization and commemoration that led to the creation of the Space for Memory and Human Rights in 2007.

Despite Menem's pardons, several factors brought back the movement for human rights in the mid-1990s. Demands for justice and denunciations of past crimes were not abandoned, but there was more emphasis on memory and commemoration with a didactic social function, in which the date of the coup—24 March—came to occupy a central place.[16] In addition to demanding action and redress from the government, human rights groups now linked "their memories of dictatorship with ongoing societal demands of various sorts (social justice, police violence, rights of minorities, demands of social policies, and so on)," effectively establishing broader connections with other social groups.[17] New groups, such as HIJOS (the Spanish acronym for Children in Search of Identity and Justice, against Oblivion and Silence) brought more active and younger groups onto the scene. At the same time, in 1995, public revelations from former participants in human rights violations contributed to the mobilization of civil society. At the level of the courts, the Mothers and Grandmothers of Plaza de Mayo brought new charges against human rights perpetrators for the crime of appropriating babies born in captivity from disappeared mothers, a crime not covered by the Due Obedience and Full Stop laws. By 2000, over a dozen active and retired military officers were in custody, and more than 100 cases of such crimes were under investigation.[18]

Parallel to all these processes, the second half of the 1990s witnessed a significant increase in terms of new initiatives for the dedication of public spaces to the commemoration and preservation of memory regarding human rights violations, including now open discussions about a museum. The twentieth anniversary of the coup in 1996 proved to be a pivotal moment for these discussions, accompanied by the republication of *Never Again* and the appearance of new books, films, and videos on human rights. Art exhibits and works of drama and film reflected more open coverage of the topic by the press. Many public spaces such as universities, unions, and schools placed plaques commemorating their "disappeared," and curricula on human rights were introduced into the public education system.[19] In this context of a more mobilized society and reinvigorated concern about memory, the discussions on memorials and museums of human rights surfaced more openly.

In 1990, human rights organizations had already participated in a proposal for the creation of a museum of human rights presented to the Buenos Aires city council. With the goal of creating a Museum of Memory "dedicated to reconstruct, protect and nurture collective memory on the horrors of state terrorism, which devastated Argentina," the proposal was turned into a resolution approved by the council that, though not converted into law, served as an important precedent.[20] Other memorials and public spaces acknowledging human rights violations soon appeared. In La Plata, a memorial at the University of La Plata, inaugurated in 1995 to honour disappeared architecture students, became one of the first such public monuments.[21] In 1998, the legislature of the now autonomous city of Buenos Aires approved a law, which had been promoted by human rights organizations, to create a Park of Memory that included a Monument to the Victims of State Terrorism.[22] These earlier projects were accompanied by discussions and tensions that mirrored debates within and among the different human rights organizations. In the case of the 1990 resolution from the city council, a person from the group Relatives of Persons Disappeared and Detained for Political Reasons expressed her initial reaction when she heard about the initiative: "We thought, 'A museum? How can we build a museum?' It seemed somewhat antiquated. How could our problem be kept in a museum?... Because for us a museum was something static, a place with rooms with objects hanging on the walls, like in the Argentine History Museum, where there are all kinds of things with a short text explaining what it is and that's it."[23] Differences erupted openly at the ceremony to set the foundation stone for the Park of Memory and the Monument to the Victims of State Terrorism in 1999. In that moment, the more radical segment of the Mothers of Plaza de Mayo, led by Hebe de Bonafini, and other organizations disrupted the ceremony in which the other association of the Mothers and Grandmothers of Plaza de Mayo were participating. They criticized the project and event as examples of collusion with politicians who had granted impunity to human rights violators and as attempts to "freeze" the past and neglect the contemporary consequences of human rights violations.[24] These two examples show

how the common struggle for human rights can feature different goals and strategies that also shape divergent ideas on what, and how, to remember.

These divisions notwithstanding, pressure for the creation of a museum advanced even during the chaotic period of the late 1990s and early 2000s, a period that would end in the severe political and economic crisis of 2001–02. In 2000, several human rights organizations that had been active in pressing for a memorial museum joined together to create Memoria Abierta (Open Memory), a group devoted to the collection, preservation, and dissemination of documentation pertaining to Argentine human rights violations and, in its words, "to raise social awareness and knowledge about state terrorism in order to enrich democratic culture."[25] These organizations continued to exert pressure for the museum at the levels of both city and national governments. At the city level, throughout 1999 and 2000, they worked toward a resolution, finally passed in 2000, to create a Commission for the Creation of a Museum of Memory, to be located in the former Navy School of Mechanics (ESMA), one of the most notorious centres of detention, torture, and murder during the dictatorship. They worked together with city officials on a proposal for a Space for Memory, presented to the city's head of government in August 2001, and in 2002 the Buenos Aires city legislature passed Law 961 creating the Institute Space for Memory, which would become organized and active in the following years.[26] Memoria Abierta supported those efforts with debates on the shape of the museum. In 2000, it organized an interdisciplinary workshop on the "institutional organization and contents of the future Museum of Memory" that brought together scholars, professionals, politicians, and human rights activists. In the introduction to the document containing the records of these sessions, Memoria Abierta expressed its vision for the museum:

> We, human rights organizations, support the creation of a
> Museum that, in an active and dynamic manner, can show
> to current and future generations what happened, how it
> happened, and the reaction of Argentine society towards
> authoritarianism. We want a Museum that fulfills the
> function of preserving historical documents and objects and
> making them accessible to the public; a Museum as a space
> for interdisciplinary research that promotes new fields of
> study; a Museum that is linked with the community through
> its essential educational function; a Museum that organizes

exhibitions that allow relating historical events with the
present, thus enriching our democratic culture.[27]

In accordance with this vision, Memoria Abierta focused on making
the museum a concrete reality in the former site of ESMA. When Menem
issued a 1998 decree targeting ESMA for demolition so that a green space
could be created to serve as a symbol of national union, human rights
organizations reacted strongly in opposition, mobilizing public opinion,
working with legislators in the National Congress on projects to preserve
the space, and arguing their case in the courts. When the Supreme Court
confirmed the unconstitutionality of Menem's decree in February 2001,
human rights groups kept the pressure on both city and national governments to reach an agreement on terms of cession of the space for creation
of the museum.

The focus on ESMA was not casual. Certainly there were many centres
scattered throughout the country where human rights abuses had been
committed during the military dictatorship, and several of them were
already dedicated or in the process of being dedicated to the memory of
those abuses. However, ESMA had been the most notorious site of those
atrocities, the place where the overwhelming majority of the approximately
5,000 people detained had been murdered. This was confirmed by CON-
ADEP's report in 1984, testimony of survivors who had been detained in
ESMA, and the 1995 revelations of the "flights of death" in which prisoners
at ESMA had been drugged and then dumped from planes into the Rio de
la Plata. Furthermore, ESMA's central location in Buenos Aires remained
a powerful physical and symbolic metaphor of the presence and (in?)vis-
ibility of state terror in Argentine society. As such, it had already become
an iconic symbol within the national memory.

With these precedents of mobilization and organization, once again
shifting historical circumstances finally made possible both a critical
breakthrough regarding the prosecution of human rights abuses and the
final creation of the Space for Memory and Human Rights at the former
ESMA. In 2003, Néstor Kirchner was elected president. Emerging out of the
economic and political crisis of 2001–02, he sought to shore up his political
support and rebuild shattered state power. As part of his political strategy, he tried to widen his base by approaching groups beyond the divided
Peronist party, including unemployed workers and human rights organizations. In fact, Kirchner made human rights a central part of the state's

agenda, echoing the broad consensus on this topic in Argentine society. He soon began inviting the Mothers and Grandmothers of Plaza de Mayo to meet with him and to attend official acts, declared himself one of the "sons" of the Mothers, and committed himself to the human rights cause. Several of the military and Federal Police officers who had opposed this policy, or who had links with human rights violations, were now retired, allowing Kirchner to push for the annulment of the Due Obedience and Full Stop laws, which the National Congress approved in 2003. In 2005, the Supreme Court finally confirmed that the two laws were unconstitutional, and this paved the way for more active judicial investigation and prosecution of human rights violations.[28] The state's critical commitment to the human rights cause, unparalleled in Latin America and beyond, has continued under the administrations of Kirchner's wife and successor, Cristina Fernández de Kirchner (2007–11, 2011–15).

This new political environment was essential in enabling the definitive move to create the museum at ESMA. In a powerful symbolic event, Néstor Kirchner held an event at ESMA on 24 March 2004, the anniversary of the coup. On that occasion, he announced that ESMA would become a museum of memory, asking forgiveness on behalf of the state for the human rights atrocities committed in the past and for the state's silence on these atrocities during twenty years of democracy.[29] The military vacated the facilities by 30 September 2007, and on 20 November an interinstitutional body composed of representatives of human rights groups, ex-ESMA detainees, and the national and city governments was established to oversee creation of the museum.[30] Over the next years, the Space for Memory and and Human Rights, as the former ESMA was renamed, would come alive in the ways discussed below.

Creation of the Space for Memory and Human Rights in the former ESMA was surrounded immediately by disputes over what and how to remember. Voices criticizing the project surfaced from conservative groups and found expression in the conservative newspaper *La Nación*, in declarations and statements by relatives of military personnel under trial, who questioned the "biased" interpretation of the past that did not account for the violence by armed leftist organizations in the 1970s, and in comments by those arguing that the state should concern itself with "current" violations of human rights defined as insecurity and crime.[31] Although human rights groups celebrated recovery of the space, debates and differences emerged regarding how to use the physical space and what should be remembered and how it should be displayed. For example, the Association of the Ex Detained and Disappeared argued that the whole space should be preserved basically intact, without allocating specific buildings to public offices or educational institutions. The argument, drawing on references to Auschwitz, was that, since the whole site had functioned as an extermination camp, preserving it as such was the right way to commemorate those who had been detained, tortured, and executed. Other human rights organizations did not share this vision. Although they agreed that the sites within the former ESMA related to detention, torture, and execution should be preserved and rededicated as historical sites, they envisioned the rest of the buildings as spaces to be used for educational purposes and to promote human rights issues, in which memory of the past would be exercised in a more dynamic manner and in connection to current debates and events.[32] Other tensions surfaced in these discussions, for example in debates over the role of human rights organizations and the state in the actual management and operation of the site.

Out of these discussions, the Space for Memory and Human Rights has evolved since 2008 into a fascinating experience, adopting a non-traditional curatorial approach reflected in its self-description:

> The Space for Memory and Human Rights (ex-ESMA)
> is proposed as a place for honouring the victims and
> condemning crimes against humanity during state terrorism.
> It also presents itself as a site of national and international
> reference for public policies regarding memory, promotion of
> democratic values, and defence of human rights. It is a place
> of cultural exchange and social debate on state terrorism
> and genocidal experience, a space for reflection on the recent
> past.... It is an integrated space where different political,
> institutional, and social representations at the regional,
> national, and local levels coexist, developing the goals of
> preservation of memory and promotion and defence of
> human rights from different perspectives and manners.[33]

The museum space clearly reflects this approach. The management of different buildings at ESMA has been divided among several organizations as well as state departments.[34] Buildings such as the former Casino de Oficiales, where the most notorious abuses of human rights were committed, have been preserved as historical sites and are open to the public for guided tours. Others have been occupied by public institutions such as the Institute Space for Memory and the National Archive of Memory. Organizations such as the Mothers of Plaza de Mayo (both segments) and Grandmothers of Plaza de Mayo occupy other buildings, devoted not only to education about human rights but also to issues such as training young people in trades. The site also includes buildings devoted to a cultural centre and to the production of state television content regarding national history. The site has become a hub of activities, including film and artistic presentations and exhibitions, and provides a dynamic approach to the commemoration and preservation of memory.

CONCLUSION

As the Argentine case shows, the struggle for human rights is connected to specific historical circumstances that, in turn, have influenced practices of memory. Debates about museums and memorials regarding traumatic events such as human rights violations during the military dictatorship are inevitably related to particular views of a nation. As the previous pages have shown, the search for truth and justice, and the related debates over a museum dedicated to the crimes of Argentina's military dictatorship, were intrinsically connected to contemporary political debates in ways that involved a particular view of the past.

Inauguration of the Space for Memory and Human Rights has not closed debates on human rights and the past in Argentina. Quite the contrary. For example, human rights organizations have been divided in terms of their relationships with the administrations of Néstor Kirchner and Cristina Fernández de Kirchner since 2003. The group of the Mothers of Plaza de Mayo led by Hebe de Bonafini, the Grandmothers of Plaza de Mayo, and HIJOS have become close to the national government and its project, in the case of Mothers receiving substantial funds from the state for a variety of projects, including building public housing. Other groups, while recognizing the advances made in terms of promoting human rights concerns, have kept their distance from the government and adopted a more critical position, understanding proximity as opening possibilities for co-optation that could compromise their causes. Those differences also surfaced around the space itself. In September 2013, news that some human rights groups close to the government as well as government officials had used the facilities to hold meetings that included music and the traditional Argentine barbeque, the *asado,* sparked outrage and a furious exchange among human rights organizations. It could not have been otherwise, since the Spanish term for the barbeque grill, *parrilla,* had been the military's slang for the bed frames on which victims had been tortured with electricity. Even more sinister, there were testimonies that bodies of victims of state terrorism had been burned at ESMA's barbeque installations, the same ones used in 2013, in what the perpetrators darkly called *asados.* In the caustic debate that followed the events, government officials and their allied human rights groups defended the events, arguing that the space was now "a site of life." On the other hand, those who opposed the events criticized them as acts of trivialization, desecration, and unspeakable affronts to the memories of those who had been killed there. Beyond these events, by rhetorically rooting the current political and economic model in the revolutionary struggles that preceded the military regimes in the 1970s, the national government has sparked new debates in Argentine society, as well as among human rights groups, over Argentine history and memory.[35] The context of increasing polarization resulting from tensions between Cristina Fernández de Kirchner's administration and allied sectors and the broad yet disunited groups in the political opposition will surely continue to influence discussions on the Argentine past.

On the other hand, and despite opposition from minority groups on the political right, it is undeniable that there is a broad consensus on the crimes committed by the military regime between 1976 and 1983 and on the importance of human rights issues related not only to the past but also to current and future problems facing the country. The military is no longer a threat, and the dramatic legal changes of the recent period are reflected in the ongoing investigations, trials, and prosecutions of human rights violators. These are not minor developments in a country such as Argentina, which has been shaken in the past by political violence and still confronts major political, economic, and social divisions. In addition to the Space for Memory and Human Rights, other former sites of human rights abuses have been opened in recent years in other places and cities in Argentina.[36] These other sites, inspired by the same varied emphasis on remembrance of past crimes as well as preservation of memory and documentation and education about human rights through the participation of multiple actors, represent an innovative approach to the delicate issue of how to construct a human rights museum.

In this sense, and going back to the opening paragraphs of this chapter, the Argentine case is related to the ongoing experience of the Canadian Museum for Human Rights. The Space for Memory and Human Rights emerged out of a fractious process of negotiations and discussions on not

only past memories and experiences but also how they should be represented in relation to specific contemporary circumstances. As Ken Norman and Dirk Moses make clear in their contributions to this volume, a
similar contentious conversation is both inevitable and necessary in order
to appropriately ground the Canadian museum in its historical, social, and
political contexts. Very much like its Argentine counterpart, the CMHR
must engage with public disagreements about the past and Canada's own
legacies of violence in order to move beyond mere curatorial exhibitions
and, instead, achieve its full meaning and importance as a site for memory,
knowledge, and education.

NOTES

1   See Bartley Kives, "Atrocities Gallery 'Too Much': Museum to Revamp Content; Ex-Workers Disparage Move," *Winnipeg Free Press,* 30 November 2012, http://www.winnipegfree-
press.com/local/atrocities-gallery-too-much-181497341.html. Helen Fallding's contribution to this volume deals specifically with media coverage of the museum's construction.

2   The chapter makes extensive use of the information and documentation provided by
Memoria Abierta, an umbrella body for the most important human rights organizations
in Argentina created in 2000 and that is of mandatory reference for any person interested
in these issues. See http://www.memoriaabierta.org.ar/eng/index.php.

3   Elizabeth Jelin, "Introducción," in *Las conmemoraciones: Las disputas en las fechas "in-
felices,"* ed. Elizabeth Jelin (Madrid: Siglo XXI, 2002), 2.

4   Elizabeth Jelin, *State Repression and the Labors of Memory* (Minneapolis: University of
Minnesota Press, 2003), xv. See also Federico Lorenz, "¿De quién es el 24 de marzo? Las
luchas por la memoria del golpe de 1976," in Jelin, *Las conmemoraciones,* 55.

5   Eric Hobsbawm, "The Invention of Traditions," in *The Invention of Traditions,* ed. Eric
Hobsbawm and Terence Ranger (New York: Cambridge University Press, 1983), 1–14.

6   For overviews of the Argentine military regime of 1976–83, see Thomas Wright, *State Terrorism in Latin America: Chile, Argentina, and International Human Rights* (Lanham, MD:
Rowman and Littlefield, 2007), 95–137; Marcos Novaro and Vicente Palermo, *La dicta-
dura militar, 1976–1983: Del golpe de estado a la restauración democrática* (Buenos Aires:
Paidós, 2003); Martin Edward Andersen, *Dossier Secreto: Argentina's Desaparecidos and
the Myth of the "Dirty War"* (Boulder, CO: Westview Press, 1993); Marguerite Fleitlowitz,
Argentina: A Lexicon of Terror (New York: Oxford University Press, 1998); and Alison
Brysk, *The Politics of Human Rights in Argentina: Protest, Change, and Democratization*
(Stanford, CA: Stanford University Press, 1994), 23–41. For the Argentine case within the
broader Latin American context during the Cold War, see Greg Grandin, *Empire's Work-
shop: Latin America, the United States, and the Rise of the New Imperialism* (New York:
Metropolitan Books, 2006).

7   In its 1984 report, the National Commission on the Disappearance of People (CONA-
DEP) documented about 9,000 murdered and disappeared people, though it is widely
acknowledged that the report underestimates the real toll. Human rights groups have
argued that at least 30,000 people were killed, a figure frequently used today.

8   Memoria Abierta, "The Road towards the Museum," http://www.memoriaabierta.org.ar/eng/camino_al_museo2.php.

9   The English version of the report is *Never Again: Report of CONADEP (National Commission on the Disappearance of Persons)—1984,* http://www.desaparecidos.org/nuncamas/web/english/library/nevagain/nevagain_001.htm.

10 For example, two of the three members of the first military junta, Jorge Rafael Videla and Emilio Eduardo Massera, were condemned to life in prison. The remaining member and two others belonging to the second military junta were condemned to different prison terms that ranged from four to seventeen years. The remaining member of the second junta and all the members of the last one were absolved, as charges against them could not be proven.

11 On the Mothers of Plaza de Mayo, see Marguerite Guzman Bouvard, *Revolutionizing Motherhood: The Mothers of Plaza de Mayo* (Wilmington, DE: SR Books, 1994); and Elizabeth Borland, "The Mature Resistance of Argentina's Madres de Plaza de Mayo," in *Latin American Social Movements: Globalization, Democratization, and Transnational Networks,* ed. Hank Johnston and Paul Almeida (Lanham, MD: Rowman and Littlefield, 2006), 115–30.

12 Wright, *State Terrorism,* 153–60.

13 Claudia Feld, "La representación de los desaparecidos en la prensa de la transición: El show del horror," in *Los desaparecidos en la Argentina: Memorias, representaciones, e ideas (1983–2008),* ed. Emilio Crenzel (Buenos Aires: Editorial Biblos-Latitud Sur, 2010), 25–41. See also Novaro and Palermo, *La dictadura militar,* 484–511.

14 Ana Ros, *The Post-Dictatorship Generation in Argentina, Chile, and Uruguay: Collective Memory and Cultural Production* (New York: Palgrave Macmillan, 2012), 17–19.

15 Guzman Bouvard, *Revolutionizing Motherhood,* 162–64; Feld, "Representación," 30; Borland, "Mature Resistance," 118, 130; Lorenz, "¿De quién?," 78.

16 Lorenz, "¿De quién?," 80.

17 Jelin, *State Repression,* 38.

18 Ros, *Post-Dictatorship,* 20; Wright, *State Terrorism,* 160–61, 166.

19 Lorenz, "¿De quién?," 82–90; Wright, *State Terrorism,* 162–64. Among the films that generated widespread attention in this period were two documentaries: *Malajunta,* on the military dictatorship, and *Cazadores de utopias* (Chasers of Utopias), on the revolutionary experience of leftist militants in the 1970s. For a catalogue of films that dealt with the military dictatorship that appeared over the years, see Memoria Abierta, "La dictadura en el cine," http://www.memoriaabierta.org.ar/ladictaduraenelcine/index.html.

20 Memoria Abierta, "The Road."

21 For an explanation and pictures of the memorial, see Verónica Capasso and Melina Jean Jean, "Memoriales en la UNLP: Análisis de diversos casos de representación del pasado reciente en distintas unidades académicas," *Aletheia* 2, 4 (2012), http://www.aletheia.fahce.unlp.edu.ar/numeros/numero-4/articulos/memoriales-en-la-unlp.-analisis-de-diversos-casos-de-representacion-del-pasado-reciente-en-distintas-unidades-academicas.

22 On the memory and the monument, see Patricia Tappatá de Valdez, "El Parque de la Memoria en Buenos Aires," in *Monumentos, memoriales, y marcas territoriales,* ed. Elizabeth Jelin and Victoria Langland (Madrid: Siglo XXI de España Editores, 2003), 97–111; and Alberto Varas, "Architecture, Site, and Memory: A Reflection on the Insertion of Architecture and the Park of Memory into the Urban Coastline of Buenos Aires," in *Architecture*

and Memory, ed. Memoria Abierta (Buenos Aires: Memoria Abierta, 2009), 37–41, http://www.memoriaabierta.org.ar/materiales/pdf/architectureandmemory.pdf.

23   Testimony of Mabel Penette de Gutiérrez, quoted in Memoria Abierta, "The Road."

24   Tappatá de Váldez, "Parque de la Memoria," 106–07; Lorenz, "¿De quién?," 92–93.

25   Memoria Abierta, "Who We Are," http://www.memoriaabierta.org.ar/eng/quienes_somos.php.

26   Memoria Abierta, "The Road"; S.P.C. van Drunen, "Struggling with the Past: The Human Rights Movement and the Politics of Memory in Postdictatorship Argentina (1983–2006)" (PhD diss., University of Amsterdam, 2010), 250–51.

27   Memoria Abierta, "Primeras jornadas de debate interdisciplinario: Organización institucional y contenidos del futuro Museo de la Memoria" (Buenos Aires: Colección "Memoria Abierta," 2000), 4, http://www.memoriaabierta.org.ar/pdf/museo_de_la_memoria.pdf.

28   Wright, *State Terrorism,* 170–71.

29   Kirchner's reference to the state's silence on human rights atrocities since 1983 was rather inaccurate, given the trials of the junta members and the other actions taken by the state to deal with human rights issues. The comment does indicate, though, the partisan element involved in the recovery of memory.

30   Instituto Espacio para la Memoria, "Escuela de Mecánica de la Armada (ESMA), http://www.institutomemoria.org.ar/exccd/esma.html.

31   Van Drunen, "Struggling," 256–57.

32   Ibid., 265–66; "Memoria en construcción: Cómo será el espacio que se está montando en la ESMA," *Página* 12 (23 March 2008), http://www.pagina12.com.ar/diario/el-pais/1-101176-2008-03-23.html. On the history of and debates surrounding the museum at ESMA, see also Emily Parsons, "The Space of Remembering: Collective Memory and the Reconfiguration of Contested Space in Argentina's ESMA," *452ºF: Electronic Journal of Theory of Literature and Comparative Literature* 4 (2011): 29–51, http://www.452f.com/index.php/en/emily-parsons.html.

33   Espacio Memoria y Derechos Humanos (ex ESMA), "El espacio hoy," http://www.espaciomemoria.ar/espaciohoy.php.

34   Plans and descriptions of the Space of Memory are available at http://www.espaciomemoria.ar/.

35   On those debates, see Alejandro Villa et al., *La sociedad Argentina hoy frente a los años '70* (Buenos Aires: Centro Cultural de la Memoria "Haroldo Conti"/EUDEBA, 2010).

36   See examples in "Experiences in the Treatment of Spaces in Recovered Sites," in Memoria Abierta, *Architecture and Memory,* 46–67.

BEYOND DIFFICULT HISTORIES: FIRST NATIONS, THE RIGHT TO CULTURE, AND THE OBLIGATION OF REDRESS

CHAPTER 16
Ruth B. Phillips

To create a national history museum that discards unitary national narratives as well as causal trajectories (the teleology of the nation)—in effect to subvert the form—is probably impossible.
— Paul Ashton and Paula Hamilton, "'Unfinished Business': Public History in a Postcolonial Nation"[1]

What is it that this government is going to do in the future to help our people? Because we are dealing with major human rights violations that have occurred to many generations: my language, my culture and my spirituality. I know that I want to transfer those to my children and my grandchildren and their children, and so on.
— Beverly Jacobs, President of the Native Women's Association of Canada, response in Parliament to House of Commons Apology to Inuit, Métis, and First Nations Peoples for Residential Schools, 11 June 2008[2]

Twenty years before the government of Canada issued its formal apology to Aboriginal people for the human rights abuses of enforced residential schooling, the Canadian museum community began to confront the legacies of its participation in the colonial project. In particular, museums began to reassess long-standing conventions that identified the authenticity of Aboriginal cultures as premodern, as well as curatorial practices that largely excluded Aboriginal peoples' voices and authorities. The initial spur to reform was an international boycott of *The Spirit Sings*, a 1988 exhibition of Aboriginal art organized for the Calgary Winter Olympics, but the response of the museum community was much more comprehensive. The Canadian Museums Association and the Assembly of First Nations commissioned a Task Force on Museums and First Peoples to develop new ethical guidelines and practices for the representation of Aboriginal cultures and histories.[3] Its report, issued in 1992, set in motion forms of redress *avant la lettre* of the United Nations Convention on the Rights of Indigenous Peoples, which Canada would sign twenty years later.

The task force report makes evident a fundamental paradox in the relationships between Indigenous people and museums in settler societies such as Canada.[4] This paradox is most evident in national institutions, which are shaped by laws and mandates designed to inscribe in the nation's citizens a distinctive and shared identity. Defined successively in Canada as British-imperial, Anglo-Canadian, bicultural, and multicultural, these collective constructs of national identity are inherently antithetical to Aboriginal affirmations of sovereignty.[5] Yet, at the same time, the national cultural institutions have preserved unique documentation of traditional Indigenous knowledge that is vital to contemporary processes of postcolonial recovery and renewal. Although much was removed to museums under the aegis of the same oppressive colonial policies that disrupted the normal transgenerational transmission of this knowledge within Aboriginal communities, many of the collectors—both Aboriginal and non-Aboriginal—worked from within the system to preserve Indigenous knowledge and material culture.[6] Access to these collections and related expertise is thus critical to the cultural strengthening that First Nations leaders have repeatedly invoked as necessary to the achievement of their larger political goals.

During the two decades that followed the release of the task force report, museums across Canada worked to implement its recommendations in partnership with Aboriginal individuals, communities, and cultural centres. They innovated new practices and models of collaboration, expanded access to collections, created culturally sensitive modes of storage and display, and set in motion processes for the repatriation of designated collections and objects.[7] National museums, granting councils, and heritage institutions were proactive participants in these processes. During the 1990s and through the first decade of this century, the Canadian Museum of Civilization (now the Canadian Museum of History), the National Gallery of Canada, Library and Archives Canada, Parks Canada, the Canadian Conservation Institute, the Department of Canadian Heritage, and the Canada Council for the Arts put in place new departments, programs, and funding to support Aboriginal research, art, and heritage preservation and reanimation.[8]

In light of this promising start, it has been astonishing to watch the rapid shrinkage and, in some cases, disappearance of these initiatives within the past few years. Museum administrators have allowed many celebrated projects and initiatives to expire through attrition by deciding not to replace curators and Aboriginal specialists who retired or left. The impact of these losses has been greatly magnified by massive staff cuts, institutional restructurings, program cancellations, and changes of mandate. Although the financial crisis that began in 2008 is usually cited as the immediate cause of these changes, the Harper government's simultaneous allocations of funding for other projects of public historical commemoration and exhibition make it clear that radical breaks with past policies are at work. A renewed focus on settler histories, often at the expense of Aboriginal heritage and demographic diversity, is evident across the federal heritage system. The changes are evidence of what Paul Ashton and Paula Hamilton have identified in the Australian context as a "politics of reaction" against postcolonial museology.[9]

The period of retrenchment and reaction in the national museums coincides almost exactly with the years during which the Canadian Museum for Human Rights (CMHR) was developing its exhibitions and programs, a coincidence central to the argument that I want to make in this chapter. I explore here the CMHR's potential role in the representation and redress of human rights abuses suffered by Aboriginal people in Canada. I premise my discussion on the notion that the museums and heritage organizations of a nation form a set. Taken together, they are designed to serve the nation's fundamental need for social reproduction through their programs of research, representation, and education. In the service of this goal, the mandates of component institutions will, ideally, interlock to span the areas of knowledge identified by the sponsoring nation as critical to the geopolitical, historical, and contemporary consciousness of its citizens. As numerous studies in critical museology have shown, the mandates of museums and heritage organizations are historically specific and change over time.[10] Imposed through the oversight of government departments and the museum boards and administrators whom they appoint, they reflect the priorities that those bodies identify as necessary to the creation of an informed citizenry.

Logically, then, the decision to create a new national museum can be understood as a response to a perceived gap in the range of representations and programs offered by the existing museum set. It also follows that the advent of the new institution will change the division of responsibilities and the internal balance that has previously been achieved; the activities of each member of the set will be influenced by, and in turn will influence, those of its sister institutions.

This chapter, written prior to the opening of the CMHR, is based on the planning documents that outline the themes and dispositions of its galleries and on the presumption that they offer accurate guides to its opening exhibitions. The documents make clear that Aboriginal people, as the group who have suffered the most long-standing and comprehensive human rights abuses at the hands of the Canadian nation, are intended to occupy a central position in its narrative of Canada's human rights record. The new museum's entry into the family of national museums thus offers an opportunity to build on the trajectory of postcolonial redress that has been arrested or slowed down in Canada's existing heritage organizations. To make this case, I first provide a more detailed review of the history of redress within the national heritage institutions and then pose three inter-related questions. What is the perceived gap that the CMHR's Aboriginal exhibits and programs are intended to fill? Which dimensions of scope and content might a human rights framework add to the decolonizing processes of access creation and representation that have already begun? And in what ways do the recent changes in the national museums shift the responsibility of redress to the CMHR?

1967–2011: INITIATING REDRESS, COUNTERING THE VANISHING INDIAN

The first major public presentation of the human rights abuses suffered by Canada's Aboriginal peoples occurred in the Indians of Canada Pavilion at Expo '67. The creation of a separate Aboriginal pavilion was achieved through the successful lobbying of Aboriginal activists within the federal civil service. Its content was the result of a palace coup that enabled them

to take curatorial control of its exhibitions and messages.[11] Two installations, one historical and one contemporary, suggested the radical nature
of the critique presented in the pavilion. In a module on religion, the curators recounted the early missionaries' attacks on traditional Aboriginal
spirituality. The installation featured a large sculpture of a bear whose
shadow fell on a Christian cross projected onto the floor of a darkened
room, suggesting the violence of a crucifixion. In another module, which
focused on contemporary work life, visitors were confronted with a near-
life-sized photograph of an Aboriginal woman and her children standing
in the doorway of their roughly built log home. The caption gave the lie
to government affirmations of progress: "And still, too many Indians are
poor, sick, cold and hungry. Three out of every four Indian families earn
2000 dollars or less a year.… The poverty line for the rest of Canada is 3000
dollars a year."[12]

Created for a world fair, the Indians of Canada Pavilion was by definition ephemeral. Although its popularity should have alerted the museum
community to the compelling importance of Aboriginal decolonization
projects, it was not until the boycott of *The Spirit Sings* that the Canadian
museum community as a whole began to consider which reforms were
needed in order to support these projects. The Assembly of First Nations and
the Canadian Museums Association gave the Task Force on Museums and
First Peoples a broad mandate "to develop an ethical framework and strategies for Aboriginal Nations to represent their history and culture in concert
with cultural institutions."[13] Funded by the Ministry of Communications
(now the Department of Canadian Heritage), its thirty-seven members met
in national and regional groups from 1989 to 1992. The report that they
produced both urged the need to change museum practices and affirmed
the importance of the collections to Aboriginal communities. It stated
that "these objects represent cultural history and values and are therefore
sources of learning, pride, and self-esteem."[14] The repatriation of certain
categories within museum collections was recommended, while the ongoing role of institutions in caring for and researching collections and their
need to engage "with living cultures, not just objects," were underlined.[15]

A key set of recommendations focused on the urgency of providing
First Nations people not only with access to artifacts, related research,
photographs, recordings of language and songs, and other cultural materials but also with funding opportunities, training, and employment in
museums. Under "Specific Recommendations to Establish Partnerships
between First Peoples and Canadian Museums," the report mandated

the involvement of Aboriginal people in the processes of "planning, re-search implementation, presentation and maintenance of all exhibitions, programs and/or projects that include Aboriginal cultures," and it asked museums to work with First Peoples "to refine the nature of information relating to their collections, activities, and practices."[16]

Four years later, in 1996, the report of the Royal Commission on Aboriginal Peoples (RCAP) returned to the subject of First Nations and museums in even more forceful terms. A "policy to affirm and support the cultural identity and expression of Aboriginal peoples" is proposed in the section on "Arts and Heritage" of the report's third volume, *Gathering Strength*. Its authors established the relationship between reclaiming cultural traditions and healing. They directly tied colonial efforts to suppress Aboriginal languages and cultures to weakened identities and youth suicide: "The legacy of our colonial history bears heavily upon Aboriginal people in the form of culture stress,"[17] they noted, linking it to "the cumulative impact of assimilative policies of the past and the failure of public institutions to reflect to Aboriginal people positive images of themselves and their cultures."[18] The RCAP report strengthened the task force's recommendations regarding repatriation, the treatment of sacred objects, and the return of human remains, and affirmed the continuing responsibility of museums to maintain Aboriginal collections and develop proactive programs:

> This makes it all the more important that Aboriginal people have access to mainstream museums and the items they hold. Aboriginal people must be involved in cataloguing museum holdings and consulted on appropriate modes of display and interpretation. This provides an opportunity for non-Aboriginal professionals to gain more insight into Aboriginal culture. Furthermore, these collections must be accessible to Aboriginal people. Here, we do not simply mean an open-door policy on the part of museums, inviting Aboriginal people to visit the displays. Rather, any facility that benefits from the display of Aboriginal culture should put something back into the Aboriginal community. This could mean bringing all or part of the exhibit directly to Aboriginal communities.[19]

The RCAP report went on to discuss specific strategies of capacity building within Aboriginal communities, training, and ongoing cooperation with museums and universities in seeking to implement these recommendations. The potential that it identified for museums to contribute to healing the psychic and other damage inflicted by colonialism thus made the relationship between postcolonial museum reform and the enactment of redress even more explicit.

When the United Nations General Assembly adopted the Declaration on the Rights of Indigenous Peoples in 2007, the international community affirmed rights to culture as integral to the discourse of human rights. The document's preliminary annex locates the need for the declaration in histories of colonial oppression and forced cultural assimilation. It recognizes, as had the RCAP report, the integral relationship between rights to liberty, security, land, and self-government and a "respect for indigenous knowledge, cultures and traditional practices [that contribute] to sustainable and equitable development."[20] Several articles spell out the scope of these rights. Article 11.1, for example, defines the Indigenous right to "maintain, protect and develop the past, present and future manifestations of their cultures, such as archaeological and historical sites, artefacts, designs, ceremonies, technologies and visual and performing arts and literature," while Article 13 affirms rights to "revitalize, use, develop and transmit to future generations their histories, languages, oral traditions, philosophies, writing systems and literatures."[21] Signatory states are instructed to provide "effective mechanisms" of redress for past infringements. In relation to Article 11, for example, such redress "may include restitution ... with respect to their cultural, intellectual, religious and spiritual property taken without their free, prior and informed consent or in violation of their laws, traditions and customs."[22] Article 31 articulates rights to culture in the broadest terms, affirming Indigenous people's "right to maintain, control and develop their cultural heritage, traditional knowledge and traditional cultural expressions, as well as the manifestations of their sciences, technologies and cultures, including human and genetic resources, seeds, medicines, knowledge of the properties of fauna and flora, oral traditions, literatures, designs, sports and traditional games and visual and performing arts."[23] When Canada ratified the declaration in 2010, it thus assumed a duty to "provide redress through effective mechanisms." The obligation has clear and direct implications for national museums, archives, and heritage institutions because, as previously noted, they are primary repositories for the Indigenous cultural and intellectual property amassed during the colonial era.[24]

As we have seen, by 2010—eighteen years after the release of the task force report— these institutions had already developed a range of "effective mechanisms" for redress. Many had established partnerships with Aboriginal communities and hired Aboriginal professionals on their permanent staffs. Volumes have been written about the specific projects developed by national and regional Canadian institutions, but space here permits only the briefest sampling of them.[25] The University of British Columbia's Museum of Anthropology (MOA), for example, has been a noted pioneer in developing collaborative models and had worked closely and collaboratively with First Nations artists, curators, and communities well before the *The Spirit Sings* crisis. The task force recommendations stimulated MOA to pursue more comprehensive forms of power sharing that would, in the words of its director, Michael Ames, respect the "rights and interests of [First Nations] partners to participate from the beginning, and [allow] projects to evolve naturally, even if awkwardly, in response to continuing participation."[26] In his account of *Written in the Earth* and *From under the Delta*, two archaeological exhibits that the museum developed with Coast Salish First Nations partners, Ames discusses the "realignment of power, achieved through a redistribution of authority," that was required and the challenge of balancing it against the deeply inscribed Western academic allegiance to the right of free enquiry.[27]

I cite the MOA exhibits in order to make clear that the responsibility for redress has been shared broadly across Canadian museums and heritage institutions. In this chapter, however, my primary focus is on national institutions, and I turn now to several outstanding projects undertaken during these years. As at MOA, Canadian Museum of Civilization (CMC) staff, including its director, George Macdonald, and its curator of Northwest Coast ethnology, Andrea Laforet, had already worked collaboratively with First Nations artists and traditional experts, notably in the creation of the museum's Grand Hall. In the late 1990s, following the release of the task force report, it developed *Threads of the Land*, a major exhibition of three Indigenous clothing traditions. The three CMC ethnology curators and their Inuit, Dene, and Nlaka'pamux partners focused on the relationships between Aboriginal technologies involved in the making of clothing and traditional knowledge of land and resources. The project broke new ground in its substance and expository style, which reflected the curators' extensive processes of consultation with originating communities.[28] Traditional experts travelled to Ottawa to study the museum's collections, and curators travelled to First Nations territories to work with the consultants on home ground. The restorative potential of the relationships established through such an exhibition became evident through additional research projects that grew out of the exhibition in the years that followed. For example, CMC curator Judy Thompson and Dene cultural worker Susan Marie worked with Dene experts to recover traditional technologies for harvesting and preparing materials and used the meticulous diagrams and technical analyses made by textile expert Dorothy Burnham through her study of the CMC's collections. Combining this museum and community-based research, Dene seamstresses were able to recreate traditional styles of clothing and container forms that had not been made since the early twentieth century.[29]

The two largest projects undertaken by national museums during this initial innovative and exploratory phase of collaboration were long-term exhibitions that opened at the CMC and the National Gallery of Canada (NGC) at the beginning of the new millennium.[30] *Art of This Land* is the title given to the 2002 reinstallation of the NGC's Canadian galleries, which, for the first time, integrated examples of Aboriginal historical arts into displays that had previously focused exclusively on settler arts. Individual installations were devised according to a number of different strategies, ranging from juxtapositions that pointed to formal and aesthetic relationships between Indigenous and Euro-Canadian works of art to displays that documented historical interconnections and borrowings among Indigenous and settler artists. Following its tradition of rotating works in the Canadian galleries every two years, the NGC proceeded to introduce new loans of Aboriginal historical arts in 2005, 2007, and 2009. After these four lively and provocative iterations, however, the Aboriginal component of *Art of This Land* was effectively brought to a halt in 2011 when budget cuts eliminated the position of Denise Leclerc, the curator in charge.

A year after the launch of *Art of This Land*, the CMC opened its permanent First Peoples Hall, a project begun in the 1980s and resumed after the completion of the task force report, to which three CMC curators had contributed. The hall communicates the themes defined by an Aboriginal Advisory Committee charged with guiding the exhibition in compliance with the new partnership model, alongside more conventional archaeological, ethnographic, and historical accounts formulated by curators trained in the Western academic disciplines. The introductory section forcefully articulates the Advisory Committee's key messages about the diversity of Aboriginal peoples, their active embrace of modernity, and the central importance of land and land rights. In the Ways of Knowing section, the authority of oral traditions is juxtaposed with that of Western science, while in the following sections visitors are presented with accounts of traditional ways of life organized according to standard anthropological culture areas but punctuated by modules introducing contemporary conflicts that have arisen over competing Indigenous and settler interests in land and resources. A final section, which narrates the radical changes introduced by contact with Europeans, includes accounts of assimilationist policies. Given the 500 years of history being recounted, only a single case could be devoted to the residential school system, and it is the only permanent installation on the topic currently presented by the national museums. As I have argued elsewhere, the sometimes uneasy juxtapositions of different perspectives, knowledges, and voices in the First Peoples Hall produce tensions that are usefully provocative because they alert viewers to the challenge of accommodating different knowledge systems that arises in the still unfolding process of decolonization.[31]

Art of This Land and the First Peoples Hall can be seen in two quite different ways that evidence the necessary and useful debates characteristically stimulated by decolonization projects. They are analyzed both as progressive and pluralist accommodations of difference and as appropriative gestures that assimilate Indigenous cultures, political agendas, and value systems to Western taxonomics of knowledge and regimes of taste and aesthetic value.[32] Both thus raise the question posed by Ashton and Hamilton in a parallel Australian context of whether a state-sponsored museum that by definition is mandated to make visible the "imagined community" of the nation can allow Indigenous cultural expressions their autonomous power. In their view, "to create a national history museum that discards unitary national narratives as well as causal trajectories (the teleology of the nation) ... is probably impossible."[33] Yet, viewed from another perspective, the gestures of inclusion and empowerment performed by the NGC and the CMC can also be understood as museological attempts to inspire respect for Aboriginal cultures and to redress the damage to cultural continuity inflicted by colonial assimilationist policies. The two possibilities present themselves in even more challenging ways in the development of the Canadian Museum for Human Rights. Before turning to that discussion, however, it is important to acknowledge, if only briefly, the attempts at redress in progress in other national heritage institutions during the 1990s and early 2000s.

Programs developed since the 1970s by the Department of Canadian Heritage (DCH) signalled the government's acceptance of Aboriginal opposition to the assimilationist policies outlined in the Trudeau government's 1969 white paper on Indian policy. In 1971, the DCH initiated the Cultural Education Centres Program and subsequently began to work toward the new policy outlined in the National Indian Brotherhood's 1972 report "Indian Control of Indian Education" (1972). During the late 1990s, as Valerie Galley has written, the DCH participated in the federal government's efforts to develop a strategy for compensating Survivors of residential schools and partnered with Indian Residential Schools Resolution Canada to "develop a 'programmatic response,' a form of restitution for the loss of language and culture."[34] In 2002, the department announced that it would create a centre with a budget of $160 million over ten years (subsequently withdrawn) and commissioned a Task Force on Aboriginal Languages and Cultures "in support of Canada's commitment to preserve, revitalize, and promote Aboriginal languages and cultures."[35] An Aboriginal Affairs Branch was set up to administer the Aboriginal Peoples' Program with stated objectives "to strengthen Aboriginal cultural identity, to encourage the full participation of Aboriginal peoples in Canadian life, and to preserve and revitalize Aboriginal languages and cultures as living elements of Canadian society."[36] Specific support has been offered for projects related to languages, broadcasting, and Aboriginal women and youth. The department's Museums Assistance Program established a separate Aboriginal Heritage granting category to support "projects related to the preservation, management and presentation of Aboriginal cultural heritage."[37] As noted earlier, the predecessor of the DCH had funded the Task Force on Museums and First Peoples, and the DCH has been assigned responsibility for delivering the government's Human Rights Program and monitoring other federal departments' compliance with the Multiculturalism Act.

The Canada Council for the Arts, following similar self-studies, set up an Aboriginal Arts Office to ensure that its "services and programs best meet the needs of Canada's First Nations, Inuit and Métis arts communities" and to advocate for the "development of Aboriginal arts practices in Canada."[38] It administers grant programs for Aboriginal practitioners of media arts, music, dance, theatre, and visual arts as well as curators, writers, publishers, and cultural institutions. Although focused primarily on contemporary arts practices, it also supports traditional arts and their transmission from elders to youth.

Other national organizations with responsibility for heritage preservation and interpretation also recognized the need to create dedicated programs that could accommodate the special needs and cultural sensitivities of Aboriginal researchers and proactively facilitate access to the national collections. In 2001, Library and Archives Canada established a team of Aboriginal and non-Aboriginal librarians, archivists, and program managers from across the institution to "recommend new ways to acquire, preserve and make known records and publications about Aboriginal documentary heritage."[39] The next year LAC hired an Aboriginal resources and services coordinator to "promote the National Library collection and encourage more individuals, communities and organizations to access Aboriginal and other resources at the Library,"[40] following the model of partnership with Aboriginal communities by then increasingly adopted throughout federal institutions. Subsequent working groups continued to study the problem of developing Aboriginal documentary heritage at LAC.

THE CHALLENGE OF MEMORIALIZATION:
STOLEN LANDS, STOLEN CHILDHOODS

Even so brief an account makes clear the difficulty of providing an easy summary of the programs and exhibitions in development in the national museums and heritage institutions during the 1990s and the first decade of the twenty-first century. Yet, at a macro level, a general pattern emerges. Programs and projects have focused on the recovery of traditional knowledge, the celebration of contemporary innovation, and the representation of Aboriginal people's active participation in modernity rather than on memorialization of past oppression and suffering.[41] Such emphases have been deemed necessary to counter persistent views among members of the public that authentic Aboriginal cultures have "disappeared," to avoid casting Aboriginal people in the role of victims, and out of a concern to avoid inflicting the further pain that public representation might cause survivors of residential schools and their families.

It was not until a federal process of compensation and reconciliation was under way that national representations of the residential schools trauma were developed by the two foundations established and funded as part of the national compensation strategy. The Aboriginal Healing Foundation (AHF) and its successor, the Legacy of Hope Foundation (LHF), partnered with Library and Archives Canada to develop two travelling exhibitions about residential schooling and its impacts. *Where Are the Children? Healing the Legacy of the Residential Schools* was curated by Onondaga photographic artist and curator Jeffrey Thomas and launched at LAC in 2002.[42] It was followed by *We Were So Far Away: The Inuit Experience of Residential Schools*, organized by the LHF and curated by Inuit artist, art historian, and curator Heather Igloliorte. It opened at LAC in 2009. Both exhibitions have since been touring nationally to large museums and small community venues.[43]

In both real and virtual space, *Where Are the Children?* chronicles the historical process of removing children, transporting them to distant schools, and disciplining them to alien routines and curricula through photographic documentation extracted by Thomas from public and church archives. *We Were So Far Away* recounts the Inuit experience through the stories, images, and artifacts of eight Survivors. In his introduction to the first iteration of the online version of *Where Are the Children?*, George Erasmus wrote of its potential to mediate Aboriginal and non-Aboriginal memory and awareness: "Some will for the first time see what Survivors of residential school abuse have never forgotten: the face of a child whose identity is a number, whose culture is forbidden, and whose future is an institutional understanding. May this exhibit provision a greater understanding."[44] He pointed to the importance of the research that both Thomas and Igloliorte undertook in working with Survivors as a vital supplement to official archival documentation: "The Archives gathers what has been as an endowment to what will be. Because no legacy is enriched by counterfeit, this project represented an attempt to tell the true and painful story of a national institution committed, not to the preservation of a people, but to their forced assimilation."[45] In addition to Survivor memory, the website for *Where Are the Children?* included an extensive list of "intergenerational impacts," accounts of exemplary Survivors who can serve as "contemporary role models," and video narratives through which Survivors shared their stories. Visitor comments, according to the Legacy of Hope Foundation, "note that the exhibition was the first time that many of them understood that there were differences and nuances between the First Nations, Métis and Inuit experience of residential school. Many also commented that the focus on individual Survivors personalized and brought home the message of the legacy of residential schools in ways that other educational resources could not."[46]

2011–? THE VANISHING INDIAN PROGRAMS

As these exhibits continue to circulate, the capacity of national heritage institutions to complement them by supporting reconnection to cultural traditions has been severely curtailed. The most radical shrinkages occurred after the Harper government won a parliamentary majority in 2011. At Library and Archives Canada, the cuts and terminations of services that followed virtually ended the institution's ability to continue its Aboriginal initiatives.[47] The deep funding cuts announced in the 2012 federal budget hit LAC particularly hard, but their paralyzing impact was the product of a longer process that had been moving it away from its traditional services and capacities. Programs designed to accommodate Aboriginal needs and those of other minorities are particularly vulnerable to budget cuts because such initiatives, compensatory by definition, can redress past deficits only if they are given dedicated resources. That funding constraints at LAC amounted to policy change was evident from the termination and non-replacement of specialist archivists, the "restructuring" out of existence of Aboriginal programs, the termination of acquisitions and collection-building programs, and the archiving of virtual exhibitions related to Aboriginal peoples.[48] LAC's staffing reductions and the disappearance of senior specialists with extensive knowledge of treaties and related textual records, maps, artworks, and photographs that shed light on Aboriginal history and culture demonstrate a serious lack of commitment in an era of active land claims negotiations in the courts and at the treaty tables.[49]

A parallel history unfolded at Parks Canada, which manages many of the most important sites of Aboriginal pre- and post-contact history. It suffered perhaps the most radical funding cuts of any heritage organization. Although it, too, had developed special Aboriginal initiatives, the draconian cuts in the 2012 federal budget—over $29 million annually, resulting in the loss of 638 positions—caused museums at its historic sites to be closed, 80 percent of its archaeologists to be fired, the six regional research labs to be closed, and their collections to be transferred to inaccessible storage locations in the national capital region.[50]

Similarly, at the Department of Canadian Heritage (DCH), key administrative units dedicated to Aboriginal programs were eliminated and their staffs folded into other divisions. In 2012, the DCH transferred the Cultural Education Centres Program to Aboriginal Affairs and Northern Development Canada, following which the budgetary allocations to this program and the major Indian, Inuit, and Métis national organizations were cut by 30 percent.

All of these cancellations and shrinkages could be interpreted as casualties of the draconian austerity imposed by the Conservative government to implement its ideology—policies which have hit funding for research and cultural programs particularly hard. However, the changes at the Canadian Museum of History, also clearly demonstrated new priorities that militate against the institution's traditional focus on Aboriginal peoples.[51] From its founding in 1911, the National Museum of Canada was charged with the major responsibility for researching, preserving, and interpreting Aboriginal cultures and histories through its two oldest and most venerable divisions, the Canadian Ethnology Service and the Archaeological Survey of Canada. In November 2012, when then Minister of Canadian Heritage James Moore announced that the museum's name would be changed to the Canadian Museum of History, he also announced that the museum would renovate and expand the Canada Hall to a huge 50,000-square-foot area at a cost of $25 million in order to retell the story of Canada's history. The new history hall is scheduled to open in time for the celebration of the 150th anniversary of Canadian Confederation in 2017. The parliamentary act necessary for the name change gave the museum a new mandate that broke with its century-old Aboriginal focus, its tradition of collections-based research, and its more recent commitment to the exploration of diasporic Canadian communities and world cultures.[52] Since the early 1980s, the mandate of the museum had been "to increase, throughout Canada and internationally, interest in, knowledge and critical understanding of and appreciation and respect for human cultural achievements and human behavior by establishing, maintaining and developing for research and posterity a collection of objects of historical or cultural interest, with special but not exclusive reference to Canada, and by demonstrating those achievements and behavior, the knowledge derived from them and the understanding they represent."[53] The museum's new mandate focuses more narrowly on Canada, replacing a plural notion of "human cultural achievements" with a more unitary construct of the nation: "The purpose of the Canadian Museum of History is to enhance Canadians' knowledge, understanding and appreciation of events, experiences, people and objects that reflect and have shaped Canada's history and identity, and also to enhance their awareness of world history and cultures."[54] The failure to acknowledge the ongoing need for research on collections in order to generate new understandings is particularly worrying, for it implies an underlying concept of knowledge as a fixed, off-the-shelf, and ready-to-use commodity.

Even before parliamentary passage of the new Museum Act, the new CMH administration had begun to marginalize research and exhibitions involving its anthropological collections—the most important of its holdings—through the attrition of its curatorial establishment. From its founding, the museum's ethnology staff was made up of specialists for each of the major Aboriginal linguistic and cultural regions of Canada, but by 2012 a series of retirements and restructurings had greatly reduced their numbers. During the next two years, the CMH reconfigured its research division, replacing the ethnology, archaeology, and history divisions with three new areas: Repatriation, First Peoples and Early Canada, and Contemporary Canada and the World. In July 2013, it issued a new research strategy that identifies the museum's priorities for the next decade. The document is evidence of a seismic shift that moves the institution away from its historical prioritization of research on Aboriginal cultures and toward a new emphasis on settler history.[55] Three general research areas—Meaning and Memory, First Peoples, and Compromise and Conflict—are further broken down into two or three sub-areas. The descriptions of the two sub-divisions of the First Peoples area—The Changing North and Aboriginal Histories—combined with the lists of objectives and examples given for the other research areas strongly suggest that the overall impact of the new strategy will be a radical compression of hundreds of complex and diverse Aboriginal cultural traditions that have developed over thousands of years and their repositioning within a framework of settler Canadian history.[56]

With the loss of so many specialists and the disconnect between staff expertise and CMH collections manifested by the new groupings and priorities for the research division, the capacity of Canada's national museum to support Aboriginal projects of cultural renewal has been seriously compromised. Ethnographic collections pose unique challenges for researchers, whether Aboriginal or non-Aboriginal. A great many objects are badly documented, either because they were assembled during periods when collectors were ignorant of or did not deem important the accurate recording of their places of origin and other critical information, or because they have lacked Aboriginal input, as mandated by the task force report. To access these collections, researchers typically need expert guidance from curators who have researched their layered and complex collecting histories. It will be much more difficult for the few remaining ethnologists at the CMH—each of whom is now responsible for vast areas of great cultural and linguistic diversity—to support collaborative research projects, to identify items that should be "on the table" in treaty negotiations, or even to provide up-to-date content for the Aboriginal stories to be told in the new history hall. The changes at CMH, furthermore, cannot be dismissed as unavoidable by-products of a normal process of generational transition, for a responsible process of change management would ensure the transmission of this knowledge to a new generation. When Moore announced the creation of the new history hall at CMH, he assured taxpayers that the $25 million cost would be paid from existing sources. In light of the developments that ensued at the CMH, the conclusion is unavoidable that key positions and research funding previously dedicated to Aboriginal histories and cultures were transferred to the new project.

MINDING THE GAPS: THE CMHR AND THE PROBLEM OF REDRESS

This very abbreviated overview suggests a widening gap between the redress to Aboriginal people called for by the reports and formal agreements completed between 1992 and 2010 and the capacity of federal institutions to respond. As we have also seen, within the national museum system, as yet there has been no permanent, national memorialization of the residential school system and no adequate public account of the devastating sequence of land appropriations, forced removals, and suppressions of Aboriginal spiritual practices that occurred during the long years of formal colonial control. *Where Are the Children?* and *We Were So Far Away* were designed as temporary travelling exhibitions, while the highly condensed accounts in the First Peoples Hall are now in need of expansion and updating. Although all set important precedents, none of these projects was planned to accommodate the scope or permanence that a serious process of redress demands.[57]

It is useful to remember in this context Jennifer Henderson and Pauline Wakeham's warning against a tendency to assume that Canada's formal apology and compensation to residential school Survivors resolve the much longer history of abuse of Indigenous human rights. In their analysis of Canada's "culture of redress," they argue that "residential schooling may be justifiably critiqued as a part-for-whole substitution which allows the state to sidestep issues of land claims and constitutional change."[58] Museums and heritage organizations, of course, operate in the realm of symbolic representation and cultural reconnection. They do not control processes of material restitution apart from the disposition of their own collections, and the kind of redress that falls within their scope involves knowledge creation and representation rather than legal action and money. These symbolic forms of redress are nevertheless important. They not only prepare the way for the substantive resolution of human rights abuses but also can actively foster processes of cultural reclamation. Henderson and Wakeham also emphasize "the vital importance and inseparability of the question of culture from a consideration of both Indigenous injuries and reparations. Culture, broadly construed, cannot be held discrete from political and legal discourse; rather, it is the means through which redress and reconciliation operate as polyvalent symbolic forms which shape and mediate past and present realities through processes of signification."[59]

I argued earlier that, at a given moment in time, the advent of a new national museum evidences a perceived gap in the coverage of histories and issues deemed important to the formation of public consciousness. I have devoted much of this chapter to tracing the deficits that have been developing in the work of redress for abuses of Aboriginal human rights in the established national museums and cultural repositories. How, then, might the CMHR's new exhibits and programs intervene in the current spectrum of representations and activist programs for cultural reconnection? Put another way, do the two gaps—the one resulting from cutbacks and policy changes in the federal heritage establishment and the other revealed by the decision to found a new national museum—map onto each other?

In a promotional video on the CMHR website, also posted to YouTube, the institution presents itself as "an 'idea' museum rooted in the past but focused on today." It is intended, we are told, to be a place where histories of human rights abuse are represented in order to create understanding for the victims and where "heroes and heroines" who have fought for human rights are celebrated. "We'll also examine our less proud moments," the video promises, concluding that "through education and understanding we will be motivated to take action and move toward a more respectful world ... to change the future."[60] The CMHR, in other words, is designed to be both historical and proactive, committed to recounting past abuses of human rights in order to serve as a site for the genesis of social action.

Paul Williams has shown that the advent of memorial museums that address specific episodes of atrocity is a relatively recent development in the museological spectrum, having begun little more than half a century ago in the aftermath of the Second World War.[61] Although they might function in part as memorials "seen to be, if not apolitical, at least safe in the refuge of history," they are also history museums "presumed to be concerned with interpretation, contextualization, and critique."[62] Williams also distinguishes the still newer and hybrid type of the peace museum, which commemorates histories of conflict with the explicit goal of inspiring visitors to advocate for peace.

Based on its web presence and mission statement, the CMHR belongs to the category of the peace museum in which historical representation is intended to perform redress and lead to future action. It commemorates through expository forms of representation a series of difficult histories and human rights abuses of specific groups of people who have connections to Canada. Its activist stance is confirmed by its institutional membership in the International Coalition of Sites of Conscience, a group of historic site museums and related institutions that share a commitment to build "lasting cultures of human rights and democracy," to initiate "new conversations about contemporary issues through a historical lens," and to harness themselves to "a self-conscious tactic in the service of human rights and civic engagement."[63]

How, then, does the CMHR plan to fulfill the challenges of representation and redress in its Aboriginal component? As noted previously, this question could not be answered prior to the museum's opening, but the Gallery Profiles document issued in 2012 and the descriptions of its eleven galleries released in February 2014 provided a clear blueprint.[64] The Aboriginal Peoples of Canada gallery is the first one that visitors encounter after experiencing the museum's introductory installation, *What Are Human Rights?* The planning document describes the 2,700-square-foot *Indigenous Perspectives* exhibit as "a circular theatre of curved wooden slats representing the multitude of Canadian aboriginal traditions, which will play a 360-degree film and serve as a space for storytelling, performance and discussion."[65] The museum's exhibition designers were asked to create an "inner space [that] evokes a sense of connectedness and equality, encouraging dialogue and the exchange of ideas between speaker and audience. It will present Aboriginal concepts of humanity and our responsibilities to each other ... in one of the most dramatic spaces of the museum."[66] Exhibits mounted around the perimeter will focus on specific topics, one of which is land and land rights. This component will be comprised of "eight community stories on the thematic wall united by a theme of land rights. The terrace interpretation will specifically highlight the connections to the land and water and the Forks at [sic] the stories of how various First Nations and Métis have lived and interacted here."[67]

This gallery is followed by the Canada's Journeys hall, whose 9,500 square feet present a video theatre, an Arc of Inclusion and several interactive spaces listed as an "interactive floor game," a Share Your Story Booth, and a Kitchen Table. The museum describes this largest of its galleries as taking "a multi-layered approach to dozens of Canadian human rights stories from French-language rights to the Chinese head tax, from voting rights to cultural dispossession in the North. A digital canvas relays stories across a 956-foot screen, while others are told in floor stations and story niches. (9,500 square feet)." Four of the eighteen niches—Cultural Dispossession in the North, Residential Schools, Métis Rights, and Stolen Sisters—focus on Aboriginal human rights abuses. The niches are described as three-sided, alcove-like structures. The description of the niche devoted to residential schools provided in the design document reads: "Small open-sided box with an evocation of a classroom from the last century. A large photo of children writing on a blackboard covers much of the back wall. Two old-style school desks are fastened to the floor and informative videos are projected on their tops. On one side wall is a map of Canada marked with places where residential schools operated. The other side wall has photos of children and families affected by the '60s scoop."[68] One hundred and thirty words are allocated for the context panel and thirty for each caption, supplemented by quotations from Survivors. The projected visitor experience and the "mood" to be generated are also described: "Visitors' curiosity is drawn by the photo on the niche's back wall.... A map of Canada studded with school locations attract[s] their attention. From a wall of personal photos they are surprised to learn about state apprehensions of children over the last few decades. They read the context panel and learn about Canada's official apology." The visitor will feel "empathy for the damage suffered by families" and be "proud of Canada's apology."[69] These small displays can provide only a nutshell version of the history that they relate. They seem designed to function like previews of full-length feature films or, if you will, a poster session provided at a conference when time does not permit the delivery of fully developed papers.

Aboriginal people and their stories will also be "woven in" to other sections of the museum. There is no specific mention in the Gallery Profiles of signal episodes of abuse such as the banning of the potlatch and the Sun Dance in the Indian Act of 1884, though these and other events might be subsumed among the examples explored in subsequent galleries, such as Turning Points for Humanity, the Canadian Stories Wall in the Human Rights Forum, Human Rights Today, or one of the CMHR's other umbrella sections. Even with such additional representations, the broad scope of the museum—universal but with specific connections to Canada—seems to have been conceived in such a way as to occlude rather than bring into relief either the special status of Aboriginal human rights histories in Canada or the nation's responsibility to perform redress and reconciliation.

The two gaps, then, do not coincide. Aboriginal people are assigned the role of host in the CMHR, but the story of their own abuses is reduced to one among many rather than being given particular prominence. Although the museum will work to meet a perceived need to raise the consciousness of Canadians about human rights and Canada's proactive role in protecting them, the symbolic redress to Aboriginal people that would be satisfied by a comprehensive narrative of their experiences as internally colonized

Indigenous people is not provided for. Such a contradiction, it seems to me, puts the larger project of confronting abuses of human rights at risk. Owning up to the past, like charity, must begin at home. The museum's introductory gallery, with its affirmative and welcoming mood, could have the effect of obscuring the great problems confronting Canada's Indigenous population that still need to be addressed: strengthening identities, improving health and education, stimulating economic development, and resolving land claims. The invitation to Canadians to "feel proud" of the government's apology for residential schools invites closure of a shameful chapter of Canadian history whose effects are still with us.

Anishinaabe political historian Dale Turner argues that reconciliation, at its base, is a political issue that arises from the denial of Aboriginal people's political sovereignty and land rights as first recognized by Great Britain in the Royal Proclamation of 1763 and as laid out in the 1996 report of the Royal Commission on Aboriginal Peoples: "Put simply, reconciliation must empower Aboriginal nations, and this empowerment necessarily involves opening the question of the sanctity of the Canadian state's unilateral assertion of sovereignty."[70] Williams comments on the difficulty that memorial museums have had in addressing such large issues. "While histories of violence and oppression towards Native Americans and Africans in the Americas are of course extremely important," he writes, "they are historically extensive and socially complicated; they suffuse so much that they lack easy representation. This does not mean they do not deserve better commemoration; rather, it is simply more difficult to imagine single institutions straightforwardly relating centuries-long histories."[71]

"Better commemoration," in the context of the symbolic forms of redress possible in a museum, demands more extended forms of representation than those envisioned for the CMHR's opening exhibitions. It requires not just mood-engendering images, sound bites, and brief texts but also detailed narratives that can provide satisfactory historical exposition and explanation. This kind of narrative—thorough, exhaustively researched, authoritative, and linear—proved to be powerful and compelling in the United States Holocaust Memorial Museum, the Asper family's inspiration in starting the process that led to the CMHR's foundation as a national museum. Without such an approach, the CMHR risks losing the opportunity to contribute to the unfinished process of redress now stalling in other national institutions. I am not suggesting, of course, that the CMHR turn itself into an ethnology museum or that it can or should perform the functions of Parks Canada or Library and Archives Canada. Rather, I am urging that it work with existing museums in possession of collections and relevant resources and serve as a site for the development of specific projects of reconnection and recovery. I am also urging the importance of such initiatives in full awareness of the tensions and contradictions inherent in efforts to recount minority histories within an overarching narrative of the nation. The challenge is to make these tensions apparent rather than mask them behind unrealized visions of harmony. A full assessment of the dynamics of revisionist and reactionary politics within the national institutions will only be possible in the years after the new representations have taken concrete form in Winnipeg and the National Capital Region. It will be important, however, to evaluate them relationally, as part of a national project devoted to recovering from colonialism.

NOTES

1   Paul Ashton and Paula Hamilton, "'Unfinished Business': Public History in a Postcolonial Nation," in *Contested Histories in Public Space: Memory, Race, and Nation,* ed. Daniel J. Walkowitz and Lisa Maya Knauer (Durham, NC: Duke University Press, 2009), 88.

2   Beverly Jacobs (President of the Native Women's Association of Canada), response in Parliament to House of Commons Apology to Inuit, Métis, and First Nations Peoples for Residential Schools, 11 June 2008, reprinted in Jennifer Henderson and Pauline Wakeham, eds., *Reconciling Canada: Critical Perspectives on the Culture of Redress* (Toronto: University of Toronto Press, 2013), 339.

3   The exhibition, *The Spirit Sings: Artistic Traditions of Canada's First Peoples,* was organized by the Glenbow Museum for the 1988 Calgary Winter Olympics and stimulated a largely polemical literature. See, for example, the debate between Bruce Trigger and Michael Ames in *Culture* 8, 1 (1988): 81–88; Robin Gillam, *Hall of Mirrors: Museums and the Canadian Public* (Banff: Banff Centre Press, 2001); and my "Moment of Truth: The Spirit Sings as Critical Event and the Exhibition Inside It," in my book *Museum Pieces: Toward the Indigenization of Canadian Museums* (Montreal: McGill-Queen's University Press, 2011), 48–70. Good starting points for reading about the task force are Trudy Nicks, "Partnerships in Developing Cultural Resources: Learning from the Task Force on Museums and First Peoples," *Culture* 12, 2 (1992): 87–94; and Stephanie Bolton, "An Analysis of the Task Force on Museums and First Peoples: The Changing Representation of Aboriginal Histories in Museums" (MA thesis, Concordia University, 2004).

4   Task Force on Museums and First Peoples, *Turning the Page: Forging Partnerships between Museums and First Peoples* (Ottawa: Canadian Museums Association and Assembly of First Nations, 1992).

5   Classic formulations of this analysis are Tony Bennett, *The Birth of the Museum: History, Theory, Politics* (New York: Routledge, 1995); and Carol Duncan, *Civilizing Rituals: Inside Public Art Museums* (New York: Routledge, 1995).

6   Stacey Loyer has recently argued for the agency of Onkwehonwe partners in collecting projects at the Six Nations of the Grand River in "Belonging and Belongings: Ethnograph-

ic Collecting and Indigenous Agency at the Six Nations of the Grand River" (PhD diss., Carleton University, 2013).

7   The task force report, like the parallel Native American Graves Protection and Repatriation Act in the United States, requires the return of human remains, illegally acquired objects, sacred objects, and items of cultural patrimony. Although lack of documentation has hampered this process in many instances, in Canada it has also been enabled by the ability of First Nations involved in land claims to negotiate for the return of cultural property held by provincial and national museums within the comprehensive claims process reinstated in the late twentieth century.

8   A sampling of these programs includes the separate Aboriginal Heritage Program within the Department of Canadian Heritage's Museums Assistance Program, the Aboriginal Training Program created by the Canadian Museum of Civilization, the Canada Council's Grants to Aboriginal Curators for Residencies in the Visual Arts, and the Canadian Conservation Institute's major 2007 conference on Preserving Aboriginal Heritage: Technical and Traditional Approaches," the proceedings of which were published.

9   Ashton and Hamilton, "'Unfinished Business,'" 85. Their discussion refers to the conservative government of Prime Minister John Howard, in power from 1996 to 2007.

10   See Bennett, *The Birth of the Museum;* and Duncan, *Civilizing Rituals.*

11   Sherry Brydon and I have discussed this history in more detail in "'Arrow of Truth': The Indians of Canada Pavilion at Expo 67," in Phillips, *Museum Pieces,* 27–47.

12   Library and Archives Canada, Canadian Corporation for the 1967 World Exhibition, fonds/e001096685. The image is reproduced in Phillips and Brydon, "'Arrow of Truth,'" Figure 1.3, 42.

13   Task Force, *Turning the Page,* n. pag.

14   Ibid., 4.

15   Ibid.

16   Ibid., 8.

17   Report of the Royal Commission on Aboriginal Peoples (RCAP), 1996, Vol. 3, *Gathering Strength* (Ottawa: Canada Communications Group, 1996), 548, http://www.collections-canada.gc.ca/webarchives/20071124060708/http://www.ainc-inac.gc.ca/ch/rcap/sg/si1_e.html#Volume%203.

18   Ibid., 547.

19   Ibid., 556.

20   United Nations Declaration on the Rights of Indigenous Peoples, http://social.un.org/index/IndigenousPeoples/DeclarationontheRightsofIndigenousPeoples.aspx, 3.

21   Ibid., 7.

22   Ibid., 6.

23   Ibid., 11.

24   I am indebted to Stacey R. Jessiman for sharing the working draft of her dissertation chapter "Analysing Respect for UNDRIP at the Canadian Museum of History," in which she argues that the new Canadian Museum of History exhibits offer an important opportunity to fulfill the cultural component of Canada's UNDRIP obligations. As she points out, signing was accompanied by a statement of support that made clear that Canada did not view UNDRIP as legally binding in relation to land claims, resources, the Constitution, and existing Canadian law.

25   A good sampling of these projects is provided by the papers in Canadian Conservation
      Institute, *Preserving Aboriginal Heritage: Technical and Traditional Approaches: Proceed-
      ings of Symposium 2007* (Ottawa: Canadian Conservation Institute, 2008); and Lynda
      Jessup and Shannon Bagg, eds., *On Aboriginal Representation in the Gallery* (Gatineau:
      Canadian Museum of Civilization, 2002).

26   Michael M. Ames, "How to Decorate a House: The Re-Negotiation of Cultural Repre-
      sentations at the University of British Columbia Museum of Anthropology," *Museum
      Anthropology* 22, 3 (1999): 49.

27   Ibid., 46.

28   For a more detailed discussion, see my review in *Archivaria: The Journal of the Association
      of Canadian Archivists* 40 (1995): 243–45.

29   Burnham's work is discussed in Judy Thompson, Judy Hall, and Leslie Tepper, eds., *Fasci-
      nating Challenges: Studying Material Culture with Dorothy Burnham* (Gatineau: Canadian
      Museum of Civilization, 2001). On the recovery of traditional Dene arts, see Ingrid
      Kritsch and Karen Wright-Fraser, "The Gwich'in Traditional Caribou Skin Clothing
      Project: Repatriating Traditional Knowledge and Skills," *InfoNorth* 55, 2 (2002): 205–13;
      Judy Thompson and Ingrid Kritsch, *Yeenoo dài' kè'tr'ijilkai' ganagwaandaii, Long Ago
      Sewing We Will Remember: The Story of the Gwich'in Traditional Caribou Skin Clothing
      Project* (Gatineau: Canadian Museum of Civilization, 2005); and Suzan Marie and Judy
      Thompson, *Whadoo Tehmi: Long Ago People's Packsack, Dene Babiche Bags: Tradition and
      Revival* (Gatineau: Canadian Museum of Civilization, 2004).

30   The following discussion summarizes my longer-analysis of this exhibition in "Modes
      of Inclusion: Indigenous Art at the National Gallery of Canada and the Art Gallery of On-
      tario," *Museum Pieces*, 252–76.

31   See my chapter "Inside-Out and Outside-In: Re-Presenting Native North America at the
      Canadian Museum of Civilization and the National Museum of the American Indian,"
      Museum Pieces, 205–27. See also Miranda J. Brady, "The Flexible Heterotopia: Indian
      Residential Schools and the Canadian Museum of Civilization," *Peace and Conflict: Jour-
      nal of Peace Psychology* 19, 4 (2013): 408–20.

32   Charles Taylor's foundational essay "The Politics of Recognition" makes the case for the
      accommodation of diversity within pluralist societies; in *Multiculturalism: Examining
      the Politics of Recognition,* ed. Amy Gutmann (Princeton, NJ: Princeton University Press,
      1994), 25–74. For critiques of inclusionary projects, see, for example, Caitlin Gordon-
      Walker, "Unity in Diversity: The Limits of Multicultural Nationalism and Museums"
      (PhD diss., Trent University, 2013); and Anne Whitelaw, "Placing Aboriginal Art at the
      National Gallery of Canada," *Canadian Journal of Communication* 31, 1 (2006), http://
      www.cjc-online.ca/index.php/journal/article/view/1775/1897.

33   Ashton and Hamilton, "'Unfinished Business,'" 88.

34   Valerie Galley, "Reconciliation and the Revitalization of Indigenous Languages," in
      Response, Responsibility, and Renewal: Canada's Truth and Reconciliation Journey, ed.
      Gregory Younging, Jonathan Dewar, and Mike DeGagné (Ottawa: Aboriginal Healing
      Foundation Research, 2009), 229.

35   Canadian Heritage website, http://www.pch.gc.ca/eng/1288015506594. See the task force
      report "Toward a New Beginning: A Foundational Report for a Strategy to Revitalize First
      Nations, Inuit, and Métis Cultures: Report to the Minister of Canadian Heritage by the
      Task Force on Aboriginal Languages and Cultures," 2005, www.afn.ca/uploads/files/edu-
      cation2/towardanewbeginning.pdf.

36   http://www.pch.gc.ca/eng/1288012444767.

37   http://www.pch.gc.ca/eng/1268597502197.

38   http://canadacouncil.ca/en/aboriginal-arts-office/about-the-aao.

39   "*All Our Relations*": *Aboriginal Resources and Services Report and Recommendations*, 2003; *Report and Recommendations of the Consultation on Aboriginal Resources and Services*, 2004.

40   The officer was Deborah Pelletier. National Library of Canada, press release, 4 October 2002, http://cnrp.ccnmatthews.com/news/releases/show.jsp?action=showRelease&action For=391536&searchText=false&showText=all.

41   On the relationship between Gerald Vizenor's notion of "survivance" and the meanings of "resilience," see Henderson and Wakeham, "Colonial Reckoning." Also see Heather Igloliorte, "Inuit Artistic Expression as Cultural Resilience," in Younging, Dewar, and DeGagné, *Response, Responsibility, and Renewal*, 113–12.

42   For a detailed summary of *Where Are the Children?*, see the Legacy of Hope website, www.legacyofhope.ca/projects/where-are-the-children. The exhibition catalogue can be downloaded at www.legacyofhope.ca/downloads/watc-catalogue.pdf.

43   For *We Were So Far Away*, see www.legacyofhope.ca/projects/we-were-so-far-away and the downloadable exhibition book. As of 2013, *Where Are the Children?* had toured to twenty-four venues, and *We Were So Far Away* had toured to thirteen sites, seven of them in the North.

44   www.wherearethechildren.ca/en/about/ahf/html. Citations in this section are to the first version of the virtual exhibition. The site has since been redesigned without Erasmus's introduction.

45   Ibid.

46   www.legacyofhope.ca/projects/we-were-so-far-away.

47   On the cuts to Library and Archives Canada, see Yves Frenette, "Conscripting Canada's Past: The Harper Government and the Politics of Memory," *Canadian Journal of History* 49 (2014): 63.

48   The archived exhibitions include one that points researchers toward holdings of value to Aboriginal research (see, e.g., http://www.collectionscanada.gc.ca/stories/index-e.html) and fourteen of the nineteen Aboriginal portal exhibitions (see http://www.collectionscanada.gc.ca/aboriginal-peoples/index-e.html#exhibitions).

49   For a detailed chronology of the cuts and shrinkages, see the backgrounder on Library and Archives Canada compiled by the Ex Libris Association based at the University of Toronto, http://exlibris.pbworks.com/w/page/63815458/Ex%20Libris%20Association%20 Backgrounder%20on%20Library%20and%20Archives%20Canada.

50   The cuts to Parks Canada were passed in the 2012 federal budget. See the Canadian Archaeological Association website, http://canadianarchaeology.com/caa/draconian-cuts-parks-canada.

51   The broader context of the changes at CMH is given in Frenette, "Conscripting Canada's Past," 59–61.

52   The Canadian Museum of History Act received royal assent on 12 December 2013.

53   Museums Act, 1990, Section 8. http://laws-lois.justice.gc.ca/eng/acts/M-13.4/section-8-20021231.html.

54   Museums Act (S.C. 1990, c. 3, Section 8) http://laws-lois.justice.gc.ca/eng/acts/m-13.4/page-3.html#h-7.

55 *Research Strategy: The Canadian Museum of History and the Canadian War Museum,*
    http://www.historymuseum.ca/research-and-collections/files/2013/07/research-strategy.
    pdf.

56 The disproportionate emphasis on research on northern First Nations also seems to be
    in line with the federal government's resource-based economic policies and its ongoing
    defence of Canada's sovereignty over the polar region. An alternative explanation is the
    outdated notion that northern peoples are more culturally "authentic" because more
    recently brought into contact with settler society. Critics have also interpreted the new
    CMH research strategy as renewing a "Victorian" emphasis on "militarism, monarchism,
    imperialism and Britishism." See Joseph Brean, "Critics Accuse the Conservative Party
    of 'Politicizing History' as National Museum Mandates Change," *National Post,* 30 July
    2013, http://news.nationalpost.com/2013/07/30/critics-accuse-the-conservative-party-of-
    politicizing-history-as-national-museum-mandates-change.

57 Two important projects of commemoration outside the national museum system should
    be noted: the National Commemorative Marker Project funded by the Indian Residential
    School Settlement Agreement announced in March 2014 and the planned Centre for
    Truth and Reconciliation at the University of Manitoba. The latter will house the archive
    of the Truth and Reconciliation Commission and include a small exhibition space.

58 Jennifer Henderson and Pauline Wakeham, "Colonial Reckoning, National Reconcili-
    ation? Aboriginal Peoples and the Culture of Redress in Canada," *English Studies in
    Canada* 31, 1: (2009): 4.

59 Ibid., 15.

60 http://museumforhumanrights.ca/media/video.

61 Paul Williams, *Memorial Museums: The Global Rush to Commemorate Atrocities* (London:
    Berg, 2007), 9.

62 Ibid.

63 http://www.sitesofconscience.org/about-us#section1.

64 CMHR, 2012 Gallery Profiles, http://s3.documentcloud.org/documents/609321/
    canadian-museum-for-human-rights-gallery-profiles.pdf; Lara Schroeder and Lauren
    McNabb, "Exclusive: Human Rights Museum Exhibits Revealed," http://globalnews.ca/
    news/1161291/human-rights-museum-to-feature-11-galleries/, posted 20 February 2014.

65 Quoted in Schroeder and McNabb, "Exclusive."

66 CMHR, 2012 Gallery Profiles, 14.

67 Ibid., 18.

68 Ibid., 30.

69 Ibid.

70 Dale Turner, "On the Idea of Reconciliation in Contemporary Aboriginal Politics," in
    Henderson and Wakeham, *Reconciling Canada,* 110.

71 Williams, *Memorial Museums,* 178.

FROM
IMAGINATION
TO INAUGURATION

AFTERWORD

Jodi Giesbrecht and Clint Curle

The legislative mandate of the Canadian Museum for Human Rights (CMHR) is found in Section 15.2 of the federal Museums Act: "The purpose of the Canadian Museum for Human Rights is to explore the subject of human rights, with special but not exclusive reference to Canada, in order to enhance the public's understanding of human rights, to promote respect for others and to encourage reflection and dialogue."[1] In translating this mandate into exhibits and museum programs, we were guided by six broad ideals. These ideals evolved in conversations among three key groups: the Board of Trustees, the museum's staff, and the academics, human rights specialists, stakeholders, and concerned citizens who provided suggestions and critiques that were carefully considered and negotiated as we developed content.

Our first ideal was to build a museum that inspired public reflection and dialogue on human rights, using an approach to content development that was participatory, inclusive, reciprocal, and empowering—in other words, using methodologies grounded in human rights concepts. We wanted to create a public space in which all people would feel safe to ask challenging and difficult questions about human rights, to agree and disagree with each other and with the CMHR, and to express their own viewpoints. This space would facilitate sharing of stories, experiences, and perspectives. This ideal was founded on the observation that human rights are defended and critiqued through ongoing processes of debate.

In keeping with this ideal, we began by asking people across Canada to tell their stories about how human rights have shaped their lived experiences. In a series of grassroots consultations, thousands of Canadians from various backgrounds shared their personal thoughts and stories. The CMHR did not impose much structure on these initial consultations; embracing the rawness and complexity of human rights, we wanted to avoid sanitizing individuals' stories and compartmentalizing their experiences within legalistic human rights frames. From this starting point, the CMHR could then integrate these deeply personal stories into broader considerations of human rights laws, practices, concepts, and debates.

One advantage of this approach is that personal stories constitute a powerful, engaging, and affective way to present complex human rights issues within museum exhibitions. Rather than placing legal texts or forensic evidence of historical atrocities on exhibit walls, we decided to tell personal stories through film and video, images and artifacts, and a host of other immersive and interactive media to encourage empathetic connections among visitors and those whose human rights stories we wanted to tell. By creating emotionally powerful exhibits that resonate with visitors' own knowledge and experiences, we can begin to bridge the gap that tends to exist between jargon-laden academic discourses and the deeply personal and intimate ways in which human rights affect our daily lives. Emphasizing lived experiences provides a broadly accessible way for people to grapple with abstract concepts such as justice, freedom, equality, and dignity.

We also faced challenges in using lived experiences as the starting point for the CMHR's exhibits. The complexity of personal stories is at odds with conventional museological frameworks that emphasize linear trajectories, predetermined learning objectives, and neat conclusions. The contradictory, open-ended, and ambiguous nature of lived experiences required us to deliberately eschew preconceived narrative frameworks in the hope that these rich stories would be able to speak for themselves. Throughout this process, we were cognizant of the ways in which curatorial practices, even those seeking democracy and public participation, are inevitably acts of power. All people are entitled to the same basic rights and freedoms, but in reality we experience justice and injustice in different ways. Although we are all implicated in the ways in which power is distributed throughout society, public institutions in particular can amplify some voices and perspectives over others. In the end, the ideal of encouraging human rights dialogue and reflection led us to content that attempts to show a diverse range of perspectives on human rights.

Our second ideal was to build a museum that paid specific attention to the development of human rights discourses in Canada and to examine honestly and critically the ways in which a kind of human rights consciousness has become engrained in the construction of Canadian identity. This ideal drew on our legislative mandate, which defines the CMHR's focus in terms of "special but not exclusive reference to Canada."[2] Canadian perspectives are integrated into all of our galleries, including those focused on international human rights themes. It was not difficult to do. From Canada's poor record of accepting Jewish refugees during the Holocaust, to John Humphrey's contributions to the Universal Declaration of Human Rights, to Canadian diasporic communities' struggles for justice in response to violations of human rights in their home countries, the many links among global human rights issues and events within Canada demonstrate the ways that human rights transcend national borders.

Our third ideal was to build a museum that worked with the dramatic architecture of the building, itself infused with human rights symbolism. Designed by architect Antoine Predock, the building's unusual geometry and textures reflect human rights ideas. The building rests on four stylized tree roots, anchoring the CMHR to its site. The museum's location at The Forks, where the Red and Assiniboine Rivers meet, has been a place of meeting, negotiation, agreement, and trade for Indigenous peoples for thousands of years. The main body of the CMHR is comprised of a sleek, light-filled glass cloud and a rocky, mountainous side. This architectural division can be understood as reflecting two aspects of human rights work. On the one hand, human rights reflect our best visions for humanity: the capacity for freedom and equality. On the other, human rights are a struggle, marked by hard toil and slow, uneven advances, like climbing a mountain. At the centre of the CMHR, exactly between the glass and the rock, a contemplative garden provides visitors with a good place to reflect on the vision and struggle of human rights. The soaring tower and the observation deck at the top of the museum point to the aspirational quality of human rights.

As our fourth ideal, we wanted the museum experience to be as accessible as possible. Inclusive design at the CMHR emphasizes physical accessibility, conceptual accessibility (e.g., text reading levels), and recognition that services must be available for people of all abilities, giving everyone the opportunity to participate in and enjoy integrated experiences. To assist us in realizing this ideal, the CMHR formed an Inclusive Design Advisory Council. This council has a diverse membership, broadly representative of Canadians with disabilities. It provides invaluable advice to the museum across its exhibits, programs, and operations. As a result of this council's input, the CMHR has tried to attain the inclusivity that one would expect from a museum for human rights.

Our fifth ideal was to ensure that the exhibits and programming of the CMHR were highly responsive to the changing human rights landscape. Human rights are dynamic and fluid, and representations of them need to be highly adaptive to changes in theory and practice. We knew that we could not be as responsive as the daily news, but we also realized that conventional museum exhibits would risk quickly becoming outdated. To respond to this challenge, the CMHR made strategic use of new technologies to enhance its exhibits and its ability to update content delivered through interactive presentations, multimedia technologies, and innovative designs.

And, finally, we wanted to be a reliable and trustworthy human rights learning resource. This ideal is expressed through several of our programs. The CMHR maintains an active oral history program, which began in 2011 with a series of interviews with people recognized for their contributions to upholding human rights. Educational programming (linked to school curriculum needs across Canada) and public programming also use tours, courses, talks, films, music, theatre, workshops, lectures, and other media to make the museum's content engaging and accessible to students and the broader public.

THE IDEA OF A HUMAN RIGHTS MUSEUM

As Karen Busby, Adam Muller, and Andrew Woolford note in their thoughtful introduction, the CMHR has been a moving target during its formative period. All of the chapters in this volume were conceived and written during earlier stages of the museum's development, prior to its opening. As such, they respond to the museum in its pre-launch phase. Nevertheless, the larger themes that they address have enduring relevance to the CMHR and representations of human rights generally.

The chapters in the first section, "The Idea of a Human Rights Museum," address several issues related to the social and political functions of ideas-based museums in liberal democracies. In their respective chapters, Ken Norman and Helen Fallding consider the ways in which transparent, participatory dialogue between the CMHR and its diverse publics is crucial to promoting the democratization of human rights knowledge. Optimistic about the museum's early efforts to encourage an inclusive and participatory approach to developing exhibition content, Norman hopes that such practices will continue to drive the CMHR's exhibits and programs. In examining the role of media in stimulating human rights dialogue, Fallding similarly encourages the museum to embrace an open model of communication, one that invites the public into the iterative debates that comprise exhibit and program development.

These chapters challenge the CMHR to use media as tools for effective communication and engagement with broader publics. In its first uses of social media, the museum used what might be called a broadcast model—essentially one-way communication from the institution to the public. As our organization matured, we began to replace this model with a more multidirectional approach to social media. This approach is in keeping with broader trends in digital culture, as participatory, user-generated platforms increasingly replace more conventional forms of disseminating information. Beyond social media, the CMHR's overall commitment to robust public engagement has been reflected in the many events and lectures hosted by the museum; in the use of peer review, consultation, and guest and tripartite models of curation used in content development; and in the growing involvement of research and curatorial staff in public media events.

The respective contributions of David Petrasek and Christopher Powell theorize the ways in which the CMHR might present broad human rights narratives. In "Illusion and the Human Rights Museum," Petrasek identifies three specific "illusions" or risks that the CMHR faces in the presentation of its content. The first illusion, which Petrasek terms the "illusion of understanding," refers to an assumption that learning about past atrocities is sufficient to prevent similar events from occurring in the future. The "illusion of progress" points to a triumphalist belief that human rights have steadily become more expansive, inclusive, and better over time. Finally, the "illusion of permanence" speaks to a conviction that we have now reached a pinnacle of achievement. Petrasek concludes by suggesting that a focus on the present and future, rather than on the past, is needed to avoid such illusions and to critique systemic inequality and marginalization.

Powell, in his chapter in the "Spatialization and Design" section, conceptualizes two competing ways—top-down versus bottom-up—that human rights narratives might be articulated within the CMHR's spaces, using poststructuralist theorizations of liberal governmentality to advocate an interpretation of human rights as social constructions. By emphasizing the fluid and negotiated character of human rights, Powell suggests, we can challenge inequality and begin to identify the ways in which top-down narratives of human rights can reproduce inequality. He concludes by noting that, despite the probable prevalence of top-down over bottom-up narratives, the CMHR will inevitably be a site of contestation over the relationship among the state, the people, and the concept of human rights.

A. Dirk Moses raises similar concerns in his chapter. Contextualizing the CMHR within a broader examination of the tensions inherent in contemporary neoliberal discourse, Moses critiques the deep resistance in countries such as Canada to recognizing the contradiction between its founding on colonial violence, on the one hand, and its constructed national identity as a global human rights defender, on the other.

We agree that the CMHR is a crystallization of this tension. Its position as a concrete embodiment of this contradiction provides the museum with an opportunity to promote public conversation on the relationship between human rights violations in Canada and definitions of national identity. From a human rights perspective, one of Canada's most pressing tasks is to grapple with historical and contemporary violations against Indigenous peoples and to consider how this reality shapes its national image as a champion of human rights. Although museums do not have the prerogative to adjudicate crimes, be they homicide or genocide, they do have the responsibility to host difficult, sustained, and public conversations on these issues.

Such conversations must also keep in mind the kinds of illusions to which Petrasek refers. In an effort to avoid a reductive narrative of teleological betterment or a smug sense of complacency, our exhibits interpret the past through a critical rather than a memorial lens, pointing to the need for continued debate, understanding, and vigilance. Our objective is to examine the many different ways that human rights are expressed. As Powell notes, while some characterize human rights as socially constructed, others view them as stable, fixed, and grounded in a shared human nature. Recognizing the spectrum of views between these poles, the CMHR's role is to examine these various perspectives without endorsing any single definition of human rights. This emphasis on multiplicity and complexity can stimulate rich and honest public conversations on human rights.

Concluding the volume's second section, on the design of museum spaces, which also contains Karen Busby's thorough account of the evolution of ideas for specific gallery content, is the chapter by Adam Muller, Struan Sinclair, and Andrew Woolford, who examine the ways in which unconventional means of creating spaces for delivering museum content—metatextual, artistic, and digital—can create affective, sensory, and bodily encounters with difficult subject matter. They discuss the use of augmented and virtual realities within museum exhibits as means of creating "empathetic communities." The model that they study is immersive and performative, yet it is inevitably representational. Focusing specifically on Indian residential schools, the authors wonder how representational immersive technology can construct a space robust yet subtle enough to bridge gaps between one's own subject position and the subject positions of others who have experienced gross violations of their rights.

This volume's third section, "Curatorial Challenges," addresses the crucial ways in which curatorial methodologies—museological pedagogy, exhibition signs, community-based research, non-textual curation, and digital technology—shape our ability to learn from difficult subject matter. In "Curatorial Practice and Learning from Difficult Knowledge," Angela Failler and Roger Simon examine the various ways in which curatorial frameworks shape not just what but also how visitors learn in museum spaces. Eschewing more conventional forms of museological pedagogy, in which knowledge is conceptualized as flowing unidirectionally from expert curators to uninformed visitors, they propose multidirectional and participatory models. Failler and Simon hope that CMHR pedagogies de-centre curatorial authority and create a kind of shared space within which meaning is constantly negotiated. Positing a form of knowing premised on multiple possibilities of interpretation grounded in Jacques Rancière's concept of "dissensus," they seek to challenge authoritarian and authoritative forms of meaning making.

In her consideration of how difficult subject matter can be exhibited in public institutions, Mary Reid reminds us that our techniques of framing, such as exhibition signage, shape and give meaning to the stories being examined. Focusing on warning labels, text panels, photo captions, and artifact labels, Reid suggests that content within museums cannot be presented in neutral or objective ways but is inevitably subject to interpretation. She concludes that a human rights museum cannot expect to provide a safe or comfortable experience and should instead embrace the discomfort involved in learning from stories of abuse and violation.

Armando Perla's chapter speaks to the many ways in which complex human rights issues can be integrated and synthesized into the spaces of a museum. Collaborating with migrant workers, unionists, and activists, Perla combined individual experiences and stories with a broader discussion of national and international human rights instruments. Through written text, artifacts, built installations, and filmed interviews, the exhibit highlights the contradictions between law and practice and between rhetoric and real-life experience.

The curatorial methodologies outlined by Failler and Simon, Reid, and Perla, respectively, summarize many issues currently debated by museologists seeking to reconceptualize conventional models of teaching and learning in museums. They also raise issues familiar to those of us who have worked on the CMHR's exhibits and programs. Many of these conversations consider how to share authority in message making, articulating a vision of museums as collaborative co-participants in active, dialogic forms of mutual engagement. Still, as the authors remind us, the process of creating exhibits is deeply fraught with political and cultural concerns, illustrating the ways in which power and privilege structure not just which stories are told but also how they are told.

For her part, Jennifer Carter provides a high-level overview of the rise of human rights–based museums in an international context. Pointing to this phenomenon as evidence of museums' changing social and political roles, from preservationist-oriented repositories of collections to active, innovative organizations promoting social justice and human rights, Carter believes that such museums can foster the kinds of museological and curatorial frameworks based on multiplicity and shared authority discussed by several authors in this volume.

The chapters in the final section, "Parallels and Obligations," examine case studies of museums around the world, focusing specifically on the responsibilities of such institutions toward their publics. Stephan Jaeger's, Amanda Grzyb's, Jorge Nállim's, and George Jacob's chapters consider how museums other than the CMHR have dealt with issues such as genocide and memorialization in their attempts to engage a wide variety of audiences. Jaeger uses the Military History Museum of the German Armed Forces in Dresden as a case study that analyzes how exhibits on violence, war, conflict, and genocide benefit from balancing a focus on historical specificity and situatedness with recognition of broader themes of universality, exhibiting past, present, and future in a way that avoids both parochialism and essentialism. Studying several memorial museums around the world, Grzyb focuses specifically on how they can encourage a "call to action" through interactivity and a framework of comparative genocide. Nállim's study of state terror and memory asks how representations of past traumas and struggles shape contemporary articulations of national identity and national history, emphasizing how efforts to link past and present are often structured by broader political concerns. In his discussion of the Khalsa Heritage Centre's efforts to connect with non-literate visitors, Jacob emphasizes the need for ideas-based museums to adapt to their local social and cultural milieus.

The capacity to encourage debate on the relationship among the state, the people, and the meaning of human rights, including the ability to grapple with contradictions between violence and national identity, is a sign of health within a democratic polity. Museums can play a crucial role in facilitating these kinds of debates, providing space for those whose experiences have typically been marginalized or erased. Our goal is to make visible that which is often invisible—the dignity within all people, the violations done in secret, the moments of resistance, and the yearning for freedom and fairness that can challenge hegemonic forms of national memory.

The concluding chapter, by Ruth Phillips, traces the tenuous relationship between federal cultural organizations and Indigenous communities in Canada over the past several decades. Phillips argues that, while some positive steps have been taken in developing collaborative, respectful programs, efforts to decolonize museum practices have been curtailed in recent years because of government cutbacks and restructuring. The CMHR, she suggests, can resume the work of decolonization and resist broader trends toward the celebration of settler colonial histories, but it has yet to demonstrate a meaningful politics of redress and reconciliation with Indigenous peoples.

Cognizant of the kinds of debates that Phillips outlines, the CMHR has attempted to develop a decolonized approach in its exhibits and programs. Indigenous content is not relegated to a single gallery but is included in all ten of the museum's galleries. The Indigenous Perspectives gallery, which contains stories and perspectives on First Nations, Métis, and Inuit concepts of rights and responsibilities, uses film, art, oral history, and other media to examine the culturally and historically specific knowledges that have sustained Indigenous nations for generations. Taken together, the Indigenous material across the galleries explores violation, dispossession, and abuse, along with resistance, cultural renewal, and the continuing relevance of traditional knowledge. These exhibits were developed in collaboration with Indigenous elders, scholars, artists, and other individuals and communities. The integration of these stories throughout the CMHR illustrates how colonialism and reconciliation involve all, Indigenous and non-Indigenous. Finally, care has also been taken not to render Indigenous peoples passive victims of colonial violence; agency, struggle, and resistance are also emphasized. By incorporating such methodologies into our practices, we hope to begin articulating a decolonizing politics of reconciliation between Indigenous and settler communities, recognizing that there is still much to be done.

CONCLUSION

As the editors note in their introduction, *The Idea of a Human Rights Museum* is "oriented to the 'idea' of the CMHR rather than its instantiation." Now that the CMHR has opened its doors to the world, it is more than an idea. It is already an active participant in national and international human rights conversations, and its role in encouraging reflection and dialogue on a variety of issues will continue to grow in the coming years. The CMHR's exhibits and program activities will continuously adapt to the changing human rights landscape. Its curatorial emphasis on personal stories, told through a variety of media channels, is an approach well suited to the ongoing evolution of human rights. Rigorous, relevant, and critical scholarship will be a significant means through which the CMHR continues to engage with human rights issues.

The important questions raised by the contributors to this volume will not easily be resolved—nor should they be. As a platform for reflection and dialogue on subjects that are inevitably contentious, the CMHR will play an ongoing role in facilitating conversations on human rights issues nationally and internationally. As many of the contributors note, the objective is not to reach an easy consensus on human rights issues. Rather, it is to provide public space for a productive exchange of diverse viewpoints on human rights. One of the most important obligations that the museum shoulders is to translate scholarly discourses on human rights and representation for public engagement, a difficult and ongoing task.

As we noted above, the CMHR's exhibits, collections, and programs are based on stories. Personal experiences, individual struggles, group and community initiatives—all have been central to the research and exhibit content development process over the past number of years. The CMHR's exhibits tell the stories of many peoples typically underrepresented in conventional historical narratives in an effort to critique the very process of marginalization. The stories are not always positive. Many speak of suffering, violence, and violation; others suggest that, despite hardship, an element of hope is often crucial in taking courageous action and mobilizing to advance human rights. As the editors of this volume note, the theme of hope, as a narrative that can inspire change, is a common thread running through the museum's stories. In the context of concrete lived experiences, this thread does not collapse into triumphalism or smug nationalism.

The CMHR's use of storytelling as a museological approach has promise to become an empowering, affective, and liberating way to share knowledge and learn from individual and community experiences. Storytelling resonates with human rights in several ways. It is guided by principles of democracy, inclusivity, fairness, respect, and justice, and it is a powerful way to cultivate affect, empathy, identification, learning, and stimulation, in ways that both settle and unsettle, comfort and discomfort. This kind of dialogic or polyphonic methodology, to use Russian literary theorist Mikhail Bakhtin's terminology, allows for the expression of multiplicity without reducing diverse voices to a singular narrative.[3]

Although storytelling, in one sense, is a profoundly personal act, it is also a collective act that mediates between subjective experience and intersubjective encounter. As Hannah Arendt reminds us, storytelling is a bridge between individuals and communities, allowing people to participate in broader social and political discourses, challenging mainstream narratives, and fostering mutual recognition and reconciliation.[4] We hope that it will be an effective means of furthering our museum's mandate to enhance the public's understanding of human rights, to promote respect for others, and to encourage reflection and dialogue.

NOTES

1   http://laws-lois.justice.gc.ca/eng/acts/M-13.4/page-6.html#docCont.

2   Ibid.

3   Mikhail Bakhtin, *Problems of Dostoevsky's Poetics*, ed. and trans. Caryl Emerson (Minneapolis: University of Minnesota Press, 1984).

4   Hannah Arendt, *The Human Condition*, 2nd ed., introduction by Margaret Canovan (Chicago: University of Chicago Press, 1958).

ACKNOWLEDGEMENTS

We would like to thank Helen Fallding and Heather Bowers of the Centre for Human Rights Research (CHRR) at the University of Manitoba for organizing the workshop that led to the publication of this book. That workshop was funded by the CHRR; the Centre for Professional and Applied Ethics; the Mauro Centre for Peace and Justice; the Faculties of Arts, Law, and Graduate Studies; the criminology and social justice research coordinator; and the Departments of Sociology, English, Film and Theatre, Philosophy, Political Studies, German and Slavic Studies, and History. In addition, we greatly appreciate the efforts of Chandra Erlendson, Heather Jusufovic, and Clint Curle in helping to arrange a tour of the Canadian Museum for Human Rights building for our workshop participants as well as Clint's and Maureen Fitzhenry's participation in the workshop.

Helen Fallding provided generous editorial advice during the process of bringing this book to life, and we wish to thank research assistants Katelin Neufeld, Danielle Barchyn, and Alex McMillan, who compiled and edited the collection's bibliography. We are also grateful for the assistance and guidance offered by the staff at the University of Manitoba Press, including David Carr, Glenn Bergen, and Jill McConkey. As well, the two anonymous reviewers for the press contributed valuable constructive suggestions that improved the manuscript greatly. Finally, we thank the CHRR for funding a portion of the publication costs.

BIBLIOGRAPHY

UNKNOWN OR CORPORATE AUTHORSHIP

"Aboriginal Arts Office: About the Aboriginal Arts Office." Canada Council for the Arts. http://canadacouncil.ca/en/aboriginal-arts-office/about-the-aao.

"About Us." Tribute to Liberty. http://www.tributetoliberty.ca/aboutus.html.

"Access Our Resources: Where Are the Children? Healing the Legacy of Residential Schools, the Exhibition Catalogue." Legacy of Hope Foundation, 2003. http://www.legacyofhope.ca/home.

"Agreement for the Employment in Canada of Commonwealth Caribbean Seasonal Agricultural Workers in British Columbia—2013." Employment and Social Development Canada. http://www.esdc.gc.ca/eng/jobs/foreign_workers/agriculture/seasonal/saw-pcc2013_bc.pdf.

"Architecture and Landscape: The Architectural Design Process." National Museum of the American Indian. http://nmai.si.edu/visit/washington/architecture-landscape/.

"Archived—Our Voices, Our Stories: First Nations, Métis, and Inuit Stories." Library and Archives Canada. Last modified May 2010. http://www.collectionscanada.gc.ca/stories/index-e.html.

"Arts and Culture: Museum Assistance Program, Eligible Applicants and Projects, Aboriginal Heritage." Government of Canada. Last modified September 2014. http://www.pch.gc.ca/eng/1268597502197#a2.

Black Rod. "The CMHR Stirs Up Hatred and Divisiveness. And It's Not Even Open." 8 August 2013. http://blackrod.blogspot.ca/2013/08/the-cmhr-stirs-up-hatred-and.html.

Canada. Department of Canadian Heritage. *Report to the Minister of Canadian Heritage on the Canadian Museum for Human Rights*. Ottawa: Department of Canadian Heritage, 1998. Catalogue No. CH4-133/2008E-PDF.

"Canadian Heritage: Cultural Diversity and Rights, Aboriginal Peoples' Program." Government of Canada. Last modified January 2014. http://www.pch.gc.ca/eng/1288012444767.

Canadian Museum for Human Rights. "2013 Annual Public Meeting." 10 December 2013. https://humanrights.ca/about/governance-and-corporate-reports/annual-public-meetings/past-annual-public-meetings.

"Canadian Museum for Human Rights to Open Exhibit on Armenian Genocide." PanARMENIAN.Net, 10 April 2013. http://www.panarmenian.net/eng/news/153580/.

"The Canadian Museum for Human Rights Responds to Misconceptions in the Media." Canadian Museum for Human Rights, 6 January 2011. http://www.humanrightsmuseum.ca/about-museum/news/canadian-museum-human-rights-responds-misconceptions-media.

"Canadians Support Museum." *Winnipeg Free Press,* 3 February 2012, A10.

"Case No 2704, Interim Report by the Committee on Freedom of Association of the ILO, November 2010." http://oppenheimer.mcgill.ca/IMG/pdf/Report_ILO_CaseNo274_UFCW_Canada__November_2010_1_.pdf.

"CEO Denies Any Political Interference in Content of Winnipeg-Based Museum." CBC News, 30 November 2012. http://www.cbc.ca/news/canada/manitoba/human-rights-museum-staff-leave-amid-interference-allegations-1.1131274.

"CMHR to Commission Inaugural Film on Ukrainian Genocide." Canadian Museum for Human Rights, 20 December 2012. https://humanrights.ca/about-museum/news/cmhr-commission-inaugural-film-ukrainian-genocide.

"CMHR Issues Call for Photos, Stories on Aboriginal Child Welfare." Canadian Museum for Human Rights, 7 May 2013. http://www.museumforhumanrights.ca/about-museum/news/cmhr-issues-call-photos-stories-aboriginal-child-welfare.

"CMHR Shines Light on 'Stalin's Secret Files' from Ukrainian Genocide." Canadian Museum for Human Rights, 15 November 2012. https://humanrights.ca/about-museum/news/cmhr-shines-light-stalins-secret-files-ukrainian-genocide.

"Code of Conduct: Values and Ethics." Library and Archives Canada, March 2013. clagov.wordpress.com/2013/03/15/lac-canada-code-of-conduct.

"Content Advisory Committee Final Report to the Canadian Museum for Human Rights." Canadian Museum for Human Rights Content Advisory Committee, 25 May 2010. http://publications.gc.ca/collections/collection_2011/mcdp-cmhr/NM104-1-2010-eng.pdf.

"Creation of Israel Must Be Included in New Museum Says B'nai B'rith Canada." B'nai B'rith Canada, 7 August 2013. http://www.bnaibrith.ca/creation-of-israel-must-be-included-in-new-museum-says-bnai-brith-canada.

"Discover the Collection: Aboriginal Peoples, Virtual Exhibitions." Library and Archives Canada. Last modified June 2013. http://www.collectionscanada.gc.ca/aboriginal-peoples/index-e.html#exhibitions.

"Dr. Catherine Chatterley Interviews CMHR about Contents of Holocaust Gallery." *Winnipeg Jewish Review*, 3 April 2013.

"Editorial: Shoah's Uniqueness." *Jewish Independent*, 16 December 2011.

"Escuela de Mecánica de la Armada (ESMA)." Instituto Espacio para la Memoria. http://www.institutomemoria.org.ar/exccd/esma.html.

"Espacio Memoria y Derechos Humanos (ex-ESMA)." http://www.espaciomemoria.ar/espacio-hoy.php.

"First Annual Report 2008–2009." Canadian Museum for Human Rights. https://humanrights.ca/sites/default/files/2008_09_Annual_Report_English.pdf.

First Nations Child and Family Caring Society of Canada et al. v. Attorney General of Canada (for the Minister of Indian and Northern Affairs Canada), 2012 CHRT 17. Canadian Legal Information Institute, 23 August 2012. http://canlii.ca/en/ca/chrt/doc/2012/2012chrt17/2012chrt17.html.

Fraser v. Ontario (Attorney General), 2011 SCC 20 [29 April 2011]. http://scc-csc.lexum.com/scc-csc/scc-csc/en/item/7934/index.do.

Gallery Profiles. Canadian Museum for Human Rights, 12 September 2012. http://s3.documentcloud.org/documents/609321/canadian-museum-for-human-rights-gallery-profiles.pdf.

"General Assembly Adopts Declaration on Rights of Indigenous Peoples: 'Major Step Forward' towards Human Rights for All, Says President." United Nations, press release, 13 September 2007. http://www.un.org/News/Press/docs/2007/ga10612.doc.htm.

"Help Write the Story of the Canadian Museum for Human Rights—by Sharing Yours. Empower Yourself and Others to Change Their Thoughts and Actions and Make the World a Better Place." Canadian Museum for Human Rights. http://share.humanrightsmuseum.ca/.

"Heritage Minister James Moore Visits News Café." *Winnipeg Free Press,* 11 September 2012. http://www.winnipegfreepress.com/breakingnews/Heritage-Minister-James-Moore-dropping-into-News-Cafe-Wednesday--169332836.html.

"The Holocaust Memorial Day Act." Government of Manitoba. Last modified 12 September 2014. http://web2.gov.mb.ca/laws/statutes/ccsm/h068e.php.

"Home, About Us: What Are Sites of Conscience?" International Coalition of Sites of Conscience. http://www.sitesofconscience.org/about-us/#section1.

"How Will the Canadian Museum for Human Rights Represent Genocide?" *Zoryan Institute News,* 17 February 2010. http://www.zoryaninstitute.org/news.html.

"Human Resources and Skills Development Canada." Employment and Social Development Canada. http://www.hrsdc.gc.ca/eng/workplaceskills/foreign_workers/sawp/description.shtml.

"Human Rights Education." UNESCO. http://www.unesco.org/new/en/education/themes/leading-the-international-agenda/human-rights-education/.

"Human Rights Museum Board behind Push for 'Positive' Stories: Canadian Museum Manager's Letter Indicates Desire for 'Optimistic Tone' for Peace Gallery." CBC News, 3 December 2012. http://www.cbc.ca/news/canada/manitoba/human-rights-museum-board-behind-push-for-positive-stories-1.1205264.

"Human Rights Museum Pushes 'Positive' Stories." CBC News, 3 December 2012. http://www.cbc.ca/player/Embedded-Only/News/Canada/Manitoba/ID/2312327648/.

"Human Rights Museum Seeks Child Welfare Materials: Canadian Museum for Human Rights Calls for Materials from First Nations on 'Sixties Scoop.'" CBC News, 7 May 2013. http://www.cbc.ca/news/canada/manitoba/story/2013/05/07/mb-cmhr-sixties-scoop-call-winnipeg.html.

"Human Rights Museum Sparks Debate over Term 'Genocide.'" CBC News, 26 July 2013. http://www.cbc.ca/1.1400154 and http://www.cbc.ca/news/canada/manitoba/story/2013/07/26/mb-cmhr-aboriginal-genocide-debate winnipeg.html.

"Human Rights Museum Staff Leave amid Interference Allegations: CEO Denies Any Political Interference in Content of Winnipeg-Based Museum." CBC News, 30 November 2012. http://www.cbc.ca/news/canada/manitoba/human-rights-museum-staff-leave-amid-interference-allegations-1.1131274.

"Human Security Report 2009/2010: The Causes of Peace and the Shrinking Costs of War." Human Security Report Project, 2 December 2010. http://www.hsrgroup.org/human-security-reports/20092010/overview.aspx.

"Indian Residential Schools Settlement—Official Court Website." http://www.residentialschool-settlement.ca/english.html.

"Interpretation at the Minneapolis Institute of Arts: Policy and Practice." Minneapolis Institute of Arts. http://www.museum-ed.org/wp-content/uploads/2010/08/mia_interpreta-tion_museum-ed.pdf.

"Irael [sic] Asper Announces Plans to Create Canadian Museum for Human Rights." Asper Foundation, 17 April 2003. http://www.friendsofcmhr.com/news_room/news_releases/index.cfm?id=23.

Justicia for Migrant Workers. http://www.justicia4migrantworkers.org.

Lord Cultural Services. "The Canadian Museum for Human Rights." http://www.lord.ca/
  project-pages/projects/regions/north-america-canada/project/canadian-museum-for-
  human-rights?back=%2Fproject-pages%2Fprojects%2Fregions%2Fnorth-america-canad
  a%3Fsb%3Ddate%26sd%3Ddesc%26.

"Mandate and Values." Canadian Museum for Human Rights. http://museumforhumanrights.
  ca/about-museum/mandate-and-values.

"Memoria en construcción: Cómo será el espacio que se está montando en la ESMA." *Página* 12
  (2008). http://www.pagina12.com.ar/diario/elpais/1-101176-2008-03-23.html.

"Mission Statement." United States Holocaust Memorial Museum. http://www.ushmm.org/
  museum/mission/.

"Museum Practice: Signage." Museums Association. http://www.museumsassociation.org/
  museum-practice/signage.

"Never Again Report of CONADEP." National Commission on the Disappearance of Persons,
  1984. http://www.desaparecidos.org/nuncamas/web/english/library/nevagain/nev-
  again_001.htm.

"Ottawa Fights Charge It Discriminates against Aboriginal Kids." CBC News, 25 February 2013.
  http://www.cbc.ca/news/politics/story/2013/02/24/pol-canadian-human-rights-tribunal-
  hearings-first-nations-children.html.

"Parental Advisory." Canadian Museum for Human Rights. http://museumforhumanrights.ca/
  legal-notices.

*Preserving Aboriginal Heritage, Technical and Traditional Approaches: Proceedings of a Confer-
  ence Symposium 2007.* Canadian Conservation Institute. Ottawa: Canadian Heritage,
  2008.

"Prime Minister Harper Receives Saul Hayes Human Rights Award." Prime Minister of Canada,
  31 May 2009. http://www.pm.gc.ca/eng/media.asp?id=2603.

"Purpose, Capacity, and Powers of the Canadian Museum for Human Rights." Justice Laws.
  http://laws-lois.justice.gc.ca/eng/acts/M-13.4/page-6.html#docConnormant.

*Québec (Commission des droits de la personne et des droits de la jeunesse) v. Centre maraîcher
  Eugène Guinois JR Inc.,* 2005-779 (TDPQ). http://caselaw.canada.globe24h.com/0/0/que-
  bec/human-rights-tribunal/2005/04/14/quebec-commission-des-droits-de-la-personne-
  et-des-droits-de-la-jeunesse-v-centre-maraicher-eugene-guinois-jr-inc-2005-11754-qc-
  tdp.shtml.

"Queen Unveils 'Magna Carta' Cornerstone for Canada Museum." *Independent,* 5 July 2010.
  http://www.independent.co.uk/arts-entertainment/art/queen-unveils-magna-carta-
  cornerstone-for-canada-museum-2019238.html.

"Raising Awareness of the Legacy of Residential Schools: Projects—Where Are the Children?"
  Legacy of Hope Foundation. http://www.legacyofhope.ca/projects/where-are-the-chil-
  dren.

"Report in Which the Committee Requests to Be Kept Informed of Development, Report No.
  363, Case No. 2704 (Canada), March 2012." International Labour Organization. http://
  www.ilo.org/dyn/normlex/en/f?p=1000:50002:0::NO::P50002_COMPLAINT_TEXT_
  ID:3057155.

*Report of the Royal Commission on Aboriginal Peoples: Volume 3, Gathering Strength: 6, Arts
  and Heritage.* Indian and Northern Affairs Canada. Last modified 8 February 2006. http://
  www.collectionscanada.gc.ca/webarchives/20071124060708/http://www.ainc-inac.gc.ca/
  ch/rcap/sg/si1_e.html#Volume%203.

Report of the Status of Migrant Workers in Canada. Toronto: United Food and Commercial Workers Canada, 2011.

Report to the Minister of Canadian Heritage on the Canadian Museum for Human Rights. Ottawa: Library and Archives Canada, 2008. http://www.uwinnipeg.ca/csrg/docs/GC-Report-to-the-Minister-of-Canadian-Heritage-on-the-CMHR.pdf.

"Research Strategy: The Canadian Museum of History and the Canadian War Museum." 15 July 2013. Canadian Museum of History. http://www.historymuseum.ca/research-and-collections/files/2013/07/research-strategy.pdf.

The Responsibility to Protect: Report of the International Commission on Intervention and State Sovereignty. Ottawa: International Development Research Centre, 2001.

"Rights Museum Facing Heat over Foreign Goods." Global News, 24 October 2012. http://www.globalwinnipeg.com/exclusive+rights+museum+facing+heat+over+foreign+goods/6442740366/story.html.

"Rights Museum Will Be 'Green': Spokeswoman." *Winnipeg Free Press,* 13 November 2008, A6.

"Rwanda." World Bank. http://www.worldbank.org/en/country/rwanda/overview.

"Section 21—Advice/Recommendations." Office of the Information Commissioner of Canada. http://www.oic-ci.gc.ca/eng/inv_inv-gui-ati_gui-inv-ati_section_21.aspx.

"Share Your Story." Canadian Museum for Human Rights. http://share.humanrightsmuseum.ca.

"Speech Delivered by Mr. Patrick O'Reilly to the Rotary International District #5550 World Peace Partners, Tuesday April 7, 2009." Canadian Museum for Human Rights. http://museumforhumanrights.ca/about-museum/speeches-our-museum-leaders/speech-delivered-mr-patrick-o-reilly-rotary-international-d - .UoJ7L-L29Ew.

"Speech Delivered by President and CEO Stuart Murray at the CMHR's First Annual Public Meeting, December 6, 2011." Canadian Museum for Human Rights. https://humanrights.ca/about-museum/news/speech-delivered-cmhr-president-and-ceo-stuart-murray-cmhrs-2012-annual-public.

"Speech Delivered by President and CEO Stuart Murray at the Memorial in Commemoration of Famines' Victims in Ukraine, July 3, 2012, Kyiv, Ukraine." Canadian Museum for Human Rights. https://humanrights.ca/about-museum/news/speech-delivered-president-and-ceo-stuart-murray-memorial-commemoration-famines.

"Speech Delivered by President and CEO Stuart Murray to University of Manitoba 'Thinking about Ideas Museums' Speaker Series, September 9, 2011." Canadian Museum for Human Rights. https://humanrights.ca/about-museum/news/speech-delivered-president-and-ceo-stuart-murray-university-manitoba-thinking.

"Statement from the Canadian Museum for Human Rights (CMHR) in Relation to Dr. Strong-Boag Blog on International Women's Day." Canadian Museum for Human Rights, 11 March 2014. https://humanrights.ca/about-museum/news/statement-canadian-museum-human-rights-cmhr-relation-dr-strong-boag-blog#.U6iqX_ldV8E.

"Statement of Reconciliation." http://www.aadnc-aandc.gc.ca/eng/1100100015725/1100100015726.

"The Status of Migrant Farm Workers in Canada, 2010–2011." United Food and Commercial Workers Canada. http://www.ufcw.ca/templates/ufcwcanada/images/awa/publications/UFCW-Status_of_MF_Workers_2010-2011_EN.pdf.

"Summary of Corporate Plan and Operating and Capital Budgets 2010–2011 to 2014–2015." Canadian Museum for Human Rights. https://humanrights.ca/sites/default/files/corporate_plan_2010-2011_to_2014-2015_en.pdf.

"Timeline on Library and Archives Canada Services Decline after 2004." Ex Libris Association. Last modified May 2014. http://exlibris.pbworks.com/w/page/63815458/Timeline%20 on%20Library%20and%20Archives%20Canada%20Service%20Decline%20after%202004.

Towards a New Beginning: A Foundational Report for a Strategy to Revitalize First Nations, Inuit, and Métis Cultures: Report to the Minister of Canadian Heritage by the Task Force on Aboriginal Languages and Cultures. Assembly of First Nations, June 2005. http://www.afn. ca/uploads/files/education2/towardanewbeginning.pdf.

"UCC Concerned over Content of Canadian Museum for Human Rights." Ukrainian Canadian Congress, 6 April 2013. http://www.ucc.ca/2013/04/06/ucc-concerned-over-content-of-canadian-museum-for-human-rights.

"UCC Welcomes Appointment of Dr. Lindy Ledohowski to Human Rights Museum Board." Ukrainian Canadian Congress, 18 March2011. http://www.ucc.ca/2011/03/18/ucc-welcomes-appointment-of-dr-lindy-ledohowski-to-human-rights-museum-board.

"Unique CMHR Theatre to Feature Immersive 'Surround' Technology." Canadian Museum for Human Rights, 10 December 2013. https://humanrights.ca/about-museum/news/unique-cmhr-theatre-feature-immersive-surround-technology.

United Nations Declaration on the Rights of Indigenous Peoples. United Nations, March 2008. http://www.un.org/esa/socdev/unpfii/documents/DRIPS_en.pdf.

"United States Holocaust Memorial Museum's New Exhibit From Memory to Action: Meeting the Challenge of Genocide Engages Visitors in Genocide Prevention Efforts." United States Holocaust Memorial Museum, 18 May 2009. http://www.ushmm.org/information/ press/press-releases/united-states-holocaust-memorial-museums-new-exhibit-from-memory-to-action-.

Universal Declaration of Human Rights. United Nations. http://www.un.org/en/documents/ udhr/.

"Vision 2020." Government of Rwanda. http://www.cdf.gov.rw/vup.html.

"Vote-Rigging Scandal Emerges." CBC Digital Archives. http://www.cbc.ca/archives/categories/ politics/provincial-territorial-politics/friendly-rivalries-manitoba-elections-since-1966/ vote-rigging-scandal-emerges.html.

"We Were So Far Away: The Inuit Experience of Residential Schools." Legacy of Hope Foundation, 2010. http://www.legacyofhope.ca/downloads/wwsfa.pdf.

"What Is Social Justice?" National Pro Bono Resource Centre, October 2011. https://wic041u. server-secure.com/vs155205_secure/CMS/files_cms/Occ_1_What Is Social Justice_FI-NAL.pdf.

"Yom ha-Shoah Holocaust Memorial Day Teacher's Guide." B'nai B'rith Canada. http://www. bnaibrith.ca/league/hh-teachers/guide00.html.

SINGLE- AND MULTI-AUTHORED WORKS

Abella, Irving, and Harold Troper. *None Is Too Many: Canada and the Jews of Europe 1933–1948.* Toronto: Lester and Orpen Dennys, 1983.

Adams, James. "Protest Grows over Holocaust 'Zone' in Canadian Museum for Human Rights." *Globe and Mail,* 14 February 2011. http://www.theglobeandmail.com/arts/protest-grows-over-holocaust-zone-in-canadian-museum-for-human-rights/article566190/.

Alembret, Bernadette. "A Bridge between Cultural Communicator and Curator." *Museum Journal UNESCO* 172, 4 (1991): 211–12.

Allen-Greil, D., and M. MacArthur. "Small Towns and Big Cities: How Museums Foster Community On-Line." In *Museums and the Web 2010: Proceedings*, edited by J. Trant and D. Bearman. Toronto: Archives and Museum Informatics, 2010.

Altmann, Susanne. "Militärhistorisches Museum Dresden: Kunst statt Militaria." *Art: Das Kunstmagazin*, 6 January 2012. http://www.art-magazin.de/kunst/47904/militaerhistorisches_museum_dresden/.

Améry, Jean. *At the Mind's Limits: Contemplations by a Survivor of Auschwitz and Its Realities.* Translated by Sidney Rosenfeld and Stella P. Rosenfeld. Bloomington: Indiana University Press, 1980.

———. *Radical Humanism: Selected Essays.* Translated by Sidney Rosenfeld and Stella P. Rosenfeld. Bloomington: Indiana University Press, 1984.

Ames, Michael. "How to Decorate a House: The Re-Negotiation of Cultural Representations at the University of British Columbia Museum of Anthropology." *Museum Anthropology* 22, 3 (1999): 41–51.

———. "The Liberation of Anthropology: A Rejoinder to Professor Trigger's 'A Present of Their Past?'" *Culture* 8, 1 (1988): 81–85.

Anaya, S. James, and Robert A. Williams. "The Protection of Indigenous Peoples' Rights over Lands and Natural Resources under the Inter-American Human Rights System." *Harvard Human Rights Journal* 14 (2001): 33–86.

Andermann, Jens. "Returning to the Site of Horror: On the Reclaiming of Clandestine Concentration Camps in Argentina." *Theory, Culture, and Society* 29 (2012): 76–98.

Andersen, Martin Edward. *Dossier Secreto: Argentina's Desaparecidos and the Myth of the "Dirty War."* Boulder, CO: Westview Press, 1993.

Andrusiak, Steve. "Letter to the Editor." *Windsor Star*, 25 April 2013.

Appadurai, A., and C.A. Beckenridge. *Museums Are Good to Think: Museums and Communities.* Edited by Ivan Karp, C.M. Kreamer, and S.D. Lavine. Washington, DC: Smithsonian Institution Press, 1992.

Arendt, Hannah. *Eichmann in Jerusalem: A Report on the Banality of Evil.* New York: Viking, 1968.

———. *The Human Condition.* 2nd ed. Chicago: University of Chicago Press, 1958.

———. *The Origins of Totalitarianism.* 1951; reprinted, New York: Schocken, 2004.

Ariew, Daniel. "Representing the Unrepresentable: The Traumatic Affect." Honours thesis, University of South Florida, 2011. http://honors.usf.edu/documents/Thesis/U35202931.pdf.

Arnoldi, Mary-Jo. *A Distorted Mirror: The Exhibition of Herbert Ward Collection of Africana: Museums and Communities.* Washington, DC: Smithsonian Institution Press, 1992.

Ashton, Paul, and Paula Hamilton. "'Unfinished Business': Public History in a Postcolonial Nation." In *Contested Histories in Public Space: Memory, Race, and Nation,* edited by Daniel J. Walkowitz and Lisa Maya Knauer. Durham, NC: Duke University Press, 2009.

Askenazi, Jacobo Dayán, Content Director at MMyT. Interview with the Author. 2 July 2013.

Asper, David. "CMHR Critics Should Back Off Gail." *Winnipeg Sun*, 11 April 2012. www.winnipegsun.com/2012/04/11/gail-not-demon-of-cmhr-asper.

Asper, Gail. "Lead by Example: A Family Motto and the Canadian Museum for Human Rights." *Think: The Lola Stein Institute Journal* 12 (2012): 14–15.

Bajovic, Mirjana. "Violent Video Game Playing, Moral Reasoning, and Attitudes towards Violence in Adolescents: Is There a Connection?" PhD diss., Brock University, 2012.

Bakhtin, Mikhail. *Problems of Dostoevsky's Poetics.* Edited and translated by Caryl Emerson. Minneapolis: University of Minnesota Press, 1984.

Bal, Mieke. "The Pain of Images." In *Beautiful Suffering: Photography and the Traffic in Pain,* edited by M. Reinhardt, H. Edwards, and E. Duganne. Chicago: University of Chicago Press, 2007.

Ball, Karyn, and Per Anders Rudling. "The Underbelly of Canadian Multiculturalism: Holocaust Obfuscation in the Debate about the Canadian Museum for Human Rights." *Holocaust Studies: A Journal of Culture and History* 20, 1 (2014).

Ball, Olivia, and Paul Gready. *The No-Nonsense Guide to Human Rights.* Oxford: New Internationalist Publications, 2006.

Barlow, Maude. "Harper Sells Canadian Human Rights to China." *Huffington Post,* 8 February 2012. http://www.huffingtonpost.ca/maude-barlow/harper-china-oil_b_1263034.html.

Barndt, Kerstin. "Layers of Time: Industrial Ruins and Exhibitionary Spaces." *PMLA* 125, 1 (2010): 134–41.

Barnes, Barry, David Bloor, and John Henry. *Scientific Knowledge: A Sociological Analysis.* Chicago: University of Chicago Press, 1996.

Barnsley, Paul. "We Can Do Better—Jewish Leader to Chiefs." *Windspeaker,* 1 August 2005.

Baron-Cohen, Simon. *The Science of Evil: On Empathy and the Origins of Cruelty.* New York: Basic Books, 2011.

Barrett, Jennifer. *Museums and the Public Sphere.* Malden, MA: Wiley-Blackwell, 2011.

Barta, Tony. "Relations of Genocide: Land and Lives in the Colonization of Australia." In *Genocide and the Modern Age: Etiology and Case Studies of Mass Death,* edited by Isidor Wallimann and Michael Dobkowski, 237–52. New York: Greenwood Press, 1987.

Barthes, Roland. *Camera Lucida: Reflections on Photography.* Translated by Richard Howard. New York: Hill and Wang, 1981.

———. *Image, Music, Text.* Translated by Stephen Heath. New York: Hill and Wang, 1977.

———. *Mythologies.* Translated by Annette Lavers. New York: Hill and Wang, 1972.

Basen, Ira. "A $310 M Battlefield/Rights and Wrongs." *Globe and Mail,* 20 August 2011, F1.

———. "Memory Becomes a Minefield at Canada's Museum for Human Rights." *Globe and Mail,* 20 August 2011.

Bauman, Zygmunt. *Modernity and the Holocaust.* Cambridge, UK: Polity, 1989.

Bell, Stewart. *Cold Terror: How Canada Nurtures and Exports Terrorism around the World.* Toronto: John Wiley and Sons, 2004.

Bellan, Bernie. "What's Happening with the Holocaust Gallery in the New Canadian Museum for Human Rights?" *Jewish Post and News,* 17 November 2010.

Bennett, Tony. *The Birth of the Museum: History, Theory, Politics.* New York: Routledge, 1995.

Berger, Peter, and Thomas Luckmann. *The Social Construction of Reality: A Treatise in the Sociology of Knowledge.* London: Penguin Books, 1966.

Bernard-Donals, Michael. "Synecdochic Memory at the United States Holocaust Memorial Museum." *College English* 44, 5 (2012): 417–36.

Bickford, Louis, and Amy Sodaro. "Remembering Yesterday to Protect Tomorrow: The Internationalization of a New Commemorative Paradigm." In *Memory and the Future:*

Transnational Politics, Ethics, and Society, edited by Yifat Gutman, Adam D. Brown, and Amy Sodaro. New York: Palgrave Macmillan, 2010.

Bitonti, Dan. "German-Canadian Group Assails Holocaust Exhibit; 'Saddens' CJC Head." *National Post,* 18 December 2010, A2.

Black, Edwin. *IBM and the Holocaust: The Strategic Alliance between Nazi Germany and America's Most Powerful Corporation.* New York: Crown Publishers, 2001.

Blake, Dale, Libby Martin, and Deborah Pelletier. "Report and Recommendations of the Consultation on Aboriginal Resources and Services." Library and Archives Canada, August 2003. https://www.collectionscanada.gc.ca/obj/020008/f2/020008-7000-e.pdf.

Bloor, David. *Knowledge and Social Imagery.* London: Routledge and Kegan Paul, 1976.

Bødker, S., and O.S. Iversen. "Staging a Professional Participatory Design Practice: Moving beyond the Initial Fascination of User Involvement." In *Proceedings of the Second Nordic Conference on Human-Computer Interaction,* 11–18. New York: ACM Press, 2001.

Bolton, Stephanie. "An Analysis of the Task Force on Museums and First Peoples: The Changing Representation of Aboriginal Histories in Museums." MA thesis, Concordia University, 2004.

Borland, Elizabeth. "The Mature Resistance of Argentina's Madres de Plaza de Mayo." In *Latin American Social Movements: Globalization, Democratization, and Transnational Networks,* edited by Hank Johnston and Paul Almeida, 115–30. Lanham, MD: Rowman and Littlefield, 2006.

Bozikovic, Alex. "Germany's First War Museum Since Fall of Berlin Wall Stirs Mixed Emotions." *Globe and Mail,* 23 February 2011.

Brady, Miranda J. "The Flexible Heterotopia: Indian Residential Schools and the Canadian Museum of Civilization." *Peace and Conflict: Journal of Peace Psychology* 19, 4 (2013): 408–20.

Brean, Joseph. "Critics Accuse the Conservative Party of 'Politicizing History' as National Museum Mandates Change." *National Post,* 30 July 2013. http://news.nationalpost.com/2013/07/30/critics-accuse-the-conservative-party-of-politicizing-history-as-national-museum-mandates-change/.

Britzman, Deborah P. *Lost Subjects, Contested Objects: Toward a Psychoanalytic Inquiry of Learning.* Albany: SUNY Press, 1998.

Brodbeck, Tom. "Bills Soaring at Rights Palace." *Winnipeg Sun,* 28 February 2011. www.winnipegsun.com/news/columnists/tom_brodbeck/2011/02/28/17446421.html.

Browning, Christopher. *The Path to Genocide: Essays on Launching the Final Solution.* Cambridge, UK: Cambridge University Press, 1992.

Brysk, Alison. *The Politics of Human Rights in Argentina: Protest, Change, and Democratization.* Stanford, CA: Stanford University Press, 1994.

Bunch, Lonnie. "The Gaigin Are Coming—the Gaigin Are Coming!" *Museum News, American Association of Museums* 73, 2 (1994): 32–35.

Byington, Judy. "Is There Government Cover-Up of Child Genocide and Mass Graves?" *Examiner,* 18 December 2013.

Cachia, F. "The Museum as a Medium for Cross Cultural Communication." *Museum Journal UNESCO* 153 (1987): 8–14.

Cameron, Fiona, and Lynda Kelly, eds. *Hot Topics, Public Culture, Museums.* Newcastle-upon-Tyne, UK: Cambridge Scholars, 2010.

Campbell, Colin. "Controversy over National Museum of Human Rights in Winnipeg." *Maclean's*, 6 December 2013. http://www.thecanadianencyclopedia.ca/en/article/controversy-over-national-museum-of-human-rights-in-winnipeg/.

Capasso, Verónica, and Melina Jean Jean. "Memoriales en la UNLP: Análisis de diversos casos de representación del pasado reciente en distintas unidades académicas." *Aletheia* 2, 4 (2012). http://www.aletheia.fahce.unlp.edu.ar/numeros/numero-4/articulos/memoriales-en-la-unlp.-analisis-de-diversos-casos-de-representacion-del-pasado-reciente-en-distintas-unidades-academicas/.

Carter, Jennifer. "Human Rights Museums and Pedagogies of Practice: The Museo de la Memoria y los Derechos Humanos." *Museum Management and Curatorship* 28, 3 (2013): 324–41.

Carter, Jennifer, and Jennifer Orange. "Contentious Terrain: Defining a Human Rights Museology." *Museum Management and Curatorship* 27, 2 (2012): 111–27.

Cassie, Angela. "Letter to Association of Manitoba Archaeologists." Association of Manitoba Archaeologists. http://www.assocmanarch.com/12.html.

———. "Letter to the Editor of the *Winnipeg Sun*." 10 January 2012. http://www.humanrights-museum.ca/about-museum/news/letter-editor-winnipeg-sun.

Cavazza, M., et al. 2005. "Intelligent Virtual Environments for Virtual Reality Art." *Computers and Graphics* 29 (2005): 852–61.

Chalk, Frank, Kyle Matthews, and Carla Barqueiro. *Mobilizing the Will to Intervene: Leadership to Prevent Mass Atrocities*. Montreal: McGill-Queen's University Press, 2010.

Chatterley, Catherine. "Canada's Struggle with Holocaust Memorialization: The War Museum Controversy, Ethnic Identity Politics, and the Canadian Museum for Human Rights." *Holocaust and Genocide Studies* (forthcoming 2015).

———. "A History of Israeli Apartheid Week." *National Post*, 3 March 2011.

———. "The War against the Holocaust." *Winnipeg Free Press*, 2 April 2011, A16.

Chatterley, Catherine, and Clint Curle. "Dr. Catherine Chatterley Interviews CMHR about Contents of Holocaust Gallery." *Winnipeg Jewish Review*, 3 April 2013. http://www.winnipegjewishreview.com/article_detail.cfm?id=3442&sec=2.

Child, Brenda J. *Boarding School Seasons: American Indian Families, 1900–1940*. Lincoln: University of Nebraska Press, 1998.

Chisvin, Sharon. "Local Institute to Combat Anti-Semitism." *Winnipeg Free Press*, 26 March 2011.

Cholewinski, Ryszard, Paul de Guchteneire, and Antoine Pecoud, eds. *Migration and Human Rights: The United Nations Convention on Migrant Worker's Rights*. Cambridge, UK: UNESCO Publishing and Cambridge University Press, 2009.

Ciolfi, L., and L. Bannon. "Designing Hybrid Places: Merging Interaction Design, Ubiquitous Technologies, and Geographies of the Museum Space." *CoDesign* 3, 3 (2007): 159–80.

Clegg, Stewart. "Bureaucracy, the Holocaust, and Techniques of Power at Work." *International Review of Management Studies* 20, 4 (2009): 326–47.

Cobb, Chris. "Fontaine Praises Bond of Jews and First Nations." *Winnipeg Free Press*, 23 June 2008.

Cohen, Roger. "The Suffering Olympics." *New York Times*, 30 January 2012.

Collins, Patricia Hill. *Black Feminist Thought: Knowledge, Consciousness, and the Politics of Empowerment*. London: Routledge, 2000.

Corrigan, Philip, and Derek Sayer. *The Great Arch: English State Formation as Cultural Revolution*. Oxford: Basil Blackwell, 1985.

Cotler, Irwin. "Universal Lessons of the Holocaust." *Times of Israel*, 5 April 2013. http://blogs. timesofisrael.com/the-holocaust-and-human-rights-universal-lessons-for-our-times.

Crooke, E. *Museums and Community: Ideas, Issues, and Challenges*. London: Routledge, 2007.

Cryderman, Kelly. "Jewish Groups Want Museum to Focus on Holocaust." *Ottawa Citizen*, 8 June 2000.

Crysler, C. "Violence and Empathy: National Museums and the Spectacle of Society." *Traditional Dwellings and Settlements Review* 17, 2 (2006): 19–38.

Culler, Jonathan. *On Deconstruction: Theory and Criticism after Structuralism*. Ithaca, NY: Cornell University Press, 1982.

Curle, Clint. "Education for Inclusive Pluralism: The Capacity of Museums and Sites of Conscience to Promote Human Rights." In *Ryerson University Conference on Prevention of Mass Atrocities*. http://iid.kislenko.com/wp-content/uploads/2013/02/Documents.pdf and http://www.ryerson.ca/news/media/General_Public/20130205_atrocitiesconference.html.

———. *Humanité: John Humphrey's Alternative Account of Human Rights*. Toronto: University of Toronto Press, 2007.

———. "Raising Awareness of Armenian Genocide." Canadian Museum for Human Rights, 2 April 2013. https://humanrights.ca/blog/raising-awareness-armenian-genocide.

Curthoys, Ann, and John Docker. "Genocide: Definitions, Questions, Settler-Colonies." *Aboriginal History* 25 (2001): 1–15.

Cywinski, Piotr. Interview with the Author. Auschwitz State Museum, June 2010.

Dan, Michael. "Seeking the Right Word for a History of Suffering." *Ottawa Citizen*, 9 April 2014.

Daschuk, James. "When Canada Used Hunger to Clear the West." *Globe and Mail*, 19 July 2013.

Dean, C. 2003. "Empathy, Pornography, and Suffering." *Differences: A Journal of Feminist Cultural Studies* 14, 1 (2003): 88–124.

———. *The Fragility of Empathy after the Holocaust*. Ithaca, NY: Cornell University Press, 2004.

de Souza e Silva, A. "From Cyber to Hybrid: Mobile Technologies as Interfaces of Hybrid Spaces." *Space and Culture* 9, 3 (2006): 261–78.

de Souza e Silva, A., and G. Delacruz. "Hybrid Reality Games Reframed: Potential Uses in Educational Contexts." *Games and Culture* 1, 3 (2006): 231–51.

Dhamoon, Rita Kaur. *Identity/Difference Politics: How Difference Is Produced and Why It Matters*. Vancouver: UBC Press, 2009.

Diamond, J. "Collaborative Multimedia." *Curator* 38, 3 (1995): 137–49.

Dison, M.E. "Taking Cultural Studies to the Streets." *Chronicle of Higher Education* 42, 20 (1996): A6.

Donnelly, Jack. "The Social Construction of International Human Rights." *Relaciones internacionales* 17 (2011): 1–30.

Doughty, Kristin. "Memorials, Human Rights, and Controversy in Post-Genocide Rwanda." *Anthropology News* (September 2011): 10.

Doyle, J., and M. Ward Doyle. "Mixing Social Glue with Brick and Mortar: Experiments Using the Mobile Web." In *Museums and the Web 2010: Proceedings*, edited by J. Trant and D. Bearman. Toronto: Archives and Museum Informatics, 2010.

Dudley, Sandra, and Kylie Message. *Museum Worlds: Advances in Research. Volume 1: 2013.* New York: Berghahn Books, 2013.

Duffy, Terence M. "Exhibiting Human Rights." *Peace Review* 12 (2000): 303–39.

———. "Museums of 'Human Suffering' and the Struggle for Human Rights." In *Museum Studies: An Anthology of Contexts,* edited by Bettina Messias Carbonell, 117–22. Chichester, UK: Blackwell Publishing, 2004.

Duitz, Mindy. "The Soul of a Museum: Commitment to the Community at Brooklyn Children's Museum." In *Museums and Communities: The Politics of Public Culture,* edited by Ivan Karp, Christine Mullen Kreamer, and Steven Levine, 242–61. Washington, DC: Smithsonian Institution Press, 1992.

Duncan, Carol. *Civilizing Rituals: Inside Public Art Museums.* New York: Routledge, 1995.

Duncan, Carol, and Alan Wallach. "The Universal Survey Museum." *Art History* 3, 4 (1980): 448–69.

Duranti, Marco. "The Human Rights Revolution and the Holocaust: Revisiting the Foundation Myth." *Journal of Genocide Research* 14, 2 (2012): 159–86.

Durkheim, Emile. *The Division of Labour in Society.* New York: Free Press, 1984.

———. *The Elementary Forms of Religious Life.* Translated by Karen E. Fields. New York: Free Press, 1995.

———. *Professional Ethics and Civic Morals.* London: Routledge, 1992.

———. "The Rules of Sociological Method." In *Durkheim: The Rules of Sociological Method and Selected Texts on Sociology and Its Method,* edited by Stephen Lukes, 31–166. New York: Free Press, 1982.

Elias, Norbert. *The Civilizing Process: The History of Manners and State Formation and Civilization.* Rev. ed. Translated by Edmund Jephcott. Oxford: Blackwell, 2000.

———. *Involvement and Detachment.* Oxford: Basil Blackwell, 1987.

———. *The Society of Individuals.* New York: Continuum, 2001.

Ellis, Clyde. *To Change Them Forever: Indian Education at Rainy Mountain Boarding School, 1893–1920.* Norman: University of Oklahoma Press, 1996.

Fanti, Kostas A., Eric Vanman, Christopher C. Henrich, and Marios N. Avraamides. "Desensitization to Media Violence over a Short Period of Time." *Aggressive Behavior* 35, 2 (2009): 179–87.

Faraday, Fay. "Made in Canada: How the Law Constructs Migrant Workers' Insecurity." Metcalf Foundation, September 2012. http://metcalffoundation.com/wp-content/uploads/2012/09/Made-in-Canada-Full-Report.pdf.

Farber, Bernie. "No Dogs and Jews Allowed." *Huffington Post,* 13 May 2012. http://www.huffingtonpost.ca/bernie-farber/human-rights-canada_b_1510399.html.

Fehr, Michael. "Art—Museum—Utopia: Five Themes on an Epistemological Construction Site." In *Thinking Utopia: Steps into Other Worlds,* edited by Jörn Rüsen, Michael Fehr, and Thomas W. Rieger, 169–73. New York: Berghahn Books, 2005.

———. "Zur Konstruktion von Geschichte mit dem Museum—fünf Thesen." In *Die Magie der Geschichte: Geschichtskultur und Museum,* edited by Martina Padberg and Martin Schmidt, 39–51. Bielefeld: Transcript, 2010.

Feld, Claudia. "La representación de los desaparecidos en la prensa de la transición: El show del horror." In *Los desaparecidos en la Argentina: Memorias, representaciones, e ideas*

(1983–2008), edited by Emilio Crenzel, 25–41. Buenos Aires: Editorial Biblos-Latitud Sur, 2010.

Ferguson, Mark. "Faculty Help Prepare Content for Canadian Museum of Human Rights." *University of Saskatchewan On Campus News,* 17 July 2009. http://news.usask.ca/archived_ocn/09-july-17/14.php.

Ferguson, T.J. "Improving the Quality of Archaeology in the United States through Consultation and Collaboration with Native Americans and Descendant Communities." In *Archaeology and Cultural Resource Management,* edited by L. Sebastian and W.D. Lipe, 169–93. Santa Fe: SAR Press, 2010.

First Nations Centre. *OCAP: Ownership, Control, Access, and Possession.* Sanctioned by the First Nations Information Governance Committee, Assembly of First Nations. Ottawa: National Aboriginal Health Organization, 2007.

Fleitlowitz, Marguerite. *Argentina: A Lexicon of Terror.* New York: Oxford University Press, 1998.

Fleming, David. "The Role of Human Rights Museums." Paper presented at the inaugural conference of the Federation of International Human Rights Museums, Liverpool, UK, 15–16 September 2010.

Fontaine, Phil, Michael Dan, and Bernie M. Farber. "A Canadian Genocide in Search of a Name." *Toronto Star,* 19 July 2013.

Fontaine, Phil, and Bernie Farber. "What Canada Committed against First Nations Was Genocide: The UN Should Recognize It." *Globe and Mail,* 14 October 2013.

Ford, Jenny. "Memo on Holodomor Fails to Quell Concern: Ukrainians Worry about Museum Space." *Winnipeg Free Press,* 10 July 2012.

Forst, Rainer. *The Right to Justification: Elements of a Constructivist Theory of Justice.* New York: Columbia University Press, 2012.

Foucault, Michel. "Confronting Governments: Human Rights." In *Power: Essential Works of Foucault 1954–1984, Volume 3,* edited by James D. Faubion, 474–75. New York: New Press, 2000.

———. *Discipline and Punish: The Birth of the Prison.* 2nd ed. Translated by Alan Sheridan. New York: Vintage Books, 1995.

———. *The History of Sexuality, Volume 1: An Introduction.* Translated by Robert Hurley. 1976; reprinted, New York: Vintage Books, 1990.

———. "The Moral and Social Experience of the Poles Can No Longer Be Obliterated." In *Power: Essential Works of Foucault 1954–1984, Volume 3,* edited by James D. Faubion, 465–73. 1994; reprinted, New York: New Press, 2000.

———. "Right of Death and Power over Life." In *The Foucault Reader,* edited by Paul Rabinow, 258–72. New York: Pantheon Books, 1984.

Freeman, Michael. *Human Rights: An Interdisciplinary Approach, Key Concepts.* Cambridge, UK: Polity, 2002.

Frenette, Yves. "Conscripting Canada's Past: The Harper Government and the Politics of Memory." *Canadian Journal of History* 49 (2014): 59–63.

Freud, Sigmund. "On the Teaching of Psycho-Analysis in Universities." In *Standard Edition of the Complete Works of Sigmund Freud,* Vol. 17, edited by J. Strachey, 159–74. London: Hogarth Press, 1918.

Funk, J., H. Baldacci, T. Pasold, and J. Baumgardner. "Violence Exposure in Real Life, Video Games, Television, Movies and the Internet: Is There Desensitization?" *Journal of Adolescence* 27 (2004): 23–39.

Galley, Valerie. "Reconciliation and the Revitalization of Indigenous Languages." In *Response, Responsibility, and Renewal: Canada's Truth and Reconciliation Journey,* edited by Gregory Younging, Jonathan Dewar, and Mike DeGagné, 241–260. Ottawa: Aboriginal Healing Foundation Research, 2009.

Galloway, Gloria. "Critics Press Ottawa to Recognize Wrongs against First Nations as Genocide." *Globe and Mail,* 30 July 2013.

Gatera, Honoré. Interview with the Author. Kigali Memorial Centre, September 2012.

Geertz, Clifford. *The Interpretation of Cultures.* New York: Basic Books-Harper Torch Books, 1973.

Gillam, Robin. *Hall of Mirrors: Museums and the Canadian Public.* Banff: Banff Centre Press, 2001.

Godfree, Tom. "Air India Flight 182 Tragedy 'Canada's Own 9/11.'" *Ottawa Sun,* 30 September 2012. http://www.ottawasun.com/2012/09/30/air-india-flight-182-tragedy-canadas-own-911.

Gordon-Walker, Caitlin. "Unity in Diversity: The Limits of Multicultural Nationalism and Museums." PhD diss., Trent University, 2013.

Gramsci, Antonio. *Selections from the Prison Notebooks.* Edited and translated by Quintin Hoare and Geoffrey Nowell Smith. New York: International Publishers, 1971.

Grandin, Greg. *Empire's Workshop: Latin America, the United States, and the Rise of the New Imperialism.* New York: Metropolitan Books, 2006.

Gray, John. "Delusions of Peace." *Prospect,* 21 September 2011. http://www.prospectmagazine.co.uk/2011/09/john-gray-steven-pinker-violence-review/.

Greenblatt, Stephen. "Resonance and Wonder." In *Exhibiting Cultures: The Poetics and Politics of Museum Display,* edited by Ivan Karp and Steven Lavine, 45–56. Washington, DC: Smithsonian Institution Press, 1991.

Greenwood, Clayton. "Muzzling Civil Servants: A Threat to Democracy." Presented at the Environmental Law Clinic, University of Victoria, 20 February 2013. www.elc.uvic.ca/press/documents/2012-03-04-Democracy-Watch_OIPLtr_Feb20.13-with-attachment.pdf.

Gregg, Benjamin. *Human Rights as Social Constructions.* Cambridge, UK: Cambridge University Press, 2011.

Gregory, Judith. "Scandinavian Approaches to Participatory Design." *International Journal of Engineering Education* 19, 1 (2003): 62–74.

Greitemeyer, Tobias, and Neil McLatchie. "Denying Humanness to Others: A Newly Discovered Mechanism by Which Violent Video Games Increase Aggressive Behavior." *Psychological Science* 22, 5 (2011): 251–55.

Grzyb, Amanda. "Mobility, Human Rights Activism, and International Intervention in Darfur." In *Mobilities, Knowledge, and Social Justice,* edited by Suzan Ilcan, 377–96. Montreal: McGill-Queen's University Press, 2013.

Guzman Bouvard, Marguerite. *Revolutionizing Motherhood: The Mothers of Plaza de Mayo.* Wilmington, DE: SR Books, 1994.

Haacke, Hans. "Museums, Managers of Consciousness." In *Institutional Critique: An Anthology of Artist's Writings,* edited by Alberro Alexander and Blake Stimson, 276–88. Cambridge, MA: MIT Press, 2009.

Hacking, Ian. *The Social Construction of What?* Cambridge, MA: Harvard University Press, 1999.

Hall, J. "Arming for the Culture Wars." *Museum News,* American Association of Museums (1992): 70–71.

Hall, Stuart. *Representation: Cultural Representations and Signifying Practice.* London: Sage Publications and the Open University, 1997.

Haney, C., W.C. Banks, and P.G. Zimbardo. "Interpersonal Dynamics in a Simulated Prison." *International Journal of Criminology and Penology* 1 (1973): 69–97.

Hanley, Wayne. "Letter to ILO Director-General Juan Somavia from UFCW Canada President Wayne Hanley, March 23, 2009." http://ufcw.ca/Theme/UFCW/files/ILO/ILO%20 PDF/LTR_%20J_%20Somavia_ILO%20re%20UFCW%20CAN%20vs_%20Ont_%20 Govt_%2003-09%20En.pdf.

Harker, John. "Human Security in Sudan: The Report of a Canadian Assessment Mission." Department of Foreign Affairs and International Trade, January 2000. http://publications. gc.ca/collections/Collection/E2-198-2000E.pdf.

Harris, M. *America Now: The Anthropology of a Changing Culture.* New York: Touchstone, 1981.

Henderson, Jennifer, and Pauline Wakeham. "Colonial Reckoning, National Reconciliation? Aboriginal Peoples and the Culture of Redress in Canada." *ESC: English Studies in Canada* 35, 1 (2009): 1–26.

———, eds. *Reconciling Canada: Critical Perspectives on the Culture of Redress.* Toronto: University of Toronto Press, 2013.

Hennebry, Jenna. "Permanently Temporary? Agricultural Migrant Workers and Their Integration in Canada." Institute for Research on Public Policy, 28 February 2012. http://irpp.org/research-studies/study-no26/.

Henteleff, Yude. "Critical Conversations with Canadians: The Work of the Content Advisory Committee." University of Manitoba, 5 January 2012. http://law.robsonhall.ca/compo nent/content/article/41-distinguished-visitors-2011-2012/753-yude-henteleff-critical-conversations-with-canadians-the-work-of-the-content-advisory-committee.

Hepburn, Bob. "Canadian Anti-Semitism Institute Aims to Fill Worldwide Void." *Toronto Star,* 9 May 2012.

Hepburn, Oksana Bashuk. "Canadian Museum for Human Rights: Right the Wrong." *Hill Times,* 16 April 2012.

Hicks, Ryan. "Palestinian-Canadians Feel Ignored in Human Rights Museum." CBC News, 4 March 2013. www.cbc.ca/news/canada/manitoba/story/2013/03/04/mb-human-rights-museum-documents-winnipeg.html.

Hilberg, Raul. *The Destruction of the European Jews.* Teaneck, NJ: Holmes and Meier, 1985.

Hillmer, Norman. "The Canadian War Museum and the Military Identity of an Unmilitary People." *Canadian Military History* 19, 3 (2010): 19–27.

Hirzy, E.C. "Excellence Equity: Education and Public Dimensions of Museums." American Association of Museums, 1992.

Hobsbawm, Eric. "The Invention of Traditions." In *The Invention of Traditions,* edited by Eric Hobsbawm and Terence Ranger, 1–14. New York: Cambridge University Press, 1983.

Hollengreen, Laura H. "Space, Seam, Scenario: The Many Operations of the Museum Label." Paper presented at the College Art Association Conference, Los Angeles, 24 June 2012.

Hooper-Greenhill, Eilean. "Changing Values in the Art Museum: Rethinking Communication and Learning." In *Museum Studies: An Anthology of Contexts,* edited by Bettina Messias Carbonell, 557–75. Chichester, UK: Blackwell Publishing, 2004.

——. *Museums and the Shaping of Knowledge.* London: Routledge, 1992.

Howard-Hassmann, Rhoda E. *Compassionate Canadians: Civic Leaders Discuss Human Rights.* Toronto: University of Toronto Press, 2003.

Hucker, John. "Antidiscrimination Laws in Canada: Human Rights Commissions and the Search for Equality." *Human Rights Quarterly* 19, 3 (1997): 547–71.

Hughes, Rachel. "The Abject Artefacts of Memory: Photographs from Cambodia's Genocide." *Media, Culture, and Society* 25 (2003): 23–43.

Humphrey, John. *Human Rights and the United Nations: A Great Adventure.* Dobbs Ferry, NY: Transnational, 1984.

Hunt, Lynn. *Inventing Human Rights: A History.* New York: W.W. Norton and Company, 2007.

Huyssen, Andreas. *Twilight Memories: Marking Time in a Culture of Amnesia.* New York: Routledge, 1995.

Igloliorte, Heather. "Inuit Artistic Expression as Cultural Resilience." In *Response, Responsibility, and Renewal: Canada's Truth and Reconciliation Journey,* edited by Gregory Younging, Jonathan Dewar, and Mike DeGagné, 311–12. Ottawa: Aboriginal Healing Foundation Research, 2009.

Ignatieff, Michael. *The Rights Revolution.* 2nd ed. Toronto: Anansi Press, 2007.

Irvin-Ericson, Douglas. "Genocide, 'Family of Mind,' and the Romantic Signature of Raphael Lemkin." *Journal of Genocide Research* 15, 3 (2013): 273–96.

Ishay, Micheline R. *The History of Human Rights: From Ancient Times to the Globalization Era.* Berkeley: University of California Press, 2008.

Itwaru, Arnold Harrichand, and Natasha Ksonzek. *Closed Entrances: Canadian Culture and Imperialism.* Toronto: TSAR Publications, 1994.

James, Stephen. *Universal Human Rights: Origins and Development.* New York: LFB Scholarly Publishing, 2007.

Janes, Robert R. *Museums in a Troubled World: Renewal, Irrelevance, or Collapse?* New York: Routledge, 2009.

Jarvie, Jenny. "Trigger Happy: The 'Trigger Warning' Has Spread from Blogs to College Classes. Can It Be Stopped?" *New Republic,* 3 March 2014. http://www.newrepublic.com/article/116842/trigger-warnings-have-spreadblogs-college-classes-thats-bad.

Jeanneret, Yves, Anneliese Depoux, Jason Luckerhoff, Valérie Vitalbo, and Daniel Jacobi. "Written Signage and Reading Practices of the Public in a Major Fine Arts Museum." *Museum Management and Curatorship* 25, 1 (2010): 53–67.

Jelin, Elizabeth. "Introducción." In *Las conmemoraciones: Las disputas en las fechas "in-felices,"* edited by Elizabeth Jelin, 1–8. Madrid: Siglo 21, 2002.

——. *State Repression and the Labors of Memory.* Minneapolis: University of Minnesota Press, 2003.

Jenkins, Richard. *Social Identity.* 3rd ed. London: Routledge, 2008.

Jessup, Lynda, and Shannon Bragg, eds. *On Aboriginal Representation in the Gallery.* Gatineau: Canadian Museum of Civilization, 2004.

Kafieh, James, and Canadians for Genocide Education. "Submission to the CMHR, Roundtable Discussion—Ottawa, June 11, 2009." Institute for Genocide. http://instituteforgenocide. org/en/wp-content/uploads/2012/03/CMHR-Submission-Nov-20-2009-2.pdf.

Kahneman, Daniel. *Thinking Fast and Slow*. New York: Doubleday, 2011.

Kaplan, E. Ann. *Trauma Culture: The Politics of Terror and Loss in Media and Literature*. New Brunswick, NJ: Rutgers University Press, 2005.

Kaufman, Jason Edward. "Renzo Piano: The World's Leading Builder of Museums." Architexturez Network, 2005. http://network.architexturez.net/pst/az-cf-162099-1081139197.

Kay, Jonathan. "Build It, and They Won't Come." *National Post*, 22 December 2011, A17.

Kazerne Dossin and Hermann Van Goethem, eds. *Holocaust and Human Rights: Kazerne Dossin Exhibition Catalogue*. Ghent: Vlaamse Overhead, 2012.

Kellow, Christine L., and Leslie Steeves. "The Role of Radio in the Rwandan Genocide." *Journal of Communication* 48, 3 (Summer 1998): 107–28.

Kelly, L. "Evaluation, Research, and Communities of Practice: Program Evaluation in Museums." *Archival Science* 4 (2004):45–69.

———. "How Web 2.0 Is Changing the Nature of Museum Work." *Curator: The Museum Journal* 53, 4 (2010): 405–10.

Kelly, L., and P. Gordon. "Developing a Community of Practice: Museums and Reconciliation in Australia." In *Museums, Society, Inequality*, edited by R. Sandell, 153–74. London: Routledge, 2002.

Kelly, Lynda. "The Impact of Social Media on Museum Practice." Paper presented at the National Palace Museum, Taipei, 20 October 2009. australianmuseum.net.au/Uploads/ Documents/9307/impact%20of%20social%20media%20on%20museum%20practice.pdf.

Kelman, Herbert, and Lee Hamilton. *Crimes of Obedience*. New Haven, CT: Yale University Press, 1989.

Kensing, Finn, and Jeanette Blomberg. "Participatory Design: Issues and Concerns." *Computer Supported Cooperative Work* 7 (1998): 167–85.

Kensing, Finn, Jesper Simonson, and Keld Bødker. "MUST—a Method for Participatory Design." In *Proceedings of the Fourth Biennial Conference on Participatory Design*, edited by J. Blomberg, F. Kensing, and E. Dykstra-Erickson, 129–40. Palo Alto, CA: Computer Professionals for Social Responsibility, 1996.

Kilb, Andreas. "Militärhistorisches Museum Dresden: Ein Minenschaf zieht in den Krieg." *Frankfurter Allgemeine Zeitung*, 13 October 2011. http://www.faz.net/aktuell/feuilleton/ militaerhistorisches-museum-dresden-ein-minenschaf-zieht-in-den-krieg-11492151. html/.

Kirbyson, Geoff. "Content Focus of Rights Museum." *Winnipeg Free Press*, 27 November 2011, A4.

Kives, Bartley. "Atrocities Gallery 'Too Much': Museum to Revamp Content: Ex Workers Disparage Move." *Winnipeg Free Press*, 30 November 2012. http://www.winnipegfreepress. com/local/atrocities-gallery-too-much-181497341.html.

———. "Canadian Museum for Human Rights Staff Exodus Tied to Content Change: Ex-Workers Blame Decision on 'Positive Stories.'" *Winnipeg Free Press*, 1 December 2012, A5.

———. "Censorship by CMHR Alleged: Blogger's Words about Tory Record on Women's Issues Pulled from Site." *Winnipeg Free Press*, 11 March 2014. www.winnipegfreepress.com/local/censorship-by-cmhr-alleged-249390631.html.

Koselleck, Reinhart. *Futures Past: On the Semantics of Historical Time*. 1979. Translated by Keith Tribe. New York: Columbia University Press, 2004.

Kovach, Margaret. *Indigenous Methodologies: Characteristics, Conversations, and Contexts*. Toronto: University of Toronto Press, 2009.

Krauß, M., and M. Bogen. "Conveying Cultural Heritage and Legacy with Innovative AR-Based Solutions." In *Museums and the Web 2010: Proceedings*, edited by J. Trant and D. Bearman. Toronto: Archives and Museum Informatics, 2010.

Kritsch, Ingrid, and Karen Wright-Fraser. "The Gwich'in Traditional Caribou Skin Clothing Project: Repatriating Traditional Knowledge and Skills." *InfoNorth* 22, 2 (2002): 205–13.

Krotz, Larry. "A Canadian Genocide?" *United Church Observer*, 23 March 2014.

Kuwanwisiwma, L.J. "Collaboration Means Equity, Respect, and Reciprocity: A Conversation about Archaeology and the Hopi Tribe." In *Collaboration in Archaeological Practice: Engaging Descendant Communities*, edited by C. Colwell-Chanthaphonh and T.J. Ferguson, 151–69. Walnut Creek, CA: AltaMira, 2008.

Labar, Wayne. "Can Social Media Transform the Exhibition Development Process? Cooking: The Exhibition—an Ongoing Case Study." In *Museums and the Web 2010: Proceedings*, edited by J. Trant and D. Bearman. Toronto: Archives and Museum Informatics, 2010. http://www.archimuse.com/mw2010/papers/labar/labar.html.

LaCapra, Dominick. *History and Its Limits: Human, Animal, Violence*. Ithaca, NY: Cornell University Press, 2009.

Lamberton, Ross. *Repression and Resistance: Canadian Human Rights Activists, 1930–1960*. Toronto: University of Toronto Press, 2005.

Lamontagne, Mireille. "Museum Archaeological Dig a Goldmine of Information." Canadian Museum for Human Rights Blog. https://humanrights.ca/blog/museum-archaeological-dig-goldmine-information.

Landsberg, Alison. "Memory, Empathy, and the Politics of Identification." *International Journal of Politics, Culture, and Society* 22 (2009): 221–29.

——. *Prosthetic Memory: The Transformation of American Remembrance in the Age of Mass Culture*. New York: Columbia University Press, 2004.

Latour, Bruno. *Reassembling the Social Sciences: An Introduction to Actor-Network Theory*. Oxford: Oxford University Press, 2005.

Lavallée, Lynn F. "Practical Application of an Indigenous Research Framework and Two Qualitative Indigenous Research Methods: Sharing Circles and Anishnaabe Symbol-Based Reflection." *International Journal of Qualitative Methods* 8, 1 (2009): 21–40.

Legge, Elizabeth. "Caroline Dukes." In *Caroline Dukes: Concealed Memories*, 13–19. Winnipeg: Winnipeg Art Gallery, 2008.

Lehrer, Erica, Cynthia E. Milton, and Monica Eileen Patterson, eds. *Curating Difficult Knowledge: Violent Pasts in Public Places*. Houndmills, UK: Palgrave Macmillan, 2011.

Lett, Dan. "CMHR Flap Shows Perils of Being Linked to Ottawa." *Winnipeg Free Press*, 29 July 2013.

——. "Conflict Is a Certainty: Museum's Challenge Is to Embrace Debate, Reject Hate." *Winnipeg Free Press*, 27 November 2010.

Levinas, Emmanuel. "Useless Suffering." In *Entre Nous: Thinking of-the-Other*, translated by Michael B. Smith and Barbara Harshav. New York: Columbia University Press, 1998.

Levine, Robert V. *A Geography of Time: On Tempo, Culture, and the Pace of Life.* New York: Basic Books, 1998.

Lewis, Charles. "Controversial Poll Flashpoint in Rights Museum Debate." *National Post,* 30 March 2011.

———. "Rights Museum Needs a Rethink, Academic Says." *National Post,* 5 April 2011.

Lewis, Jason, and Skawennati Tricia Fragnito. "Aboriginal Territories in Cyberspace." *Cultural Survival Quarterly* Summer (2005): 29–31.

Lindqvist, Sven. *"Exterminate All the Brutes": One Man's Odyssey into the Heart of Darkness and the Origins of European Genocide.* New York: New Press, 1996.

Linfield, Susie. *The Cruel Radiance: Photography and Political Violence.* Chicago: University of Chicago Press, 2010.

Lister, M., J. Dovey, S. Giddings, I. Grant, and K. Kelly. *New Media: A Critical Introduction.* London: Routledge, 2008.

Locke, Stefan. "Das neue Antikriegsmuseum der Bundeswehr." *Frankfurter Allgemeine Zeitung,* 18 May 2011.

Logan, Tricia. "National Memory and Museums: Remembering Settler Colonial Genocide of Indigenous Peoples in Canada." In *Remembering Genocide,* edited by Nigel Eltringham, and Pam MacLean, 112–30. New York: Routledge, 2014.

Lomawaima, K. Tsianna. *They Called It Prairie Light: The Story of Chilocco Indian School.* Lincoln: University of Nebraska Press, 1994.

Lonetree, Amy. *Decolonizing Museums: Representing Native America in National and Tribal Museums.* Chapel Hill: University of North Carolina Press, 2012.

———, ed. *The National Museum of the American Indian: Critical Conversations.* Lincoln: University of Nebraska Press, 2008.

Lorenz, Federico. "¿De quién es el 24 de marzo? Las luchas por la memoria del golpe de 1976." In *Las conmemoraciones: Las disputas en las fechas "in-felices,"* edited by Elizabeth Jelin, 53–100. Madrid: Siglo 21, 2002.

Love, Myron. "Shoah Education Still Key for Human Rights Museum." *Canadian Jewish News,* 28 March 2013.

———, "Ukrainian Groups Oppose Museum's Holocaust Exhibit." *Canadian Jewish News,* 20 January 2011.

Loyer, Stacey. "Belonging and Belongings: Ethnographic Collecting and Indigenous Agency at the Six Nations of the Grand River." PhD diss., Carleton University, 2013.

Lübbe, Hermann. *Der Fortschritt und das Museum: Über den Grund unseres Vergnügens an historischen Gegenständen.* London: Institute of Germanic Studies, University of London, 1982.

Luciuk, Lubomyr. "All Genocide Victims Must Be Hallowed." *Ukrainian Weekly,* 7 March 2004.

———. "The Canadian Museum for Human Rights: A Canadian Ukrainian Perspective." Ukrainian Civil Liberties Association, 11 June 2009. http://www.uccla.ca/CMHR_11June09.pdf.

MacDonald, David B., and Graham Hudson. "The Genocide Question and Indian Residential Schools in Canada." *Canadian Journal of Political Science* 45, 2 (2012): 427–49.

Mahabir, Mark. "Bill C-42, An Act to Amend the Museums Act and to Make Consequential Amendments to Other Acts." Parliament of Canada, 22 February 2008. www.parl.gc.ca/About/Parliament/LegislativeSummaries/bills_ls.asp?lang=E&ls=c42&Parl=39&Ses=2&source=library_prb.

Mahoney, Jack. *The Challenge of Human Rights: Origin, Development, and Significance.* Oxford: Blackwell Publishing, 2006.

Manatee, Hugh. "Cash-Strapped Rights Museum to Be Converted to Water Park." *Winnipeg Sun,* 31 March 2012. www.winnipegsun.com/2012/03/31/cash-strapped-rights-museum-to-be-converted-to-water-park.

Manovich, L. "The Poetics of Augmented Space." *Visual Communication* 5, 2 (2006): 219–40.

Margalit, Avishai. *Ethics of Memory.* Cambridge, MA: Harvard University Press, 2002.

Marie, Suzan, and Judy Thompson. *Whadoo Tehmi: Long Ago People's Packsack, Dene Babiche Bags: Tradition and Revival.* Gatineau: Canada Museum of Civilization, 2004.

Martinkuk, Susan. "Native Leaders' Talk of Genocide Just Fuels Anger." *Calgary Herald,* 9 August 2013.

Marx, Karl. *Capital: A Critique of Political Economy, Volume 1.* Translated by Ben Fowkes. London: Penguin Books, 1976.

———. "Economic and Philosophical Manuscripts of 1844." In *Karl Marx, Frederick Engels Collected Works Volume 3,* translated by Martin Milligan and Dirk J. Struik, 229–348. New York: International Publishers, 1975.

Matas, David. "Remembering the Holocaust." In *Genocide Watch,* edited by Helen Fein. New Haven, CT: Yale University Press, 1992.

———. "Remembering the Holocaust Can Prevent Future Genocides." In *Genocide,* edited by William Dudley, 119–23. San Diego: Greenhaven Press, 2001.

———. "The Struggle for Justice: Nazi War Criminals in Canada, from Immigration to Integration." In *The Canadian Jewish Experience: A Millennium Edition,* edited by Ruth Klein and Frank Dimant. Toronto:: Institute for International Affairs B'nai B'rith Canada, 2001.

Matthews, Robert O. "Sudan's Humanitarian Disaster: Will Canada Live Up to Its Responsibility to Protect?" *International Journal* 60, 4 (2005): 1049–64.

Mazower, Mark. *Governing the World: The History of an Idea.* New York: Penguin, 2012.

McClintock, Anne. *Imperial Leather: Race, Gender, and Sexuality in the Colonial Contest.* London: Routledge, 1995.

McDonnell, Michael A., and A. Dirk Moses. "Raphael Lemkin as Historian of Genocide in the Americas." *Journal of Genocide Research* 7, 4 (2005): 501–29.

Mcguire, Joan M., Sally S. Scott, and Stan F. Shaw. "Universal Design and Its Applications in Educational Environments." *Remedial and Special Education* 27, 3 (2006): 166–75.

McLaughlin, Janet. "Those Who Construct, Care, and Cultivate: A Synopsis of Issues Facing Past and Present Migrant Workers in Canada." Prepared for the Canadian Museum for Human Rights, 2011.

McManus, Paulette M. "Oh Yes, They Do: How Museum Visitors Read Labels and Interact with Exhibit Texts." *Curator* 32, 3 (1989): 174–89.

Meierhenrich, Jens. "Through a Glass Darkly: Genocide Memorials in Rwanda 1994–Present." http://genocidememorials.cga.harvard.edu.

———. "The Transformation of *Lieux de mémoire:* The Nyabarongo River in Rwanda, 1992–2009." *Anthropology Today* 25 (2009): 13–19.

Memoria Abierta. "Architecture and Memory." 2009. http://www.memoriaabierta.org.ar/materiales/pdf/architectureandmemory.pdf.

————. "Primeras jornadas de debate interdisciplinario: Organización institucional y contenidos del futuro museo de la memoria." 2000. http://www.memoriaabierta.org.ar/pdf/museo_de_la_memoria.pdf.

Milgram, Paul, and Fumio Kishino. "Taxonomy of Mixed Reality Visual Displays." *IEICE Transactions on Information and Systems* E77-D12 (1994): 1321–29.

Milgram, Stanley. *Obedience to Authority: An Experimental View.* New York: HarperCollins, 1974.

Miller, J.R. *Shingwauk's Vision: A History of Native Residential Schools.* Toronto: University of Toronto Press, 1996.

Miller, James, and Edmund Danziger Jr. "'In the Care of Strangers': Walpole Island First Nation's Experiences with Residential Schools after the First World War." *Ontario History* 92, 2 (2000): 71–88.

Monod, David. "'Who Owns History Anyway?': The Political Assault on North American History." *Ahornblätter: Marburger Beiträge zur Kanada-Forschung* 90 (1999). http://archiv.ub.uni-marburg.de/sum/90/sum90-5.html.

Montpetit, Raymond. "Making Sense of Space." *Museum International* 47, 1 (1995): 41–45.

Morsink, J. *Inherent Human Rights: Philosophical Roots of the Universal Declaration.* Philadelphia: University of Pennsylvania Press, 2009.

Mosby, Ian. "Administering Colonial Science: Nutrition Research and Human Biomedical Experimentation in Aboriginal Communities and Residential Schools, 1942–1952." *Histoire sociale/Social History* 46, 91 (2013): 145–72.

Moses, A. Dirk. "An Antipodean Genocide? The Origins of the Genocidal Moment in the Colonization of Australia." *Journal of Genocide Research* 2, 1 (2000): 89–106.

————. "The Canadian Museum for Human Rights: The 'Uniqueness of the Holocaust' and the Question of Genocide." *Journal of Genocide Research* 14, 2 (2012): 215–38.

————. *Colony, Empire, Genocide: Conquest, Occupation, and Subaltern Resistance in World History.* New York: Berghahn Books, 2008.

————. "Conceptual Blockages and Definitional Dilemmas in the Racial Century: Genocide of Indigenous Peoples and the Holocaust." *Patterns of Prejudice* 36, 4 (2002): 7–36.

————. "*Das römische Gespräch* in a New Key: Hannah Arendt, Genocide, and the Defense of Republican Civilization." *Journal of Modern History* 85, 4 (2013): 867–913.

————. "Does the Holocaust Reveal or Conceal Other Genocides? The Canadian Museum of Human Rights and Grievable Suffering." In *Hidden Genocides: Power, Knowledge, and Memory,* edited by Doug Irvin, Alexander Hinton, and Tom LaPointe, 21–51. New Brunswick, NJ: Rutgers University Press, 2013.

————, ed. *Empire, Colony, Genocide: Conquest, Occupation, and Subaltern Resistance in World History.* New York: Berghahn Books, 2008.

————. "Empire, Colony, Genocide: Keywords and the Philosophy of History." In *Empire, Colony, and Genocide: Conquest, Occupation, and Subaltern Resistance in World History,* ed. A. Dirk Moses, 3–54. New York: Berghahn Books, 2008.

————, ed. *Genocide and Settler Society: Frontier Violence and Stolen Indigenous Children in Australian History.* New York: Berghahn Books, 2004.

————. "Genocide and Settler Society in Australian History." In *Genocide and Settler Society: Frontier Violence and Stolen Indigenous Children in Australian History,* ed. A. Dirk Moses, 4–48. New York: Berghahn Books, 2004.

——. "Genocide and the Terror of History." *Parallax* 17, 4 (2011): 90–108.

Moyne, Samuel. *The Last Utopia: The Holocaust in History.* Cambridge, MA: Harvard University Press, 2010.

Muller, Adam. "Holocaust Was Not Primarily an Antisemitic Experience." *Winnipeg Jewish Review,* 7 April 2012.

Muller, Michael. "Participatory Design: The Third Space in HCI." In *Human-Computer Interaction: Development Process,* edited by Andrew Sears and Julie Jacko,165–85.Cleveland: CRC Press, 2009.

Murray, John P. "Media Violence: The Effects Are Both Real and Strong." *American Behavioral Scientist* 51 (2008): 1212–30.

Murray, Stuart. First Critical Conversations Seminar. 9 September 2011.

——. "'Genocide' Will Have Its Place." *Winnipeg Free Press,* 28 July 2013.

Narine, Shari. "Missing and Dead Residential School Children." *Windspeaker* 30, 4 (2012).

Nevins, J. "The Abuse of Memorialized Space and the Redefinition of Ground Zero." *Journal of Human Rights* 4 (2005): 267–82.

Nicks, Trudy. "Partnerships in Developing Cultural Resources: Learning from the Task Force on Museums and First Peoples." *Culture* 12, 2 (1992): 87–94.

Nightingale, Eithne, and Richard Sandell. "Introduction." In *Museums, Equality, and Social Justice,* edited by Richard Sandell and Eithne Nightingale, 1–9. London: Routledge, 2012.

Nora, Pierre. "Between Memory and History: *Les lieux de mémoire.*" *Representations* 26, 1 (1989): 7–24.

Novaro, Marcos, and Vicente Palermo. *La dictadura militar, 1976–1983: Del golpe de estado a la restauración democrática.* Buenos Aires: Paidós, 2003.

Nussbaum, Martha. *The Fragility of Goodness: Luck and Ethics in Greek Tragedy and Philosophy.* Cambridge, UK: Cambridge University Press, 2001.

——. *Poetic Justice: The Literary Imagination and Public Life.* Boston: Beacon, 1997.

O'Brien, David. "Jewish Suffering Is Unique in History." *Winnipeg Free Press,* 22 April 2009.

——. "Museum to Respect Ukrainian Rights." *Winnipeg Free Press,* 1 December 2003.

Oliver, S. "Simulating the Ethical Community: Interactive Game Media and Engaging Human Rights Claims." *Culture, Theory, and Critique* 51, 1 (2010): 93–108.

Orange, Jennifer, and Jennifer Carter. "'It's Time to Pause and Reflect': Museums and Human Rights." *Curator* 55, 3 (2012): 259–66.

Orford, Anne. *Reading Humanitarian Intervention.* Cambridge, UK: Cambridge University Press, 2003.

Oxford English Dictionary. "Savage, adj. and n. 1." 2014. http://www.oed.com.

Palmer, Alison. *Colonial Genocide.* Adelaide: Crawford House, 2000.

Parsons, Emily. "The Space of Remembering: Collective Memory and the Reconfiguration of Contested Space in Argentina's ESMA." *452°F: Electronic Journal of Theory of Literature and Comparative Literature* 4 (2011): 29–51. http://www.452f.com/pdf/numero04/04_452f_completo.pdf.

Paul, Alexandra. "Donations Won't Sway Content, CMHR Declares." *Winnipeg Free Press,* 8 August 2013.

——. "Genocide Never Debated: Chief." *Winnipeg Free Press,* 10 August 2013.

———. "It's the Million-Dollar Question: Manitoba Chiefs Say Donation Gives Them a Say on 'Genocide.'" *Winnipeg Free Press,* 6 August 2013.

Perkel, Colin. "At Least 3,000 Native Children Died in Residential Schools: Research." *Globe and Mail,* 18 February 2013.

Philipps, Mark Salber. "Distance and Historical Representation." *History Workshop Journal* 57 (2004): 123–41.

Phillips, Ruth B. "Community Collaboration in Exhibitions: Toward a Dialogic Paradigm." In *Museums and Source Communities: A Routledge Reader,* edited by L. Peers and A.K. Brown, 155–70. London: Routledge, 2005.

———. "Inside-Out and Outside-In: Re-Representing Native North America at the Canadian Museum of Civilization and the National Museum of the American Indian." In *Museum Pieces: Toward the Indigenization of Canadian Museums,* edited by Ruth B. Phillips, 205–27. Montreal: McGill-Queen's University Press, 2011.

———. "Modes of Inclusion: Indigenous Art at the National Gallery of Canada and the Art Gallery of Ontario." In *Museum Pieces: Toward the Indigenization of Canadian Museums,* edited by Ruth B. Phillips, 252–76. Montreal: McGill-Queen's University Press, 2011.

———. "Moment of Truth: The Spirit Sings as Critical Event and the Exhibition Inside It." In *Museum Pieces: Toward the Indigenization of Canadian Museums,* edited by Ruth B. Phillips, 48–70. Montreal: McGill-Queen's University Press, 2011.

———, ed. *Museum Pieces: Toward the Indigenization of Canadian Museums.* Montreal: McGill-Queen's University Press, 2011.

———. "Review of *Threads of the Land: Clothing Traditions from Three Indigenous Cultures.*" *Archivaria* 40 (1995): 243–44.

Phillips, Ruth B., and Sherry Braydon. "'Arrow of Truth': The Indians of Canada Pavilion at Expo 67." In *Museum Pieces: Toward the Indigenization of Canadian Museums,* edited by Ruth B. Phillips, 27–47. Montreal: McGill-Queen's University Press, 2011.

Pieken, Gorch, and Matthias Rogg, eds. *The Bundeswehr Museum of Military History: Exhibition Guide.* Dresden: Sandstein, 2012.

Pinker, Stephen. *Better Angels of Our Nature: The Decline of Violence in History and Its Causes.* New York: Viking, 2011.

Pitt, Alice, and Deborah Britzman. "Speculations on Qualities of Difficult Knowledge in Teaching and Learning: An Experiment in Psychoanalytic Research." *International Journal of Qualitative Studies in Education* 16, 6 (2003): 755–76.

Pontanilla, Bernice. "Guatemalan Partnership to 'Break Long Silence,' Says CMHR President." *Metro News,* 20 June 2013.

Povinelli, Elizabeth. *The Cunning of Recognition: Indigenous Alterities and the Making of Australian Multiculturalism.* Durham, NC: Duke University Press, 2002.

Powell, Christopher. *Barbaric Civilization: A Critical Sociology of Genocide.* Montreal: McGill-Queen's University Press, 2011.

———. "Crisis of Co-Optation: Human Rights Social Movements and Global Politics." *Alternate Routes* 15 (1999): 5–34.

———. "Sinclair Is Correct: It Was Genocide." *Winnipeg Free Press,* 24 February 2012.

Pursaga, Joanne. "Plans for Human Rights Museum Galleries Revealed." *Winnipeg Sun,* 4 March 2013.

Rabson, Mia. "Chief Operating Officer Leaves Rights Museum." *Winnipeg Free Press,* 3 March 2011. http://www.winnipegfreepress.com/local/chief-operating-officer-leaves-rights-museum-117302453.html.

Rancière, Jacques. *Dissensus: On Politics and Aesthetics.* Edited and translated by Steven Corcoran. London: Continuum, 2010.

———. *The Emancipated Spectator.* Translated by Gregory Elliot. London: Verso, 2009.

———. *Politics of Aesthetics: The Distribution of the Sensible.* Translated by Gabriel Rockhill. London: Continuum, 2004.

Razack, Sherene H. "Stealing the Pain of Others: Reflections on Canadian Humanitarian Responses." *Review of Education, Pedagogy, and Cultural Studies* 27, 4 (2007): 375–94.

Regan, Paulette. *Unsettling the Settler Within: Indian Residential Schools, Truth Telling, and Reconciliation in Canada.* Vancouver: UBC Press, 2011.

Remy, Ruane. "Human Rights Museum in the Wrong, Say Ukrainians." *Catholic Register,* 24 May 2013.

Richmond, J., and J.C. Wilson. "Are Graphic Media Violence, Aggression, and Moral Disengagement Related?" *Psychiatry, Psychology, and Law* 15, 2 (2008): 350–57.

Riney, Scott. *The Rapid City Indian School 1898–1933.* Norman: University of Oklahoma Press, 1999.

Rollason, Kevin. "Discontent Remains on CMHR, Holodomor." *Winnipeg Free Press,* 9 April 2013, A5.

Rorty, Richard. "Human Rights, Rationality, and Sentimentality." In *On Human Rights: The 1993 Oxford Amnesty Lectures,* edited by Susan Hurley and Stephen Shute, 112–34. New York: Basic Books, 1993.

Ros, Ana. *The Post-Dictatorship Generation in Argentina, Chile, and Uruguay: Collective Memory and Cultural Production.* New York: Palgrave Macmillan, 2012.

Ross, William. "Draconian Cuts to Parks Canada." Canadian Archaeological Association. http://canadianarchaeology.com/caa/draconian-cuts-parks-canada.

Rothmund, T., M. Gollwitzer, and C. Klimmt. "Of Virtual Victim and Victimized Virtues: Differential Effects of Experienced Aggression in Video Games on Social Cooperation." *Personality and Social Psychology Bulletin* 37, 1 (2011): 107–19.

Rudling, Per Anders. "Multiculturalism, Memory, and Ritualization: Ukrainian Nationalist Monuments in Edmonton, Alberta." *Nationalities Papers* 39, 5 (2011): 733–68.

Sachs, Andrea. "The Spirit of Manitoba, Canada's Mystery Province." *Washington Post,* 3 August 2012. http://www.washingtonpost.com/lifestyle/travel/the-spirit-of-manitoba/2012/08/02/gJQAduVZUX_story.html.

Samyn, Paul. "$125-M Holocaust Museum for City?" *Winnipeg Free Press,* 3 April 2002.

———. "Asper-Led Museum Sets Off Alarm Bells: View of Genocide Said Too Exclusive." *Winnipeg Free Press,* 27 February 2003.

———. "Aspers Got Grant for Lobbyist." *Winnipeg Free Press,* 22 November 2004.

———. "Museum Price Tag May Hit $200M." *Winnipeg Free Press,* 4 April 2002.

———. "Rights Museum Faces Cash Crunch." *Winnipeg Free Press,* 3 January 2005.

Sandell, Richard. *Museums, Society, Inequality.* London: Routledge, 2002.

Sanders, Carol, and Nick Martin. "Archeologists Dig for Information: 'Buried' Findings at Forks Excavation Site." *Winnipeg Free Press,* 16 December 2011.

———. "CMHR Won't Flip on Armenian Genocide." *Winnipeg Free Press,* 8 April 2013, A6.

Sanders, Elizabeth B.N. "From User-Centred to Participatory Design Approaches." In *Design and Social Sciences,* edited by J. Frascera. London: Taylor and Francis Books, 2002.

Santin, Aldo. "Most Oppose Separate Holocaust Gallery: Boosts Those Pushing Museum to Change Genocide Treatment." *Winnipeg Free Press,* 24 March 2011.

Sather-Wagstaff, Joy, and Rebekah Sobel. "From Memory to Action: Multisited Visitor Action at the United States Holocaust Memorial Museum." *Museums and Social Issues* 7 (2012): 293–305.

Saunders, Doug. "A Fight over the Word 'Genocide' Is No Way to End the Aboriginal Crisis." *Globe and Mail,* 19 October 2013.

Schlereth, Thomas J. "Collecting Ideas and Artifacts: Common Problems of History Museums and History Texts." In *Museum Studies: An Anthology of Contexts,* edited by Bettina Messias Carbonell, 335–47. Chichester, UK: Blackwell Publishing, 2004.

Schnädelbach, H., B. Koleva, M. Paxton, M. Twidale, S. Benford, and R. Anastasi. "The Augurscope: Redefining Its Design." *Presence* 15, 3 (2006): 278–93.

Schroeder, Lara, and Lauren McNabb. "Exclusive: Human Rights Museum Exhibits Revealed." Global News Winnipeg, 20 February 2014. http://globalnews.ca/news/1161291/human-rights-museum-to-feature-11-galleries/.

Schwartz, Bryan. "Centrality of Antisemitism in Producing the Holocaust Is Known and Settled." *Winnipeg Jewish Review,* 24 April 2012.

Sen, A. *The Idea of Justice.* Cambridge, MA: Harvard University Press, 2009.

Serrell, Beverly. *Exhibit Labels: An Interpretive Approach.* Altamira, CA: Rowman, 1996.

Sezirahiga, Gilbert, Director of Murambi Genocide Memorial. Interview with the Author. September 2012.

Sharma, Arvind. *Are Human Rights Western? A Contribution to the Dialogue of Civilizations.* Oxford: Oxford University Press, 2006.

Shirinian, George. "Canadian Museum for Human Rights and the Armenian Community." *Asbarez,* 21 February 2012.

Short, Damien. "Cultural Genocide and Indigenous Peoples: A Sociological Approach." *International Journal of Human Rights* 14, 6 (2010): 833–48.

Siebers, Tobin. "What Can Disability Studies Learn from the Culture Wars?" *Cultural Critique* 55 (2003): 182–216.

Silverman, Lois H. *The Social Work of Museums.* New York: Routledge, 2010.

Simon, Roger I. "A Shock to Thought: Curatorial Judgment and the Public Exhibition of 'Difficult Knowledge.'" *Memory Studies* 4, 4 (2011): 432–49.

———. "The Terrible Gift: Museums and the Possibility of Hope without Consolation." *Museum Management and Curatorship* 21 (2006): 187–204.

———. *The Touch of the Past: Remembrance, Learning, and Ethics.* Houndmills, UK: Palgrave Macmillan, 2005.

Simon, Roger I., Sharon Rosenberg, and Claudia Eppert, eds. *Between Hope and Despair: Pedagogy and the Remembrance of Historical Trauma.* Lanham, MD: Rowman and Littlefield Publishers, 2000.

Smith, Laurajane, and Kalliopi Fouseki. "The Role of Museums as 'Places of Social Justice': Community Consultation and the 1807 Bicentenary." In *Representing Enslavement and*

Abolition in Museums: Ambiguous Engagements, edited by Laurajane Smith, Geoff Cubitt, Kalliopi Fouseki, and Ross Wilson, 97–115. New York: Routledge, 2011.

Smith, Linda Tuhiwai. *Decolonizing Methodologies: Research and Indigenous Peoples.* 2nd ed. London: Zed Books, 2012.

Spivak, Gayatri Chakravorty. "Can the Subaltern Speak?" In *Marxism and the Interpretation of Culture,* edited by Cary Nelson and Lawrence Grossberg. London: Macmillan, 1988.

Spivak, Rhonda. "CISA Announces Its First Year of Programming." *Winnipeg Jewish Review,* 2 October 2011.

———. "Open Letter to Lubomyr Luciuk, Director of Research, Ukrainian Civil Liberties Association, Re: CMHR." *Winnipeg Jewish Review,* 31 March 2011.

———. "Tanenbaum Donates \$1 Million to Rights Museum." *Canadian Jewish News,* 13 March 2008.

Stammers, Neil. "Social Movements and the Social Construction of Human Rights." *Human Rights Quarterly* 21, 4 (1999): 980–1008.

Stannard, David E. *American Holocaust: The Conquest of the New World.* Oxford: Oxford University Press, 1992.

Stanton, Kim. "Canada's Truth and Reconciliation Commission: Settling the Past?" *International Indigenous Policy Journal* 2, 3 (2011). http://ir.lib.uwo.ca/iipj/v012/iss3/2.

Steiman, Lionel. "Muller Advances a Conception of the Holocaust Different from that Recognized by Most Other Scholars." *Winnipeg Jewish Review,* 5 April 2012.

Stephen, A. "Intrinsic Information in the Making of Public Space: A Case Example of the Museum Space." *Space and Culture* 6, 3 (2003): 309–29.

Stock, O., M. Zancanaro, P. Busetta, C. Callaway, A. Kruger, M. Kruppa, T. Kuflik, E. Not, and C. Rocchi. "Adaptive, Intelligent Presentation of Information for the Museum Visitor in PEACH." *User Modeling and User-Adapted Interaction* 17 (2007): 257–304.

Straus, Scott. "What Is the Relationship between Hate Radio and Violence? Rethinking Rwanda's 'Radio Machete.'" *Politics and Society* 35 (2007): 609–37.

Strong, Pauline Turner. "Exclusive Labels: Indexing the National 'We' in Commemorative and Oppositional Exhibitions." *Museum Anthropology* 21, 1 (1997): 42–56.

Sunstein, Cass. "Some Effects of Moral Indignation on Law." *Vermont Law Review* 33, 3 (2009): 405–34.

Syms, Leigh. "Accelerated Destruction of First Nations Heritage Beneath the Canadian Museum of Human Rights, 2009." Association of Manitoba Archaeologists. http://www.assocmanarch.com/12.html.

Tadjo, Veronique. "Genocide: The Changing Landscape of Memory in Kigali." *African Identities* 8 (2010): 379–88.

Tai, Eika. "Local and Global Efforts for Human Rights Education: A Case from the Osaka Human Rights Museum." *International Journal of Human Rights* 14, 5 (2010): 771–88.

Tappatá de Valdez, Patricia. "El Parque de la Memoria en Buenos Aires." In *Monumentos, memoriales, y marcas territoriales,* edited by Elizabeth Jelin and Victoria Langland, 97–111. Madrid: Siglo XXI de España Editores, 2003.

Task Force on Museums and First Peoples. *Turning the Page: Forging Partnerships between Museums and First Peoples.* Ottawa: Canadian Museums Association and Assembly of First Nations, 1992.

Taylor, Charles. *Multiculturalism and "The Politics of Recognition": An Essay.* Edited by Amy Gutmann. Princeton, NJ: Princeton University Press, 1992.

———. "The Politics of Recognition." In *Multiculturalism: Examining the Politics of Recognition,* edited by Amy Gutmann, 25–74. Princeton, NJ: Princeton University Press, 1994.

Taylor, J. "Teaching African American History through Museum Theatre." *The Councilor: The Journal of the Illinois Council for the Social Studies* 72, 2 (2011): 1–11.

Thiemeyer, Thomas. *Fortsetzung des Krieges mit anderen Mitteln: Die beiden Weltkriege im Museum.* Paderborn: Schöningh, 2010.

Thompson, Judy, Judy Hall, and Leslie Tepper, eds. *Fascinating Challenges: Studying Material Culture with Dorothy Burnham.* Gatineau: Canadian Museum of Civilization, 2001.

Thompson, Judy, and Ingrid Kritsch. *Yeenoo Dài' Kè'tr'ijilkai' Ganagwaandaii, Long Ago Sewing We Will Remember: The Story of the Gwich'in Traditional Caribou Skin Clothing Project.* Gatineau: Canadian Museum of Civilization, 2005.

Thomson, Janice E. *Mercenaries, Pirates, and Sovereigns: State-Building and Extraterritorial Violence in Early Modern Europe.* Princeton, NJ: Princeton University Press, 1994.

Tilly, Charles. "War Making and State Making as Organized Crime." In *Bringing the State Back In,* edited by Peter Evans, Dietrich Rueschemeyer, and Theda Skocpol, 169–91. Cambridge, UK: Cambridge University Press, 1985.

Todorov, Tzvetan. "The Abuses of Memory." *Common Knowledge* 5 (1996): 6–26.

Trennert, Robert A. *The Phoenix Indian School: Forced Assimilation in Arizona, 1891–1935.* Norman: University of Oklahoma Press, 1988.

Trigger, Bruce G. "A Present of Their Past? Anthropologists, Native People, and Their Heritage." *Culture* 8, 1 (1988): 71–79.

———. "Reply to Michael Ames." *Culture* 8, 1 (1988): 87–88.

Troper, Harold, and Morton Weinfield. *Old Wounds: Jews, Ukrainians, and the Hunt for Nazi War Criminals in Canada.* Chapel Hill: University of North Carolina Press, 1989.

Truth and Reconciliation Commission of Canada. *They Came for the Children: Canada, Aboriginal Peoples, and Residential Schools.* Winnipeg: Truth and Reconciliation Commission of Canada, 2012.

Turenne, Paul. "CMHR Not Worth the Trip: Canadians." *Winnipeg Sun,* 31 January 2012. http://www.winnipegsun.com/2012/01/31/cmhr-not-worth-the-trip-canadians.

Turner, Bryan S. *Vulnerability and Human Rights.* University Park: Pennsylvania State University Press, 2006.

Turner, Dale. "On the Idea of Reconciliation in Contemporary Aboriginal Politics." In *Reconciling Canada: Critical Perspectives on the Culture of Redress,* edited by Jennifer Henderson and Pauline Wakeham, 100–14. Toronto: University of Toronto Press, 2013.

Tyburczy, Jennifer. "Warning: Explicit Display in Museums." Paper presented at the College Art Association Conference, Los Angeles, 24 June 2012.

Van Drunen, S.P.C. "Struggling with the Past: The Human Rights Movement and the Politics of Memory in Postdictatorship Argentina (1983–2006)." PhD diss., University of Amsterdam, 2010.

Vanderhart, Tessa. "Genocide Exhibit Too Close to Bathroom: Ukrainians." *Winnipeg Sun,* 29 March 2013.

Varas, Alberto. "Architecture, Site, and Memory: A Reflection on the Insertion of Architecture and the Park of Memory into the Urban Coastline of Buenos Aires." In *Architecture and*

Memory, edited by Memoria Abierta, 37–41. Buenos Aires: Memoria Abierta, 2009. http://www.memoriaabierta.org.ar/materiales/pdf/architectureandmemory.pdf.

Veracini, Lorenzo. *Settler Colonialism: A Theoretical Overview.* New York: Palgrave Macmillan, 2010.

Vesely, Caroline, and Carol Sanders. "New Museum Head under Fire." *Winnipeg Free Press,* 19 September 2009, B1.

Villa, Alejandro, Claudia Medvescig, Rocío Otero, and Valentina Salvi. *La sociedad Argentina hoy frente a los años '70.* Buenos Aires: Centro Cultural de la Memoria "Haroldo Conti"/EUDEBA, 2010.

Vizenor, Gerald. *Survivance: Narratives of Native Presence.* Lincoln: University of Nebraska Press, 2008.

Waldie, Paul, and Daniel LeBlanc. "Canadian Human Rights Museum Dogged by Controversy." *Globe and Mail,* 20 December 2011. http://www.theglobeandmail.com/news/politics/canadian-human-rights-museum-dogged-by-controversy/article2278785/.

———. "A Ukrainian Quest to Shed Light on Horror Soviets Kept in the Dark." *Globe and Mail,* 18 November 2012. http://www.theglobeandmail.com/news/world/a-ukrainian-quest-to-shed-light-on-horror-soviets-kept-in-the-dark/article5414086.

Waller, James. *Becoming Evil: How Ordinary People Commit Genocide and Mass Killing, Second Edition.* Oxford: Oxford University Press, 2007.

Ward, Olivia. "Canada Gets Human Rights Failing Grade from Amnesty International." *Toronto Star,* 19 December 2012.

Weber, Bob. "Atleo Calls on PM to Acknowledge 'Horrors' of Nutrition Tests on Native Children." *Globe and Mail,* 17 July 2013.

Weber, Max. *Economy and Society, Volume 1.* Berkeley: University of California Press, 1978.

———. "'Objectivity' in Social Science and Social Science Policy." In *The Methodology of the Social Sciences,* edited by Edward A. Shils and Henry A. Finch, 50–112. Glencoe, IL: Free Press, 1949.

Weedon, Chris, and Glenn Jordan. "Collective Memory: Theory and Politics." *Social Semiotics* 22, 2 (2012): 143–53.

Weinberg, Jeshajahu. "From the Founding Director." In *The World Must Know: The History of the Holocaust as Told in the United States Holocaust Memorial Museum,* 2nd ed., edited by Michael Berenbaum. Washington, DC: United States Holocaust Memorial Museum, 2006.

Welch, Mary A. "CMHR Rejects Genocide for Native Policies." *Winnipeg Free Press,* 26 July 2013. http://www.winnipegfreepress.com/local/cmhr-rejects-genocide-for-native-policies-217061321.html.

Welsh, Jennifer, ed. *Humanitarian Intervention and International Relations.* Oxford: Oxford University Press, 2004.

Whitelaw, Ann. "Placing Aboriginal Art at the National Gallery of Canada." *Canadian Journal of Communication* 31, 1 (2006): 197–214.

Williams, Paul. *Memorial Museums: The Global Rush to Commemorate Atrocities.* London: Berg, 2007.

———. "Witnessing Genocide: Vigilance and Remembrance at Tuol Sleng and Choeung Ek." *Holocaust and Genocide Studies* 18 (2004): 234–55.

Wolfe, Patrick. "Settler Colonialism and the Elimination of the Native." *Journal of Genocide Research* 8, 4 (2006): 387–409.

Wong, A. "Ethical Issues of Social Media in Museums: A Case Study." *Museum Management and Curatorship* 26, 2 (2011): 97–112.

Wood, Aylish. "Recursive Space: Play and Creating Space." *Games and Culture* 7 (2012): 87–105.

Woolford, Andrew, Jeff Benvenuto, and Alexander Laban Hinton, eds. *Colonial Genocide in Indigenous North America.* Durham, NC: Duke University Press, 2014.

———. "Ontological Destruction: Genocide and Aboriginal Peoples in Canada." *Genocide Studies and Prevention* 4, 1 (2009): 81–97.

Wright, Thomas. *State Terrorism in Latin America: Chile, Argentina, and International Human Rights.* Lanham, MD: Rowman and Littlefield, 2007.

Yakel, Elizabeth. "Who Represents the Past? Enabling Reuse and Recreation of Digital Objects in Cyberspace." In *Controlling the Past: Documenting Society and Institutions (Essays in Honor of Helen Willa Samuels),* edited by Terry Cook. Society of American Archivists, 2011.

Yamane, K. "Peace Education through Peace Museums." In *International Security, Peace, Development, and Environment—Volume 2.* http://www.eolss.net/Sample-Chapters/C14/E1-39B-21-00.pdf.

Young, G., and Monica Whittey. "Games without Frontiers: On the Moral and Psychological Implications of Violating Taboos within Multi-Player Virtual Spaces." *Computers in Human Behavior* 26, 6 (2010): 1228–36.

Young, James. *The Texture of Memory: Holocaust Memorials and Meaning.* New Haven, CT: Yale University Press, 1993.

Young-Seok, K., T. Kesavadas, and S.M. Paley. "The Virtual Site Museum: A Multi-Purpose, Authoritative, and Functional Virtual Heritage Resource." *Presence: Teleoperators and Virtual Environments* 15, 3 (2006): 245–61.

Zahavi, Dan. "Simulation, Projection, and Empathy." *Consciousness and Cognition* 17 (2008): 514–22.

Zalaquett, José. "Balancing Ethical Imperatives and Political Constraints: The Dilemma of New Democracies Confronting Past Human Rights Violations." *Hastings Law Journal* 43, 6 (1992): 1425–38.

———. "Introduction to the English Edition." In *Report of the Chilean National Commission on Truth and Reconciliation.* Notre Dame, IN: University of Notre Dame Press, 1993. Posted by the United States Peace Institute Library (www.usip.org) on 4 October 2002.

Zimmerman, L.J. "First, Be Humble: Working with Indigenous Peoples and Other Descendant Communities." In *Indigenous Archaeologies: Decolonizing Theory and Practice,* edited by C. Smith and H.M. Wobst. London: Routledge, 2005.

CONTRIBUTORS

KAREN BUSBY is a law professor and director of the University of Manitoba's Centre for Human Rights Research. Her research focuses on law and sex, including sexual assault, sex work and prostitution, sexual representations, queer rights, and assisted reproduction, and, more recently, on the right to water in First Nations communities. She has served on the governing boards of various visual arts organizations, including a ten-year stint on the board of the Winnipeg Art Gallery, where she chaired the Building Committee and the Works of Art Committee.

JENNIFER CARTER is director of the graduate museology program at the Université du Québec à Montréal, where she is also professor of new museologies, intangible heritage, and cultural objects in the Department of Art History. Her praxis consists of research and teaching in the areas of the history and theory of museums and museum practices, exhibition theory, and human rights museology. Her current research focuses on a comparative analysis of how social justice and human rights are negotiated curatorially, pedagogically, and semantically in cultural institutions dedicated to human rights in Asia, North America and South America. She is the author of essays in English and French on human rights museology, exhibition design, national museums, and museological practice. She is associate editor of the international journal *Museum Management and Curatorship*, published by Taylor and Francis / Routledge.

CLINT CURLE is the former curator of the Holocaust gallery and current director of stakeholder relations at the Canadian Museum for Human Rights. He is a lawyer and former academic, and among his publications is *Humanité: John Humphrey's Alternative Account of Human Rights* (University of Toronto Press, 2007).

ANGELA FAILLER is Chancellor's Research Chair, an associate professor, and chair of the Department of Women's and Gender Studies at the University of Winnipeg. Her current research is focused on public memory of the 1985 Air India bombings. She is also interested in phenomena at the intersection of culture, embodiment, and psychic life, and she has published writings on anorexia and self-harm in this vein. She is the lead researcher of a collaborative project on public engagement with the Canadian Museum for Human Rights. Her areas of teaching include cultural studies, feminist theory, queer theory, and sociology of the body.

HELEN FALLDING manages the Centre for Human Rights Research at the University of Manitoba. She has a master's degree in journalism and was a reporter and then editor for the *Winnipeg Free Press* from 1998 to 2011. Helen has won awards from Amnesty International Canada and the Sidney Hillman Foundation for her reporting on human rights issues.

JODI GIESBRECHT is currently the Acting Manager of Research at the Canadian Museum for Human Rights. She has provided research and content direction for numerous museum exhibitions that integrate oral history, material culture, new media, and digital platforms in the examination of Canadian and international human rights issues. Jodi earned her PhD and MA in Canadian history from the University of Toronto and her BAH in history from the University of Winnipeg. Her research interests include the history of human rights and social movements in Canada, public history and collective memory, identity politics and multiculturalism, and the workings of affect in human rights discourse.

AMANDA GRZYB is an associate professor of information and media studies at Western University, where her teaching and research interests include comparative genocide studies, social movements, and media and the public interest. She is editor of *The World and Darfur: International Response to Crimes against Humanity in Western Sudan* (McGill-Queen's University Press, 2009) and co-editor (with Samuel Totten) of *The Nuba Mountains of Sudan: From Genocide-by-Attrition to the Contemporary Crisis* (Routledge, 2014). She has also published extensively on media coverage of genocide and anti-genocide activism. Her current research projects include an ethnographic study of genocide memorial sites and museums in Rwanda and a study of post-communist Holocaust museums in Eastern Europe. She holds a PhD in English from Duke University.

GEORGE JACOB was trained at the Smithsonian and educated at the Birla Institute of Technology and Science, the University of Toronto, and Yale School of Management. He is known internationally for spearheading over 108 stellar museum and exhibit planning/design-build assignments and is one of the leading museum thinkers of our time. A Canadian Commonwealth Scholar, his design-build portfolio spans eleven countries. Founding director of four museums in his distinguished career, including the Khalsa Heritage complex, he is the author of seminal books on the future of museum practice and design. He taught Canada's first Masters Studio on Museum Design at the University of Manitoba's Faculty of Architecture, first American Cultural Leadership and Diplomacy Executive Program at the University of Texas (PB), and currently serves on the Peer Review Committee of American Alliance of Museums. He was honoured to be the project director for the production of the *Star Spangled Banner* permanent exhibit—the Smithsonian's most treasured icon, rededicated to the nation by President George W. Bush. He is, at present, the founding president and CEO of the award-winning Philip J. Currie Dinosaur Museum—Canada's newest world-class facility scheduled for a Fall 2015 opening in Grande Prairie, Alberta.

STEPHAN JAEGER is a full professor of German studies at the University of Manitoba and head of the Department of German and Slavic Studies. He has published extensively on narratology, history and literature, documentary history in historiography, film, and the museum, representations of war, and romantic and modern poetry. He has written two monographs: *Theory of Lyrical Expression* (Fink, 2001) and *Performative Historiography in the Late-Eighteenth Century* (de Gruyter, 2011) and five co-edited books, including *Fighting Words and Images: Representing War across the Disciplines* (University of Toronto Press, 2012), and a special issue of *Seminar* 50, 1 (2014) on *Representations of German War Experiences from the Eighteenth Century to the Present*. He is a co-coordinator of the Interdisciplinary Network on War and Violence of the German Studies Association. Currently, he is working on a comparative research project on twenty-first-century museum representations of the Second World War in North America and Europe (Germany, Poland, United Kingdom, Belgium, Canada, and United States).

A. DIRK MOSES is a professor of global and colonial history at the European University Institute, Florence, and an associate professor of history at the University of Sydney. He is the author of *German Intellectuals and the Nazi Past* (Cambridge University Press, 2007) and many essays and anthologies on genocide and colonialism, including most recently *Colonial Counterinsurgency and Mass Violence: The Dutch Empire in Indonesia* (Routledge, 2014), co-edited with Bart Luttikhuis.

ADAM MULLER is an associate professor in the Department of English, Film, and Theatre at the University of Manitoba. In addition to the present volume, he is the editor of *Concepts of Culture: Art, Politics, and Society* (2005) as well as a co-editor of *Fighting Words and Images: Representing War across the Disciplines* (2012). Muller is a specialist in cultural studies, critical theory, and war and genocide studies, and he has a particular research interest in the way in which episodes of mass violence are represented in museums, literature, film, and the visual arts.

JORGE A. NÁLLIM is an associate professor of history at the University of Manitoba, where he teaches Latin American and world history. His research has focused on modern Latin America and Argentina in the fields of cultural, intellectual, political, and social history. He has published articles and contributions on Argentine liberalism, anti-fascism, and anti-Peronism, including *Transformations and Crisis of Liberalism in Argentina, 1930–1955* (University of Pittsburgh Press, 2012). He has also worked on human rights in Argentina and contemporary Indigenous mobilization in Latin America. He is currently working on a comparative research project on anti-communist intellectual networks in Latin America during the Cold War.

KEN NORMAN is emeritus professor of law at the University of Saskatchewan, sometime first chief commissioner of the Saskatchewan Human Rights Commission, and principal draftsperson of the Saskatchewan Human Rights Code (1979). His recent publications include "Saskatchewan's One Bright Shining Moment, at Least It Seemed So at the Time," Chapter 3 in *14 Arguments in Favour of Human Rights Institutions,* ed. Shelagh Day, Lucie Lamarche, and Ken Norman (Toronto: Irwin Law, 2014); "A Forecast for Human Rights Commissions and Tribunals: Overcast, with a Chance of Furies," Pitblado Lecture, Winnipeg, 22 November 2013, http://www.pitbladolectures.ca; "Free Speech: 'The Right to Be Stupid' v. 'Words Matter,'" *Jurist Forum,* 19 March 2013, http://jurist.org/forum/2013/03/ken-norman-hate-speech.php; "Promoting and Protecting Human Rights: Snakes and Ladders," Association for Canadian Studies, Canadian Issues, *The Constitution, the Charter: Federalism and Identities* (Spring 2013); and Mary Eberts, Alex Neve, and Ken Norman, "The Wrong Moves for Saskatchewan Human Rights," *Human Rights Digest* (June 2012).

ARMANDO PERLA is a researcher/curator at the Canadian Museum for Human Rights. A lawyer, he specializes in human rights issues connected to migrant workers and displaced peoples.

DAVID PETRASEK is an associate professor in the Graduate School of Public and International Affairs, University of Ottawa. Formerly a special advisor to the secretary-general of Amnesty International, he has worked extensively on human rights and humanitarian and conflict resolution issues, including for Amnesty International (1990–96), for the Office of the UN High Commissioner for Human Rights (1997–98), for the International Council on Human Rights Policy (1998–2002), and as director of policy at the HD Centre (2003–07). He has taught international human rights and/or humanitarian law courses at the Osgoode Hall Law School, the Raoul Wallenberg Institute at Lund University, Sweden, and at Oxford University. David has also worked as a consultant or advisor to several NGOs and UN agencies.

RUTH B. PHILLIPS holds a Canada Research Chair in modern culture and is a professor of art history at Carleton University, Ottawa. Her research and publications focus on African and Aboriginal art and critical museology, and she has curated exhibitions and served as director of the University of British Columbia Museum of Anthropology. Her books include *Trading Identities: The Souvenir in Native North American Art from the Northeast, 1700–1900* and *Museum Pieces: Toward the Indigenization of Canadian Museums* (2011).

CHRISTOPHER POWELL is an assistant professor in the Department of Sociology at Ryerson University. His work uses contemporary social theory to examine the interrelations among violence, knowledge, and identity. In the field of genocide studies, he is the author of *Barbaric Civilization: A Critical Sociology of Genocide* (McGill-Queen's University Press, 2011) as well as "What Do Genocides Kill? A Relational Conception of Genocide," *Journal of Genocide Studies* (2007); "Genocidal Moralities: A Critique," in *New Directions in Genocide Research,* ed. Adam Jones (Routledge, 2011); and, with Julia Peristerakis, "Genocide in Canada," in *Colonial Genocide in Indigenous North America,* ed. Andrew Woolford, Jeff Benvenuto, and Alexander Laban Hinton (Duke University Press, 2014). Christopher is also a co-editor, with François Dépelteau, of *Conceptualizing Relational Sociology: Ontological and Theoretical Issues and Applying Relational Sociology: Relations, Networks, and Society* (Palgrave Macmillan, 2013).

MARY REID is currently the director/curator of the Woodstock Art Gallery. She was formerly the director/curator of the School of Art Gallery at the University of Manitoba (2011–2014) and the curator of contemporary art and photography at the Winnipeg Art Gallery (2004–11). In 2010, she worked with the Winnipeg Arts Council as part of the Cultural Capital program of events to coordinate My City's Still Breathing, a symposium that explored the many dimensions of the arts, artists, and the city. In addition to exhibition coordination, Mary has project-managed and contributed essays to several catalogues, brochures, journals, and magazines that support her various projects.

ROGER I. SIMON was professor emeritus of the Ontario Institute for Studies in Education at the University of Toronto, where he taught for more than forty years, the last decade in the Department of Sociology and Equity Studies in Education. He served as director of the Centre for Media and Culture in Education and was a founder of the Critical Pedagogy and Cultural Studies Forum. Roger published broadly on critical approaches to culture and education. His research addressed questions of the pedagogical and ethical dimensions of practices of cultural memory, particularly as they apply to the remembrance of mass systemic violence.

STRUAN SINCLAIR is an associate professor in the Department of English, Film, and Theatre and the director of the Media Lab at the University of Manitoba. He has conferenced and published widely on topics in literature and computing and cognitive approaches to narrative. He is also the author of *Everything Breathed* (Granta), *Automatic World* (Doubleday), and the forthcoming graphic novel *Tomorrowless* as well as the interactive novel *If/Then*.

ANDREW WOOLFORD is a professor of sociology and criminology and the social justice research coordinator at the University of Manitoba. His forthcoming book *"This Benevolent Experiment": Indigenous Boarding Schools, Genocide, and Redress in the United States and Canada* will be co-published by the University of Nebraska Press and the University of Manitoba Press in 2015. He is the author of *The Politics of Restorative Justice: A Critical Introduction* (Fernwood, 2009) and *Between Justice and Certainty: Treaty-Making in British Columbia* (UBC Press, 2005). He is also a co-author, with R.S. Ratner, of *Informal Reckonings: Conflict Resolution in Mediation, Restorative Justice, and Reparations* (Routledge, 2007). Andrew is a co-editor, with Jeff Benvenuto and Alexander Hinton, of *Colonial Genocide in Indigenous North America* (Duke University Press, 2014). His research interests lie in the areas of genocide studies, settler-colonial studies, and transitional justice.